# VICTIMOLOGY

## SECOND EDITION

William G. Doerner
Florida State University

Steven P. Lab
Bowling Green State University

**anderson publishing co.**
2035 Reading Road
Cincinnati, OH 45202
800-582-7295

## Victimology, Second Edition

Copyright © 1995, 1998
Anderson Publishing Co.
2035 Reading Rd.
Cincinnati, OH 45202

Phone 800.582.7295 or 513.421.4142
Web Site www.andersonpublishing.com

### Library of Congress Cataloging-in-Publication Data

Doerner, William G., 1949-
     Victimology / William G. Doerner, Steven P. Lab. -- 2nd ed.
          p.     cm.
     Includes bibliographical references and index.
     ISBN 0-87084-226-9 (pbk.)
     1. Victims of crimes.  2. Criminal statistics.  I. Lab, Steven P.
     II. Title.
     HV6250.25.D64    1998
     362.88--DC21
                                                          98-12333
                                                          CIP

Cover design by Tin Box Studio/Cincinnati, OH
Cover photo credit: Tony Latham/Tony Stone Images

EDITOR  Ellen S. Boyne
ASSISTANT EDITOR  Elizabeth A. Shipp
ACQUISITIONS EDITOR  Michael C. Braswell

*To our loved ones:*
*Rita, Billy, Chris and Susan, Danielle*

# Table of Contents

Chapter 10
**Victim Rights**                                                        255

**References**                                                           283

# List of Figures

# List of Tables

# LEARNING OBJECTIVES

After reading Chapter 1, you should be able to:

- Explain how early society handled victim problems.

- Understand the meaning of retribution and restitution.

- Discuss the change from a victim justice system to a criminal justice system.

- Outline the early interest in victim typologies.

- Account for the attention paid to victim precipitation.

- Summarize what Wolfgang found out about homicide victims.

- Report on Amir's victim precipitation study.

- Evaluate the reaction to Amir's victim precipitation study.

- Critique the shortcomings that underlie victim precipitation.

- List the areas that fall under "general victimology."

- Provide an overview of the broad topics studied by victimologists.

- Talk about the victim movement and tell how it increased public interest in crime victims.

Chapter 1
Chapter 1
Chapter 1
Chapter 1
Chapter 1
Chapter 1
Chapter 1

# The Scope of Victimology

## INTRODUCTION

Something not very funny happened on the way to a formal system of justice. The victim got left out. As strange as it may sound, the bulk of history has seen crime victims become further removed as an integral part of dealing with criminals. Fortunately, this trend is beginning to reverse itself. Recent years have seen an increased interest in the plight of victims of crime and an increase in moves toward reintegrating the victim into the criminal justice system. This chapter will look at the role of the victim throughout history and will trace the elimination of the victim from social processing of criminal acts. We will see how victimology emerged and we will investigate the resurgence of interest in the victim.

## KEY TERMS

agent provocateur

critical victimology

deterrence

gemeinschaft

general victimology

gesellschaft

lex talionis

mala in se

restitution

retribution

typology

victim compensation

victim precipitation

## THE VICTIM THROUGHOUT HISTORY

Most people take for granted the existence of the formal criminal justice system. They do not realize that this method of handling deviant activity has not been the norm throughout history. Indeed, the modern version of criminal justice is a relatively new phenomenon. In days gone by, responsibility for dealing with offenders fell to the victim and the victim's kin. There were no "authorities" to turn to for help in "enforcing the law." Victims were expected to fend for themselves, and society acceded to this arrangement.

This state of affairs was not outlined in any set of laws or legal code. With rare exceptions, written laws did not exist. Codes of behavior reflected prevailing social norms. Society recognized murder and other serious affronts as *mala in se* (totally unacceptable behavior). However, it was up to victims or their survivors to decide what action to take against the offender. Victims who wished to respond to offenses could not turn to judges for assistance or to jails for punishment. These institutions did not exist yet. Instead, victims had to take matters into their own hands.

This does not suggest that there were no provisions for victims to follow. Society recognized a basic system of retribution and restitution for offenders. In simplest terms, *retribution* meant that the offender would suffer in proportion to the degree of harm caused by his or her actions. Often times, retribution took the form of *restitution*, or making payment in an amount sufficient to render the victim whole again. If the offender was unable to make restitution, his or her kin were forced to assume the liability.

This response system emphasized the principle known as *lex talionis*—an eye for an eye, a tooth for a tooth. Punishment was commensurate with the harm inflicted upon the victim. Perhaps the most important feature of this system was that victims and their relatives handled the problem and were the beneficiaries of any payments. This arrangement was truly a "victim justice system."

This basic system of dealing with offensive behavior found its way into early codified laws. The Law of Moses, the Code of Hammurabi (2200 B.C.) and Roman law all entailed strong elements of individual responsibility for harms committed against others. Restitution and retribution were specific ingredients in many of these early codes. Part of the rationale behind this response was to deter such behavior in the future.

The major goal of *deterrence* is to prevent future transgressions. The thinking is that the lack of any enrichment or gain from criminal activity would make these acts unattractive. Retribution and restitution attempt to reestablish the status quo that existed before the initial action of the offender. Thus, removing financial incentives would make it not profitable to commit crimes.

This basic system of dealing with offensive behavior remained intact throughout the Middle Ages. Eventually, though, it fell into disuse. Two factors signaled the end of this victim justice system. The first change was the move by feudal barons to lay a claim to any compensation offenders paid their victims (Schafer, 1968). These rulers saw this money as a lucrative way to increase their own riches. The barons accomplished this goal by redefining criminal acts as violations against the state, instead of the victim. This strategy recast the state (the barons being the heads of the state) as the aggrieved party. The victim diminished in stature and was relegated to the status of witness for the state. Now the state could step in and reap the benefits of restitution.

A second factor that reduced the victim's position was the enormous upheaval that was transforming society. Up until this time, society was predominantly rural and agrarian. People lived in small groups, eking out an existence from daily labor in the fields. Life was a rustic struggle to meet day-to-day needs.

People, for the most part, were self-sufficient and relied heavily upon their families for assistance. Families often lived in relative isolation from other families. Whenever a crime took place, it brought physical and economic harm not only to the individual victim, but also to the entire family network. This simple *gemeinschaft* society (Toennies, 1957) could rely on the individual to handle his or her own problems.

As the Middle Ages drew to a close, the industrial revolution created a demand for larger urbanized communities. People took jobs in the new industries, leaving the rural areas and relocating to the cities. They settled into cramped quarters, surrounded by strangers. Neighbors no longer knew the people living next door. As faces blended into crowds, relationships grew more depersonalized. The interpersonal ties that once bound people together had vanished.

As this *gesellschaft* type of society continued to grow, the old victim justice practices crumbled even further. Crime began to threaten the delicate social fabric that now linked people together. At the same time, concern shifted away from making the victim whole to dealing with the criminal. Gradually, the *victim* justice system withered and the *criminal* justice system became its replacement.

Today, crime victims remain nothing more than witnesses for the state. Victims no longer take matters into their own hands and extract retribution and restitution from their offenders. The victim must call upon society to act. The development of formal law enforcement, courts and correctional systems in the past few centuries has reflected an interest in protecting the state. For the most part, the criminal justice system simply forgot about victims and their best interests.

## THE REEMERGENCE OF THE VICTIM

The criminal justice system spends the bulk of its time and energy trying to control criminals. It was within this preoccupation of understanding criminal activity and identifying causes of criminal behavior that the victim was "rediscovered" in the 1940s. Interestingly, the victim emerged not as an individual worthy of sympathy or compassion, but as a possible partner or contributor to his or her own demise. Students of criminal behavior began to look at the relationship between the victim and the offender in the hopes of better understanding the genesis of the criminal act.

As interest in victims began to sprout and attract more scholarly attention, writers began to grapple with a very basic issue. What exactly was victimology? Some people believed that victimology was a specialty area or a subfield within criminology. After all, every criminal event by definition included a criminal and a victim. Others countered that victimology was so broad and encompassing that it deserved to stand as a separate field or discipline in its own right. They foresaw the day when college catalogs would list victimology as a major area of study along with such pursuits as biology, psychology, mathematics, political science, and other subjects.

Early scholarly work in victimology focused considerable energy upon creating victim typologies. A *typology* is an effort to categorize observations into logical groupings to reach a better understanding of our social world (McKinney, 1950; McKinney, 1969). As we shall see in the following sections, these early theoretical reflections pushed the field in a direction that eventually created an explosive and haunting reaction.

## The Work of Hans von Hentig:
### *The Criminal and His Victim*

An early pioneer in victimology was a German scholar, Hans von Hentig. As a criminologist, von Hentig spent much time trying to discover what made a criminal a criminal. As he focused on crime victims, von Hentig began to wonder what it was that made a victim a victim. The key ingredient, according to von Hentig, was the criminal-victim dyad.

In an early publication, von Hentig (1941) claimed that the victim was often a contributing cause to the criminal act. One example would be an incident in which the ultimate victim began as the aggressor. However, for some reason, this person wound up as the loser in the confrontation. Von Hentig's message was clear. Simply examining the outcome of a criminal event sometimes presents a distorted image of who the real victim is and who the real offender is. A closer inspection of the dynamics underlying the situation might reveal that the victim was a major contributor to his or her own victimization.

Von Hentig expanded upon the notion of the victim as an *agent provocateur* in a later book called *The Criminal and His Victim*. He explained that "increased attention should be paid to the crime-provocative function of the victim. . . . With a thorough knowledge of the interrelations between doer and sufferer new approaches to the detection of crime will be opened" (1948: 450).

Von Hentig was not naive enough to believe that all victim contribution to crime was active. Much victim contribution results from characteristics or social positions beyond the control of the individual. As a result, von Hentig classified victims into 13 categories depending upon their propensity for victimization.

**FIGURE 1.1**
**Hans von Hentig's Victim Typology**

| Type | Example |
| --- | --- |
| 1. The Young | children and infants |
| 2. The Female | all women |
| 3. The Old | elderly persons |
| 4. The Mentally Defective and Deranged | the feeble-minded, the insane, drug addicts, alcoholics |
| 5. Immigrants | foreigners unfamiliar with the culture |
| 6. Minorities | racially disadvantaged persons |
| 7. Dull Normals | simple-minded persons |
| 8. The Depressed | persons with various psychological maladies |
| 9. The Acquisitive | the greedy, those looking for quick gains |
| 10. The Wanton | promiscuous persons |
| 11. The Lonesome and the Heartbroken | widows, widowers and those in mourning |
| 12. The Tormentor | an abusive parent |
| 13. The Blocked, Exempted, or Fighting | victims of blackmail, extortion, confidence games |

Source: Adapted from von Hentig, H. (1948), *The Criminal and His Victim: Studies in the Sociobiology of Crime.* New Haven: Yale University Press, pp. 404-438.

Many of von Hentig's victim types reflect the inability to resist a perpetrator due to physical, social or psychological disadvantages. For example, very young people, females and the elderly are more likely to lack the physical power to resist offenders. Immigrants and minorities, because of cultural differences, may feel they are outside the mainstream of society. This lack of familiarity may lead them into situations in which the criminal preys upon them. Individuals who are mentally defective or deranged, "dull normal," depressed, lonesome or blocked may not understand what is occurring around them or may be unable to resist. The acquisitive person and the tormentor are individuals who, due to their own desires, are either directly involved in the criminal act or place themselves in situations in which there is a clear potential for victimization.

The typology suggested by von Hentig does not imply that the victim is always the primary cause of the criminal act. What he does suggest is that victim characteristics may contribute to the victimization episode. According to von Hentig (1948: iii), we must realize that "the victim is taken as one of the determinants, and that a nefarious symbiosis is often established between doer and sufferer. . . ."

## The Work of Beniamin Mendelsohn: *Further Reflections*

Some observers credit Beniamin Mendelsohn, a practicing attorney, with being the "father" of victimology. Mendelsohn, like von Hentig, was intrigued by the dynamics that take place between victims and offenders. Before preparing a case, he would ask victims, witnesses and bystanders in the situation to complete a detailed and probing questionnaire. After examining these responses, Mendelsohn discovered that usually there was a strong interpersonal relationship between victims and offenders. Using these data, Mendelsohn (1956) outlined a six-step classification of victims based on legal considerations of the degree of the victim's blame.

The first type was the "completely innocent victim." This victim type exhibited no provocative or facilitating behavior prior to the offender's attack. The second grouping contained "victims with minor guilt" or "victims due to ignorance." These unfortunate people inadvertently did something that placed themselves in a compromising position before the victimization episode.

Mendelsohn reserved the third category for the "victim as guilty as the offender" and the "voluntary victim." Suicide cases and parties injured while engaging in vice crimes and other victimless offenses were listed here.

The next two categories address some of von Hentig's earlier concerns. Mendelsohn's fourth type, "victim more guilty than the offender," represents the situation where the victim provokes the criminal act. A person who comes out on the losing end of a punch after making an abusive remark or goading the other party would fit here. Similarly, a victim who entered the situation as the offender and, because of circumstances beyond his or her control, ended up the victim is considered the "most guilty victim." An example of this category would be the burglar shot by a home owner during an intrusion.

The last category is the "simulating or imaginary victim." Mendelsohn reserves this niche for those persons who pretend that they have been victimized. The person who claims to have been mugged, rather than admitting to gambling his or her paycheck away, would be an example.

Mendelsohn's classification is useful primarily for identifying the relative culpability of the victim in the criminal act. Besides developing this typology, he also coined the term "victimology" and proposed the terms "penal-couple" (a criminal-victim relationship), "victimal" and "victimity" (as opposed to criminal and criminality) and "potential of victimal receptivity" (an individual's propensity for being victimized). Figure 1.2 lists some common terms used by victimologists.

**FIGURE 1.2**
**The Vocabulary of Victimology**

| | |
|---|---|
| Victimhood | the state of being a victim |
| Victimizable | capable of being victimized |
| Victimization | the act of victimizing, or fact of being victimized, in various senses |
| Victimize | to make a victim of; to cause to suffer inconvenience, discomfort, annoyance, etc., either deliberately or by misdirected attentions; to cheat, swindle, or defraud; to put to death as, or in the manner of, a sacrificial victim; to slaughter; to destroy or spoil completely |
| Victimizer | one who victimizes another or others |
| Victimless | the absence of a clearly identifiable victim other than the doer, for example, in a criminal situation |

Source: Viano, E.C (1976b). "From the Editor: Victimology: The Study of the Victim." *Victimology* 1:1-7. Reprinted by permission from *Victimology: An International Journal*, Victimology, Inc. All rights reserved.

## The Work of Stephen Schafer: *The Victim and His Criminal*

Scholarly interest in victims and the role they played in their own demise evoked little interest throughout the 1950s and 1960s. Stephen Schafer, in a playful twist on Hans von Hentig's seminal work, revisited the victim's role in his book *The Victim and His Criminal*. The key concept that undergirds Schafer's thinking was what he termed "functional responsibility." Once again, the victim-offender relationship came under study.

As Figure 1.3 shows, Schafer (1968) provided a typology that builds upon victim responsibility for the crime. In many respects, Schafer's groupings are a variation of those proposed by von Hentig (1948). The difference between the two schemes is primarily one of emphasis on the culpability of the victim. Where von Hentig's listing identifies varying risk factors, Schafer explicitly sets forth the responsibility of different victims.

## Other Scholarly Efforts

Von Hentig, Mendelsohn and Schafer were not the only persons to produce significant analyses regarding victims during this time. Most assuredly, some other scholars began recognizing the importance of a victim-based orientation. These early attempts at probing the victim-offender relationship signaled the beginning of renewed interest in the victim.

**FIGURE 1.3**
**Schafer's Victim Precipitation Typology**

| | |
|---|---|
| 1. Unrelated Victims (no victim responsibility) | Instances where the victim is simply the unfortunate target of the offender. |
| 2. Provocative Victims (victim shares responsibility) | The offender is reacting to some action or behavior of the victim. |
| 3. Precipitative Victims (some degree of victim responsibility) | Victims leave themselves open for victimization by placing themselves in dangerous places or times, dressing inappropriately, acting or saying the wrong things, etc. |
| 4. Biologically Weak Victims (no victim responsibility) | The aged, young, infirmed, and others who, due to their physical conditions, are appealing targets for offenders. |
| 5. Socially Weak Victims (no victim responsibility) | Immigrants, minorities, and others who are not adequately integrated to society and are seen as easy targets by offenders. |
| 6. Self-Victimizing (total victim responsibility) | Individuals who are involved in such crimes as drug use, prostitution, gambling, and other activities in which the victim and the criminal act in concert with each another. |
| 7. Political Victims (no victim responsibility) | Individuals who are victimized because they oppose those in power or are made victims in order to be kept in a subservient social position. |

Source: Adapted from Schafer, S. (1968). *The Victim and His Criminal: A Study in Functional Responsibility.* New York: Random House.

This interest, however, was lopsided. The early victimologists generally failed to look at the damage that offenders inflicted upon their victims, ignored victim recuperative or rehabilitative efforts and bypassed a host of other concerns. In an attempt to understand the causes of crime, they concentrated on how the victim contributed to his or her demise. Eventually, the idea of victim precipitation emerged from this preoccupation with "blaming the victim." As we shall see later in this chapter, the assumption that somehow the victim shared responsibility for or instigated the criminal episode would spark a major ideological confrontation.

# EMPIRICAL STUDIES OF VICTIM PRECIPITATION

*Victim precipitation* deals with the degree to which the victim is responsible for his or her own victimization. That involvement can be either passive (as much of von Hentig's typology suggests) or active (as seen in Mendelsohn's classification). Each typology presented in this chapter implicates victim contribution as a causative factor in the commission of crime. However, none present any empirical evidence to support that point of view. The first systematic attempt to overcome this objection was Wolfgang's (1958) analysis of police homicide records. A few years later, one of Wolfgang's students, Menachem Amir, applied this framework to forcible rape cases and met with a barrage of criticism.

## The Work of Marvin E. Wolfgang: *Patterns in Criminal Homicide*

Using homicide data for the city of Philadelphia, Wolfgang reported that 26 percent of the homicides that occurred from 1948 through 1952 resulted from victim precipitation. Wolfgang (1958: 252) defined victim-precipitated homicide as those instances in which the ultimate victim was:

> the first in the homicide drama to use physical force directed against his subsequent slayer. The victim-precipitated cases are those in which the victim was the first to show and use a deadly weapon, to strike a blow in an altercation—in short, the first to commence the interplay of resort to physical violence.

Wolfgang identified several factors as typical of victim-precipitated homicides. First, the victim and the offender usually had some prior interpersonal relationship. Typical examples include relationships of spouses, boyfriends-girlfriends, family members and close friends or acquaintances. In other words, victims were more likely to die at the hands of someone they knew rather than those of a complete stranger.

Second, the homicide act is often the product of a small disagreement that escalates until the situation bursts out of control. That change in degree could be either short-term or may be the result of a longer, drawn-out confrontation. For instance:

> A husband had beaten his wife on several previous occasions. In the present instance, she insisted that he take her to the hospital. He refused, and a violent quarrel followed, during which he slapped her several times, and she concluded by stabbing him (Wolfgang, 1958: 253).

Third, alcohol consumed by the victim is a common ingredient in many victim-precipitated homicides. Several possibilities surface here. It may be that as intoxicated persons lose their inhibitions, they vocalize their feelings more readily. Eventually, these inebriated parties grow more obnoxious and belligerent, and unwittingly provoke their assailants into a deadly confrontation. Another alternative is that alcohol consumption renders these people so impaired that they lose the physical ability to defend themselves in a skirmish. In any event, Wolfgang (1958: 265) points out that "connotations of a victim as a weak and passive individual, seeking to withdraw from an assaultive situation, and of an offender as a brutal, strong, and overly aggressive person seeking out his victim, are not always correct."

## The Work of Menachem Amir: *Patterns in Forcible Rape*

Several years later, Menachem Amir undertook what perhaps became the most controversial empirical analysis of rape. Amir (1971) gathered information from police records on rape incidents that took place in Philadelphia between 1958 and 1960. Based on details contained in the files, he claimed that 19 percent of all forcible rapes were victim-precipitated.

According to Amir (1971: 266), victim-precipitated rape referred to those situations in which:

> the victim actually, or so it was deemed, agreed to sexual relations but retracted before the actual act or did not react strongly enough when the suggestion was made by the offender. The term applies also to cases in risky situations marred with sexuality, especially when she uses what could be interpreted as indecency in language and gestures, or constitutes what could be taken as an invitation to sexual relations.

Amir proceeded to list a variety of factors that helped precipitate the criminal act. Similar to Wolfgang's homicide findings, alcohol use—particularly by the victim—was a major factor in a precipitated rape. The risk of sexual victimization intensified if both parties had been drinking.

Other important factors include seductive actions by the victim, wearing revealing clothing, using risqué language, having a "bad" reputation and being in the wrong place at the wrong time. According to Amir, such behaviors could tantalize the offender to the point that he simply "misread" the victim's overtures. At one point, Amir (1971) even suggested that some victims may have an unconscious need to be sexually controlled through rape.

In the concluding remarks of the section on victim precipitation, Amir (1971: 275-276) commented:

These results point to the fact that the offender should not be viewed as the sole "cause" and reason for the offense, and that the "virtuous" victim is not always the innocent and passive party. Thus, the role played by the victim and its contribution to the perpetration of the offense becomes one of the main interests of the emerging discipline of victimology.

## Criticisms and Reactions

The notion of victim precipitation, particularly regarding Amir's claims about rape, came under swift attack. Weis and Borges (1973; 1976), for example, attribute Amir's conclusions to faults implicit in relying upon police accounts, to a host of procedural errors as well as to ill-conceived theoretical notions. For example, Amir suggested that victims may *psychologically* prompt or desire the rape as a means of rebelling against accepted standards of behavior. In contrast, though, the male is simply responding to *social* cues from the female. Despite these contrasting origins of behavior, Amir does not provide any justification for why female behavior stems from psychological factors while male actions derive from social variables. In any event, Amir's study attracted blistering rebuttals from academic quarters, along with enraged reactions from women's groups and victim advocates. This reception made many victimologists uncomfortable with the precipitation argument as it had developed.

Cooler heads soon prevailed. Rather than abandoning the idea of victim precipitation, some scholars began a more sensitive probing. Curtis (1974), for one, suggested that what was needed was a more accurate definition of victim precipitation. For example, one set of researchers might define hitchhiking as a precipitating factor. Other studies may not make such a blanket assumption or may view hitchhiking as substantively different from other precipitating actions.

A more productive approach came from a critical examination of the underpinnings of the victim-precipitation argument. Franklin and Franklin (1976) exposed four major assumptions behind this victimological approach. First, victim precipitation assumes that criminal acts can be explained by the behavior of the victim. However, many factors often identified as precipitous also appear in instances where no criminal act takes place. For example, many people go to bars at night. Sometimes they drink excessively and then stagger home alone without becoming victimized. Thus, supposedly precipitating acts are not enough, in and of themselves, to cause criminal behavior.

Second, victim precipitation assumes that the offender becomes activated only when the victim emits certain signals. This belief ignores the fact that many offenders plan their offenses ahead of time and do not simply react to another person's behavior. For these criminals, crime is a rational, planned enterprise.

Third, Franklin and Franklin (1976) disagree with the assumption that a victim's behavior is necessary and sufficient to trigger the commission of a criminal act. In fact, the opposite is probably closer to the truth. Many offenders commit crimes despite any specific action by the victim. Other individuals will not seize the opportunity to commit a crime, for whatever reason, although a potential victim presents himself or herself.

Finally, victim precipitation arguments assume that the intent of the victim can be gauged by the victimization incident. Unfortunately, if intent is equivalent to action, there would be no need for criminal court proceedings beyond the infallible identification of the person who perpetrated the crime. Our criminal system, however, explicitly assumes possible variation in intent, regardless of the action.

Although each of these assumptions shows how the victim-precipitation argument falters, there is a much larger issue requiring attention. Studies of victim involvement tend to be myopic. That is, they do not address the offender. Instead, they imply that all offenders are equal in their drive and desire to engage in deviant activity. This assumption, however, is untenable. Some offenders may actively hunt for the right situation, while others display little or no prior intent. What was needed is an integrated approach that takes both the victim and the offender into account.

Curtis (1974) attempted to do just this when he sketched a simple grid that allows the degree of victim precipitation to vary. As Figure 1.4 shows, Curtis (1974) merged victim provocation with offender intent. This strategy results in recognizing five degrees of precipitation, ranging from pure victim precipitation to total offender responsibility. This presentation shows that even in the position of clear outright provocation by the victim, the offender may still be an equally responsible partner in the final outcome. What is important to remember here is that, at best, one should conceive of victim precipitation as a contributing factor and certainly not as the predominant force.

## A NEW APPROACH: GENERAL VICTIMOLOGY

The preoccupation with victim precipitation, along with its divisiveness and ensuing fragmentation, threatened to stagnate this fledgling area of interest. The lack of theoretical advances brought genuine worries from some quarters that victimology was bogging down in an academic quagmire (Bruinsma and Fiselier, 1982; Levine, 1978). However, an antidote emerged from the discussions held at an international conference in Bellagio, Italy, during the summer of 1975 (Viano, 1976a). It was the term "general victimology."

**FIGURE 1.4**
**Precipitation Grid Outlining the Relative Responsibility of Both Victim and Offender**

| Degree of Offender Intent | Degree of Victim Involvement | | |
|---|---|---|---|
| | Clear Provocation | Some Involvement | Little or No Involvement |
| Deliberate Premeditation | Equal | More Offender | Total Offender Responsibility |
| Some Intent | More Victim | Equal | More Offender |
| Little or No Intent | Pure Victim Precipitation | More Victim | Equal |

Source: Adapted from Curtis, L.A., *Criminal Violence: National Patterns and Behavior,* p. 95, Copyright © 1974 Jossey-Bass Inc., Publishers. First published by Lexington Books. Reprinted with permission. All rights reserved.

The remedy proposed by Beniamin Mendelsohn called for victimology to move out of the provincial backwaters of criminology and into its own rightful domain. As mentioned earlier, some scholars wondered whether victimology was a discipline in its own right or if it was merely an attractive subfield of criminology. Mendelsohn attempted to assure victimology of its independence from criminology by devising the term "general victimology."

According to Mendelsohn (1982: 59), victimologists aim to "investigate the causes of victimization in search of effective remedies." Since human beings suffer from many causal factors, focusing on criminal victimization is too narrow a perspective. A more global term, like general victimology, is needed to convey the true meaning of the field.

According to Mendelsohn (1976), *general victimology* subsumes five types of victims. They include:

1. the victim of a criminal
2. the victim of one's self
3. the victim of the social environment
4. the victim of technology
5. the victim of the natural environment.

The first category (crime victims) is self-explanatory. It has been the traditional subject matter that victimologists have grown accustomed to studying. Self-victimization would include suicide as well as any other suffering induced by victims themselves. The term "victims of the social environment" refers to individual, class or group oppression. Some common examples here would include racial discrimination, caste relations, genocide and war atrocities. Technological victims are those who fall prey to society's reliance upon scientific innovations. Nuclear accidents, improperly tested medicines, industrial pollution and transportation mishaps provide fodder for this category. Finally, victims of the natural environment would include those affected by such events as floods, earthquakes, famine, and the like.

In line with Mendelsohn's formulations, Smith and Weis (1976) proposed a broad overview of the areas subsumed by general victimology. As Figure 1.5 illustrates, there are four major areas of concern. They include the creation of definitions of victims, the application of these definitions, victim reactions during the postvictimization period, and societal reactions to victims.

When viewed in this context, general victimology becomes a very broad enterprise with extensive implications. As Mendelsohn (1976: 21) explains:

> Just as medicine treats all patients and all diseases, just as criminology concerns itself with all criminals and all forms of crime, so victimology must concern itself with all victims and all aspects of victimity in which society takes an interest.

## CRITICAL VICTIMOLOGY

One recent trend in victimology is to shift the focus from the more general approach outlined above to what some people call *critical victimology*. Proponents of this move maintain that victimology fails to question the basic foundations of what crime is, overlooks the question of why certain acts are sanctioned, and, consequently, has developed in the wrong direction. Mawby and Walklate (1994: 21) define critical victimology as:

> an attempt to examine the wider social context in which some versions of victimology have become more dominant than others and also to understand how those versions of victimology are interwoven with questions of policy response and service delivery to victims of crime.

Central to critical victimology, therefore, is the issue of how and why certain actions are defined as criminal and, as a result, how the entire field of victimology becomes focused on one set of actions instead of another. This notion is not entirely different from Mendelsohn's category of "victim of the social environment" outlined previously under the rubric of general victimology. Mawby and Walklate (1994) point out that many crimes committed by the powerful in society are not subjected to the criminal code. Consequently, the victims of those crimes do not enter the average discussion of victimology.

**FIGURE 1.5**
**General Model of the Areas of Research and Application in the Field of Victimology**

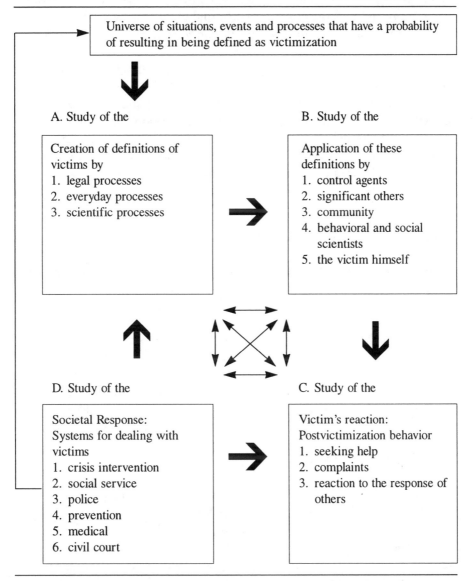

Source: Smith, D.L. and K. Weis (1976). "Toward an Open-System Approach to Studies in the Field of Victimology." In E.C. Viano (ed.), *Victims & Society*. Washington, DC: Visage Press, Inc., p. 45.

Under critical victimology, most victim-oriented initiatives tend to perpetuate the existing definitions of crime by failing to question the underlying social factors that give rise to the action and the response (Elias, 1990). The reason for this failure is multifaceted. One contributing factor is the reliance on official definitions and data in most analyses of victim issues. This subjugation inevitably leads to solutions that do not question the underlying social setting. Another factor is the ability of existing agencies to co-opt and incorporate emerging movements (such as children's rights) into existing social control systems. A more radical argument posits that the control of criminal justice and victimology rests in the hands of a powerful few who would view a critical approach as a threat to the status quo.

While critical victimology offers an interesting viewpoint and carries much potential for victimology, debating its merits is beyond the scope of this text. Various points throughout this text, however, will raise issues that are relevant to a critical approach. Examples of this include sociocultural discussions of why violence occurs and investigations of impediments to victim programs. A deeper and more intense examination of critical victimology will be left for other forums.

## THE VICTIM MOVEMENT

While academicians were debating the victim-precipitation argument, practitioners had pinpointed the victim as someone who deserved assistance from society and the criminal justice system. To some extent, this grassroots concern for the victim's well-being was a reaction to the charges of victim complicity in the offense. Several different movements occurred simultaneously and contributed to the renewed interest in the plight of the victim. Among them were (1) the women's movement, (2) efforts to establish children's rights, (3) concerns over the growing crime problem, (4) the advocacy of victim compensation, (5) legal reforms, and some other factors.

### The Women's Movement

The women's movement, especially in the mid- to late-1960s, included a large component dealing with victims. Victim-blaming arguments often dealt with rape and sexual assault. The female victim found herself and her lifestyle on trial when an offender was apprehended. Reformers complained that the system dealt with sexual assault victims as if they themselves were the offenders. Advocates called for equal treatment. They found the actions of the criminal justice system to be strong ammunition for their arguments. Beyond simply calling for changes in the formal system of justice, the women's movement made many gains. A short list would include the development of rape crisis centers, shelters for battered women, counseling for abused women and their children, and other forms of assistance. As women demanded an equal place in society, they worked to overcome the disadvantages of the criminal justice system.

## Children's Rights

A growing concern over the needs and rights of youth blossomed during the mid- to late 1960s. Many writers point to this period as the time when child abuse was "discovered." It was around this time that society decided to define abuse against children as a social problem. However, that does not mean that child abuse was a new phenomenon. Child abuse is an age-old practice and, by many accounts, may have been much worse in the past than today. The difference in the 1960s, however, was that many physical and psychological actions used with children began to be questioned and labeled as abuse. States enacted legislation outlining the limits to which a child could be physically "disciplined." Specific children's bureaus within criminal justice agencies were either established or expanded to deal with the growing recognition of child maltreatment. Shelters were established to house children from abusive situations.

Runaways also gained publicity as a serious problem in the late 1960s. The general rebellion of youth in the United States enticed many juveniles to seek freedom from authority. Consequently, runaway shelters appeared in most large cities for the purpose of assisting the youths rather than returning them to their homes. Children were emerging as a new class of victims—both of abuse at home and of society in general.

## The Growing Crime Problem

The level of crime in the United States began to register giant strides in the 1960s and the early 1970s. According to Uniform Crime Report (UCR) data, crime in the United States more than doubled from 1960 to 1980. Along with concern over the Vietnam War, crime was the most important issue of the day. Presidential and local elections targeted the problem of law and order as a major concern. In an attempt to identify the causes of the growing problem and possible solutions, President Johnson appointed a commission to examine crime and the criminal justice system. Victim issues were a major focus of the President's Commission (1967) report. Among the victim components of the report were the beginnings of systematic victimization surveys, suggestions for the means of alleviating the pain and loss of victims, ideas for community programs aimed at providing victim services, and calls for involving victims further in the criminal justice system.

Some 15 years after this report was aired, another national task force concluded that victims still had substantial needs that were still unfilled. Many of the identified problems were similar to those noted by the earlier commission.

## Victim Compensation

One suggestion made by the President's Commission (1967) was the establishment of methods for compensating crime victims for their losses. Among these methods were restitution and *victim compensation*. Neither of these ideas, however, originated with the Commission. As was mentioned earlier in this chapter, restitution was the common method for dealing with crime throughout most of history. Victim compensation (state payments made to the victims of crime) was first introduced in Great Britain by Margery Fry in 1957. Although that early attempt failed, victim compensation fast became a major issue around the world.

New Zealand passed the first compensation legislation in 1963, closely followed by England in 1964. In the United States, California established victim compensation in 1965, New York in 1966, Hawaii in 1967 and Massachusetts in 1968. The federal government enacted legislation in 1984 that outlined compensation in instances in which federal crimes were committed. The statute also provided for monetary assistance to states with compensation programs. By 1989, 45 states had enacted compensation statutes. Other countries, such as Australia and Finland, have also established compensation programs. While each program may differ in its particulars, the basic premise of assisting crime victims remains the same.

## Legal Reforms

In addition to the establishment of compensation legislation, a variety of legal reforms aimed at protecting and helping crime victims has appeared since the 1960s. Among the changes that have emerged are statutes that protect the rape victim's background and character in court proceedings, laws designed to protect battered spouses and their children, legislation mandating doctors and teachers to report suspected cases of child abuse, guidelines for informing victims about court proceedings and the legal system, and provisions that allow victim impact statements in sentencing and parole decisions. In some instances, states have passed what is known as a "Victim's Bill of Rights." These provisions outline the rights of the victim in a manner similar to those appearing in the U.S. Bill of Rights, which focuses on the accused. This type of legislation has started to bring the plight and role of the victim back into the criminal justice system and, as Figure 1.6 indicates, has the support of the United Nations in its efforts to ease the plight of victims throughout the world.

**FIGURE 1.6**
**Selected Portions of the United Nations Declaration Regarding Victims of Crime**

Cognizant that millions of people throughout the world suffer harm as a result of crime and the abuse of power and that the rights of these victims have not been adequately recognized,

Recognizing that the victims of crime and the victims of abuse of power, and also frequently their families, witnesses and others who aid them, are unjustly subjected to loss, damage or injury and that they may, in addition, suffer hardship when assisting in the prosecution of offenders,

1. Affirms the necessity of adopting national and international measures in order to secure the universal and effective recognition of, and respect for, the rights of victims of crime and of abuse of power;

2. Stresses the need to promote progress by all States in their efforts to that end, without prejudice to the rights of suspects or offenders;

3. Adopts the Declaration of Basic Principle of Justice of Victims of Crime and Abuse of Power . . . which is designed to assist Governments and the international community in their efforts to secure justice and assistance for victims of crime and victims of abuse of power;

4. Calls upon Member States to take the necessary steps to give effect to the provisions contained in the Declaration. . . .

   (a) To implement social, health, including mental health, educational, economic and specific crime prevention policies to reduce victimization and encourage assistance to victims in distress;

   (b) To promote community efforts and public participation in crime prevention;

   (c) To review periodically their existing legislation and practices in order to ensure responsiveness to changing circumstances, and to enact and enforce legislation proscribing acts that violate internationally recognized norms relating to human rights, corporate conduct, and other abuses of power;

   (d) To establish and strengthen the means of detecting, prosecuting and sentencing those guilty of crimes.

Source: United Nations (1985). *Declaration of Basic Principles of Justice for Victims of Crime and Abuse of Power.* Adopted November 29, 1985.

# OTHER FACTORS

Other factors have played either a direct or indirect role in emphasizing victim issues. One such source of influence has been the mass media. Rarely a week goes by in which a "crime of the week" does not appear in a special movie or as part of an ongoing series. Shows such as "Rescue 911," "Unsolved Mysteries" and "America's Most Wanted" portray not only the offender but the harm to the victim, often relying on interviews with the victim or victim's family. Such media attention and interest in the victim naturally influences some of those who watch.

Another factor not to be overlooked is the increasing interest in victims among academics. Thirty years ago, there were virtually no books specifically focusing on victims. The publication of Schafer's (1968) *The Victim and His Criminal* signaled an era of increasing interest in victimology. Many texts have appeared since then. They range from general victim topics to specific discussions of compensation, spouse abuse, child abuse, victim services and other areas of interest. The first International Symposium on Victimology was held in Jerusalem in 1973. Since then, there have been several more worldwide gatherings and an uncounted number of national, state and local meetings of academics and professionals working with crime victims. The growth in college courses devoted to victimology or topical victim issues is encouraging. Some campuses even offer a specialized program in victim services. As Figure 1.7 shows, a variety of specialty journals devoted to victim issues now exist.

**FIGURE 1.7**
**Selected Journals Devoted to Victim Issues**

---

*Child Abuse & Neglect*
*Child Maltreatment*
*Homicide Studies*
*International Review of Victimology*
*Journal of Child Sexual Abuse*
*Journal of Elder Abuse & Neglect*
*Journal of Family Violence*
*Journal of Interpersonal Violence*
*Violence Against Women*
*Violence & Abuse Abstracts*
*Violence and Victims*

---

## SUMMARY AND OVERVIEW OF THIS BOOK

As you have read, Mendelsohn (1976) saw general victimology as addressing five distinct types of victims. In addition to crime victims, he saw self-victimization, social victims, technological victims and victims of the natural environment as legitimate focal concerns. All these victims suffer some degree of social or physical pain or loss. Each deserves assistance to offset the devastating effects of the victimization episode.

While Mendelsohn's vision of general victimology is quite impressive, it does cover a huge territory. Because Mendelsohn's approach is such a large undertaking, we will confine ourselves to a more manageable task. For that reason, this text must restrict itself to only the first category—crime victims. By the time you finish this book, we think you will agree with us. Victimology is so broad and complex that it makes sense to look at it in slices.

A glimpse of what lies ahead reveals an ambitious range of topics. This first chapter has laid the foundation for a host of issues and ideas that we will take up in greater detail in later chapters. Many topics will appear in the context of more than one discussion. Chapter 2 examines the extent of victimization and the development of victimization surveys. Victim surveys have become a key measure of crime and contribute a great deal of information to the study of victimization. Chapter 3 looks at the costs associated with being a crime victim and the additional burdens of becoming involved with the criminal justice system. As you will see, many people wrongly assume that victims do not cooperate with the authorities because of apathy. That chapter will demonstrate that the real reason reflects a very sensible cost-benefit analysis. Sometimes it is just too costly and too painful to be a "model citizen." Chapter 4 examines how the criminal justice system responds to victimization, the impact of those responses and the continuing needs of victims.

Chapters 5 through 9 turn to discussions of particular forms of criminal victimization. These special topics include sexual assault, spouse abuse, child maltreatment, elderly abuse and homicide. Each of these specific victim groupings has developed its own literature about causes and possible remedies. Finally, the book concludes with a look at the changing landscape of legal rights for crime victims.

An additional feature that appears toward the end of each chapter is the inclusion of selected internet sites devoted to various victimological topics pertinent to that chapter. People in criminology and criminal justice are becoming much more aware of the wealth of information available through this medium (Gerstenfeld, 1997; Lively, 1996; Lively and Reardon, 1996). In order to take advantage of these technological developments, Figure 1.8 contains a listing of sites to get you started in this direction.

**FIGURE 1.8**
**Selected Internet Sites Dealing with General Victim Issues**

---

California State University-Fresno, National Victim Assistance Academy
    http://csufresno.edu/criminology/victim.htm

National Crime Victim's Research and Treatment Center
    http://www.musc.edu/cvc

National Criminal Justice Reference Service
    http://www.ncjrs.org/

National Organization for Victim Assistance
    http://www.access.digex.net/~nova/

National Victim Center
    http://www.nvc.org/

9th International Symposium on Victimology
    http://www.victimology.nl

Office for Victims of Crime
    http://www.ojp.usdoj.gov/ovc/

Office of International Criminal Justice
    http://www.acsp.uic.edu/

---

# LEARNING OBJECTIVES

After reading Chapter 2, you should be able to:

- Describe three major data sources for measuring crime.
- Tell what the UCR does.
- Outline three advantages of the UCR.
- Explain three disadvantages of the UCR.
- List the contents of the Index offenses.
- Differentiate personal offenses from property offenses.
- Give a definition of the "dark figure of crime."
- Talk about the level of crime and crime trends using the UCR.
- Specify what a victimization survey is.
- Summarize and criticize the findings from the 1967 NORC survey.
- Give an example of telescoping.
- Explain how memory decay affects victim surveys.
- Compare and contrast reverse record checks and forward record checks.
- Identify three assumptions behind the record-check strategy.
- Define the term "panel design."
- Reveal why bounding is important for victim surveys.
- Distinguish a self-respondent from a household respondent.
- Outline the contributions of second-generation victim surveys.
- Tell why the development of NCS was so important.
- Address the mover-stayer problem in the NCS.
- Relay a prime difficulty with business victimization surveys.
- Discuss redesign efforts behind fourth-generation victim surveys.
- Provide an example of a screen question in a victim survey.
- Know what the initials NCVS represent.
- List some suggested improvements for the NCVS.
- Convey the goals and objectives behind the NCVS.
- Explain how the redesign has affected victimization estimates.
- Talk about victimization trends uncovered by the NCVS.
- Link victim characteristics to victimization rates.
- Compare and contrast results from the NCVS with the UCR.
- Explain what "repeat victimization" means.

# Gauging the Extent of Criminal Victimization

## INTRODUCTION

Gauging the extent of criminal victimization has long been a goal of the criminal justice system and those who study crime. Researchers and policymakers typically rely upon three major data sources for measuring the level of crime (O'Brien, 1985). The first source, official records of police departments, are the traditional depositories for crime information. However, dissatisfaction with police records prompted researchers to look elsewhere. Surveys that ask people about offenses they have committed became a popular alternative. For our purposes, however, this approach is very limited. These surveys are not conducted on an annual or national basis. A third tactic is to question individuals about instances in which they were victimized. As we shall see in this chapter, this approach holds much promise.

Despite the common goal of measuring crime, none of these strategies alone yields a definitive answer to the question of how much victimization occurs in society. Each scheme provides a slightly different angle from which to view the crime problem. Each one of these methods has its own distinct advantages and inherent flaws.

## KEY TERMS

bounding
"dark figure" of crime
forward record check
gray-area event
hot spots
household respondent
incidence data
index offenses
memory decay
mover-stayer problem
National Crime Survey (NCS)
National Crime Victimization Survey (NCVS)
NORC Survey
panel design
personal offenses
prevalence data
property offenses
repeat victimization
reverse record check
screen questions
self-respondent
series victimizations
telescoping
Uniform Crime Reports (UCR)
victimization survey

This chapter examines some issues involved in measuring victimization, paying particular attention to the development and use of victimization surveys. We also will examine the level of crime and victimization presented by the Uniform Crime Reports and the National Crime Victimization Survey. As you will see, victim surveys provide a wealth of data that are quite useful for studying victims and related issues.

## THE UNIFORM CRIME REPORTS

The system of *Uniform Crime Reports* (UCR) began in 1931 as a mechanism by which police departments in different jurisdictions could exchange relevant information about crime. Police administrators around the country were very supportive of this effort. They felt that such knowledge could help identify the magnitude of the crime problem, map changes over time and guide actions to combat the criminal element. This reporting system was meant to be a tool for the law enforcement community throughout the United States. As a result, the task of developing and carrying out this innovative program fell to the Federal Bureau of Investigation.

The UCR is characterized by a number of interesting and advantageous features. First, crime data are compiled annually from jurisdictions throughout the country. Such consistency and broad geographical coverage allows crime comparisons from year to year and from place to place. The fact that the UCR has been in operation since 1931 means that it is one of the longest-running systematic data collection efforts in the social sciences.

Second, the UCR has been influential in providing standardized crime definitions. Common definitions make it possible to draw comparisons across different times and jurisdictions. To achieve this goal, the FBI introduced what it calls the *index offenses*. The FBI divides these serious crimes into two groups. *Personal offenses* include murder, forcible rape, robbery and aggravated assault. *Property offenses* consist of burglary, larceny-theft, motor vehicle theft and arson. While state statutes and local codes are not bound to these definitions, the UCR does introduce a common metric among the 50 states.

Third, the UCR gathers a large amount of information and details about particular crimes. These data are especially useful when attempting to identify patterns and trends about crime and criminals. In addition, the FBI has developed some specialized databases, such as the Supplemental Homicide Reports, which are useful to researchers and practitioners.

The UCR is not immune from problems or disadvantages. Perhaps the greatest concern is that the UCR overlooks the *"dark figure" of crime.*

In other words, these tabulations reflect only offenses that are known to the police. Any incidents in which victims or witnesses opt not to call the police are excluded from UCR figures. This drawback prompts critics to argue that the UCR grossly underreports the true level of crime in society. The UCR reflects police—and not necessarily criminal—activity.

Another concern revolves around agency reporting practices. In the past, some departments have manipulated their UCR reports or provided incomplete data to boost their image or to mask problems (McCleary et al., 1982; O'Brien, 1985). These actions are readily understandable when one considers that crime can hinder the economic growth and well-being of an area by "chasing away" potential businesses and residents.

A third shortcoming is the lack of information about victims and offenders. The UCR gathers detailed data primarily on the more serious personal offenses (murder, forcible rape, robbery and aggravated assault). Even then, though, most of these items chronicle only persons who are arrested. There is very little information about the victim, the victim's circumstances, the context of the offense, and other potentially valuable information. This fact should not be surprising because law enforcement is oriented more toward dealing with offenders than with crime victims.

Despite the problems with the UCR, the data do have a long history and are helpful in answering a variety of questions. In order to reach a fuller understanding of how the UCR contributes to our knowledge of crime, the following section highlights some recent materials published by the FBI.


## STATISTICS FROM THE UCR

According to Table 2.1, the Uniform Crime Reports state that there were more than 13.8 million index offenses known to the police in 1995. If personal and property crimes are grouped together, that number amounts to a crime rate of roughly 5,280 offenses for every 100,000 people in the United States. A closer examination shows that the most common threat of crime comes in larceny: 3,045 individuals out of every 100,000 are victimized. Murder is the least common offense, with slightly more than eight victims per 100,000 population.

As mentioned earlier, one great advantage of the UCR is the ability to look at crime over time. Figure 2.1 graphs violent crime rates for the nation from 1986 until 1995. Figure 2.2 presents similar information for property offenses.

**TABLE 2.1**
**National Index Offenses, UCR, 1995**

| Offense Category | Number | Rate per 100,000 |
|---|---|---|
| **Violent Crimes:** | | |
| Murder | 21,597 | 8.2 |
| Rape | 97,464 | 37.1 |
| Robbery | 580,545 | 220.9 |
| Aggravated Assault | 1,099,179 | 418.3 |
| **Property Crimes:** | | |
| Burglary | 2,594,995 | 987.6 |
| Larceny | 8,000,631 | 3,044.9 |
| Motor Vehicle Theft | 1,472,732 | 560.5 |
| **Total Offenses** | 13,867,143 | 5,277.6 |

Note: Arson is not included under property crimes due to insufficient reporting by agencies.

Source: Federal Bureau of Investigation (1996). *Uniform Crime Reports for the United States 1995.* Washington, DC: U.S. Government Printing Office.

**FIGURE 2.1**
**Violent Index Offense Rates, UCR, 1986-95**

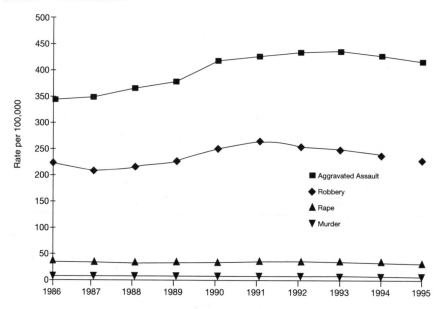

Source: Federal Bureau of Investigation (1996). *Uniform Crime Reports for the United States 1995.* Washington, DC: U.S. Government Printing Office, p. 58.

**FIGURE 2.2**
**Property Index Offense Rates, UCR, 1986-95**

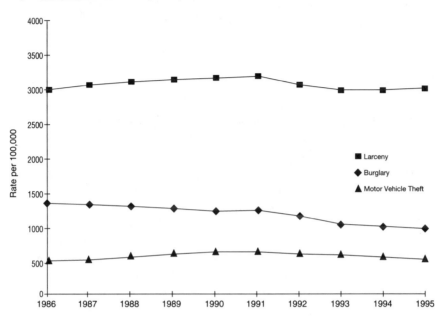

Source: Federal Bureau of Investigation (1996). *Uniform Crime Reports for the United States 1995.* Washington, DC: U.S. Government Printing Office, p. 58.

Both aggravated assault and robbery showed a distinct upward trajectory until 1991-1992 and have begun to decrease in recent years. Overall murder and rape rates remain flat, while larceny and motor vehicle theft have inched upward. Burglary has evidenced a subtle decline during the past 10 years.

The UCR and similar official records provide interesting, but limited, data for those interested in studying crime victims. Very little information is gathered about victims and even less is reported in the summary UCR reports. One key area of interest for victimology is the relationship between the victim and offender. Unfortunately, the UCR offers information on the victim-offender relationship only for homicide events. Based on 1995 data, roughly 15 percent of the homicides were committed by family members (including boyfriends and girlfriends), 31 percent by acquaintances and 15 percent by strangers. No information is known about the victim-offender relationship in the remaining 40 percent of the homicide events (Federal Bureau of Investigation, 1996). Little additional information is provided about the victims and offenders in homicides. Coupled with the lack of victim-offender information for any other offense, the UCR offers little insight for understanding victimization. As a result of the shortcomings of official data, researchers have moved toward other data collection methods for capturing the kind of details important for the study of victimization.

## VICTIMIZATION SURVEYS

While the UCR has a long history, victimization surveys are only about 30 years old. Victim surveys got their start with the work of the President's Commission in the mid-1960s. The Commission came about because of problems with increasing crime and civil unrest during that era. From its inception, the President's Commission (1967) recognized that an accurate description of the crime problem was lacking. As a result, it authorized a number of independent projects to gather information about crime victims.

From that modest beginning point, victimization surveys have grown into an invaluable data source. A *victimization survey*, instead of relying upon police reports or other official information, entails contacting people and asking them if they have been crime victims. In looking at the development of victimization surveys, one can divide them into various stages or "generations" (Hindelang, 1976). Each successive wave is marked by the way it grappled with several methodological problems raised in earlier phases.

The first generation consisted of the initial pilot studies conducted for the 1967 President's Commission. These surveys documented discrepancies between official crime counts and the daily experiences of many Americans. The second generation identified and addressed flaws discovered in the original survey designs. These follow-up studies involved pretesting instruments that would form the basis for the National Crime Survey (NCS). The establishment of the NCS in the early 1970s represents the third generation. The recent redesign now puts victimization surveys well into their fourth generation.

## First-Generation Victim Surveys

The initial victim surveys, undertaken at the behest of the President's Commission, represented little more than a set of extensive feasibility studies. These efforts tested whether such an approach could elicit sensitive information from the public. The researchers also wanted to determine how the criminal justice system could use these victim-based findings.

## The NORC Survey

Perhaps the best known of all the initial pilot studies was the poll sponsored by the National Opinion Research Center (NORC) and reported by Ennis (1967). This effort was the first national victim survey and targeted 10,000 households throughout the country. Interviewers initially asked participants to report on incidents that happened to them during the preceding 12-month period. Then, the interviewer sought more detailed information on the two most recent and most serious offenses.

What made this survey so well-known was the subsequent claim that the UCR underreported by roughly 50 percent the crime rate indicated by the *NORC Survey*. Table 2.2 contains a comparison of crime rates based upon the NORC data and the UCR figures. The NORC Survey uncovered almost four times as many rapes and more than three times as many burglaries as did the UCR. The lone exception to reporting discrepancies was motor vehicle theft, for which both data sources produced comparable rates. This similarity was probably due to the fact that most auto insurance companies will not issue a reimbursement check unless the victim files a police report. Combining the offenses into broader categories gave a much clearer picture. The NORC Survey unearthed 1.9 times as many violent episodes and 2.2 times more property offenses than official crime statistics had logged. Critics quickly pointed to the NORC findings as definitive proof that official crime records were inaccurate and unreliable because they neglected the "dark figure" of crime (Biderman and Reiss, 1967).

**TABLE 2.2**
**Comparison of NORC Victimization Rates with UCR Rates**

| Crime Category | NORC | UCR | Ratio of NORC to UCR |
|---|---|---|---|
| Homicide | 3.0 | 5.1 | 0.6 |
| Rape | 42.5 | 11.6 | 3.7 |
| Robbery | 94.0 | 61.4 | 1.5 |
| Aggravated Assault | 218.3 | 106.6 | 2.0 |
| Burglary | 949.1 | 299.6 | 3.2 |
| Larceny $50+ | 606.5 | 267.4 | 2.3 |
| Auto Theft | 206.2 | 226.0 | 0.9 |
| Violent Crimes | 357.8 | 184.7 | 1.9 |
| Property Crimes | 1,761.8 | 793.0 | 2.2 |

Source: The President's Commission on Law Enforcement and Administration of Justice (1967). *Task Force Report: Crime and Its Impact—An Assessment.* Washington, DC: U.S. Government Printing Office, p. 17.

## *Some Methodological Considerations*

While the NORC results were dramatic, there were enough problems to compromise their usefulness. First, the claim that there was twice as much crime than what the police acknowledged was based on a very small number of victim accounts. Under normal conditions, someone conducting a victim survey might anticipate uncovering only a handful of rape and robbery incidents. Deriving estimates from a few observations can yield some questionable figures. Garofalo (1981: 99) explained:

> if a researcher were interested in studying robbery victimiza-
> tions during the past year in a city, and (unbeknown to the
> researcher) 3% of the residents have been victims of personal
> robbery during that time, he or she would locate only about 60
> robbery victims in a sample of 2,000 persons. For the analyst
> who is interested in subdividing the robbery victimizations
> according to criteria such as the age of the victim, when the
> incident occurred, whether a weapon was used, how much
> property was stolen, and so forth, 60 cases are a very small
> number with which to work.

Second, the crime instances that victims reported were submitted to a panel of experts to assess whether these events were really crimes. Ultimately, the panel excluded more than one-third of the victim reports. An example of misclassification would be a person who returns home, finds all the furniture gone, and exclaims "Help—I've been robbed!" The real crime here is a burglary, not a robbery. Employing a panel to check victim reports may help validate the results and impart a greater sense of confidence, but it also alerts us to the fact that the survey design had some major flaws in terms of question wording.

A third set of problems dealt with subject recall. Some participants experienced difficulties with telescoping. *Telescoping* means that respondents may mistakenly bring criminal events that occurred outside the time frame into the survey period. For example, suppose that you are taking part in a victimization survey. The interviewer asks whether you had a car stolen during the past 12 months. In actuality, your automobile was taken 14 months ago. However, since you cannot remember exactly when the incident took place, you advise the interviewer that you were the victim of such a crime.

A related hindrance is faulty memory. *Memory decay* means that respondents were victimized during the survey time frame, but they forgot the event and did not provide the correct answer to the question. Researchers also found that respondent fatigue could influence the results. For example, the level of crime reporting decreased as the length of the survey increased. Because of these considerations, victimization estimates derived from these efforts contained an unknown margin of error.

The question of accuracy is really a matter of balance between these different sources of error. As one research team explained:

> [F]orgetting and telescoping both influence the accuracy of survey-generated estimates. Incidents that are telescoped into the time period (when they actually occurred prior to it) inflate the estimated rate; incidents that are forgotten depress the rate. Unless these two exactly offset one another, the survey estimate of the amount of crime that occurred is inaccurate (Schneider et al., 1978: 18-19).

Another major concern emerged from the selection of respondents from each household. The study did not randomly select respondents from households. In addition, individuals under the age of 18 were excluded unless they were married. Finally, all household offenses were counted as crimes against the head of the household. Each of these facts could add more bias to the results.

Besides the concerns highlighted in this section, a host of other imperfections contaminated the findings. There were definitional problems in the survey questions, an inability to locate where the crime actually took place, a problem in having a count of victims rather than offenses, and other nagging obstacles that plagued first-generation efforts. Despite these weaknesses, an important contribution had emerged. Criminologists and victimologists learned that the public was willing to answer questions about their victimization experiences. These early pilot studies clearly established the need for more refined victimization surveys and the avenues they should travel.

## Second-Generation Victim Surveys

Preparations for the second generation of victim surveys began with several exploratory projects conducted during 1970 and 1971. These preliminary studies investigated a variety of methods for addressing the problems noted earlier with the first-generation surveys. Once these concerns received treatment, then it would be time to move on to running the surveys themselves.

### Recall Problems

To test the accuracy of respondent recall, researchers in two different locations (Washington, DC and Baltimore) conducted their own record checks. The strategy here was to compare information derived from police records with victimization survey data. Two types of record checks were involved. They were reverse record checks and forward record checks.

A *reverse record check* starts by locating crime victim names in police files. The next step is to contact these people and administer a victim survey to them. Then, survey responses are checked against police records to assess the degree to which a respondent confirms offense characteristics that appear in the official files.

The reverse record check comparisons revealed that memory decay grew more problematic as the time period increased. The best recall usually occurred within three months of the incident. After that point, victims became more forgetful about the incident and its details. The results also showed that recall was better for some offenses than others and that there was a noticeable degree of telescoping. In other words, victims erroneously moved up events that occurred outside the time frame and placed them inside the targeted interval. In addition, the wording of some questions and their order of presentation also affected the responses (Hindelang, 1976: 46-53).

Schneider and her associates (1978) approached the very same issues with the exact opposite methodology. They opted to conduct a *forward record check*. After asking respondents in a victim survey whether they had contacted the police about the incident, the researchers then combed police records for a written case report. Police reports could not be found for about one-third of the victims who said they had filed such a report. When case records were located, police reports and victim accounts showed a great deal of similarity. However, there was evidence that telescoping could produce some major distortions unless specific steps were taken to counteract this tendency.

Despite the gains that record check studies had provided, there was still a need for caution. Skogan (1981: 13-14) warned of three assumptions imbedded within this strategy. First, there is an assumption that police incident records are the appropriate benchmark against which to assess victim accounts. Just because an officer scribbles some entries into a notebook while talking with a victim does not mean that this information will become parlayed into an official report. Second, record check studies can deal only with situations that have come to the attention of the record keeper. Third, crime victims are a very mobile group whose frequent address changes make recontact difficult. As Skogan (1981: 14) explained, "It is prosecutor's lore that the first response of many victims of crime is to arrange an unlisted telephone number or to move to a new address."

The problem of telescoping received further consideration in a panel study of households undertaken as part of the Quarterly Household Survey conducted by the Bureau of the Census in 1971. A *panel design* allows for the same group of households or respondents to be surveyed at regular intervals over a period of time. The repetition in the study group allows for *bounding*. In other words, the first survey serves as the calendar reference point for the second, the second for the third, and so on. The earlier interview gives the respondent a solid referent for separating one time period from the next. It also permits the researcher to check for the same victimization instance from one time period to another. This provision can eliminate any obvious repetition in the events that victims report. The Quarterly Household Survey found more accurate recall and less telescoping in a six-month time frame than over a 12-month format (Hindelang, 1976).

## *The San Jose-Dayton Surveys*

Incorporating recommendations from earlier exploratory pretests, surveys in San Jose and Dayton sought to compare information gathered from self-respondents with that from household respondents. A *self-respondent* is a person who reports victimization incidents for himself or herself. On the other hand, a *household respondent* relays information about crimes committed against all members of his or her household. Of course, any data obtained from a household respondent is subject to limitations typically associated with secondhand information. In any event, the San Jose and Dayton surveys revealed that self-respondents reported more personal crimes and experienced less recall problems than did household respondents (Hindelang, 1976: 57-68).

In addition to interviewing victims from the general population, surveys of businesses and commercial establishments were also being developed at this time. Many of the very same issues arose in these studies. Problems with such things as telescoping, memory decay, question wording, and bounding existed in these evaluations. Sometimes, particular problems loomed even larger. For example, most reports of a business burglary or robbery would come from an employee who knew about the incident firsthand. Quite often, subsequent efforts to recontact the original informant were hampered by personnel turnover. The contact person, as well as anyone familiar with the episode, sometimes was no longer an employee of the business at the time of the second interview. Thus, the quality of record checks suffered from a lack of continuity among respondents.

The second-generation surveys were useful in identifying several factors that became incorporated into later survey instruments. First, it was found that more specific questions elicited more accurate information and better recall than did very general questions about prior victimization. Second, shorter recall periods (six months or less) significantly limited the problems of telescoping and memory decay. Third, bounding the time period by some concrete event (such as the last interview in a panel design) helped to limit the problem of telescoping. Fourth, interviewing individuals themselves about their victimization experiences was preferable to asking a proxy (a household respondent) about the experiences of others. Finally, through careful wording of questions, it was possible to approximate UCR offense definitions in order to enable comparisons across the two data sources.

## Third-Generation Victim Surveys

The third generation of victim surveys sustained an ambitious schedule of activity. The federal government launched a national victimization survey, a survey of commercial businesses and a special victimization survey in 26 American cities. The following subsections outline each of these endeavors.

### The National Crime Survey

The *National Crime Survey* (NCS) was launched in 1972 with a probability sample of 72,000 households set up in a panel format. The plan was to interview each member within these households. This strategy would produce a study group of approximately 100,000 people after eliminating problems such as refusals to cooperate, incorrect addresses, and others.

Workers contacted each household every six months over a three-year period for a total of seven interviews during this time. To avoid replacing the entire sample at the end of three years, the NCS staggered the beginning and ending points for each wave. Every six months, one-sixth of the households departed the study group and their replacements underwent the initial interview. Roughly 12,000 households were interviewed each month, making the survey process a year-round endeavor.

The NCS incorporated many features uncovered in the earlier exploratory studies. The panel design, for example, established a six-month bounding period for the study. The first interview was not used to estimate crime rates. Instead, it became the starting point or boundary. To guard against telescoping and memory decay, each subsequent interview was checked against previous reports.

One burden that confronted the NCS was the *mover-stayer problem*. Sample plans were built on the residence, not the respondent. If the original survey participants vacated the premises and somebody else moved in, the new tenants automatically joined the sample for the balance of the study period. Responses from the new residents were used even though bounding was not possible. The NCS made no effort to track the original respondents. Instead, it assumed that the impact of relocation upon victimization estimates and the comparability of stable versus changed residences were minimal.

Unlike earlier generations, interviewers talked with each household member rather than just a single household representative. Exceptions to this rule occurred when the contact person was a child, when the parent objected to an interview with a minor or when repeated attempts to contact an individual family member proved futile. In these cases, one person acted as a proxy for the entire household.

While the above is true regarding individual victimizations, crimes against the household were solicited from only one household representative. This procedure aimed to reduce interviewing time and to eliminate the overlap from talking with more than one person about the same things. Unfortunately, the selected household respondent may not always be aware of all crimes against the household or may not know all the details needed for accurate reporting.

### The Business Victimization Survey

Along with the national survey, the NCS also launched a commercial victimization survey. This undertaking gathered information from businesses to assess their level of risk. The commercial survey, though, was discontinued in 1977 for two primary reasons. First, the sample of 15,000 businesses was too small to project reliable estimates. Second, the costs of the survey were not commensurate with the potential payoff.

### City Surveys

Twenty-six large cities were selected for special surveys of both residents and businesses. A total of 12,000 households and 2,000 businesses were targeted for interviews in each city. While the single-city findings were interesting, there was a great deal of overlap with the national survey. The costs associated with these multiple projects were astronomical. Eventually, the city surveys were discontinued in 1975 after only three years of operation.

## Fourth-Generation Victim Surveys

Today, we are in the fourth generation of victimization surveys. To emphasize this transition, the format and title of the national victim surveys has changed. The new name is the *National Crime Victimization Survey* (NCVS).

The redesign efforts began in 1979, partly as a response to issues raised in a National Academy of Sciences report (Penick and Owens, 1976). As before, a number of exploratory analyses were undertaken to test potential adjustments. Some of these considerations covered such items as improving accuracy of responses, identifying information by subgroups, adding new questions to tap different dimensions of crime and victim responses, and making the data more useful for researchers (Skogan, 1990; Whitaker, 1989). Figure 2.3 spells out some of the objectives that the Bureau of Justice Statistics hopes the victim survey efforts will achieve.

**FIGURE 2.3**
**Objectives and Intended Uses for the NCVS**

- To provide trend data that will serve as a set of continuous and comparable national social indicators for the rate of victimization for selected crimes. . . .

- To provide policy makers at the national, state and local levels as well as the research community with a database that constitutes the best available empirical information concerning crime victims and victimization.

- To facilitate analytical research on issues of public concern and of consequence to the development of national, state and local criminal justice policy.

- To provide empirical information relevant to understanding the differences between the rates of crime reported to the police and the victimization rate.

- To provide empirical information concerning the characteristics of victims and the consequences of the victimization that will be useful in designing, implementing and maintaining victim assistance programs.

- To provide empirical information that assists individuals and households in avoiding victimization.

- To assist state and local governments in evaluating the feasibility and utility of local victimization surveys.

- To provide empirical information on perceived satisfaction with the criminal justice system.

- To gather information on a regular basis concerning attitudes toward crime, criminals and crime control.

Source: Taylor, B.M. (1989). *Bureau of Justice Statistics Technical Report: New Directions for the National Crime Survey.* Washington, DC: U.S. Government Printing Office.

Concern over recall accuracy returns to issues of question wording, bounding, memory decay and telescoping. There was some worry that the *screen questions*—those inquiries that probe possible victimization experiences—could be misleading and in need of revision (Dodge, 1985). Redesign analysts found that improved screen questions resulted in a 28 percent increase in reported crime (Taylor, 1989: 23). This gain stemmed from an enhanced ability to prod the memory of respondents. To see how the NCVS does this, Figure 2.4 displays the household screen questions and Figure 2.5 contains the revised individual screen questions. Each respondent is asked the questions in Figures 2.4 and 2.5 as a means of probing victimization experiences in the past six months. These responses are then used as the basis for in-depth questions about the specific victimization occurrences.

**FIGURE 2.4**
**Household Screen Questions from the National Crime Victimization Survey**

| HOUSEHOLD SCREEN QUESTIONS | | | |
|---|---|---|---|
| 36. Now I'd like to ask some questions about crime. They refer only to the last 6 months – <br><br> between _____ 1, 19___ and <br> _____, 19___. During the last 6 months, did anyone break into or somehow illegally get into your (apartment/home), garage, or another building on your property? | ☐ Yes – How many times? <br><br> ☐ No <br> _____ | 39. Did anyone take something belonging to you or to any member of this household, from a place where you or they were temporarily staying, such as a friend's or relative's home, a hotel, or motel, or a vacation home? | ☐ Yes – How many times? <br><br> ☐ No <br> _____ |
| 37. (Other than the incident(s) just mentioned) Did you find a door jimmied, a lock forced, or any other signs of an ATTEMPTED break in? | ☐ Yes – How many times? <br><br> ☐ No | 40. What was the TOTAL number of motor vehicles (cars, trucks, motorcycles, etc.) owned by you or any other member of this household during the last 6 months? Include those you no longer own. | 511 <br> 0 ☐ None – SKIP to 43 <br> 1 ☐ 1 <br> 2 ☐ 2 <br> 3 ☐ 3 <br> 4 ☐ 4 or more |
| 38. Was anything at all stolen that is kept outside your home, or happened to be left out, such as a bicycle, a garden hose, or lawn furniture? (other than any incidents already mentioned) | ☐ Yes – How many times? <br><br> ☐ No <br> _____ | 41. Did anyone steal, TRY to steal, or use (it/any of them) without permission? | ☐ Yes – How many times? <br><br> ☐ No |
| | | 42. Did anyone steal, or TRY to steal parts attached to (it/any of them), such as a battery, hubcaps, tape-deck, etc.? | ☐ Yes – How many times? <br><br> ☐ No <br> _____ |

Source: U.S. Department of Justice (1992). *Criminal Victimization in the United States, 1991.* Washington, DC: U.S. Government Printing Office, p. 122.

A shorter reference period was also examined as a means to improve recall. This option, however, was rejected. The increased costs were simply too prohibitive.

The problem of bounding came up in reference to the mover-stayer issue. If you recall, newly relocated respondents at a household marked for inclusion in the NCVS provide unbounded information during their initial interview. One solution called for basing the sample on respondents, as opposed to household addresses. However, such a move would require interviewers to follow sample members to their new residences for subsequent questioning. This option was not feasible because it substantially increased survey costs.

Another exasperating problem has been the inability to examine subgroups within the survey data. Because of legal restrictions protecting respondent identities, it is difficult to analyze victimization data in anything but the national aggregate. The redesign efforts have demonstrated that it is possible to produce limited information based on cities or states without violating subject confidentiality. Such an ability will allow for more direct and meaningful comparisons with the UCR and other data sources.

**FIGURE 2.5**
**Individual Screen Questions from the National Crime Victimization Survey**

| INDIVIDUAL SCREEN QUESTIONS | |
|---|---|
| 43. The following questions refer only to things that happened to YOU during the last 6 months – between _____ 1, 19___ and _____, 19____. Did you have your (pocket picked/purse snatched)? <br> ☐ Yes – How many times? <br> ☐ No | 54. Did you call the police during the last 6 months to report something that happened to YOU which you thought was a crime? (Do not count any calls made to the police concerning the incidents you have just told me about.) [512] ★ <br> ☐ No – *SKIP to 55* <br> ☐ Yes – **What happened?** |
| 44. Did anyone take something (else) directly from you by using force, such as by a stickup, mugging or threat? <br> ☐ Yes – How many times? <br> ☐ No | |
| 45. Did anyone TRY to rob you by using force or threatening to harm you? (other than any incidents already mentioned) <br> ☐ Yes – How many times? <br> ☐ No | **CHECK ITEM C** Look at 54. Was HHLD member 12 + attacked or threatened, or was something stolen or an attempt made to steal something that belonged to him/her? <br> ☐ Yes – How many times? <br> ☐ No |
| 46. Did anyone beat you up, attack you or hit you with something, such as a rock or bottle? (other than any incidents already mentioned) <br> ☐ Yes – How many times? <br> ☐ No | 55. Did anything happen to YOU during the last 6 months which you thought was a crime, but did NOT report to the police? (other than incidents already mentioned) [513] ★ <br> ☐ No – *SKIP to Check Item E* <br> ☐ Yes – **What happened?** |
| 47. Were you knifed, shot at, or attacked with some other weapon by anyone at all? (other than any incidents already mentioned) <br> ☐ Yes – How many times? <br> ☐ No | |
| 48. Did anyone THREATEN to beat you up or THREATEN you with a knife, gun, or some other weapon, NOT including telephone threats? (other than any incidents already mentioned) <br> ☐ Yes – How many times? <br> ☐ No | **CHECK ITEM D** Look at 55. Was HHLD member 12 + attacked or threatened, or was something stolen or an attempt made to steal something that belonged to him/her? <br> ☐ Yes – How many times? <br> ☐ No |
| 49. Did anyone TRY to attack you in some other way? (other than any incidents already mentioned) <br> ☐ Yes – How many times? <br> ☐ No | **CHECK ITEM E** Who besides the respondent was present when screen questions were asked? *(If telephone interview, mark box 1 only.)* [514] ★ <br> 1 ☐ Telephone interview – *Go to Check Item F* <br> **Personal interview** – *Mark all that apply.* <br> 2 ☐ No one besides respondent present <br> 3 ☐ Respondent's spouse <br> 4 ☐ HHLD member(s) 12 +, not spouse <br> 5 ☐ HHLD member(s) under 12 <br> 6 ☐ Nonhousehold member(s) <br> 7 ☐ Someone was present – Can't say who <br> 8 ☐ Don't know if someone else was present |
| 50. During the last 6 months, did anyone steal things that belonged to you from inside ANY car or truck, such as packages or clothing? <br> ☐ Yes – How many times? <br> ☐ No | |
| 51. Was anything stolen from you while you were away from home, for instance at work, in a theater or restaurant, or while traveling? <br> ☐ Yes – How many times? <br> ☐ No | **CHECK ITEM F** *If self-response interview, SKIP to Check Item G* <br> Did the person for whom this interview was taken help the proxy respondent answer any screen questions? [515] <br> 1 ☐ Yes <br> 2 ☐ No <br> 3 ☐ Person for whom interview taken not present |
| 52. (Other than any incidents you've already mentioned) was anything (else) at all stolen from you during the last 6 months? <br> ☐ Yes – How many times? <br> ☐ No | |
| 53. Did you find any evidence that someone ATTEMPTED to steal something that belonged to you? (other than any incidents already mentioned) <br> ☐ Yes – How many times? <br> ☐ No | **CHECK ITEM G** Do any of the screen questions contain any entries for "How many times?" <br> ☐ Yes – *Fill Crime Incident Reports* <br> ☐ No – *Interview next HHLD member. End interview if last respondent.* |

Source: U.S. Department of Justice (1992). *Criminal Victimization in the United States, 1991.* Washington, DC: U.S. Government Printing Office, p. 122.

Despite the wealth of information contained in the NCVS, many researchers would like to capture data on other related topics. The redesign team considered the feasibility of adding special supplements that would supply data on selected topics. Two examples of these efforts are the Victim Risk Supplement conducted in 1983 and the School Crime Supplement carried out in 1989. Both projects addressed meaningful issues (crime prevention activities, fear of crime, and victimization within schools). The NCVS plans to append other supplemental questions from time to time (Taylor, 1989).

The final major goal of the redesign is to enhance the analytical worth of the survey. Two possible ways to meet this expectation are probing various outcomes of victimization and conducting longitudinal analyses. The problem of longitudinal study is a fundamental concern. To date, victimization studies have been restricted to cross-sectional approaches. It has not been possible to match a person's file with responses from an earlier interview. The redesign team strongly recommended that procedures for more longitudinal analyses be adopted.

The redesign also suggested other improvements (Taylor, 1989). One idea is to move to Computer-Assisted Telephone Interviews (CATI). This technique uses a computer to prompt the interviewer with the proper questions. It automatically skips questions whenever appropriate. Computerization should also eliminate miscoded data by accepting only legitimate responses during the interview. At the present time, roughly 30 percent of the NCVS interviews are completed using the CATI technology (Bureau of Justice Statistics, 1997).

Another suggestion is to eliminate questions that have proven to be of limited use in past analyses. It also may be possible to ask other questions on a less frequent basis. The overriding consideration, and one of immense importance, is to keep survey costs reasonable in light of the other proposed changes.

The NCVS began carrying out the redesigned survey in 1988 and had the full survey overhauled and in place by the end of 1992. Figure 2.6 presents a condensed version of some other prominent changes.

As mentioned earlier, a major goal of the redesign efforts that began in 1992 was to improve screening questions so as to stimulate better respondent recall and to provide clearer definitions of criminal victimization. To assess the impact of these changes, one-half of the interviews in 1992 were conducted using the old questions while one-half of the subjects were asked the new questions. A comparison of the two formats showed that the revamped queries produced 44 percent more personal victimization reports and 49 percent more property incidents (Kindermann et al., 1997). As expected, reports for robbery, personal theft and motor vehicle theft did not show substantial gains. However, rapes jumped by 157 percent, assaults rose by 57 percent, burglaries increased by 20 percent and theft moved upward by 27 percent. Inspection of the data led the analysts to believe that the new instrument made inroads into gray-area events. A *gray-area event* pertains to a victimization that does not conform to the usual common stereotype. For example, episodes involving nonstrangers as the aggressors showed marked increases with the new questions. It would appear, then, that the revisions are working as intended.

**FIGURE 2.6**
**Selected National Crime Victimization Survey Redesign Features**

---

**Questionnaire:**

- Revise Industry and Occupation items to target victim-related occupational characteristics.
- Begin to collect data on vandalism.
- Adopt victim-related lifestyle items.
- Continue to collect household incident data from one household respondent.
- Retain the six-month reference period.
- Adopt new self-protection items detailing consequences and bystander behavior.
- Adopt items on substance abuse by offenders.
- Adopt items on long-term contacts with the criminal justice system.
- Provide greater detail in "place of occurrence."
- Adopt item measuring threats before actual attacks.
- Provide greater detail in "type of property taken."
- Expand codes for items measuring reasons for reporting or not reporting crimes to the police.
- Raise threshold for defining series crimes to six incidents.

**Data Collection Procedures:**

- Eliminate proxy interviews for twelve- and thirteen-year-old respondents when possible.
- Implement "maximum telephone" usage data collection.

**Sample Design:**

- Stratify sample by areal UCR data to improve sample accuracy.

**Estimation:**

- Develop models to incorporate bounding interview data in estimates.

**Other Issues:**

- Release of county-level NCS data.
- Adopt full, person-based longitudinal design.
- Implement CATI.
- Design and schedule longitudinal supplement.

---

Source: U.S. Department of Justice (1989). *Redesign of the National Crime Survey.* Washington, DC: U.S. Government Printing Office.

Undoubtedly, the NCVS will undergo further modification as victimization surveys continue to evolve and as the need for different sorts of information becomes more apparent. Victimization surveys have become a valuable tool within a very short time. As the next section will show, the information gathered by this approach offers a much different view of criminal victimization than that given by the official records.

## STATISTICS FROM THE NCVS

Recent years have witnessed a growing reliance on victimization survey data for assessing the crime problem. Perhaps the greatest reason for this change is the realization that the UCR suffers from systematic limitations. For some time now, criminologists have recognized that official reports underestimate how much crime there really is. Even the primitive early victim surveys uncovered much more crime than the UCR did. In addition, victim surveys capture data on the victim and the circumstances surrounding the criminal event. As a result, victimization surveys have earned an important niche in the measurement of crime.

According to the National Crime Victimization Survey (Bureau of Justice Statistics, 1997), there were 38.4 million crimes committed in 1995. In comparison, the UCR tabulated almost 14 million index offenses in 1995 (Federal Bureau of Investigation, 1996). Even when one takes definitional differences into account, the gap between these two data sources is quite large.

Table 2.3 presents national victimization figures according to incident type. The table reveals that the risks of becoming a property crime victim are far greater than being involved in a violent encounter. This finding mirrors the UCR information discussed earlier.

**TABLE 2.3**
**National Victimization Levels, NCVS, 1995**

| Offense Category | Number of Victimizations (in thousands) | Victimization Rate per 1,000 |
|---|---|---|
| **Personal Crimes:** | | |
| Rape | 234 | 1.1 |
| Robbery | 1,142 | 5.3 |
| Aggravated Assault | 1,892 | 8.8 |
| Simple Assault | 6,227 | 28.9 |
| Personal Theft[a] | 365 | 1.7 |
| **Household Crimes:** | | |
| Burglary | 4,825 | 47.4 |
| Theft | 22,002 | 215.9 |
| Motor Vehicle Theft | 1,614 | 16.2 |

[a] Includes pocket picking, purse snatching, and attempts.

Source: Taylor, B.M. (1997). *Bureau of Justice Statistics: National Crime Victimization Survey: Changes in Criminal Victimization, 1994-95.* Washington, DC: U.S. Government Printing Office, p. 2.

Victimization surveys also provide additional information not addressed by the UCR. For example, Table 2.4 shows that males are more likely to be violent crime victims than females. Like the UCR, the NCVS reveals that people under the age of 24 are a very vulnerable group. Blacks have higher robbery and aggravated assault victim rates than do whites, as well as higher burglary rates. However, they share almost identical chances of becoming simple assault and household theft victims. In every category except household theft, persons with lower incomes have a higher risk of becoming crime victims than people who are wealthier. Finally, victimization is much more likely to occur in urban areas than in either suburban or rural areas.

**TABLE 2.4**
**Victimization Rates by Selected Characteristics, NCVS, 1995**

| Victim Characteristic | Robbery | Aggravated Assault | Simple Assault | Burglary | Household Theft |
|---|---|---|---|---|---|
| **Sex** | | | | | |
| Male | 7.5 | 11.9 | 33.5 | | |
| Female | 3.2 | 5.9 | 24.6 | | |
| **Age** | | | | | |
| 12-15 | 9.5 | 15.4 | 80.1 | | |
| 16-19 | 9.0 | 24.4 | 68.6 | | |
| 20-24 | 10.8 | 15.4 | 49.6 | | |
| 25-34 | 6.9 | 11.7 | 34.1 | | |
| 35-49 | 4.7 | 6.8 | 20.9 | | |
| 50-64 | 1.8 | 2.6 | 9.5 | | |
| 65+ | 1.3 | 1.3 | 3.3 | | |
| **Race** | | | | | |
| White | 4.2 | 8.2 | 29.1 | 45.4 | 213.6 |
| Black | 12.5 | 12.6 | 28.7 | 61.6 | 230.3 |
| Other | 6.3 | 9.2 | 24.2 | 46.4 | 224.3 |
| **Family Income** | | | | | |
| $    0- 7,499 | 11.8 | 16.5 | 39.2 | 71.4 | 205.4 |
| $ 7,500- 9,999 | 9.1 | 10.0 | 27.7 | 55.0 | 185.5 |
| $10,000-14,999 | 6.5 | 9.1 | 30.4 | 48.7 | 222.4 |
| $15,000-24,999 | 5.1 | 8.9 | 30.8 | 42.0 | 224.5 |
| $25,000-29,999 | 3.6 | 8.8 | 30.1 | 42.6 | 232.6 |
| $30,000-49,999 | 3.1 | 8.5 | 29.9 | 41.8 | 258.1 |
| $50,000+ | 2.4 | 5.5 | 27.6 | 43.3 | 273.7 |
| **Residence** | | | | | |
| Urban | 9.7 | 11.7 | 33.4 | 59.9 | 263.3 |
| Suburban | 4.0 | 8.1 | 28.4 | 39.0 | 213.0 |
| Rural | 2.6 | 6.6 | 24.5 | 46.8 | 164.8 |

Source: Taylor, B.M. (1997). *Bureau of Justice Statistics: National Crime Victimization Survey: Changes in Criminal Victimization, 1994-95.* Washington, DC: U.S. Government Printing Office, pp. 3-4.

The NCVS has collected victimization data for several years now. This practice permits an inspection of trends. Figure 2.7 graphs personal victimization rates since the NCVS redesign in 1992. A glance at the figure shows that victimization rates for robbery, personal theft and rape have remained stable over the past four years. Simple and aggravated assault, though, exhibit modest increases followed by small decreases. Both rape and aggravated assault patterns are consistent with what we saw earlier when we looked at trends with the UCR data. Unfortunately, the short time span since the 1992 redesign makes any trend analyses suspect. Rand and associates (1997) have attempted to make adjustments in the earlier NCS data that will allow inspection of trends spanning the two survey forms. While they admit to some tenuous assumptions, their results do show general declines in victimization throughout the early to mid-1980s, followed by increases in the late 1980s and early 1990s, with declines following that.

**FIGURE 2.7**
**Personal Victimization Rates, NCVS, 1992-95**

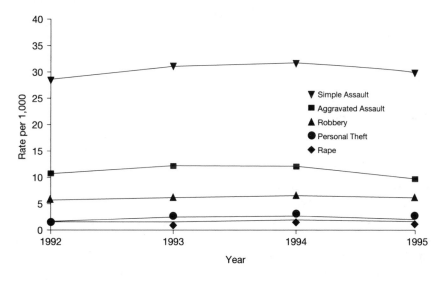

Source: Taylor, B.M. (1997). *Bureau of Justice Statistics: National Crime Victimization Survey: Changes in Criminal Victimization, 1994-95.* Washington, DC: U.S. Government Printing Office, p. 2.

Similar information for household property victimization appears in Figure 2.8 for the 1992-95 period. Again, the graphs show no major disturbances over time. Household theft and burglary display small declines, while motor vehicle theft has remained constant. Again, these patterns are somewhat consistent with conclusions derived from our earlier examination of UCR crime rates.

**FIGURE 2.8**
**Household Victimization Rates, NCVS, 1992-95**

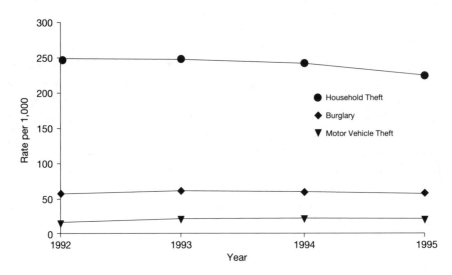

Source: Taylor, B.M. (1997). *Bureau of Justice Statistics: National Crime Victimization Survey: Changes in Criminal Victimization, 1994-95.* Washington, DC: U.S. Government Printing Office, p. 2.

One obvious distinction between the UCR and the NCVS is that victims reveal to interviewers incidents that have not come to the attention of the police. Figure 2.9 contains a visual presentation of reporting practices for 1994. Overall, less than one-half of the victimization episodes identified by the NCVS resulted in police notification. Motor vehicle theft leads the pack with the highest reporting rate, probably due to insurance company expectations. Cases of household theft lag far behind typical reporting patterns.

Compared to the UCR, victimization data provide a great deal of information about the victim-offender relationship. This information, however, is primarily for crimes in which the victim and offender have personal contact. In 1994, 46 percent of all violent crimes were committed by nonstrangers. Strangers were involved in a high of 78 percent of all robberies to a low of 36 percent of all sexual offenses (Bureau of Justice Statistics, 1997). The victim-offender relationship is specified further as spouse, ex-spouse, parent, child, other relative, well-known acquaintance, casual acquaintance, stranger or unknown. These categories will be useful in many of the discussions in later chapters.

**FIGURE 2.9**
**Percent Victimizations Reported to the Police, NCVS, 1994**

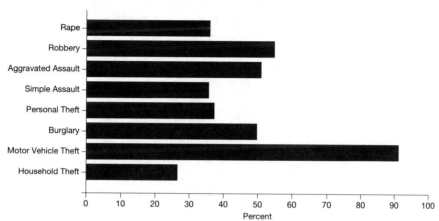

Source: Perkins, C. and P. Klaus (1996). *Bureau of Justice Statistics Bulletin: National Crime Victimization Survey: Criminal Victimization, 1994.* Washington, DC: U.S. Government Printing Office, p. 6.

## REPEAT VICTIMIZATION

The growth of victimization surveys and the development of new data analysis techniques, particularly through the use of computer mapping, has generated increased interest in repeat victimization or revictimization. *Repeat victimization* can be defined as the repeated occurrence of crime either involving the same victim or the same location. Even casual observation demonstrates that victim recidivism is common with some crimes. For example, it is not unusual for domestic violence victims to drop charges or refuse to cooperate with the prosecution, despite records of ongoing violent episodes. Sherman (1995) points out that police often receive repeated calls for service stemming from domestic violence at the same addresses.

Revictimization can be gleaned from a variety of data collection and analytic techniques. The NCVS provides some insight through its questions dealing with *series victimizations*. These are instances where a respondent reports six or more separate victimization episodes occurring within the time frame of the survey. Hindelang et al. (1978) and Reiss (1980), using NCS data, report evidence of repeat victimization in the data. Other analyses of juvenile victimization data (Lauritsen and Quinet, 1995) and the British Crime Survey (Osborn et al., 1996) also show that multiple victimization episodes are concentrated among relatively few victims.

Another way of demonstrating revictimization using victimization data is to compare prevalence and incidence data. *Prevalence data* include the number of individuals who experience victimization over a period of time, whereas *incidence data* represent the total number of offenses that are reported during the same period. Any point at which the number of incidents exceed the number of victims would indicate revictimization. Farrell (1995) notes that this is a routine finding in analyses of both the NCVS and the British Crime Survey (BCS), despite the fact that a six-month or one-year recall period should limit such findings. Longer recall periods would undoubtedly increase the finding of repeat victimizations.

Various analyses of survey data demonstrate the often concentrated nature of victimization. Mayhew and associates (1993) report that 17 percent of all burglaries involve only 6 percent of the burglary victims, and almost one-half of all violent victimizations are experienced by only 17 percent of the victims of violent crimes. Similarly, Gottfredson (1984) notes that, of those victimized two or more times in the 1982 BCS data, 14 percent of the survey participants suffered 70 percent of the offenses. The 1988 BCS data reveal that 20 percent of the respondents are repeat victims accounting for more than 80 percent of all reported offenses (Shah, 1991).

Evidence of repeat victimization, victim recidivism or chronic victimization is not restricted to survey data or to individuals. Efforts to improve police effectiveness and efficiency have prompted the development of various techniques to identify what are known as crime "hot spots." *Hot spots* are "small places in which the occurrence of crime is so frequent that it is highly predictable" (Sherman, 1995: 36). The use of computer mapping has enhanced the ability of most police departments to identify such places. Sherman et al. (1989) note that all domestic disturbance calls in Minneapolis come from only 9 percent of the places in town, all assaults occur at 7 percent of the locations, and all burglaries transpire at 11 percent of the places. Similar concentrations of offenses and calls for police service have been found in many other locations (see, for example, Block and Block, 1995; Spelman, 1995). What is not always demonstrated is whether the calls involve the same victims. While domestic violence calls to the same address probably have the same victim, repeated assault calls to a bar may involve different patrons every time. In either case, the value of the information is in its ability to inform responses to victimization.

Revictimization information can be useful for developing responses by both potential victims and community agencies. Pease and Laycock (1996) point out that past victimization is a good predictor of future victimization. This finding does not mean that every victim will be victimized again in the future; rather, it indicates that victims may be more vulnerable because of circumstances or lifestyle. Past victimization should be used by a victim to assess what factors contributed to the crime and what actions can be taken to mitigate future vulnerability. Just as people use knowledge of the victimization of others as a warning sign, so should a victim take heed. Unfortunately, for many victims, "Lightning *does* strike twice!"

**FIGURE 2.10**
**Selected Internet Sites Dealing with Victimization Statistics**

Bureau of Justice Statistics
      http://www.ojp.usdoj.gov/bjs/

FBI Uniform Crime Reports
      http://www.fbi.gov/

Rate Your Risk
      http://www.telalink.net/~police/risk/index.html

Sourcebook of Criminal Justice Statistics
      http://www.albany.edu/sourcebook/

# SUMMARY

How much criminal victimization is there in our society? One thing that should be evident after working your way through this chapter is that criminologists and victimologists cannot provide an exact answer. However, by using different data sources, they can give some estimates as to the nature and extent of the victimization problem.

No matter which approach a researcher takes when he or she tackles this question, certain systematic problems have the potential to hamper those measurement efforts. The materials in this chapter shed light on what some of these obstacles are, how they impinge upon the data and what can be done to minimize these intrusions. As you can see, victim surveys are very much like any other consumer product. People are constantly tinkering, updating and refining these instruments to take advantage of the most current technology available.

# LEARNING OBJECTIVES

After reading Chapter 3, you should be able to:

- Talk about why some people do not want to call the police after being victimized.

- Explain how there is no "truth in sentencing."

- Catalog the costs victims sustain as a result of their criminal experience.

- Relay what is meant by "the second insult."

- Chronicle the development of victim-witness management projects.

- Identify some of the recommendations issued by the President's Task Force on Victims of Crime.

- Understand some of the recommendations that the U.S. Attorney General issued for strengthening local criminal justice systems.

- Outline the planning preparations for instigating a victim-witness assistance program.

- List different types of services usually provided by victim-witness programs.

- Explain how a victim-witness program blunts the "prosecutory assembly line" mentality.

- Talk about the two assumptions that underlie victim-witness service projects.

- Explain how derivative victims have come under the umbrella of victim services.

- Evaluate whether victim-witness projects work.

- Address the criticism that witness management is simply a tool with which to manipulate victims.

# The Costs of Being a Victim

## Introduction

This chapter takes a look at some of the costs associated with becoming a crime victim. As we all know, victims suffer at the hands of their offenders. Some people may be injured physically; others may lose property during the attack. All will be gripped to some extent with fear and mental anguish. This aspect of their victimization experience will affect their quality of life and probably will not subside for quite a while.

### Key Terms

cost-benefit analysis

derivative victims

double victimization

victim advocates

victim-witness
(victim/witness) projects

Victims who turn to the criminal justice system for comfort and solace quickly learn that they run the risk of being exploited. The system, through its impersonal and detached mechanisms for sorting through cases, aggravates the victim's condition. For example, inconsiderate habits may force some victims to wait in hallways for a hearing to start, only to learn later that it has been canceled already. No one may bother to telephone them. Other victims are bewildered by what is transpiring around them. No one may have taken the time to explain what is happening in the case or why. Instead, these victims find system officials quickly shepherding them through the courthouse doors without so much as a simple "thank you."

As victim complaints intensified, officials began to worry that continued mishandling would jeopardize the role victims played when the state presented its case. Prosecutors needed victim testimony to make charges stick. As a result, victim-witness assistance programs materialized. Their goal was to soften the impact of system participation so that victims would make good witnesses at the trial stage.

This chapter will visit some of the problems that victims and witnesses encounter during their treks through the system. We will then focus on what the system is doing to alleviate these problems. Finally, our attention will turn to some criticisms that have surfaced.

## THE CONSEQUENCES OF VICTIMIZATION

The American criminal justice system is facing a critical loss of citizen trust and support. Results from the National Crime Victimization Surveys indicate that almost two of every three victimizations now go unreported to the police (Perkins and Klaus, 1996: 6). When interviewers ask these victims why they did not call the police, several consistent refrains emerge. Most often, victims report that the suspect was not successful and that nothing was lost. Others claim the police would not do anything or feel that the police would not want to get involved in the matter. In short, many victims see no benefits to be gained from initiating contact with system representatives.

These sentiments are not confined to the police. Many people harbor genuine doubts that the courts will sufficiently punish an offender once he or she is apprehended and prosecuted (Maguire and Pastore, 1996: 174; Schneider et al., 1976: 102). They realize that there is no "truth in sentencing" for convicted felons. Homicide offenders, for example, usually net a 21-year state prison term from the courts. However, they typically spend only about one-half of this amount of time behind bars. Judges solemnly pronounce 14-year terms for rapists, but often they are out in less than five years. Robbers can expect to fulfill maybe four years out of a 10-year sentence. Aggravated assault convicts often serve four years, although their sentences officially extend for eight years (Maguire and Pastore, 1996: 507). What this boils down to is that the system is not making good on its promises.

Given this climate, citizen reluctance to become involved in the criminal justice system continues to reach epidemic heights. A substantial number of victims and witnesses who have gone through the criminal justice process confide that they would not return if they could avoid doing so in the future (Cannavale and Falcon, 1976; Finn and Lee, 1987: 8; Knudten et al., 1976; Norton, 1983). System personnel complain that citizens are growing increasingly apathetic. However, such a self-serving portrayal is difficult to accept. An alternative description is that victims have grown disenchanted and are rebelling against further abuse. Because of past mistreatment, they are making a very deliberate and rational decision to bypass the criminal justice system.

Victims sustain costs from at least two different sources. In this sense, they face *double victimization*. First, they suffer at the hands of their offenders. Then, by participating in the criminal justice system, they risk even more damage. By making a choice to avoid the system, victims are able to minimize their losses. As one victim's mother put it:

> You have already been victimized, and you end up going through the victimization again from the system you are in. So what happens is, with all these choices, you end up trying to maintain integrity and security and sanity in hopes that the truth will come out and you feel good about the result. It is very hard. I don't know if we would go through it again (Cassell, 1997).

Before we go any further, though, let us review just what some of these costs entail. We will start by looking at the costs associated with criminal victimization. Then, we will proceed to examine the costs that stem from system involvement.

## The First Insult: Criminal Victimization

Early victim studies concentrated on documenting the calamity and woes that accompany the victimization experience. The Milwaukee Victim/Witness Project, for example, was undertaken to assess the difficulties stemming from the criminal episode (Knudten et al., 1976; Knudten et al., 1977; Knudten and Knudten, 1981). In addition to sustaining physical injury and property loss or damage, a sizable proportion of victims reported losing time from work and their normal routines. They also endured emotional anguish and interpersonal complications with family members and friends. Despite their perception that these problems were serious, most victims forged ahead alone. Even though many social service agencies were in operation, victims remained largely unaware of service availability. As a result, relatively few victims received help coping with their crime-induced problems (Doerner et al., 1976a), a finding that persists even today in other jurisdictions (Jerin et al., 1995; Johnson, 1996).

Recent efforts have focused more sharply on cataloging the costs involved in criminal victimization. Miller and his colleagues (1996) combed through a variety of data sources, including the National Crime Victimization Survey, to get a fuller picture of the costs and consequences of criminal victimization. The researchers began by compiling a lengthy list of costs extracted by the victimization experience. As Figures 3.1 and 3.2 show, some of the costs associated with victimization extend far beyond just the immediate victim and indirectly affect a host of other people.

**FIGURE 3.1**
**List of Costs Associated with Crime**

| Costs of Crime | Party Who Directly Bears Cost |
|---|---|
| Direct Property Losses | |
|     Losses not reimbursed by insurance | Victim |
|     Losses reimbursed by insurance | Society |
|     Administrative cost of insurance reimbursement | Society |
|     Recovery by police | Society |
| Medical and Mental Health Care | |
|     Costs not reimbursed by insurance | Victim/Family/Society |
|     Costs reimbursed by insurance | Society |
|     Administrative overhead of insurance coverage | Society |
| Victim Services | |
|     Expenses charged to victim | Victim |
|     Expenses paid by agency | Society |
|     Temporary labor and training of replacements | Society |
| Lost Workdays | |
|     Lost wages for unpaid workday | Victim |
|     Lost productivity | Society/Employer |
| Lost School Days | |
|     Foregone wages due to lack of education | Victim |
|     Foregone nonpecuniary benefit of education | Victim |
|     Foregone social benefits due to lack of education | Society |
| Lost Housework | Victim |
| Pain and Suffering/Quality of Life | Victim |
| Loss of Affection/Enjoyment | Family |
| Death | |
|     Lost quality of life | Victim |
|     Loss of affection/enjoyment | Family |
|     Funeral and burial expenses | Family |
|     Psychological injury/treatment | Family |
| Legal Costs Associated with Tort Claims | Victim or Family |
| "Second Generation Costs" | |
|     Future victims of crime committed by earlier victims | Future Victims |
|     Future social costs associated with above | Society/Victims |

Source: Miller, T.R., M.A. Cohen and B. Wiersema (1996). *Victim Costs and Consequences: A New Look.* Washington, DC: National Institute of Justice, p. 11.

**FIGURE 3.2**
**List of Costs Associated with Society's Response to Crime**

| Costs of Society's Response to Crime | Party Who Directly Bears Cost |
| --- | --- |
| Precautionary Expenditures/Effort | Potential Victim |
| Fear of Crime | Potential Victim |
| Criminal Justice System | |
| Police and investigative costs | Society |
| Prosecutors | Society |
| Courts | Society |
| Legal fees | |
| Public defenders | Society |
| Private lawyers | Offenders |
| Incarceration costs | Society |
| Nonincarcerative sanctions | Society |
| Victim time | Victim |
| Jury and witness time | Jury/Witness |
| Victim Services | |
| Victim service organizations | Society |
| Victim service volunteer time | Volunteers |
| Victim compensation programs | Society/Offender |
| Victim time | Victim |
| Other Noncriminal Programs | |
| Hotlines and public service announcements | Society |
| Community treatment programs | Society |
| Private therapy/counseling | Society/Offender |
| Incarcerated Offender Costs | |
| Lost wages | Offender/Family |
| Lost tax revenue and productivity | Society |
| Value of lost freedom | Offender |
| Psychological cost to family/loss of consortium | Family of Offender |
| "Overdeterrence" Costs | |
| Innocent individuals accused of offense | Innocent Individuals |
| Restriction of legitimate activity | Innocent Individuals |
| Actions taken by offenders to avoid detection | Victim |
| "Justice" Costs | |
| Constitutional protections to avoid false accusations | Society |
| Cost of increasing detection rate to avoid differential punishment | Society |

Source: Miller, T.R., M.A. Cohen and B. Wiersema (1996). *Victim Costs and Consequences: A New Look.* Washington, DC: National Institute of Justice, p. 11.

Using these cost categories enabled Miller and associates (1996) to produce estimates of crime-related losses according to type of crime. As Table 3.1 shows, the annual loss due to just these 10 crime classifications reached $450,000 million each year during the 1987-1990 period. This number works out to $1,800 for each individual in this country.

**TABLE 3.1**
**Annual Losses Due to Crime During 1987-1990, in Millions, Expressed in 1993 Dollars**[a]

| Type of Crime | Medical | Other Tangible[b] | Quality of Life | Total |
|---|---|---|---|---|
| Fatal Crime | $    700 | $32,700 | $ 60,000 | $ 93,000 |
| Child Abuse | $ 3,600 | $ 3,700 | $ 48,000 | $ 56,000 |
| Rape and Sexual Assault | $ 4,000 | $ 3,500 | $119,000 | $127,000 |
| Other Assault or Attempt | $ 5,000 | $10,000 | $ 77,000 | $ 93,000 |
| Robbery or Attempt | $    600 | $ 2,500 | $  8,000 | $ 11,000 |
| Drunk Driving | $ 3,400 | $10,000 | $ 27,000 | $ 41,000 |
| Arson | $    160 | $ 2,500 | $  2,400 | $  5,000 |
| Larceny or Attempt | $    150 | $ 9,000 | $      0 | $  9,000 |
| Burglary or Attempt | $     30 | $ 7,000 | $  1,800 | $  9,000 |
| Motor Vehicle Theft or Attempt | $      9 | $ 6,300 | $    500 | $  7,000 |
| Total | $18,000 | $87,000 | $345,000 | $450,000 |

[a] Totals may appear not to add up due to rounding.

[b] "Other Tangible" includes property damage and loss, mental health care, police and fire services, victim services, and productivity.

Source: Miller, T.R., M.A. Cohen and B. Wiersema (1996). *Victim Costs and Consequences: A New Look*. Washington, DC: National Institute of Justice, p. 17.

Of course, these monetary estimates would escalate considerably if there were no "dark figure of crime" and if complete information were available on every single incident. At the same time, one should realize that these figures refer to only a handful of street crimes. Other statutory violations, tax evasion, white-collar crime, corporate crime, and the like need to be factored in to arrive at a more comprehensive assessment.

To help appreciate the magnitude of victimization costs, consider the following information (Miller et al., 1996: 1):

- Violent crime causes 3 percent of U.S. medical spending and 14 percent of injury-related medical spending.

- Violent crime results in wage losses equivalent to 1 percent of American earnings.

- Violent crime is a significant factor in mental health care usage. As much as 10 to 20 percent of mental health care expenditures in the United States may be attributable to crime, primarily for victims treated as a result of their victimization.

- Personal crime reduces the average American's quality of life by 1.8 percent. Violence alone causes a 1.7 percent loss.

Beyond such obvious costs as injury, medical expenses, lost days from work and economic loss, victimization generates a broader public impact. Many citizens, whether or not they have been victimized, report being afraid of crime and respond to that fear in a variety of ways. Surveys report that more than 40 percent of the public is fearful of crime (Gallup, 1992; Skogan and Maxfield, 1981; Toseland, 1982). The National Victim Center (1991), surveying a national cross-section of U.S. adults, found that 60 percent said they avoided going out alone, 32 percent changed their shopping routine (time and/or place), 25 percent installed home security systems, 22 percent altered their work routine and 18 percent purchased a gun—all due to fear of crime. Thus, fear of crime becomes an added burden affecting both those victimized and the general public.

These figures suggest that many victims, as well as the general public, become the "walking wounded." They endure their problems and tribulations in silence often without help from external sources. On top of these crime-related losses come more difficulties when a victim's case finds its way into the criminal justice system. As the following section explains, these costs can be substantial.

## The Second Insult: System Participation

A victim's problems have only just begun if the case is processed through the criminal justice system. The system extracts further costs as soon as people enter into the halls of justice. In fact, the plight of victims and witnesses has led at least one prosecutor to chastise the system for victimizing its own patrons. Ash (1972: 390) describes typical system encounters in the following terms:

> [T]he witness will several times be ordered to appear at some designated place, usually a courtroom. . . . Several times he will be made to wait tedious, unconscionable long intervals of time in dingy courthouse corridors or in other grim surroundings. Several times he will suffer the discomfort of being ignored by busy officials and the bewilderment and painful anxiety of not knowing what is going on around him or what is going to happen to him. On most of these occasions he will never be asked to testify or to give anyone any information, often because of a last-minute adjournment granted in a huddled conference at the judge's bench. He will miss many hours from work (or school) and consequently will lose many hours of wages. In most jurisdictions he will receive at best only token payment in the form of ridiculously low witness fees for his time and trouble.

One feature of the Milwaukee Victim/Witness Project (discussed earlier) was to identify problems that the criminal justice system provoked for victims and witnesses (Doerner et al., 1976a; Knudten et al., 1976; Knudten et al., 1977; Knudten and Knudten, 1981). Interviewers learned that common problems for system participants included time loss, a corresponding reduction in income, time wasted waiting needlessly inside the courthouse, and transportation problems getting to and from the courthouse. In addition, court appearances for subpoenaed witnesses translated into lost wages—a significant concern for many people. Waiting conditions were another critical problem. At the time of the study, all victims and witnesses reported to a large waiting room at the courthouse. Bailiffs would retrieve witnesses when it was time for their testimony. In one particular case, a sexual assault victim took a seat before the trial began. A number of other people shuffled in and out waiting for their cases to begin. A few minutes later, much to her chagrin, the victim realized her suspected assailant was sitting next to her. Intimidation tactics can be very discomforting (Healey, 1995). Needless to say, situations such as the one described here do nothing to alleviate the stress and anxiety associated with system participation.

The time and the delays that materialize as a case winds its way through the system can be frustrating. Figure 3.3 illustrates the number of hearings, postponements, delays and other sacrifices one victim and her family endured during the prosecution of a child sexual assault case. All told, it took more than 15 months for the case to come to a conclusion, despite provisions in that state's laws entitling victims to the right to a speedy trial.

Probably the best way to characterize the reactions of victims and witnesses would be to say that their courthouse experiences leave them bewildered and frustrated. They have gone there to discharge a civic duty, yet they learn the hard way that the system takes undue advantage of their goodwill. They spend time away from work, lose money and are not treated courteously (Norton, 1983: 146-147). As one research team explained:

> [T]here is a serious gap between . . . problems faced by crime victims and the help available to them. Unless this gap is bridged, victims may come to realize they stand a good chance of incurring even greater financial losses if they cooperate with the criminal justice system. The anticipated financial loss due to entrance into the system may be sufficient to deter such citizen involvement. It is ironic that the system which is designed to protect the constitutional rights of the offender fails even to recognize the victim's position and then turns around and wonders why its citizenry is apathetic (Doerner et al., 1976a: 489).

**FIGURE 3.3**
**Time Line from One Criminal Case**

| | |
|---|---|
| June 1995 | Victim's family reports abuse to the proper authorities. |
| November 3, 1995 | Defendant arraigned. |
| November 21, 1995 | Roll call for defendant; preliminary hearing set for December 19, 1995. |
| December 19, 1995 | Victim comes to court. Preliminary hearing canceled because defense counsel was considering a settlement and wanted to talk over details. New preliminary hearing set for February 8, 1996. |
| February 8, 1996 | Victim comes to District Attorney's (DA) office for preliminary hearing. Defense attorneys call DA to request continuance. DA's office rejects in view of victim's preparation to testify. Then DA's office receives another call that defense counsel is sick. Deputy DA (DDA) appears along with another member of defense counsel's firm and previous attorney for defendant. DDA cites victims' rights provisions to speedy conclusion. Preliminary hearing canceled because of illness of defense counsel. Judge continued the case but attempts to accommodate victim's interests. New preliminary hearing set for February 13. |
| February 13, 1996 | Preliminary hearing held. Victim testifies. Victim's mother testifies. Defense counsel asks for recess because of time of day (4:00 P.M.) and because two more hours of questions for the mother were anticipated and because of scheduling conflict. Preliminary hearing continued until February 23. |
| February 22, 1996 | DDA notified that defense counsel could not appear for February 23rd preliminary hearing because of other scheduling problems. (Victim's family had canceled a trip to San Francisco to attend the February 23rd preliminary hearing, as previously mentioned in open court). |
| February 23, 1996 | Preliminary hearing canceled. New preliminary set for April 16, 1996. |
| April 16, 1996 | Victim's mother cross-examined for less than 10 minutes. Defense counsel did not have extensive questions. Briefing on bindover established. Hearing set for May 28, 1996. |
| May 28, 1996 | DDA appears. Defense counsel not prepared to proceed; had not filed memorandum. New briefing set for June 13, 1996. |
| June 13, 1996 | Briefs filed; hearing held; defendant bound over. |
| June 24, 1996 | Defendant appeared before District Court. Trial date set for October 29, 1996. October 29th date canceled because defense counsel involved in another trial and has not had time to prepare. |
| October 21, 1996 | Court meeting to schedule new trial. January 7, 1997 trial date set. |
| December 23, 1996 | Pre-trial conference (not on the record—in chambers). Defense counsel asks for continuance. Wanted more time to respond to prosecution's motion (filed three weeks earlier) and because new prosecutor would need more time. DDA says victim's family wants closure and promises to remain on the case if her absence (new job) would in any way delay proceedings. Defense counsel also indicates he typically takes vacation the week after Christmas. Judge refuses to continue. |

**FIGURE 3.3**—*continued*

| Early January 1997 | Case reassigned to new judge. |
|---|---|
| January 7, 1997 | Trial starts before new judge and new DDA. Victim testifies and concludes testimony. Trial ends for the day at noon. Victim's mother scheduled to be the next witness. Husband and two sisters all there. Judge says motions will be considered the next morning. |
| January 8, 1997 | Defense counsel asks for dismissal based on inadequate evidence to support the bindover. Denied. Judge agrees to allow appeal of issue of standard of review for bindover determinations. Further trial proceedings stopped. |
| January 16, 1997 | Meeting to review appeal in judge's chambers. DDA and defense counsel present. Advocate enters appearance on behalf of the victim, requests expedited hearing on victim's speedy trial rights. Asks for hearing to be scheduled while all attorneys are present. Judge says that scheduling, if a hearing is necessary, can be done by phone. |
| January 17, 1997 | Hearing on victim's motions scheduled for January 21 at 2:00 P.M. |
| January 21, 1997 | Hearing held. Judge agrees that victim has the right to be heard, but delays start of trial for unspecified period of time. Sets later hearing to schedule resumption of trial date. |
| February 3, 1997 | Further hearings held on resumption of trial. Advocate attempts to assert victim's right to be heard on speedy trial issue, but told by judge "we're fully staffed now" with prosecutor and defense attorney arguing the issue. Case set for trial at a time when victim had previously scheduled vacation. |
| February 28, 1997 | Bench trial resumes. |
| Early March 1997 | Defendant acquitted. |

Source: Cassell, P.G. (1997). *Statement before the Committee on the Judiciary, United States Senate, Concerning a Constitutional Amendment Protecting the Rights of Crime Victims on April 16, 1997.* Washington, DC: U.S. Government Printing Office.

Rather than claim apathy on the part of victims, it is more realistic to view the lack of participation in the criminal justice system as a rational choice. That is, victims make a *cost-benefit analysis* and see exacerbated costs accruing from system participation. Unless these financial needs are addressed, victims and witnesses will continue to boycott the criminal justice system.

## VICTIM-WITNESS MANAGEMENT PROJECTS

The criminal justice community has recognized the need to address the looming problem of citizen noncooperation in order to save the system from crumbling. Starting in the mid-1970s, the federal government provided funding for victim-witness assistance programs housed in prosecutor offices. There were more than 265 such programs in place by the end of the decade (Viano, 1979).

Observers refer to these efforts as *victim-witness projects* or *victim/witness projects*. The underlying ideological thrust is witness management. Many feel that prosecutors render services to crime victims not out of compassion, but to cultivate or preserve the worth of the victims as witnesses for the state (Chelimsky, 1981: 83). Thus, the focus is on minimizing witness discontent with system treatment in order to retain testimonial value.

Revised budget priorities and funding shifts saw the federal monies that underwrote victim-witness projects dry up by the beginning of the 1980s. The original federal strategy was to build in funding obsolescence. In other words, the federal government would provide the initial seed money to get new local victim-witness efforts up and running. Then, over the next three or four years, contributions to these projects would dwindle in specific decrements. The goal behind these prearranged cutbacks was to wean these fledgling programs away from a complete reliance upon federal funding sources. It was hoped that the early success of these seedling efforts would attract local fiscal support, enabling the projects to become self-sufficient.

To nurture the expansion of victim-witness programs from one jurisdiction to the next, the federal government developed several prescriptive packages. These booklets were blueprints that interested officials could adopt and mold to fit the local terrain. In this way, the government could avoid "reinventing the wheel," could bypass obstacles that others had faced already and would be able to get these programs fully operational with a minimal amount of delay.

Despite a modicum of success, local victim-witness projects languished as federal funds withered. They had not been very adept in becoming institutionalized as permanently funded fixtures within local criminal justice budgets. However, the political landscape underwent significant changes with the release of the report from the President's Task Force on Victims of Crime (1982).

The President's Task Force traveled throughout the country holding public hearings and securing testimony. Time after time, the Task Force received disturbing accounts of how the criminal justice system routinely mishandled victims and witnesses. Citizens relayed the tragic details of their victimization experiences, and further explained how their misfortunes had intensified when they turned to the criminal justice system for relief. Victims told how system officials shunned them, how becoming involved in the system had exacerbated or heightened their suffering and how the halls of justice became just another ordeal to undergo.

Task Force members came to the conclusion that the criminal justice system had become a monstrous operation in dire need of immediate reform. If the plight of victims and witnesses was to be corrected, then the system needed improvement. For this reason, the Task Force issued a number of recommendations aimed directly at victim and witness concerns. As Figure 3.4 illustrates, the Task Force had formed some definite ideas for victim-witness management. Specifically, it urged prosecutors to communicate more closely with victims, seek greater victim input, protect them against any harassment, honor scheduled case appearances, return property promptly and improve the overall quality of client services.

**FIGURE 3.4**
**Selected Recommendations to Prosecutors by the President's Task Force on Victims of Crime**

- Prosecutors should assume ultimate responsibility for informing victims of the status of a case from the time of the initial charging decision to determinations of parole.

- Prosecutors have an obligation to bring to the attention of the court the views of victims of violent crime on bail decisions, continuances, plea bargains, dismissals, sentencing, and restitution. They should establish procedures to ensure that such victims are given the opportunity to make their views on these matters known.

- Prosecutors should charge and pursue to the fullest extent of the law defendants who harass, threaten, injure, or otherwise attempt to intimidate or retaliate against victims or witnesses.

- Prosecutors should strongly discourage case continuances. When such delays are necessary, procedures should be established to ensure that cases are continued to dates agreeable to victims and witnesses, that those dates are secured in advance whenever possible, and that the reasons for the continuances are adequately explained.

- Prosecutors' offices should use a victim and witness on-call system.

- Prosecutors' offices should establish procedures to ensure the prompt return of victims' property, absent a need for the actual evidence in court.

- Prosecutors' offices should establish and maintain direct liaison with victim/witness units and other victim service agencies.

Source: The President's Task Force on Victims of Crime (1982). *Final Report*. Washington, DC: U.S. Government Printing Office, pp. 63-64.

In 1986, the U.S. Department of Justice issued its assessment *Four Years Later: A Report on the President's Task Force on Victims of Crime*, which monitored compliance with the Task Force's recommendations. The overall tone of the report was quite positive—almost buoyant. Victims and witnesses were making significant strides. Many efforts were underway to address the concerns raised by the Task Force. Assistant Attorney General Lois Herrington (U.S. Department of Justice, 1986: ii-iii) wrote the following message in her transmittal letter to the President of the United States:

When you created the President's Task Force on Victims of Crime, the Nation began to listen and respond. . . . To date, nearly 75 percent of the proposals have been acted upon, led by a new Office for Victims of Crime in the Justice Department created expressly to implement the Task Force reforms. . . . We hope this document will help assure that the victim of crime will never be overlooked as an integral part of the criminal justice system.

Attention to victim-witness services did not die with these pronouncements. Federal officials have continued to monitor these efforts and make adjustments wherever necessary. In fact, in 1992, the U.S. Attorney General released a directive exhorting state and local governments to make their criminal justice systems more user-friendly. As Figure 3.5 shows, these recommendations look to encourage modifications and to keep victim-witness concerns in the forefront.

**FIGURE 3.5**
**Selected Recommendations from the U.S. Attorney General for Strengthening State Criminal Justice Systems**

- Provide for hearing and considering the victims' perspective at sentencing and at any early release proceedings.

- Provide victim-witness coordinators.

- Provide for victim restitution and for adequate compensation and assistance for victims and witnesses.

- Adopt evidentiary rules to protect victim-witnesses from courtroom intimidation and harassment.

- Permit victims to require HIV testing before trial of persons charged with sex offenses.

- Notify the victim of the status of criminal justice proceedings and of the release status of the offender.

Source: Office of the United States Attorney General (1992a). *Combating Violent Crime: 24 Recommendations to Strengthen Criminal Justice.* Washington, DC: U.S. Government Printing Office, pp. 50-55.

In order to ensure that the hard-fought gains won on behalf of victims and witnesses would not be just a temporary fad, the Attorney General's report contained a checklist of questions. The instructions called for interested citizens to query their officials about what was being done in their hometowns to secure victim-witness rights. Some of these questions are reprinted in Figure 3.6.

**FIGURE 3.6**
**Citizen's Checklist: Questions About Criminal Justice to Ask Your State and Local Leaders**

- Do victims have the right to address the court at sentencing in our state, or may only the defendant do so? Do victims have the right to attend all court proceedings in our state? Is the victim's perspective considered before early release is granted to a convicted felon?

- In a death penalty case where the defendant puts on evidence of his background and family life to evoke sympathy, can our prosecutors present evidence about the victim and the victim's family to give the jury a sense of their loss?

- Does our state have victim-witness coordinators?

- Does our state provide for victim restitution and assistance for victims and witnesses?

- If a criminal profits from his crime by writing a book or giving a paid interview, does our law require that some of that money go to the victim?

- Does our state provide professional assistance or counselors to assist victims and witnesses in the criminal process? Are adequate witness fees paid to cover food, travel, and lost work time?

- Do our evidence laws protect rape victims against courtroom attacks on their reputations and revelation of irrelevant details of their private sex lives? Does our state provide for protection of child witnesses by allowing closed-circuit televised testimony where testifying in the presence of the defendant would cause the child serious emotional trauma?

- Can victims of sex offenses in our state require HIV testing of the accused before trial?

- Are victims in our state notified of the status of criminal justice proceedings and the release status of the offender?

Source: Adapted from Office of the United States Attorney General (1992a). *Combating Crime: 24 Recommendations to Strengthen Criminal Justice.* Washington, DC: U.S. Government Printing Office, p. 58.

## Project Development

A very important step in any planning preparation is to determine the feasibility of program implementation. A three-pronged approach is advisable. The first priority is to identify appropriate target groups. The next step is to learn what needs and expectations these clients hold. The final course of action is to assemble a staff to set these plans into motion (Finn and Lee, 1987: 5; Tomz and McGillis, 1997: 11-33).

A major task in any needs assessment is to gain a sense of the size and characteristics of the client population in the area. An important starting block in many instances is to locate or construct demographic projections for the entire population. Analyzing population trends permits profiling by race, age and gender. As we saw in the last chapter, victimization patterns track demographic variables. Focusing on shifts in various age categories becomes an important exercise. For example, it may be more expedient for an agency housed in a retirement community to concentrate upon crimes against the elderly. Certainly, it would not make good managerial sense to inaugurate an array of services aimed at child maltreatment victims to the exclusion of services for the aged.

Other local resources can provide a wealth of information. For example, crime statistics can indicate some of the more immediate and recurrent problems. Talking with criminal justice professionals, people who have been victimized and existing social service providers can isolate the gaps between what is being accomplished and what clients need. These preliminary efforts can prevent unnecessary duplication.

Following such a series of steps can lead to some very fundamental recommendations. When city officials in Jacksonville, Florida, decided to establish a Crime Victim Intake Center, they turned to a research team for guidance. To assess unmet concerns, Blomberg and his colleagues (1989) analyzed population growth estimates and city crime statistics, and interviewed staff members from local victim and witness services as well as workers in the criminal justice system. Armed with this information, the evaluators were able to provide officials with an image of what goals and objectives this new agency should strive to achieve.

The decision regarding what services a project should provide must begin with an overview of the models that currently exist. Most victim-witness assistance programs offer a very similar core of services (Finn and Lee, 1987: 17; Tomz and McGillis, 1997: 8; U.S. Department of Justice, 1986: 121-125; Webster, 1988). While the actual blend or mix may be adjusted to reflect particular local conditions, the essential elements remain relatively constant from one place to the next. These basic provisions include:

- Emergency Services
  - Shelter/Food
  - Security Repair
  - Financial Assistance
  - On-Scene Comfort
  - Medical Care
- Counseling
  - 24-Hour Hotline
  - Crisis Intervention

- ▸ Follow-Up Counseling
- ▸ Mediation
- Advocacy and Support Services
  - ▸ Personal Advocacy
  - ▸ Employer Intervention
  - ▸ Landlord Intervention
  - ▸ Property Return
  - ▸ Intimidation Intervention
  - ▸ Victim Impact Reports
  - ▸ Legal/Paralegal Counsel
  - ▸ Referral
- Claims Assistance
  - ▸ Insurance Claims Aid
  - ▸ Restitution Assistance
  - ▸ Compensation Assistance
  - ▸ Witness Fee Assistance
- Court-Related Services
  - ▸ Witness Reception
  - ▸ Court Orientation
  - ▸ Notification
  - ▸ Witness Alert
  - ▸ Transportation
  - ▸ Child Care
  - ▸ Escort to Court
- Post-Sentencing Services
  - ▸ Orientation
  - ▸ Notification
  - ▸ Victim-Offender Reconciliation Program
  - ▸ Restitution
- Systemwide Services
  - ▸ Public Education
  - ▸ Legislative Advocacy
  - ▸ Training

A national survey of victim-witness assistance programs was conducted to determine typical organizational structures and the umbrella of services delivered by these programs (Roberts, 1991). Agency autonomy meant that agencies could tailor their offerings to local client needs. It was learned that regardless of what combination of services a victim-witness program dispenses, these efforts usually fall into four general categories. According to one reviewer (Roberts, 1992: 14), program staff aim to:

- Explain to victims and witnesses that their cooperation is essential to crime control efforts and successful criminal prosecution;

- Inform victims and witnesses of their rights to receive dignified and compassionate treatment from criminal justice professionals;

- Furnish information to witnesses on the court process, the scheduling of the case, the trial and the final disposition; and

- Provide orientation to court proceedings and tips on how best to recall the crime scene accurately and testify.

## Project Performance

Victim-witness projects, like many other social service agencies, keep statistics to track their performance and to justify their continued existence. Reports typically contain such items as the number of persons who used different project features, measures of client satisfaction, individual testimonials praising staff efforts, commendations from system officials, and the like. These process-oriented figures are helpful when describing the level of service delivery and the type of activities in which staff members engage.

When these accounts stretch over time or multiple sites, one can obtain a better idea of the direction in which these ventures are moving. A number of states require prosecutors' offices to make services available to victims and witnesses. While Table 3.2 explains what type of services prosecutors offer, it is also instructive to see the range of services these offices provide. Gaps here could suggest possible areas needing improvement.

Another national assessment surveyed 347 assistance programs to unearth a "state of the art" picture of these efforts (Webster, 1988). One of the more striking regularities that surfaced from these reports is that victim-witness projects are starting to become swamped with referrals. Both the police and prosecutors are sending more clients to these projects for help, and there has been a sharp rise in victim self-referrals. The number of inquiries has risen so dramatically that some managers have had to expand the number of service providers on staff. In short, these programs seem to have become institutionalized fixtures within the criminal justice system.

**TABLE 3.2**
**Types of Victim Services Prosecutors' Offices Are Required to Provide**

| | | Full-Time Office Serving Population | | |
| --- | --- | --- | --- | --- |
| Type of Services | All Offices | 500,000 or more | Under 500,000 | Part-Time Offices |
| **Notification/Alert:** | | | | |
| Notify Victim | 82% | 87% | 85% | 73% |
| Notify Witness | 55 | 67 | 59 | 42 |
| **Orientation/Education:** | | | | |
| Victim Restitution Assistance | 60% | 62% | 62% | 55% |
| Victim Compensation Procedures | 58 | 73 | 65 | 41 |
| Victim Impact Statement Assistance | 55 | 78 | 60 | 40 |
| Orientation to Court Procedure | 41 | 57 | 48 | 24 |
| Public Education | 15 | 20 | 17 | 9 |
| **Escort:** | | | | |
| Victim | 23% | 39% | 28% | 9% |
| Witness | 17 | 31 | 19 | 9 |
| **Counseling/Assistance:** | | | | |
| Property Return | 38% | 46% | 39% | 35% |
| Referral | 32 | 46 | 37 | 18 |
| Personal Advocacy | 17 | 26 | 22 | 5 |
| Counseling | 10 | 21 | 12 | 5 |
| Crisis Intervention | 10 | 19 | 14 | 0 |
| **Number of Offices** | 2,282 | 119 | 1,480 | 683 |

Source: DeFrances, C.J., S.K. Smith and L. van der Does (1996). *Prosecutors in State Courts, 1994.* Washington, DC: U.S. Department of Justice, p. 9.

Among other things, the survey addressed unmet victim needs and areas that needed improvement. An overwhelming number of respondents felt that victim notification about case status at different junctures of the justice process was a key area of concern (Webster, 1988: 5). Agency directors noted that other prominent concerns included: protection from intimidation in domestic violence situations, more victim participation in case decisions and better training for victims preparing to testify in court proceedings.

## Project Evaluation

In the past, some prosecutor offices were so clinical in how they handled witnesses that commentators (Cannavale and Falcon, 1976) dubbed these operations "the prosecutory assembly line." In stark contrast, victim-witness projects now concentrate on making the criminal justice system more user-friendly. For example, prosecutors have redesigned waiting areas to make them more comfortable, and efforts are expended in returning property quickly to owners, filing applications for victim compensation, registering system participants for witness fees and explaining court procedures to those with questions. Notifying victims and witnesses about cancellations eliminates many unnecessary trips to the courthouse (as well as the frustration that accompanies such trips).

Two assumptions have guided these attempts at witness service provision (Davis, 1983: 289; Weigend, 1983: 93-94). First, prosecutors want to ameliorate witness conditions because they feel that witness cooperation is essential to winning convictions. Second, the popular view is that victims and witnesses refuse to cooperate with system officials because the anticipated costs are too high. Thus, evaluation efforts gather data aimed at empirically refuting or supporting these two lines of thinking.

Despite the intuitive appeal behind these assumptions, there is some question as to whether these efforts actually carry a commensurate payoff. Davis (1983: 290), for example, advises that the Vera Institute's Victim/Witness Assistance Project was unable to affect victim-witness attendance rates at court hearings. Furthermore, improved notification practices did not alter the rate at which prosecutors were forced to dismiss cases due to no-shows. Nor was there any improvement in victim-witness attitudes toward the system. All in all, there were no appreciable changes that could be attributed to better victim-witness management.

In another jurisdiction, the establishment of a victim-witness unit that handled only child sexual abuse cases provided another opportunity to assess whether witness cooperation could improve prosecution performance (Dible and Teske, 1993). The victim counselor who was assigned to this unit would follow a case throughout the entire process. This person would meet several times with the victim to establish a rapport with the child and to evaluate the validity of the complaint. Anatomically correct dolls were available so the child could explain what had happened to him or her. Whenever the case went to the grand jury, judges allowed the victim counselor to take the place of the child on the witness stand and explain the details of the case. Finally, the counselor would accompany the child to the trial and offer support in whatever way was necessary.

The researchers decided to evaluate the performance of this program by using a before-and-after intervention strategy. It was felt that comparing case outcomes prior to this effort with case outcomes after the program was in place would give some indication as to whether the specialized unit had the desired impact. The results showed strong support for the program. Once the program was operational, guilty trial verdicts increased from 38 percent to 72 percent, the severity of the convicted charges increased and the number of sentences resulting in imprisonment rose. In short, the program was a prosecutorial success.

What is the key to program success? Why do some offices appear to be more effective than others? One possible explanation is that witnesses seek only humane treatment, and giving them that will increase program effectiveness. Satisfied clients who have had a comfortable experience inside the halls of justice tend to express no reservations about returning again if the need arises (Kelly, 1984; Norton, 1983; O'Grady et al., 1992). As one observer (Davis, 1983: 297) put it:

> Victim/witness programs had little success in increasing cooperation because they perpetuated the treatment of victims as nothing more than witnesses for the prosecution. In doing so, they failed to come to grips with the fundamental issue of the role of the victim in criminal proceedings that may be at the crux of the widespread failure of citizens to cooperate with officials in lower criminal courts.

## Expanding the Boundaries

While project staff often struggle to keep pace with staggering caseloads and mounting piles of paperwork, they now find themselves fielding more requests to apply their expertise to nontraditional clients. Many service providers recognize that the victimization experience and its aftermath has ramifications that extend beyond just the person who is victimized. The victim's support system of family members and friends are affected as well. Since these people form an integral support foundation for the victim, extension of sevices was sensible in these instances. In one respect, then, this outreach beyond just the immediate crime victim paved the way for expansion.

Many victim advocates now offer their expertise to nontraditional victims. *Derivative victims*, while not direct crime victims, usually include persons whose lives have been touched by some other tumultuous event (Tomz and McGillis, 1997: 25). The trauma that survivors of an attempted suicide undergo, the processes induced from witnessing a traumatic event, or the emotional upheaval triggered by the unexpected death of a young person are sufficient to propel people into a morass of emotions. Victims of environmental mishaps or other disasters may experience an emotional collapse in the wake of such unfortunate calamaties. Rescue workers exposed to a critical incident may find debriefing exercises to be beneficial as they try to sort through and juggle their own emotions. In short, victim advocates are learning that many skills are transferrable to kindred forms of human suffering.

This mantle of expertise has prompted some concern to make sure that *victim advocates*, the people who service victim clients, have an appropriate background before they engage in helping behavior. When victim services first emerged as a fledgling area, many service providers were simply well-intended persons with a concern for others. Formal credentials, particularly when victimology was in its infancy, were nonexistent. Today, though, greater attention is being paid to formal pre-service and in-service training for staff members and others who come into contact with victims. California, for example, requires service providers to sit through a training curriculum if they wish to achieve certification as a victim advocate. Essentially, then, there is a growing recognition that employee preparation is one mechanism to ensure that quality services are being delivered to those in need of assistance.

**FIGURE 3.7**
**Victim Advocate: An Emerging Profession?**

As the number of victim advocates nationwide continues to increase, and as advocates' expertise becomes more sophisticated, there is a growing movement to professionalize the position. The movement in part reflects increased pressure from Federal and State funding sources for uniform standards among victim assistance programs. In addition, many victim advocates believe that, in order to accomplish program activities more effectively, they need to be perceived as professionals—not just do-gooders—by lawyers, judges, and other professionals with whom they work.

To facilitate the professionalization of the position of victim advocate, many victim assistance networks and program administrators are placing increased emphasis on staff qualifications and training program standards, and public recognition of program accomplishments. Also supporting the professionalization of victim services is the growing body of research regarding victimology and victim services. The National Organization of Victim Assistance (NOVA) has proposed a code of ethics to guide victim assistance providers in professional conduct with crime victims, colleagues, other professionals, and the public. The organization is also strongly encouraging colleges and universities to offer courses and specialized degrees in victim assistance.

Accreditation is another increasingly prevalent method of standardizing and professionalizing victim services. The California Victim and Witness Coordinating Council established a system of victim advocate certification in 1993 to recognize the professional standing of victim advocates in the State. Victim assistance program employees apply for certification by completing a form that lists their educational background, the number of months or years employed by a comprehensive victim services agency, and any specialized training sessions or courses the employee has taken. The director of the program for which the employee works must recommend employees for certification by signing their application.

Source: Tomz, J.E. and D. McGillis (1997). *Serving Crime Victims and Witnesses*, 2nd ed. Washington, DC: U.S. Department of Justice.

## DISSENTING VOICES

Not everyone is enamored with the direction that these system-based victim-witness projects have taken. Critics charge that bureaucrats, more interested in organizational survival than in client needs, have replaced zealous advocates. They contend that victim-witness projects have changed so that they no longer remain victim-oriented. In other words, virtually no effort is expended to address what this chapter labels as "the first insult." Instead, these projects concentrate on blunting only "the second insult," problems that stem from becoming involved with the criminal justice system.

Shapland (1983) cautions that many victim-witness programs are based on what officials think their clients need—not necessarily what victims themselves want or need. Improvement of waiting conditions, provision of witness notification services, distribution of brochures outlining the criminal justice process, and similar strategies can be viewed as peripheral to clients—props designed to appease and manipulate people for ulterior purposes.

Under "ideal" conditions, victim programs would reach out to all victims (Weigend, 1983). However, current operations confine attention to preselected types of criminal victims. This client group is restricted to just those victims who report the incident to the authorities. As we saw in Chapter 2, the attrition here is considerable. However, the pool becomes even smaller. Eligibility is reserved for those cases in which the police have identified and apprehended a suspect. Ultimately, the only victims who do get served are those whose cases culminate in the halls of justice.

Skeptics point out that the only value these victims hold depends upon how well they can serve criminal justice officials. As McShane and Williams (1992: 264) explain, "That which is passed off as victim assistance is, in reality, predicated on the needs of the prosecution rather than on the needs of the victim." Cries of foul from defendant quarters reinforce these concerns. A common complaint from defense attorneys is that granting concessions to victims affords the prosecutor an unfair advantage (Kelly, 1987; Kelly, 1991). While the evidence to date does not support such an assertion, these statements serve as ongoing evidence to the tensions elicited by victim-witness services.

**FIGURE 3.8**
**Selected Internet Sites Dealing with Victim/Witness Services**

Federal Judicial Center
    http://www.fjc.gov/

National District Attorney's Association
    http://www.ndaa.org/

## SUMMARY

It is easy to see why victims are reluctant to invoke or to reenter the criminal justice system. Victims initially come into the halls of justice with hopes of minimizing their losses. However, after they complete the circuit and exit the system they often realize they have maximized their losses instead. As a result, it should come as no surprise that system veterans claim they will avoid the system in the future whenever possible.

This decision to boycott the legal system is not the product of an apathetic citizenry. It is a calculated and rational assessment—a silent protest. Avoiding system participation reduces victim exposure to further hardships and liabilities.

System officials have tried to counter this trend by introducing victim-witness management projects into the system. These efforts, though, are reserved for only the small number of victims who eventually testify against their suspects. In addition, they do very little to address economic losses that victims incur from cooperating with the system. As we shall learn in the following chapter, the system has crafted a number of financial incentives designed to lure victims back. It remains to be seen whether these efforts will be sufficient to maintain victim interest in current system operations.

# LEARNING OBJECTIVES

After reading Chapter 4, you should be able to:

- Define "offender restitution."

- Know what a civil restitution lien is.

- Explain the rationale behind restitution.

- Outline four types of offender restitution.

- Evaluate the impact of restitution.

- Explore the ramifications of net-widening.

- Point out some drawbacks of restitution.

- Grasp why civil litigation is gaining popularity.

- Comment on the benefits of civil litigation.

- Sketch some limitations of civil litigation.

- Recognize the role of private insurance.

- Explain what victim compensation is.

- Understand the philosophical bases of compensation.

- Know what acts are compensable.

- Define "Good Samaritan" provisions.

- Discuss eligibility restrictions for compensation.

- Define "unjust enrichment" and "contributory misconduct."

- Tell about the awards and funding structures of compensation.

- Debate whether victim compensation works.

- Distinguish macro-level from micro-level effects.

- Describe some program operations.

# Chapter 4

# Remedying the Plight of Victims

## INTRODUCTION

Those in the criminal justice system are aware that victims are growing increasingly disenchanted with the system's workings. Participation in the criminal justice system frequently aggravates the victim's losses. At the same time, the system alienates the victim, making him or her feel like an outsider to both the offense and the system processes. In the past, victims could make themselves whole by exacting payment from the offender or the offender's family. Today, however, the victim has evolved into nothing more than a key witness for the state. The emphasis is no longer on restoring the victim back to his or her original pre-crime state. Judging from citizen disillusionment with the current status quo, there is a clear need to take some bold steps to ameliorate the victim's suffering.

The recent proliferation of victim-witness assistance projects represents an attempt to reduce victims' adverse experiences with the criminal justice system. Some of these projects provide child care facilities, transportation to and from the courthouse, waiting rooms, counseling, prompt notification of court postponements, property recovery assistance, preparation for courtroom testifying, orientation to criminal proceedings and notification of

## KEY TERMS

civil restitution lien
contributory misconduct
defendant
"Good Samaritan" provisions
macro-level effects
micro-level effects
monetary-community restitution
monetary-victim restitution
net-widening
offender restitution
outcome evaluations
plaintiff
process evaluations
service-community restitution
service-victim restitution
social contract
social welfare
"Son of Sam" provisions
source of last resort
third-party civil suit
tort
unjust enrichment
victim compensation
Victims of Crime Act (VOCA)

case disposition. Usually, though, victim-witness assistance programs are not geared toward reducing the economic calamity of the victimization experience. Instead, these projects try to soften or reduce the harsh treatment that victims encounter once inside the legal system. Although victim-witness assistance projects provide meaningful services, their efforts may be somewhat misdirected. If the victim's decision to avoid formal contact with the criminal justice system stems from a rational cost-benefit assessment, then the system needs to entice victims back into the system with economic incentives.

There are a variety of ways whereby victims may recoup some of their monetary losses stemming from the victimization episode. Some alternatives include restitution, civil litigation, insurance payments and victim compensation. While each method has the potential to restore the victim to his or her pre-crime state, the victim faces new obstacles when using these methods. Likewise, each option holds a different potential for drawing victims back into the criminal justice system. This chapter will look at restitution, civil litigation, insurance payments and victim compensation as means of both restoring the victim's losses and bringing the victim back into the criminal justice system.

## OFFENDER RESTITUTION

*Offender restitution* involves the transfer of services or money from the offender to the victim for damages inflicted by the offender. As seen in our discussion of the history of the victim in Chapter 1, restitution predates the formal criminal justice system. Prior to the advent of societal action against offenders, the victim was responsible for apprehending the offender and exacting payment for any loss or harm. Restitution was clearly outlined in various early laws, such as the Code of Hammurabi and the Justinian Code. The idea of offenders making restitution to their victims largely disappeared once the state assumed responsibility for apprehending and prosecuting offenders. While this new system of justice did not prohibit restitution, the practice gradually fell into disuse and was largely ignored.

The 1960s saw a renewed interest in offender restitution. A variety of factors contributed to this movement. They included the recognition of the victim in the 1967 President's Commission's reports, the growing concern for identifying alternative methods for dealing with offenders, and the societal movement toward concern for crime victims. The awakening acceptance of restitution was not accompanied by a myriad of new legislation at that time. Rather, it was pointed out that restitution was an already existing sentencing option that the courts very rarely invoked.

The 1982 President's Task Force on Victims of Crime recommended that restitution become the norm in criminal cases. Later that same year, the Victim/Witness Protection Act went so far as to require federal judges to give a written explanation for why they did not require full restitution in a case. Today, 48 states have specific legislation dealing with restitution as a separate sentence or as an additional requirement to another sentence (Shapiro, 1990).

Some states have followed the federal lead and now require judges to make offender restitution a mandatory part of sentencing. At least one state, Florida, now imposes a civil restitution lien order upon convicted criminal offenders. A *civil restitution lien* means that the sentencing court, at the request of the victim, levies a claim against any real or personal property the convicted offender currently possesses or may come to own during the next 20 years (Florida Statutes, 1997: §960.29-960.297). What this entry means is that victims can recover any damages or losses from any assets the offender accrues over the following two decades.

## The Rationale for Restitution

The rationale for restitution involves the needs of victims. Victim losses are a key driving force behind the growth of restitution legislation and the use of court-ordered restitution. Other factors, however, are also apparent in the adoption of restitution as a sentencing alternative.

Many restitution programs are couched in terms of benefits for the offender. Rehabilitation is hailed as the most potent outcome (Barnett, 1981; Galaway, 1981; Hofrichter, 1980; Hudson and Galaway, 1980). Forcing the offender to pay or perform service to the victim allows the offender to see the pain and suffering that his or her actions caused. Rather than simply punishing the individual, restitution is supposed to provide a therapeutic or rehabilitative response to deviant actions. The rehabilitative argument is particularly appealing whenever restitution is tied to maintaining gainful employment or entering a job training program (Hillenbrand, 1990). In these instances, offenders help their victims while positioning themselves for legitimate opportunities in the future.

Proponents tend to regard restitution as a less restrictive alternative than normal processing, which most often would take the form of incarceration. Labeling arguments, which fault system intervention as the cause of further deviance, support restitution as a means of mitigating future offending. Rather than leading to deviance, restitution assists the offender in refraining from subsequent criminal activity.

Restitution also carries a deterrence effect (Tittle, 1978). Deterrence assumes that people will continue to commit deviant acts only as long as there is a positive payoff. By mandating repayment to the victim, restitution returns the offender—at least financially—to the exact same position held prior to the unlawful act. Coupling restitution with a fine or imprisonment can produce a negative balance between the outcome of the offense (assumed pleasure) and the system's response (pain). Following the basic hedonistic arguments underlying deterrence, the offender would be better off not committing the offense in the first place. Restitution, therefore, can produce a specific deterrent effect on the punished offender and may even provide general deterrence (i.e., influencing others through example).

## Types of Restitution

Galaway (1981) outlines four variations on the general theme of restitution. The first, *monetary-victim restitution*, most closely fits the general public's impression of restitution. Under this arrangement, the offender makes direct monetary repayment to the victim for the actual amount of harm or losses incurred. While this is considered direct payment, in practice payments actually are routed through the court or probation office, which then turns the funds over to the victim. This process is particularly useful in cases in which the victim does not wish to have any further contact with the offender.

A second form is referred to as *monetary-community restitution*. This type of restitution entails payment by the offender to the community rather than to the actual victim. This option may be used for several reasons. For example, it may not be possible to identify a tangible victim in cases involving vandalism of public property; a victim may be unwilling to participate in a restitution program; or the court may be reluctant to use restitution to the victim in the sentencing of an offender. In some instances, this monetary-community restitution may actually be a method whereby the community simply recoups funds it previously made available to the victim. In essence, the community provided "up-front" restitution to the victim that would now be replaced by the offender.

The remaining restitution categories are closely aligned with the first two, except that they substitute service in place of financial payments. Both *service-victim restitution* and *service-community restitution* require the perpetrator to perform a specified number of hours or types of service (or both) in lieu of making cash payments. These forms of restitution are most common in situations in which the offender does not have the ability to make monetary compensation (such as in the case of unemployed individuals and juveniles). Service to the community may act as repayment for restitution that the community made on behalf of the offender, or may be a way to pay for court costs and/or harm to the general populace. In any event, the important feature is that the offender must satisfy the debt established through his or her victimizing behavior.

## Evaluating the Impact of Restitution

As with many new programs, evaluations of restitution have evolved from simple examinations of attitudes and processes to studies of such outcomes as recidivism, cost savings and diversion. In general, restitution has enjoyed a warm reception from victims, offenders, the general public and system personnel (Gandy, 1978; Gandy and Galaway, 1980; Hudson and Galaway, 1980; Keldgord, 1978; Kigin and Novack, 1980; Novack et al., 1980). Support for restitution is qualified only by concerns over the use of restitution for serious personal offenses. Survey respondents appear to favor more punitive sanctions (either in place of or in combination with restitution) when offenders commit violent crimes.

The initial wave of restitution evaluations were mostly *process evaluations;* that is, the emphasis was on the number of offenders handled, the amount of time participants took to make restitution, the completion rate for restitution orders, and other similar program achievements. Many courts quickly embraced restitution and imposed these orders with great frequency (Hudson and Chesney, 1978).

Most programs report a high offender compliance rate with restitution orders (Kigin and Novack, 1980; Lawrence, 1990; Schneider and Schneider, 1984). However, success varies according to the type and level of supervision provided to probationers (Schneider and Schneider, 1984). The simultaneous imposition of other sanctions, such as fines and imprisonment, may hinder or delay offender payments. Finally, restitution programs have been found to be quite economical. They can handle a large number of individuals at a relatively low cost (Hudson and Galaway, 1980).

Studies that look at the impact of restitution on victims and offenders are known as *outcome evaluations.* The amount of money collected and funneled to victims is one key result that has been assessed. While the average amount of restitution ordered in the Bronx hovered around $100, individual orders ranged from a low of $7 up to $4,000 (Zalichin et al., 1980). This program collected roughly $97,000 in its first year, even though only 59 percent of the offenders completed their restitution orders. A Minnesota restitution program for youths took in more than $25,000 during its first two years (Kigin and Novack, 1980). Restitution orders in Texas averaged more than $1,000, for a total collection of almost $61,000 during 1987 (Lawrence, 1990). It appears that restitution can be big business.

Another major outcome to assess is offender recidivism. Challeen and Heinlen (1978) report 2.7 percent recidivism for restitution clients, compared to 27 percent for similar offenders sentenced to jail. Recidivism declined in three of four programs by 10 fewer offenses per 100 youths (Schneider, 1986). A six-year follow-up of offenders who were diverted into a restitution program also showed significantly lower recidivism (Rowley, 1990).

While these results appear encouraging, Schneider and Schneider (1984) caution that the value of restitution depends upon how well the program is administered. When restitution becomes an agency priority, the results are promising. However, outcome measures lag when restitution is handled as an added-on condition and is not a top agency concern. Programs that aggressively target restitution generate more successful performances and lower recidivism rates (Ervin and Schneider, 1990).

Other outcome measures may involve diversion away from normal processing and the savings created by this move. An early project claimed that there was little evidence that restitution resulted in lower numbers of individuals under custodial care (Hudson and Galaway, 1980). More recently, though, figures from Texas show that more than 3,000 offenders were diverted from prison to restitution centers during a seven-year period (Lawrence, 1990). While this number is substantial, the overall impact on Texas' incarceration efforts was minimal. One possibility is that some net-widening was at work. *Net-widening* occurs when new programs allow the system to absorb more clients than before, rather than displacing clients.

Another way of looking at restitution is in terms of cost-effectiveness. Rowley (1990) notes that restitution is a much less expensive alternative than imprisonment. The mean cost for restitution was $215, compared to $750 for prison. What this means is that restitution entails less than one-third the cost of incarceration. Other studies (Hudson and Galaway, 1980; Lawrence, 1990; Patterson, 1978) also report that restitution is a more economical alternative to normal system processing.

## Problems and Concerns with Restitution

Despite both the theoretical attractiveness and positive outcomes of restitution, there are a variety of problems and concerns facing the practice. At the outset is the need to apprehend and adjudicate the offender (Galaway, 1981; Hillenbrand, 1990). The Uniform Crime Reports show that only approximately 20 percent of crimes are cleared by an arrest, with property crimes (which are most amenable to restitution) having even lower clearance rates. Restitution, therefore, is possible a maximum of one-fifth of the time. Beyond arrest statistics, many offenders are not convicted, thereby mitigating any possibility of restitution.

A second stumbling block is the ability of offenders to pay restitution (Barnett, 1981; Shapiro, 1990). Most offenders come from lower-class segments of society. It is naive to assume that these individuals will have the necessary means to make restitution. The potential solutions to this problem—providing service to the victim or locating jobs for offenders—are not always ideal. The provision of jobs to offenders requires either public funds or substantial cooperation from the private sector.

The first may not be available and the second faces the argument that more worthy law-abiding citizens are denied jobs in favor of offenders. Another potential problem may be that offenders refuse or are unable to work (Barnett, 1981).

A third major issue is the determination of harm and the appropriate level of restitution (McAnany, 1978; Thorvaldson, 1989). While some aspects of crime are readily quantifiable, others are difficult to determine. At first glance, a dollar figure for stolen or damaged property should be easy to identify. However, questions arise concerning depreciation for older property already in use for a period of time. Some items may hold sentimental value for which monetary compensation is hard to determine. Some offenses may leave victims with both physical and psychological damage. While one can equate physical injuries with medical costs and lost wages, setting a dollar figure for the psychological impact may be more demanding. More difficulty arises when attempting to set a level of service for restitution (Harland and Rosen, 1990). How much work or time offsets monetary loss, physical pain or psychological suffering? This problem is especially acute when the court decides to order community service. How does the court factor in harm to the victim? In almost every attempt to order restitution, the court is asked to go beyond its legal expertise and become involved in the decisions that would be better made by a doctor, psychiatrist, economist or accountant.

A fourth worry revolves around program administration. Florida, for instance, decided to decentralize restitution by assigning responsibility for program management to county clerks of court and state probation officers. Soon thereafter, victim advocates encountered a number of problems with restitution programs. These concerns ranged from an inability to collect offender payments to a failure to disburse already collected monies to crime victims. An independent evaluation (Crew and Vancore, 1994) revealed some interesting findings. While judges ordered more than $31 million in restitution during fiscal year 1991-92, collections only amounted to slightly more than $11 million. Officials were not always able to locate the victims for whom restitution was intended. Given the variety of accounting techniques used throughout the state, it is estimated that more than $500,000 did not get disbursed to victims. While some agencies forwarded undistributed restitution funds to the state crime compensation fund, others handled these monies under abandoned property laws, returned them to local or state government or stopped collecting payments altogether from offenders. What these practices amount to is that unclaimed dollars originally intended to go to crime victims are routinely diverted to other uses.

Another major area of concern deals with the question of the proper philosophy of the criminal court. Thorvaldson (1990) argues that restitution moves the emphasis of the criminal justice system from society to the victim. Under restitution, the victim is seeking personal redress rather than acting on behalf of society. Consequently, restitution diminishes the importance of criminal processing and sentencing (Thorvaldson, 1990). The basic premise of restitution shifts the court from a criminal orientation to a civil orientation. Society is no longer appeased or vindicated (Barnett, 1981). Rather, the victim becomes the focus of the process.

Several other issues carry potential problems for restitution. The current criminal justice system is not set up to administer such programs (Shapiro, 1990). Offenders with the financial means have a better chance of receiving restitution sentences. Victimless crimes are not amenable to restitution. Moreover, restitution will have little deterrent effect (Barnett, 1981). Clearly, there are still many reasons to question the efficacy of restitution.

## CIVIL LITIGATION

Another method of redress for crime victims is the civil litigation arena. Civil lawsuits are the modern version of retribution/restitution practices from the past. The victim or the victim's family has the right to take civil action against offenders to recoup losses and to exact punitive damages. A civil lawsuit is sometimes called a tort. A *tort* refers to a wrongful act that the *defendant* (the criminal) has committed against the *plaintiff* (the victim). This act has produced some type of loss, usually an injury or damage. The purpose of a tort action or civil litigation is for the plaintiff to recover monetary compensation from the defendant for any physical or psychological harm inflicted by the offender (Berliner, 1989). Thus, any civil lawsuit must be concerned with issues surrounding liability of the defendant and collectability or recovery of damages (Office for Victims of Crime, 1997).

There are some important benefits from filing civil suits (Dawson, 1989). Perhaps the most important aspect is the sense of control the victim regains through the court action. As long as the state is prosecuting the case in a criminal court, the prosecutor makes all the key decisions. The prosecutor, not the victim, decides whether to take the case to trial. The prosecutor, not the victim, can negotiate a plea settlement. The prosecutor, not the victim, decides what evidence to bring into court. Once the venue switches from the criminal court to a civil proceeding, the victim is no longer an outsider in the case. Instead, the victim and his or her ensuing problems are the central concern of the court case.

There are other advantages to pursuing a tort action. Civil suits use a more relaxed level of proof compared to criminal cases ("a preponderance of evidence" versus "proof beyond a reasonable doubt"). Even if the defendant is not found guilty in a criminal trial or if the prosecutor elects not to file charges, civil action may remain a viable alternative. In addition, a unanimous jury decision is not necessary in a civil proceeding. A majority or two-thirds decision is enough to gain a favorable verdict. Berliner (1989) notes that juries tend to be sympathetic to victims in civil cases. Furthermore, the defendant (offender) can no longer refuse to testify by invoking the self-incrimination protection (Brien, 1992; Dawson, 1989; Office for Victims of Crime, 1997). The constitutional privilege against self-incrimination pertains to criminal proceedings, not civil action.

Despite these advantages, there are a number of drawbacks to civil remedies. First, as with restitution, the offender must be identified and located. There may be no possibility for civil action if the offender is unknown. Second, civil cases require the victim to hire an attorney and pay some filing fees before the proceedings begin (Barbieri, 1989). Therefore, in effect, lower-income victims are barred from the civil system. Unless the victim is awarded a sizable sum of money, he or she may actually lose money after paying a guaranteed minimum fee to the attorney. Even with large awards, attorneys typically secure at least one-third of the award as a fee. Third, some victims suffer further damage as a result of the lawsuit. Information about the victim's past behavior, character and personal situation are all open to detailed scrutiny. This type of examination may cause further psychological and emotional harm to the victim (Barbieri, 1989). Fourth, civil suits are time-consuming and may take a period of years to resolve. During this interval the victim must have continued contact with the offender, which could bring further discomfort. Finally, because a great many offenders have little or no income, there is little reason to expect any recovery even if the victim wins his or her suit.

**FIGURE 4.1**
**Possible Defendant Resources to Consider When Recovering a Civil Judgment**

Source of Income:
   Wages
   Benefits (pension payments and annuities)
   Unearned income
   Trust fund income
   Tax refunds
   Government entitlements

Property and Holdings:
   Personal property (cars, jewelry, etc.)
   Real property (home, land, etc.)
   Bank accounts
   All debts owed to the defendant
   Financial holdings (stocks, bonds, etc.)
   Partnership interests
   Future interests in real and personal property through wills, trusts, etc.

Source: Office for Victims of Crime (1997). *Civil Legal Remedies for Crime Victims,* 2nd ed. Washington, DC: U.S. Department of Justice. *URL: http://www.ncjrs.org/txtfiles/clr.txt*

Another possible avenue for victims is to file a *third-party civil suit* (Carrington, 1981; Castillo et al., 1979). In these instances, a victim sues a government entity, a business or corporation, such as a landlord, the managing corporation of a shopping center or any other responsible body.

The argument developed during litigation of a third-party suit concerns the issue of whether the defendant's negligence failed to establish or to maintain a safe and protected environment. Here the victim must demonstrate two things. First, the criminal episode must be a foreseeable event. One can satisfy this requirement by documenting other offenses that have occurred on the premises or by showing that the area has a reputation for being a high-risk location. Second, the third party must have either failed to take appropriate steps to curtail further criminal events or its efforts must have fallen woefully short.

Suppose, for example, an unknown offender assaults and robs a tenant who is returning to his apartment in a housing complex. Neighbors have complained to the landlord on several occasions that the lighting in the halls is broken, nonresidents have been seen roaming the area and there have been other similar criminal incidents in the past. Despite this information, the property manager has taken no remedial actions. Under these circumstances, a victim may be able to hold the landlord responsible for ignoring a known hazard.

## PRIVATE INSURANCE

Another method for alleviating the losses due to crime entails private insurance. Most homeowner insurance policies have provisions for recovery of lost and damaged property. Likewise, health insurance policies typically allow payments for injuries sustained as a result of criminal incidents.

The use of insurance to offset the effects of crime does have several shortcomings. Foremost among these is that citizens must purchase the insurance. The fact that many people cannot afford insurance premiums effectively places such protection beyond their reach. Of course, this observation assumes that insurance is available to purchase in the first place. Many inner-city locations are in such crime-infested areas that private insurance companies refuse to do business there. This problem carries enormous ramifications. Lack of insurance leads to more urban decline in these blighted areas. This situation became so grave that the Federal Emergency Management Agency stepped in to fill the gap. The federal government now underwrites crime insurance for commercial enterprises and residents in high-crime areas. There were more than 15,000 such policies in effect at the end of calendar year 1995. These recipients paid approximately $3.3 million in premiums. During the same year, 456 claims were paid out, amounting to a $1.4 million expenditure (Maguire and Pastore, 1996: 390).

Some people also argue that viewing insurance as a means of offsetting crime losses actually penalizes the victim further by assuming that it is the victim's responsibility to take action and avoid crime. A further problem is that most insurance policies have a deductible amount that reduces the cash outlay to victims. Deductibles of $200 or $500 effectively eliminate any insurance payments for many crimes. In general, while insurance is a possible method for recouping losses, it is not an appealing means in many instances.

## VICTIM COMPENSATION

*Victim compensation* takes place when the state, rather than the perpetrator, reimburses the victim for losses sustained at the hands of the criminal. While it is true that some victim compensation operations derive money from offender restitution, the state is the entity that has direct contact with the victim.

Victim compensation is not a new concept. These remedies once existed in such historical places as ancient Greece and Rome, biblical Israel, Teutonic Germany and Saxony England (Jacob, 1976: 35-36; Schafer, 1970: 3-7). For a variety of reasons, this practice fell into disuse during the Middle Ages. Modern interest in victim compensation came about as a result of the advocacy efforts of Margery Fry. Fry, an English magistrate, played a prominent role in the passage of victim compensation laws in New Zealand in 1963 and in Great Britain in 1964 (Edelhertz and Geis, 1974: 10-11). In the United States, California launched its victim compensation program in 1966, followed next by New York and Hawaii. As one might imagine, there are a number of parallels between the British legislation and the American programs (Greer, 1994).

Federal efforts in the United States for victim compensation began in 1964, but did not win approval until passage of the *Victims of Crime Act (VOCA)* in 1984. VOCA initiated a process whereby the federal government would provide victim compensation for federal offenses and federal funds for state compensation programs. The source of these funds were fines, bond forfeitures and special assessments levied on convicted individuals and businesses.

As Figure 4.2 shows, VOCA has been responsible for the flow of significant amounts of money into state compensation programs. In 1996, the Crime Victims Fund generated more than $528 million for distribution to the states. Fund disbursements follow a set formula. The first

$10 million is set aside for the investigation and prosecution of child abuse cases. The remaining monies are earmarked for replenishing state victim compensation accounts, underwriting state victim assistance programs, and aiding in training and expansion of victim services.

**FIGURE 4.2**
**Annual Deposits to the Federal Crime Victims Fund, 1985-1996**

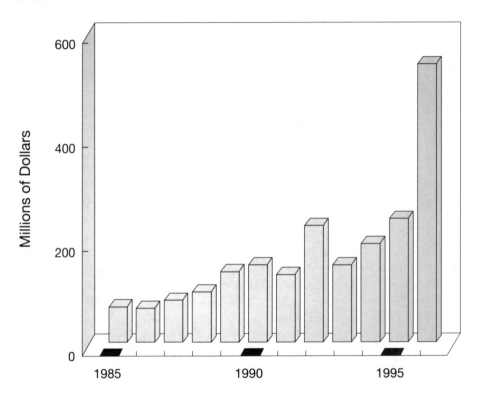

Source: Office for Victims of Crime (1996). *OVC Fact Sheet: Victims of Crime Act: Crime Victims Fund Fact Sheet.* Washington, DC: U.S. Department of Justice.

In addition to providing money, VOCA helped standardize state crime compensation laws. The initial flurry to pass compensation provisions produced a variety of rules and regulations that differed from one state to the next. To be eligible to receive the federal VOCA funds, states had to follow a series of program guidelines. For instance, some states were granting compensation only to victims who were state residents. VOCA regulations called for the removal of state residency requirements among other things. In order to reach a better understanding of just what victim compensation entails, the following sections describe some of the more salient characteristics of these statutes.

## Philosophical Bases

Proponents of victim compensation believe that the government has the obligation to provide victim compensation for two distinct reasons. The first view is the *social contract* argument. This perspective maintains that the government, through its system of taxation and provision of services, engages in an unwritten contract to care for the safety and well-being of its citizens. Citizens, according to this perspective, have relinquished the power of law enforcement to the government in exchange for protection. The experience of being a crime victim, through no fault of one's own, represents an affront to this agreement because the government has failed to keep its promise. As a result, it is incumbent upon the government to restore victimized citizens to their former status.

The second philosophical position is the notion of *social welfare*. The government attempts to provide a minimum standard of living for its disabled, deprived and unfortunate citizens. The position holds that innocent crime victims fall into this category because they suffer deprivations that are not self-induced. As a result, the government should extend its welfare practices and come to the rescue of crime victims because they are, in effect, deprived.

The argument one chooses to embrace carries important ramifications for other features of victim compensation. For example, if one adheres to the social welfare view, one might endorse a "financial means test." In this scheme, only poor people should be eligible for compensation benefits. However, if one adopts the social contract notion, then compensation should be available to everybody, regardless of their financial status.

A third reason offered for victim compensation deals with the use of compensation as an enticement to lure victims back to the criminal justice system. Earlier we noted that many victims refrain from contacting the authorities because of the additional costs inherent in doing so. They are responding to a simple cost-benefit analysis. Compensation, however, can alleviate much of the monetary loss associated with the offense. Therefore, it is possible that compensation can tip the balance of the cost-benefit equation and bring victims back into the system. Not only does compensation carry the potential to promote goodwill between the criminal justice system and citizens/victims, it may also result in more crime clearances and (eventually) lower crime through the apprehension of more offenders.

## Compensable Acts

Most states restrict victim compensation to three categories of victims. The first group includes family survivors and the estates of victims who suffer death, and victims who suffer physical injuries that require medical attention. Family survivors and the victim's estate also are included here. The important limiting factor is the exclusion of property crimes and the inclusion of violent criminal acts only. Only a handful of states have provisions allowing payment for property loss or damage (Parent et al., 1992).

The second group falls under the *"Good Samaritan" provisions*. The term "Good Samaritan" originates from the biblical story of a traveler who came across a person who had been robbed, beaten and left by the roadside. Rather than ignore this victim, the traveler nursed the injured man and transported him to an inn. The stranger graciously disappeared before the victim could thank or repay him for his troubles.

In terms of victim compensation, a "Good Samaritan" is a person who is hurt or killed during an attempt to prevent a crime from taking place or while attempting to capture a suspected criminal. The thinking here is that society owes a special duty to anybody who acts above and beyond the normal duties of citizenship—that altruism should be encouraged, not discouraged.

The final category specifically includes anyone who is injured while coming to the aid of a law enforcement officer. Some states stipulate that people who do not help a police officer when he or she asks for their assistance are guilty of a misdemeanor. Thus, it makes sense to compensate citizens when they act on behalf of a police officer.

While statutes outline who is eligible, there are some people who are specifically not eligible. For example, most states prohibit compensation for law enforcement officers and fire fighters. The thinking here is that their actions are part of the job and that other programs, such as workers' compensation, are more appropriate sources (Parent et al., 1992). Other excluded persons are prison or jail inmates and individuals involved in organized crime.

Initially, almost every state stipulated in such statutes that the crime must have occurred within its geographical boundaries. For example, suppose a Floridian was visiting San Francisco and was shot during a robbery. The Florida resident could not receive victim compensation from California because that person was not a Californian. Similarly, this victim was not eligible for compensation from Florida because that event took place outside state boundaries. Prior to 1988, some jurisdictions decided to waive the in-state residency requirement if other states reciprocated by providing compensation to nonresidents. The federal VOCA, as amended in 1988, mandated that states must lift the residency clause if they wished to participate in the federal compensation program. Parent and associates (1992) report that roughly 40 states now comply with this regulation, and others are in the process of amending their statutes accordingly.

## Eligibility Restrictions

Most states scrutinize the victim-offender relationship quite carefully. In the past, a violent crime victim was ineligible for benefits if the offender was a relative, a sexual partner or a resident of the same household. As a result, victims of spouse abuse were patently ineligible in many states. The primary rationale for this restriction was the concern that compensating a spouse-abuse victim would also benefit the offender. Such *unjust enrichment* was anathema to proponents of victim compensation.

Rather than make a blanket exclusion for domestic violence victims, the VOCA and its 1988 amendments required states to establish guidelines for determining whether compensation should be denied (Office for Victims of Crime, 1990). These new guidelines were designed to apply to *all* crimes, not just domestic violence offenses. The requirements are supposed to consider the extent of enrichment derived by the offender. One way to alleviate such concerns are provisions, such as in Minnesota, that allow compensation if a domestic violence victim will prosecute the offending party or is in the process of seeking a legal separation or a divorce.

A number of states have a financial means test on the books. In other words, the victim must suffer a serious financial hardship before an award will be forthcoming. As we mentioned earlier, one philosophical basis for establishing a victim compensation program is the social welfare argument. While a financial hardship test stems from this orientation, it is also a mechanism to cap program expenditures. Critics dislike this criterion. In fact, if a state compensation program operates under a financial hardship restriction, it is not eligible for federal victim compensation funds.

Another condition that affects eligibility is victim involvement or *contributory misconduct*. The victim must not share any criminal responsibility for the event. In other words, victim precipitation reduces one's standing for a compensation award. For example, suppose that John challenges Peter to a fight. Peter accepts the challenge and during this pugilistic event breaks John's nose. Depending upon on how the state's provisions read, the compensation board may deny John's claim completely or it may reduce the size of the award in proportion to the amount of victim contribution to the criminal incident.

One additional eligibility criterion concerns the availability of other forms of assistance. Victim compensation is universally viewed as a *source of last resort*. That is, all other avenues for compensation must be exhausted before compensation benefits are forthcoming. Payments go to victims only after all alternate sources of funds are exhausted. Other sources include workers' compensation, disability benefits, insurance policies, offender restitution, private donations and possibly civil lawsuit awards. Any payments from a state compensation program are reduced by an appropriate amount corresponding to funds received from such alternate sources. In order to avoid undue hardship on victims, programs typically make awards and subsequently recover any funds available from other sources.

## Awards

States vary in the cap or limit they will pay per claim. Minnesota, for example, will award up to $50,000, while Tennessee has a $5,000 ceiling. Some states require a minimum loss in order to prevent the program from being inundated by frivolous claims that are costly to investigate.

Crime compensation covers such items as lost wages, medical bills, prosthetics, funeral expenses and, in some instances, mental health counseling. Most programs do not set aside any monies for pain and suffering or for property damage. Indeed, Parent et al. (1992) reported that only five allow for pain and suffering, and eight make awards for property damage.

A recent addition to the items for which victim compensation can pay are costs that arise from forensic medical examinations. A standard police investigatory practice is to transport sexual assault victims to a medical facility for physical examination. As Chapter 5 will explain, this examination consists of two parts, gathering physical evidence from the victim and providing medical treatment to the victim. Some compensation boards reimburse applicants for the medical portion of the examination, but reject payment for the evidentiary aspects. This practice led a U.S. Department of Justice report (1986: 17) to comment that "Forcing sexual assault victims to bear this cost is tantamount to charging burglary victims for collecting fingerprints." In response to this situation, the President's Task Force on Victims of Crime (1982) urged states to pass laws exempting victims from shouldering these costs. The Victims of Crime Act of 1984 makes funds available for qualifying victim compensation programs to pay for forensic examinations.

The award itself can take several forms. The payout can be in a lump sum, periodic installments or in partial amounts. Some states permit victims in dire need to receive a small emergency award, pending the outcome of a full investigation. Some compensation agencies pay vendors (such as doctors and hospitals) directly to prevent victims from skipping out on their bills.

## Funding

An important political issue for many people concerns funding sources. While some states extract monies from the general tax structure to underwrite victim compensation, a more popular funding mechanism is the offender. According to the Office for Victims of Crime (1990), 64 percent of state victim compensation funds are derived solely from the criminal population. These funds appear in the form of fines or mandatory additional surcharges assessed on every convicted criminal defendant. This type of funding also includes monies recouped through offender restitution payments to the state. Appropriations from state general revenue funds account for about 22 percent of compensation funding. The remaining 14 percent of funds come from a combination of fines/surcharges and general revenues (Office for Victims of Crime, 1990).

Another innovative source of funding is the implementation of so-called *"Son of Sam" provisions.* After New York serial murderer David Berkowitz (nicknamed "Son of Sam") was apprehended, he stood to gain millions of dollars by selling book and media rights to his story while his victims and their families received nothing. The idea that a criminal could gain a small fortune from his heinous acts prompted passage of a new law. To prevent criminals from profiting from their misdeeds, the state decided to confiscate any royalties and to compensate victims with these proceeds. Other states soon followed suit. Laws that restricted the profits a criminal received from writing a book, selling movie rights, granting interviews or any other financial arrangements became known as "Son of Sam" provisions.

Despite a flurry of similar legislation, these regulations did not generate the windfall that some people had expected (McGillis and Smith, 1983: 126). More recently, the U.S. Supreme Court declared the New York "Son of Sam" law unconstitutional (*Simon & Schuster v. Members of the New York State Crime Victims Board et al.,* 1991). The Court ruled that this statute violated the First Amendment protections against censorship because it "singles out income derived from expressive activity for a burden the State places on no other income, and it is directed only at works with a specified content" (p. 487). As a result, these monies are no longer earmarked for confiscation and payment to crime victims. However, this decision does not preclude the state from exacting funds from offenders to compensate victims. It simply means that you cannot single out a certain source of revenue, in this case speech or writing, for compensation (Alexander, 1992). Since the *Simon & Schuster* ruling, many states have moved to revise their statutes in such a way that *any* assets of an offender, including those derived from books, speeches or movies, can be attached by the state for use in compensating crime victims. Figure 4.3 displays the revised New York "Son of Sam" legislation.

**FIGURE 4.3**
**The Revised New York "Son of Sam" Provisions**

---

1. (b) "Profits from the crime" means (i) any property obtained through or income generated from the commission of a crime of which the defendant was convicted; (ii) any property obtained by or income generated from the sale, conversion or exchange of proceeds of a crime, including any gain realized by such sale, conversion or exchange; and (iii) any property which the defendant obtained or income generated as a result of having committed the crime, including any assets obtained through the use of unique knowledge obtained during the commission of, or in preparation for the commission of the crime, as well as any property obtained by or income generated from the sale, conversion or exchange of such property and any gain realized by such sale, conversion or exchange.

2. (a) Every person, firm, corporation, partnership, association or other legal entity which knowingly contracts for, pays, or agrees to pay, any profit from a crime, as defined in subdivision one of this section, to a person charged with or convicted of that crime shall give written notice to the crime victims board of the payment, or obligation to pay as soon as practicable after discovering that the payment or intended payment is a profit from a crime.

   (b) The board, upon receipt of notice of a contract, an agreement to pay or payment of profits of the crime shall notify all known victims of the crime of the existence of such profits at their last known address.

3. [A]ny crime victim shall have the right to bring a civil action in a court of competent jurisdiction to recover money damages from a person convicted of a crime of which he or she is a victim, or the legal representative of that convicted person, within three years of the discovery of any profits of the crime. . . . Any damages awarded in such action shall be recoverable only up to the value of the profits of the crime.

---

Source: *McKinney's Consolidated Laws of New York Annotated* (1997), Executive Law §632-a.

## Other Provisions

One prominent feature of victim compensation is its close alliance with the criminal justice system. As we shall see in a moment, these provisions have become the stepping-stone for research concerning the impact of victim compensation. Virtually every state requires that the crime be reported to the police, that the victim cooperate fully with the police investigation and that the victim cooperate completely with the prosecution of the case should the state attorney or district attorney pursue that option. Failure to abide by any of these requirements results in an automatic claim denial and the repayment of any compensation benefits that the victim may have already received. It is clear that victim compensation represents a very calculated attempt to bring victims back into the criminal justice system.

Victim compensation statutes normally contain other provisions dealing with agency composition, powers, the appeal process, attorney payments and a host of other items. The interested reader can become more attuned to these considerations by examining some of the references cited at the end of this text.

## DOES VICTIM COMPENSATION WORK?

As discussed earlier, victims who enter the criminal justice system become twice-victimized. First, they lose time from work, suffer physical injury and mental anguish, incur medical expenses, have property damaged or taken, and endure a variety of other inconveniences because of the criminal episode. Then, when these victims enter the halls of justice, they are subject to a second set of problems. They give up more time from work, lose more money and must travel to the courthouse for different sets of proceedings. Once inside the courthouse, they are beset by feelings of uncertainty and bewilderment. For many victims, reliving the painful episode elicits many suppressed and unresolved emotions.

One result of this double victimization is that many victims have come to boycott the criminal justice system. As pointed out in Chapter 2, a substantial number of victims elect not to report their victimizations to the police. Those victims who do contact the police may choose not to prosecute. One reason for this lack of involvement in the criminal justice process appears to be that victims realize they can minimize their losses by avoiding the legal system. If the decision to not cooperate with the system stems from an economic appraisal, then the system needs to lure victims back with financial incentives.

Some observers contend that victim compensation fits this bill. Because failure to satisfy the requirements (that the crime be reported to the police, that the victim assist in the police investigation and that the victim cooperate completely with the prosecution of the offender) can automatically produce a compensation claim denial, victim compensation amounts to an economic incentive that serves to entice the victim back into the legal process.

Victim compensation administrators routinely tout their programs as promoting greater victim cooperation with the legal machinery. If these officials are correct, then certain *macro-level effects* should appear. A macro-level effect refers to a change in some group or organizational characteristic. Such logical outcomes would include higher crime-reporting rates, higher clearance rates, higher prosecution rates and higher conviction rates. In addition, certain *micro-level effects* should materialize. A micro-level effect refers to any changes in a person. One expected micro-level effect stemming from victim compensation would be more satisfied victims. As we shall see, however, program officials appear to be a bit overzealous in their attribution of success to victim compensation programs.

## Macro-Level Effects

Victim compensation administrators generally assume that their programs increase victim participation in the criminal justice system. Because victim compensation laws mandate crime reporting, cooperation with the authorities and participation in court cases, certain systematic effects should surface. Victim compensation programs should produce an increased rate of violent crimes known to the police, a higher proportion of known crime that is violent and an increased proportion of violent crimes cleared by the police.

An examination of four states operating a victim compensation program found no support for any of these expectations (Doerner et al., 1976a). A replication using victim compensation programs from several Canadian provinces did not uncover any evidence for the proposed effects (Doerner, 1978a). Because both studies utilized official data, it is possible that shortcomings within the data influenced the findings. As a result, another analysis examined self-reported victimization data (Doerner, 1978b). Utilizing the National Crime Panel Surveys from 26 cities made it possible to test two hypotheses. First, it was anticipated that compensating jurisdictions would record higher rates of violent crime-reporting than would noncompensating areas. Second, it was expected that reporting rates for property crime in compensating and noncompensating jurisdictions would be similar in both types of jurisdictions because these offenses were not compensable. The findings revealed that areas with compensation programs had similar rates of reporting violent crime and reporting property crime. Thus, these studies suggest that victim compensation did not stimulate an increase in crime reporting.

Moreover, another analysis of Canadian provinces revealed similar conviction rates for violent offenses and property offenses in both compensating and noncompensating jurisdictions (Silverman and Doerner, 1979). As a result, the researchers concluded that victim compensation did not alter conviction rates.

In sum, these studies do not provide any consistent empirical evidence in support of the contention that victim compensation positively affects other components of the criminal justice system. This conclusion takes on much greater importance in view of the fact that the evidence is derived from studies conducted in two different countries and with data from official, as well as nonofficial, sources. Despite the conclusion of no macro-level or organizational effects, it still remains to be seen whether victim compensation programs generate any micro-level or individual effects.

## Micro-Level Effects

Several researchers have pointed out that a definitive verdict about compensation programs requires an examination of client reaction (Brooks, 1975; Chappel and Sutton, 1974; Silverman and Doerner, 1979). Doerner and Lab (1980) mailed a questionnaire to victims who had applied for crime compensation from a program in Florida. Following the advice of program officials, they divided the study participants into a group who received compensation and a group who was denied compensation. The expectation was that compensated victims would express more favorable attitudes toward criminal justice personnel and would be more likely to cooperate with these personnel in the future than would noncompensated applicants.

The results showed that compensated victims were more satisfied with the crime compensation program officials than were noncompensated victims. However, a similar sense of satisfaction did not accrue to the police, the state attorney or the judge. While compensated victims were more likely to say that they would register a claim with the crime compensation program in the event of a future victimization, they were not inclined to cooperate with other system personnel. Thus, it would seem from this study that victim compensation programs do not generate a "spill-over" or a halo effect to the remainder of the criminal justice system.

The foregoing results suggest that victim compensation programs have had little impact on the attitudes and views of the public toward the criminal justice system in general. This suggests that the future of compensation must not rely on arguments that it benefits the criminal justice system or society. Rather, an appeal to the social welfare and social contract arguments holds much more promise.

## Problems and Concerns with Compensation

Besides the potential impact of compensation on the criminal justice system, it is possible to evaluate these operations in terms of the number of victims served and the extent of services provided. Early program evaluations found a number of readily identifiable deficiencies (Brooks,

1975; Doerner, 1977; Meiners, 1978). Just about every program was deluged by the number of claims it had received. Given the small number of staff, some claims required more than a year for processing. Rejection rates exceeded the 50 percent mark and the availability of victim compensation remained a well-kept secret. These observations led one researcher to forecast that unless these problems were corrected, "victim compensation programs will not significantly reduce the plight of the crime victim in our society and will remain a prime example of a misguided social program" (Doerner, 1977: 109).

Apparently, these concerns have not diminished as the programs have matured. A review of the Bureau of Victim Compensation operations in Florida reveals an enormous backlog of claims. Because of the sluggish processing pace, victims often must wait more than one full year to receive a compensation check. As one victim advocate quipped, "Our experience has been that you can have a baby faster than getting paid" (No Author, 1993: 6B).

The federal government helped set standards when it began to offer funds to these state programs. Parent et al. (1992) noted that 75,900 victims in the United States filed compensation claims and 65,799 applicants received awards in 1987. Recognizing that some victims may have filed their paperwork during the previous year and that some 1987 claims may still be in the processing stage, these figures suggest that more than 85 percent of claimants receive compensation. Reasons for denying compensation mainly involve victim contribution to the crime, failure to cooperate with the criminal justice system and lack of adequate information with which to process the claims (Parent et al., 1992).

While these figures appear impressive, they fail to tell us the extent to which all eligible victims are being reached and served by compensation programs. Considering the total number of compensable offenses reported to police, whether the victim was culpable and the availability of insurance to cover losses, there were roughly 168,000 victims eligible for compensation in 1987 (Parent et al., 1992). Less than one-half of these crimes, however, resulted in a compensation claim. Many victims are not applying for or receiving compensation. One reason for this gap may be the relative anonymity within which many compensation programs operate. That is, most victims do not know about the programs (McCormack, 1991). Thus, while compensation has the potential to help victims, it still only reaches a portion of those in need.

**FIGURE 4.4**
**Selected Internet Sites Dealing with the Financial Plight of Victims**

Campaign for Equity-Restorative Justice
http://www.cerj.org/

Federal Office of Child Support Enforcement
http://www.acf.dhhs.gov/

Florida Association of Court Clerks & Comptrollers
http://www.flclerks.com/

National Center for State Courts
http://www.ncsc.dni.us/

Office for Victims of Crime
http://www.ojp.usdoj.gov/ovc/

Society of Professionals in Dispute Resolution
http://www.spidr.org/

Victim Offender Mediation Association
http://www.igc.org/voma/

# SUMMARY

Crime victims face a host of problems, not the least of which are the financial costs accruing from the crime. This chapter has examined several mechanisms that victims can use to recoup some of their losses. There has been a great deal of resurgent interest in restitution over the past few decades. The problems with restitution, however, have prompted moves to other forms of recompense. Both civil litigation and insurance represent methods by which the victim takes an active role. Unfortunately, each requires a monetary outlay on the part of the victim beyond the loss due to the crime. Many victims simply cannot afford to turn to these alternatives. The final possibility discussed here is the use of state victim compensation. Under this scheme, the state makes payments to crime victims. Innocent victims who cooperate with the criminal justice system receive compensation for their crime-related losses. Many victims, however, do not know about these programs and therefore fail to take advantage of these funds. The recent increase in federal participation and funding of victim compensation suggests that this scheme could well become the primary source of monetary aid to crime victims in the foreseeable future.

# LEARNING OBJECTIVES

After reading Chapter 5, you should be able to:

- Give the common law definition of rape.
- Contrast rape with sexual assault.
- Tie the notion of spousal immunity to the idea of male power and domination
- Differentiate between acquaintance rape and stranger rape.
- Assemble a picture of rape based on FBI UCR statistics.
- Sketch out the characteristics of rape based upon victimization survey results.
- Compare and contrast UCR and NCVS statistics regarding rape.
- Discuss the shortcomings of the UCR and NCVS databases.
- Forecast what NCVS reforms will mean for sexual assault statistics.
- Critique independent efforts to gauge the extent of sexual assault among women.
- Talk about why psychopathology is a popular explanation for rape.
- Link a physiological explanation to rape behavior.
- Relate the theme of male domination or power to rape.
- Comment on the categories produced by rape typologies.
- Talk about what a crisis means.
- Understand the stages in the crisis reaction repair cycle.
- Analyze the rape trauma syndrome.
- Amplify some of the concerns surrounding compulsory HIV testing for sexual assault suspects.
- Explain consent and corroboration.
- Outline the purpose that shield provisions serve.
- Talk about sex offender registration laws.
- Distinguish macro-level effects from micro-level effects.
- Evaluate whether rape reforms are working as intended.
- Provide an overview of the steps involved in the system's response to sexual assault cases.
- Differentiate the medical examination from a forensic examination.
- Raise some issues pertaining to the use of "rape kits."
- List some common pitfalls that the prosecutor's office should avoid in the handling of sexual assault cases.
- Discuss sexual harassment.

# Chapter 5

# Sexual Assault

## INTRODUCTION

Sexual assault is a devastating, dehumanizing experience. What makes this crime so crushing is that it is a direct attack on the person's self. Many victims suffer tremendous feelings of humiliation and degradation because of their assailants. Later, many of these same emotions are rekindled when the victim turns to the criminal justice system expecting comfort and assistance.

This chapter opens with a brief look at some of the theories that purport to explain why rape occurs. To get a better sense of the prevalence of sexual battery in this country, we will look at official and unofficial data sources. A comparison of information contained in the Uniform Crime Reports with materials from the National Crime Victimization Survey reinforces the discussion held in Chapter 2. Underreporting is a major drawback with this crime category.

The system is not unaware of the widespread reluctance to report this offense and to become involved with the authorities. Many states have rewritten their laws in an effort to dismantle the traditional barriers to victim cooperation. For example, rape has become redefined as sexual assault and attention has been given to concerns with

## KEY TERMS

absolute exemption

acquaintance rape

anger rape

crisis

crisis reaction repair cycle

date rape

forensic examination

gang rapes

impact

impulsive rapes

in camera

macro-level effect

micro-level effect

nonstranger rapes

partial exemption

physiological explanations

post-traumatic stress
  disorder (PTSD)

psychopathology

rape kit

rape myths

rape trauma syndrome

recoil

reorganization

consent, the types of proof necessary to substantiate an allegation of sexual assault, and the character assassination tactics used to discredit victim testimony in court. Whether these reforms are working is an empirical question that we will probe.

Our discussion of sexual assault will delve into the personal tragedy that victims experience, the healing process these people face and common coping strategies. This material will provide a backdrop for discussing how the police, hospital personnel and the prosecutor respond to the victim. Finally, we will examine sexual harassment in the workplace.

## DEFINING SEXUAL ASSAULT

The definition of rape traditionally has been a matter of utmost concern. The common law view of rape dominated most state statutes well into the 1970s. Common law defines rape to be carnal knowledge by a male of a female, who is not his wife, forcibly and against her will (Dane, 1991: 148; Gross, 1991; Snelling, 1975; Weis and Borges, 1973).

This definition is notable for several reasons. First, the victim status is restricted to females and only males can be offenders. Second, the only act controlled under this approach is penile penetration. Third, husbands enjoy an automatic exemption from offender status. Fourth, an important element or ingredient is that the victim did not submit voluntarily to the act.

Over the years, lawmakers have altered the legal terminology involved with rape in a variety of ways. Many states have replaced the term "rape" with such phrases as "sexual battery," "deviant sexual conduct" and "sexual assault." These changes are more than just semantic. For one thing, they eliminate the gender bias inherent in the common law formulation. Today, it is possible for males to be victims and for females to be offenders. In addition, other forms of sexual abuse now fall under the purview of unwanted criminal intrusions (Largen, 1988). Some such acts would include oral, anal and digital penetration, as well as fondling and the application of any other foreign objects to the victim's body. Finally, varying degrees of sexual assault replace the former all-inclusive single category of rape. As Figure 5.1 shows, the degree of a criminal act can be distinguished by the extent of injury, use of weapons, presence or absence of penetration, multiple versus lone offenders, and other factors. These aggravating circumstances can raise the applicable penalty allowed under the sentencing guidelines.

## Spousal Rape

Under common law, a wife cannot accuse her husband of raping her while they are legally married. Many states continue to embrace this thinking apparently without hesitation (Frieze and Browne, 1989). The underlying assumption is that the marriage vows provide an irretractable contractual arrangement to deliver exclusive sexual services upon demand. The marriage ceremony marks the formal transfer of the woman from her father's possession to the ownership of the husband. The practice of placing a premium on virginity, the institution of the dowry and the tradition of relinquishing one's maiden name to assume the husband's surname all further reinforce the image of women as a commodity that males can buy and trade. This orientation maintains that a husband is free to do with his "property" as he sees fit.

**KEY TERMS**
—*continued*

sadistic rape

seropositive

sex offender registration

sexual conquest rape

sexual harassment

sexually transmitted disease (STD)

sociocultural explanations

spousal immunity

**FIGURE 5.1**
**An Example of a Sexual Battery Statute Containing Provisions Regarding Aggravating Circumstances**

A person who commits sexual battery upon a person 12 years of age or older without that person's consent, under any of the following circumstances, commits a felony of the first degree, punishable as provided in §775.082, §775.803, or §775.084:

(a) When the victim is physically helpless to resist.

(b) When the offender coerces the victim to submit by threatening to use force or violence likely to cause serious personal injury on the victim, and the victim reasonably believes that the offender has the present ability to execute the threat.

(c) When the offender coerces the victim to submit by threatening to retaliate against the victim, or any other person, and the victim reasonably believes that the offender has the ability to execute the threat in the future.

(d) When the offender, without the prior knowledge or consent of the victim, administers or has knowledge of someone else administering to the victim any narcotic, anesthetic, or other intoxicating substance which mentally or physically incapacitates the victim.

(e) When the victim is mentally defective and the offender has reason to believe this or has actual knowledge of this fact.

(f) When the victim is physically incapacitated.

Source: Florida Statutes (1997), §794.011(4).

Despite this legal barrier, society recognizes that some uncon-scionable husbands do force their spouses to engage in unwanted sexu-al activity. It is not uncommon for coerced sexual behavior to occur in at least one of every 10 marriages (Finkelhor and Yllo, 1983; Russell, 1982). According to the 1994 NCVS, 5.5 percent of all actual and attempted sexual assaults were committed by the victim's spouse. How-ever, a common perception is that a sexual assault by a husband is not as serious as an attack by a complete stranger (Monson et al., 1996).

Some states continue to adhere to the common law interpretation that renders a husband incapable of raping his wife. These jurisdictions grant husbands an *absolute exemption* and do not allow prosecution for spousal rape under any condition. Other states have relaxed their statutes to reflect the growing awareness that marital rape does exist and can have deep traumatic effects for the victim. These states may allow prosecution if the parties are separated, are in the process of obtaining a divorce or have taken other steps to void or nullify the marriage. These laws grant what is known as a *partial exemption*. While this modifica-tion may appear to be an enlightened and progressive move, it does have its limits. A national survey of rape reform legislation cautions that states that "have removed the traditional immunity for spouses . . . have offset this change by providing relatively low penalties for conviction" (Berger et al., 1988: 342). Thus, what may appear at first to be a signif-icant gain is sometimes really a very small concession.

## Date or Acquaintance Rape

Another form of sexual assault that has emerged as a major topic of study is the category of *date rape* or *acquaintance rape*. These instances have garnered attention because they do not fit the stereotypical view of rape. To a large degree, many people assume that sexual assault occurs between individuals who do not know one another. They think the offender either stalks his or her prey or happens upon a victim and vio-lently attacks that person. Date rape, however, does not fit that conve-nient mold. Rather, the victim and offender know one another and are engaged in friendly, noncombative interaction up until the attack. In many analyses, being "talked into" having sexual relations when the vic-tim did not want to, submitting when inebriated, being made to feel guilty if refusing to have sex, or submitting after being given false promises (such as marriage) fall into the realm of sexual assault, although physical force or threats may not have been involved. The absence of the traditional stranger-to-stranger relationship and physical force sometimes leads some people to believe there must be some degree of consent in date or acquaintance instances, thereby negating a valid claim of rape.

# Measuring the Extent of Rape

As we learned in Chapter 2, estimates concerning the nature, extent and distribution of crime vary considerably depending upon the source of that information. The category of forcible rape or sexual battery is no exception. The typical forums for gathering data on these criminal incidents are the Uniform Crime Reports (UCR) and the National Crime Victimization Survey (NCVS). Information from both these databases (as well as other undertakings) follows in this chapter.

## UCR Information

The UCR describes forcible rape as "the carnal knowledge of a female forcibly and against her will" (FBI, 1996: 23). This category excludes statutory rape and other sex offenses. Using this definition, the UCR reveals there were 97,460 rapes known to the police in 1995. This figure reflects a decrease of roughly 10.5 percent from the peak of 109,060 incidents reported during 1992 (FBI, 1995: 58). When one transforms the 1995 numbers into crime rates, the resulting figure is 37.1 offenses per 100,000 persons. Despite the recent decrease in official rape figures, an examination of crime trends shows that rape increased by more than 31 percent from 1980 to 1992, and is still up by 17.4 percent from the 1980 figures (FBI, 1996: 58).

## NCVS Information

The emerging women's movement in the 1960s and 1970s assailed official rape statistics as being too low and patently inaccurate. This position garnered a great deal of support from the early victimization surveys. The NORC (National Opinion Research Center) victimization survey, undertaken on behalf of the 1967 President's Commission, uncovered almost four times more rapes than what police reports had tallied. Despite a host of methodological problems with first-generation victim surveys, the issue of underreporting fueled skepticism about the reliability and validity of official crime counts.

After a great deal of refinement, the NCVS has emerged as a recognized source of information on crime victims. As you will recall from Chapter 2, the recent redesign of the NCVS modified the screen questions so as to more fully measure the extent of certain types of offenses, including sexual assault. Rather than simply probe sexual assault under a general question dealing with being attacked "in some other way," the redesigned survey specifically asks about rape, attempted rape or any other type of sexual assault (Bachman and Saltzman, 1995). The expectation was that the new survey would uncover substantially more rape and sexual assault incidents than have materialized in the past (Kindermann et al., 1997).

As expected, the level of sexual assault has increased under the redesigned format. According to the 1990 NCVS, there were 67,430 attempted rapes and 62,830 completed rapes in the United States. These figures jump to 148,610 attempted rapes and 167,550 completed rapes in 1994, roughly a 243 percent increase for the combined categories (Bureau of Justice Statistics, 1997: 6). Furthermore, there were 116,590 other sexual assaults in this country during 1994. These recent figures translate into a combined rape/sexual assault victimization rate of 200 per 100,000 population age 12 and above, compared to a rate of roughly 60 in 1990.

Two important points must be considered when interpreting these recent results. First, these figures include both males and females as victims. An examination of just female rape victims, which would more closely approximate UCR data, further increases the rate to 270 offenses per 100,000 female population. A cursory comparison with the UCR rates, while not perfectly parallel, shows a noticeable gap between the two data sources. If one accepts the NCVS as more realistic, then the police are very much unaware of the true extent of sexual victimization. Second, because of the redesign, trends in the NCVS are difficult to discern, especially for rape, and should be made with great caution (Rand et al., 1997). The reason for this warning is due partly to the failure to probe specifically for sexual offenses in earlier years.

Table 5.1 presents some selected characteristics of rape incidents outlined in the NCVS. According to this data source, there were 432,710 rapes (completed and attempted) and sexual assaults in 1994. Younger females, particularly those under 24 years old, are more likely to become rape victims. *Nonstranger rapes* (which include "date rape" and "acquaintance rape," among other things) account for almost 70 percent of these sexual victimizations. Sexual assaults, besides rape, are almost equally distributed between strangers and nonstrangers. More nonstranger rapes are completed than are rapes in which the victim does not know the offender. Roughly one-third of these incidents occur at or near the victim's home. Finally, more than one-half of all rapes are not reported, with completed episodes being more likely to come to the attention of the police.

**TABLE 5.1**
**Selected Characteristics of Rape Victimization, NCVS, 1994**

**Rape Incidents:**

| Type | Number | Rate per 1,000 |
|------|--------|----------------|
| Completed Rape | 167,550 | 0.8 |
| Attempted Rape | 148,610 | 0.7 |
| Sexual Assault | 116,590 | 0.5 |
| Total | 432,750 | 2.0 |

**Rape Rate by Victim Age:**

| | | | |
|------|-----|-------|-----|
| 12-15 | 3.1 | 35-49 | 1.6 |
| 16-19 | 5.1 | 50-64 | 0.2 |
| 20-24 | 5.0 | 65+ | 0.1 |
| 25-34 | 2.9 | | |

**Victim-Offender Relationship:**

| | STRANGERS | | NONSTRANGERS | |
|------|--------|------|--------|------|
| Type | Number | Rate | Number | Rate |
| Completed Rape | 37,720 | 0.2 | 129,830 | 0.2 |
| Attempted Rape | 58,620 | 0.3 | 89,990 | 0.2 |
| Sexual Assault | 59,060 | 0.3 | 57,530 | 0.3 |

**Time of Incident:**

| | |
|------|------|
| 6 AM – 6 PM | 34% |
| 6 PM – Midnite | 3% |
| Midnite – 6 AM | 64% |

**Location of Incident:**

| | |
|------|------|
| At or In Victim's Home | 34% |
| Near Victim's Home | 3% |
| Away From Victim's Home | 64% |

**Incidents Reported to Police:**

| | |
|------|------|
| Completed Rape | 36% |
| Attempted Rape | 20% |
| Sexual Assault | 41% |

Source: Adapted from U.S. Department of Justice (1997). *Criminal Victimization in the United States, 1994.* Washington, DC: U.S. Government Printing Office.

# Comparing the UCR with the NCVS Over Time

One way to address any similarities and disparities between police-derived and survey-derived victimization rates is to look at these data over time. If both sets of crime statistics are subject to similar influences, then they ought to move in unison. Should different forces affect one data set but not the other, then one should observe uncorrelated trends. Unfortunately, the implementation of the redesigned NCVS in 1992 introduces a significant change in the victimization figures. As noted earlier, the redesign increased the number of rapes reported by respondents. Figure 5.2 presents the rape victimization rates for both the UCR and the NCVS from 1976 through 1995. The vertical line at 1992 indicates the point at which the revised NCVS appears.

**FIGURE 5.2**
**NCVS and UCR Rape Rates, 1976-95**

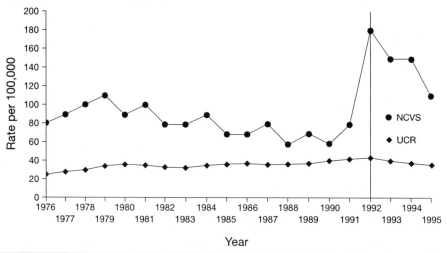

Source: U.S. Department of Justice (1992). *Criminal Victimization in the United States, 1991.* Washington, DC: U.S. Government Printing Office, p. 6; U.S. Department of Justice (1996). *National Crime Victimization Survey, 1995: Preliminary Findings.* Washington, DC: U.S. Government Printing Office, p. 6; and Federal Bureau of Investigation, *Uniform Crime Reports for the United States, 1995.* Washington, DC: U.S. Government Printing Office, p. 62.

The UCR forcible rape rates display a relatively steady climb from 1976 until 1992, at which point the rates began a steady decline. On the other hand, the victimization rape rates evidence a general downward trend throughout the data, even when considering the sudden jump due to the survey redesign. Both the data from 1976 to 1991 and those from 1992 to 1995 display a downward pattern. While the UCR pattern is smooth, the NCVS exhibits steep bounces in both directions. Because the two data sources do not track each other, the next step is to find what systematic influences affect each data set.

One possibility is that changes in traditional sex-role attitudes have relaxed the taboos once associated with rape. This liberalization, in turn, paves the way for greater reporting of such incidents. The underlying argument is that before this attitudinal shift, women were reluctant to report episodes that departed from "classic rape" stereotypes. For example, victims may have found it easier to report attacks in which the perpetrator brandished a weapon, was a complete stranger or beat the victim. At the same time, however, victims would hide from public view incidents involving acquaintances or relatives.

To see if this notion was plausible, Orcutt and Faison (1988) analyzed attitudinal trends and victimization reporting habits from 1973 until 1985. They found that broader or more liberated perceptions of acceptable female behavior greatly affected whether the police were notified in nonstranger rape situations. Thus, Orcutt and Faison (1988) maintained that increases in rapes known to the police during this period could very well be a function of changing social mores. More recent research by Bachman (1993; 1995) lends support to this line of thinking.

Although the notion of an attitudinal shift carries considerable appeal, another alternative is just as lucrative. Criminologists know that organizational changes within the police bureaucracy influence the quantity and composition of official crime. Drawing upon this outlook, Jensen and Karpos (1993) counter that an increased presence of female law enforcement employees changes the quality of police interaction with victims. This gain, in turn, influences agency recording practices. More precisely, dispatchers and officers who are female have a heightened sensitivity toward sexual assault victims. These employees are in a better position to anticipate victim needs. A more sensitive posture, coupled with specialized investigatory units and connections with rape crisis centers, fosters greater citizen reporting and better police documentation of sexual assault cases.

A third reason for the UCR-NCVS discrepancy prior to 1992 is the realization that the victimization survey instrument did not contain any inquiries that deal directly with rape (Bachman and Taylor, 1994; Eigenberg, 1990). The individual screen questions eliciting reports of rape victimization were vague and evasive. This may have been because survey administrators regarded this area as delicate and highly sensitive. The NCVS redesign addresses this deficiency by including an item that uses a screen question asking about rape, attempted rape or other type of sexual assault. Follow-up questions on any incidents are then conducted. This new procedure has resulted in a 157 percent increase in identified incidents compared to the older approach (Kindermann et al., 1997). Consequently, data since the redesign have a better chance of mirroring the patterns in UCR data.

## Other Information on Sexual Assault Levels

In addition to the information and comparisons available from the UCR and NCVS, independent researchers have attempted to gauge the extent of rape among the total female population for various subgroups of females as well as for different types of rape. One of the most researched areas deals with date or acquaintance rape. Interest in date rape is not new. In one early survey, one-fourth of the responding college women reported experiencing forcible intercourse over a one-year period of time (Kanin, 1957). More recently, surveys of college students have revealed sexual victimization levels that range from 10 percent to more than 50 percent (Abbey et al., 1996; Bernard and Bernard, 1983; Cate et al., 1982; Kilpatrick et al., 1985; Koss, 1995; Koss et al., 1987; Makepeace, 1983; Schwartz and Pitts, 1995; Shapiro and Schwarz, 1997). Quite often, the aggressor is characterized as an acquaintance. Indeed, Abbey et al. (1996) claim that 95 percent of sexual assaults are committed by an acquaintance. It is also important to note that several studies find significant levels of sexual coercion reported by male respondents (Hogben et al., 1996; Poppen and Segal, 1988; Struckman-Johnson, 1988; Waldner-Haugrud and Magruder, 1995). These figures for both females and males bespeak of a much greater problem than that suggested by either official data or large national survey data.

In evaluating this information, however, there are several issues that should be kept in mind. First, the magnitude of many figures is inflated by focusing on "lifetime" occurrences or college surveys asking about "since you were 14" or any other similar ages. The data, therefore, appear high when compared to official and NCVS measures that tap only the past year.

Second, while often discussed as "date rape," the actions under consideration typically reflect a much broader category of "sexual coercion." For example, verbal persuasion to engage in sex, promises of marriage, and making someone feel guilt are often lumped together with the use or threat of physical force in defining an experience as sexual assault. While these actions may entail coercion, there is a clear difference in magnitude and potential harm involved in the actions.

Third, most studies of date rape restrict their inquiries to just college students. Furthermore, researchers often rely upon very select groups of students, such as undergraduates enrolled in psychology or criminal justice classes. A college sampling frame, while convenient, is not representative of society, nor of the 18- to 22-year-old general population.

Finally, caution must be used in blindly accepting interpretations advanced by "advocates." Gilbert (1993), while reviewing research on the magnitude of date rape, notes that in one study almost three-quarters of the respondents whom the researchers regarded as victims actually reported that they themselves did not think they had been a victim. He also points out that some "rape" questions fail to address whether the behavior was consensual or not—an important criterion to consider. Reliance upon such questionable assumptions results in incidence and prevalence rates that not only dwarf official data, but belie even the experiences of crisis assistance groups (Gilbert, 1993). Clearly, rape and sexual assault are greater problems than what official data would lead us to believe. At the same time, though, advocacy data probably err on the other extreme end of the spectrum by making unreasonable assumptions when measuring the problem. A safe conclusion is that rape is a much larger and more pervasive problem than the UCR and the NCVS figures indicate.

# THEORIES OF SEXUAL ASSAULT

Attempts to understand the occurrence of sexual assault must grapple with the cause of such behavior. As with virtually every form of deviant behavior, there is no consensus about the exact etiological or causative factors that underlie sexual assault. A variety of potential explanations have been put forth as capable explanations of this behavior. The following materials highlight selected explanations grounded in the pathology and physiology of the offender as well as the social development of society, with the latter being instrumental in the growth of the women's movement and public interest in sexual assault.

## Intraindividual Explanations

Most early explanations portrayed rape and sexual assault as stemming from *psychopathology,* or mental imbalances within the offender. The perpetrator was seen as a disturbed or maladjusted individual who failed to exert sufficient control over his actions. Sexual assault was a reaction to repressed desires, past domination by a female figure, or other forces beyond the offender's control (Brownmiller, 1975; Lottes, 1988; Scully, 1990).

These explanations gained quick acceptance because they painted rape as a social aberration. One could attribute such undesirable behavior to the few deranged individuals who committed these acts. What made this perspective so lucrative was that it deflected attention away from society and the victim. In essence, they were blameless for the offense.

*Physiological explanations* also locate the cause of rape within the individual offender. According to these views, an uncontrollable sex drive, compounded by the lack of available partners, compels the offender to rape (Lottes, 1988). According to Ellis (1989), rape is a consequence of the natural selection process endemic to society. This evolutionary approach maintains that males need frequent copulation as a substitute for the lengthy gestation period experienced by females. According to this theory, females contribute to the species through gestation, while males do so through multiple copulation with more than one partner. Thus, this model contends that rape is the product of a distinctive physiological need on the part of the male.

## Sociocultural Explanations

*Sociocultural explanations* have gained prominence as viable explanations for sexual assault. Sociocultural explanations, frequently labeled as feminist in orientation, focus on the traditional roles of males and females in society.

Brownmiller (1975) brought these arguments to the forefront when she pointed out that the historical place of women in society was one of subservience. Women belonged either to their fathers or to their husbands. Females were property; as such, they were subject to the wishes of the owner. In this context, any attack on a female was actually an affront against her master. Any compensation or retribution due to the possession's devaluation went to the owner, not to the female who was victimized. It is for similar reasons that warring armies use rape as a weapon to terrorize, intimidate and taunt opposing forces (Brownmiller, 1975).

In updating the sociocultural explanation, rape is simply a means of showing and promoting male domination in a society in which formal ownership of females is no longer permitted. Rape is a means of guaranteeing the inequality between the sexes, with males occupying the upper niches of power. The sociocultural approach emphasizes the argument that rape is *not* a sexual offense. Instead, rape is an offense of *power*—a tool that enables men to exert power and control over women.

The sociocultural explanation borrows heavily from the arena of learning theory. In this approach, behavior is learned through both formal and informal mechanisms, such as imitation, modeling, reinforcement and explicit training. Proponents who embrace this viewpoint see rape as the result of stereotypical role expectations in society (Brownmiller, 1975; Griffin, 1971; Makepeace, 1981; Sanders, 1980; Schwendinger and Schwendinger, 1983). The "proper" place of males and females is passed down from one generation to the next in everyday behavior and expectations. Rape is a result of males exerting their learned position in society.

As one would expect, the sociocultural explanation gained a great deal of support from the women's movement. It became a clear challenge to the dominant male structure within society. Rape was also identifiable as perhaps the most heinous example of what was wrong with traditional sex roles. The sociocultural problems surrounding rape were highlighted further by the callous methods used by the criminal justice system when handling victims (Brownmiller, 1975; Holmstrom and Burgess, 1978) and by rape myths believed by many individuals (Koss and Leonard, 1984; Lottes, 1988).

The sociocultural approach also receives a great deal of support from discussions of date or acquaintance rape among college populations. Numerous authors point to the influence of peer support in sexual assault (see, for example, DeKeseredy and Kelly, 1995; Koss and Cleveland, 1997; Koss and Gaines, 1993; Martin and Hummer, 1989; Worth et al., 1990). Two peer networks often linked to sexual aggression are fraternities and athletics (Koss and Gaines, 1993; Martin and Hummer, 1989; Stombler, 1994). In both cases, it is argued that offenders are challenged to prove their masculinity, maintain confidentiality and support one's peers. Intertwined with these peer associations is the use of alcohol. Alcohol contributes to sexual assault in numerous ways. It can reduce inhibitions, thwart the ability of a person to resist advances, increase the possibility of misreading another person's desires or intent, diminish any feelings of responsibility, heighten miscommunication and promote "rape myths" (Abbey et al., 1996; Ehrhart and Sadler, 1985; Harrington and Leitenberg, 1994; Lundberg-Love and Geffner, 1989; Martin and Hummer, 1989). It is important to note that alcohol influences *both* the offender and the victim. Harrington and Leitenberg (1994) note that the victim was "somewhat drunk" in 55 percent of the sexually aggressive situations they uncovered and that alcohol increased the degree of "acceptable sexual contact" (according to the victim) before the assault. While it is common to assume that most offenders consciously attempt to get the victim drunk, it is probably more likely that alcohol is used willingly by both parties, which, in turn, produces more opportunities for assault. The social setting of college life, coupled with broader social expectations for male and female behavior, enhances the probability of sexually aggressive activity.

## Typological Efforts

As discussed in Chapter 1, typologies attempt to organize or classify observations according to what they share or have in common. The goal of a typology is to reach a better understanding of the phenomenon under study by grouping similar items together.

There have been several efforts to construct typologies to reach a fuller understanding of sexual assault. Based upon their clinical experience with offenders, Groth and Birnbaum (1980: 21) warned:

> Rape is complex and multidetermined. It serves a number of psychological aims and purposes. Whatever other needs and factors operate in the commission of such an offense, however, we have found the components of anger, power, and sexuality always present and prominent. Moreover, in our experience, we find that either anger or power is the dominant component and that rape, rather than being primarily an expression of sexual desire, is, in fact, the use of sexuality to express power and anger. Rape, then, is a pseudosexual act, a pattern of sexual behavior that is concerned much more with status, hostility, control, and dominance than with sexual pleasure or sexual satisfaction.

Drawing upon a scheme developed by Groth and Birnbaum (1980), Schneider (1987) delineates several different kinds of rape. *Anger rape* makes up roughly 20 percent of all sexual battery cases. It involves a conscious attempt to harm and humiliate the victim. *Sexual conquest rape* (more than 50 percent of all rape offenses) entails the offender's desire to conquer and possess the victim. Offenders feel an overwhelming degree of inadequacy. While not very common (comprising less than 5 percent), *sadistic rape*, in which sexual gratification is achieved through tormenting the victim, typically involves serious physical harm and sometimes even death. Rapes that are fueled by a desire to prove oneself to peers are considered *gang rapes*. These represent 5 to 10 percent of the cases. The remaining 20 percent of the cases are classified as *impulsive rapes* because they lack any other clear motivating factors.

The ability of these and other typological efforts to alert us to different kinds of sexual assaults has important theoretical ramifications. For example, Ellis has taken the next logical step in understanding rape by promoting a synthesized theoretical model. In essence, Ellis (1989) argues that because no single theory is capable of explaining every case of sexual assault, social scientists must combine a wide variety of variables that hold differing degrees of explanatory power. Some of these key ingredients involve motivational, learning, biological, psychological and social factors. In short, despite advances in our knowledge, there is still room for continued improvement before we are able to understand what prompts this form of criminal victimization.

## A Model of Sexual Assault

Lundberg-Love and Geffner (1989) have developed a model that attempts to explain the occurrence of sexual assault. While primarily targeted at date rape, the model incorporates factors that apply to many forms of sexual aggression. Figure 5.3 outlines four preconditions to date rape, many of which have been discussed already in this chapter. The assumption is that date rape can occur when a motivated offender is faced with few or reduced inhibitions (both internal and external) and a victim who fails to resist or take proper precautions. The authors point out that such a framework can assist in understanding both the offender and the victim in sexual assault situations, and can inform modes of intervention.

## Summary of Theories

As with any other form of behavior, the causes of sexual assault are multifaceted. It is unlikely that any of the various explanations presented above is sufficient in and of itself to explain sexual aggression. The most plausible explanation probably incorporates a variety of factors, such as that suggested by the Lundberg-Love and Geffner model. While most critics would favor a sociocultural orientation, one should not dismiss physiological and psychopathological perspectives out of hand. Indeed, the use of drugs to achieve a "chemical" castration of male sexual offenders has been and continues to be advocated and used as a means of reducing testosterone-driven sexual assaults. These approaches, however, require a great deal of additional attention before widespread use of such techniques is justified.

**FIGURE 5.3**
**The Lundberg-Love and Geffner Model**

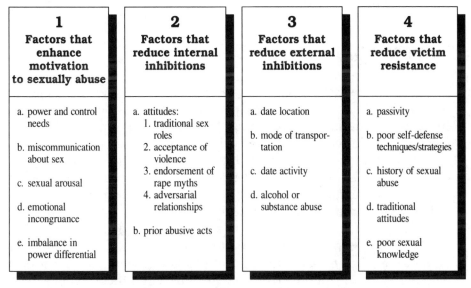

| 1<br>Factors that enhance motivation to sexually abuse | 2<br>Factors that reduce internal inhibitions | 3<br>Factors that reduce external inhibitions | 4<br>Factors that reduce victim resistance |
|---|---|---|---|
| a. power and control needs<br><br>b. miscommunication about sex<br><br>c. sexual arousal<br><br>d. emotional incongruance<br><br>e. imbalance in power differential | a. attitudes:<br>  1. traditional sex roles<br>  2. acceptance of violence<br>  3. endorsement of rape myths<br>  4. adversarial relationships<br><br>b. prior abusive acts | a. date location<br><br>b. mode of transportation<br><br>c. date activity<br><br>d. alcohol or substance abuse | a. passivity<br><br>b. poor self-defense techniques/strategies<br><br>c. history of sexual abuse<br><br>d. traditional attitudes<br><br>e. poor sexual knowledge |

## 1 + 2 + 3 + 4 = DATE RAPE

Source: Lundberg-Love, P. and R. Geffner (1989). "Date Rape: Prevalence, Risk Factors, and a Proposed Model." In M.A. Pirog-Good and J.E. Stets (eds.), *Violence in Dating Relationships: Emerging Social Issues.* New York: Praeger. Reproduced with permission of Greenwood Publishing Group, Inc., Westport, CT.

## THE AFTERMATH OF RAPE

Although they are enlightening, statistics about the number of offenses, debate over whether one data source is superior to another and theoretical musing about the causes of sexual assault present a rather sterile view of the problem. Such a focus loses sight of the victim's personal feelings and experiences. One key area of concern is the emotional repercussion that sexual assault unleashes upon the victim.

As soon as the sexual attack is over, the victim begins the task of facing a bewildering mixture of emotions and concerns. Perhaps the most immediate reaction is one of upheaval and confusion. The victim generally does not know what to do; nor does she know to whom to turn for assistance. Many victims do not call the police right away, particularly if the offender was an acquaintance. If they do talk with anyone, it is often a family member, a close friend or possibly someone at a rape crisis center.

A great deal of fear and anxiety can accompany this initial disorientation. The victim may second-guess her actions prior to and during the attack. She may fear potential retaliation from the assailant. She may envision disapproval, and even condemnation, from those who learn of the incident. Many victims worry about what will happen if the police and criminal justice system become involved, and how people will respond to them afterward.

## Crisis Reaction

Over the years, psychologists have learned that all these reactions are normal and follow a very typical pattern. A variety of events can contribute to or trigger a state of crisis. They may range from the bereavement or grief associated with death, the loss of a job, an unwanted pregnancy or any other traumatic event that may surface throughout the course of life (Bassuk, 1980; Lindemann, 1944; Rapoport, 1962). What makes sexual victimization so disturbing is that it is the penultimate violation. As one team of psychological experts explains, "Short of being killed, there is no greater insult to the self" (Bard and Sangrey, 1986: 21).

A *crisis* develops whenever a situation poses a serious danger or threat to the person's self. This hazard is so monumental that the person who is at the center of this crisis has a great deal of difficulty coping with the circumstances. This imbalance, or lack of equilibrium, between what it takes to resolve the problem and the resources to combat the crisis renders the victim unable to climb out of the situation. As Bard and Sangrey (1986: 33) put it:

> The sudden, arbitrary, unpredictable violation of self leaves victims feeling so shattered that they cannot continue to function the way they did before the crime. Things fall apart, and victims are unable to pull themselves back together right away.

The severity and duration of a crisis depends upon three conditions. The first consideration is the degree to which the person's self is threatened. Insignificant events require very little, if any, attention or redirection. Devastating intrusions, on the other hand, command many more resources. They need constant attention and can be exhausting. The second factor is the person's ability at that precise moment to deal with a problem of such magnitude. Some people might be worn out from facing a series of calamities prior to this unexpected intrusion. Others might be refreshed and able to muster considerable inner strength to meet the challenge. Finally, the kind of intervention or help that a person receives immediately after the tragedy strikes can determine how long it takes to propel out of this helplessness and into recovery.

## The Crisis Reaction Repair Cycle

While the time it takes to recuperate may vary from one person to the next, victims go through a very predictable sequence during their recovery. The *crisis reaction repair cycle* consists of three distinct stages. The first phase is called impact. The second phase is the recoil period. The final stage, reorganization, marks the end of the crisis reaction repair cycle. Although some people contend that this model neglects to explain which victims have these experiences and who will recover more quickly than another (Resick, 1990: 76-77), it does provide a convenient backdrop for understanding the plight of the victim.

### *Impact*

A single word that summarizes the *impact* stage is "shock"; "distress" is another appropriate descriptor. Victims run the entire gamut of emotions during this period. Some people go through denial. Expressions like "I can't believe this happened to me" are common. Other victims blame themselves and ask what they did to deserve this humiliation. Sometimes there are expressions of outrage, anger and revenge. Confusion, fear, helplessness, guilt, self-pity and feelings of worthlessness, if left unchecked, can ravage victims during this stage.

Many victims seek security and strong emotional support while dealing with and sorting out these feelings. Victims sense that they are vulnerable. They know they have lost control over themselves and their surroundings. As a result, victims sometimes interpret insensitive or judgmental comments as strong condemnations. Remarks such as "I can't believe you went there" or "What do you mean you don't know what happened?" can elicit harsh negative responses and devastate a person in need of some compassionate understanding.

The fear, anxiety and shame that victims endure during the impact stage are not ill-founded. Sexual assault victims must combat various notions associated with rape and sexual assault. As Chapter 1 explained, the perception of victim precipitation is very much alive—especially in sexual assault situations. One common reaction is to "blame the victim" for the assault by claiming that she was in the wrong place at the wrong time. There might be other hints that the victim acted suggestively, dressed provocatively or that she originally consented and later changed her mind.

Many victims have to grapple with a number of *rape myths*. These beliefs basically shift responsibility away from the offender and onto the victim. Far from relieving the victim's feelings and problems, they exacerbate them. Among these myths are such ideas as "many women wish to be raped" (Burt and Estep, 1981), "victims who fail to report to the police right away were not really raped" (Costin and Schwarz, 1987; Ehrhart and Sandler, 1985) and the "just world" hypothesis that "only those who deserve to be raped get raped" (Lerner, 1980).

## *Recoil*

The second phase of the victim's recovery is known as the *recoil* period. At this point, victims begin to adapt to the fact that the violation took place. The mending process helps reduce the sting of the emotions that appeared earlier. While these feelings still resurface from time to time, they are not as intense or devastating as they once were. In some cases, victims may move back and forth between the impact and the recoil stages. Over time, these swings become less frequent and less intense.

Many rape victims experience a condition known as *post-traumatic stress disorder* (PTSD). Clinicians who deal with sexual assault victims sometimes refer to these symptoms more narrowly as the *rape trauma syndrome* (Bassuk, 1980; Burgess and Holmstrom, 1974; Frazier and Borgida, 1992; Giannelli, 1997). In any event, this condition refers to a response to major, sudden tragedies. Figure 5.4 outlines the four key criteria involved in PTSD. First, the stressor or event is such that it brings about a similar result in most people who experience it. Second, the individuals relive the initial experiences through flashbacks, nightmares and other recollections. Third, those suffering PTSD display a lack of responsiveness and reduced involvement in everyday activities. Finally, the individuals experience a variety of potential problems, such as sleeplessness, headaches, self-blame, fear and anxiety (Burgess, 1995). Victims often make major lifestyle changes so as to avoid situations similar to that involved in the earlier experience.

Rape significantly affects the victim's self-esteem (Resick, 1987; Shapiro and Schwarz, 1997). Its impact has a lasting effect that diminishes very slowly over time (Murphy et al., 1988; Resick, 1993). Depression is another common problem for sexual assault victims (Atkeson et al., 1982; Marhofer-Dvorak et al., 1988; Murphy et al., 1988; Norris and Feldman-Summers, 1981; Resick et al., 1981; Siegel et al., 1990; Ullman and Siegal, 1993). Sometimes, suicide is a response to the depression brought on by rape experiences (Kilpatrick et al., 1985).

**FIGURE 5.4**
**Criteria for Post-Traumatic Stress Disorder**

1.  A stressor "of significant magnitude as to evoke distinguishable symptoms in almost everyone."

2.  "Re-experiencing of the trauma."
    —Examples: day dreams, nightmares, recollections.

3.  Reduced "responsiveness to or . . . involvement with the environment."
    —Examples: withdrawal, feeling numb, shock, constrained behavior.

4.  Evidence of at least two of the following:
    —exaggerated startle response
    —disturbed sleep
    —feelings of guilt about survival or activity during the event
    —impaired memory or concentration
    —avoidance behavior
    —recurring symptoms related to non-rape sexual events

Source: Adapted from Burgess, A.W. (1995). "Rape Trauma Syndrome." In P. Searles and R.J. Berger (eds.), *Rape and Society: Readings on the Problem of Sexual Assault.* Boulder, CO: Westview Press.

## *Reorganization*

The last stage in the crisis reaction repair cycle is *reorganization*. Victims reach this point once they have sorted through their feelings and are able to place this traumatic event into perspective. As the intensity of their reaction begins to diminish, they are able to move on to other activities. Although from time to time victims will drift back to their unfortunate episode and think about what happened to them, they are no longer preoccupied with these memories as they once were. They have coped with the situation, reached a point of adjustment and are now emerging out of the crisis.

Victims never attain a total or complete cure. They carry their emotional scars with them for the remainder of their days. Victims who do complete the repair cycle, however, are able to proceed with the rest of their lives. For those victims who are not able to complete this transition, the future may consist of a continuing struggle to find the answer to the question of "Why me?"

## LEGAL REFORMS

As sexual assault and related concerns have grown over the years, societal and criminal justice responses have also changed. One area of change has entailed the alteration of statutes governing rape or sexual battery. This section will focus on some of the other more prominent revisions. We have already discussed changes in the definition of rape and the issue of spousal immunity earlier in this chapter. Compulsory AIDS testing for offenders, removal of the corroboration requirement and the enactment of shield provisions are additional areas of concern that will be taken up below. After we explore just what these changes are, we will take a look at whether they brought about the desired effect.

## Compulsory AIDS Testing

A health concern that worries some sexual assault victims is the threat of sexually transmitted diseases (STDs). Sparking many policy considerations is the growing awareness of the acquired immunodeficiency syndrome (AIDS) caused by the HIV virus—and its devastating effects. One issue is whether the criminal justice system should mandate testing for the HIV virus in sex offenders. According to the National Victim Center (1996), 44 states have some type of law governing mandatory HIV-testing of sexual offenders. Some states have enacted pretrial compulsory testing for assailants while others restrict this procedure to convicted offenders only.

AIDS is spread through interpersonal contact. The usual sources of contamination include contact with tainted blood, sexual intercourse with an infected person and the sharing of needles for injecting drugs. Medical advances have made it possible to determine whether HIV, a marker for AIDS, is present within the bloodstream. When a person tests *seropositive*, he or she is a carrier and has the potential to infect others.

Despite medical progress, there is still some ambiguity surrounding HIV laboratory testing. For one thing, the presence of HIV antibodies does not mean that a seropositive person has developed AIDS already. At the same time, a seronegative reading, while reassuring, is not necessarily conclusive. Once infection occurs, the virus requires an incubation period. What this means is that it may take several months for medical screening to detect any antibodies present in the carrier's bloodstream. Thus, a negative report from one or two points in time offers no guarantee that a person is disease-free.

What are the odds that sexual assault victims will become contaminated after the attack? One way to answer that question is to focus upon two related aspects. The first is to calculate the percentage of HIV cases within the offender population. The second is to determine the risk of viral infection from one act of intercourse.

National health tests administered to military recruits fix the HIV infection rate at 0.15 percent (Blumberg, 1989: 458). Approximately 90 percent of these seropositive readings come from two groups that are highly unlikely to attack women: homosexual males and intravenous drug users (Blumberg and Langston, 1991: 7). It has also been estimated that there is a one in 500 chance of contracting AIDS from a contaminated person during a single act of unprotected intercourse (Hearst and Hulley, 1988). Taking all these variables into account suggests that the odds of a sexual battery victim contracting AIDS from a single incident are minimal. While the Centers for Disease Control and Prevention have identified isolated cases in which a sexual assault victim has contracted HIV, the incidence is so low that statistics are not kept for this means of infection.

An assessment of this situation has led to some protests against mandatory HIV-testing policy as an invasion of constitutional rights. For example, objections have surfaced concerning the suspect's right to privacy, the presumption of innocence and whether preconviction testing violates search and seizure standards (McGuire, 1991; Smotas, 1991). At the same time, more than one-half of the states have enacted legislation making the intentional spread of HIV through sexual contact a crime. Florida, in 1996, convicted an HIV-positive man for attempted murder based on his forced sodomy with three boys (Stine, 1996). The case law developing in this area is worth watching over the next few years.

## Consent and Corroboration

The common law looked for corroborative or supporting evidence to validate a woman's claim that she had been the victim of a rape. Many juries hesitated to convict solely on the basis of the victim's testimony. They were afraid that the accuser might be harboring a vendetta and, for whatever reason, may try to "railroad" the man into prison (Ellis, 1992).

Typical supporting evidence would involve such things as timely notification to the police, the presence of semen, the use of a weapon by the offender and, most notably, physical harm (Bourke, 1989; Spears and Spohn, 1996). The assumption was that any victim subjected to a sexual attack should resist to her utmost capacity. It was expected that a woman would submit only if her struggles would bring her to the brink of death. Under this reasoning, the "perfect" case would be the woman who was brutally beaten and exhibited massive physical injuries. Indeed, some people assumed that the absence of physical harm was tantamount to *prima facie* evidence that a rape did not take place.

Legal reforms eliminated the requirement that rape victims must fight ferociously for their lives. The reasoning employed was that no other victims are held to this defensive standard. For example, robbery victims are not expected to resist the robber before giving up their valuables. In the interest of justice, then, it is not fair to impose this extra burden upon sexual assault victims. As a result, when new sexual battery legislation was drafted, the resistance requirement was dropped. Of course, this move is beginning to raise new questions that have yet to be resolved (Stitt and Lentz, 1996).

The modification in the need for corroborative evidence also shows the change in the response to victims. Many jurisdictions no longer require proof of penetration or maximum resistance to the point of physical force. However, as Figure 5.5 demonstrates, there is still a reluctance to convict solely on the testimony of the victim for fear of a false claim (Bourke, 1989).

**FIGURE 5.5**
**Polygraph Tests Used to Corroborate Victim Allegations**

Ms. Sloan backs up her advocacy with chilling statistics, which she collected from 83 rape-crisis centers in 19 states. Thirty-one of the centers reported that women had to take polygraph tests before police investigations began. Twenty-two reported that if a woman refused to take the test, there were no subsequent investigations into her claims.

Only Illinois and New York have statutes prohibiting law-enforcement officials from requesting or requiring a rape victim to take a polygraph exam. . . . "As long as polygraphing of rape victims can still be requested, then it is not much better than having nothing at all . . . because police can say, 'Well, you're not required to take, and we're not required to investigate or prosecute, either.'"

Polygraphers argue that lie-detector tests help weed out false allegations. According to a Texas examiner, "If a victim is telling the truth, then the polygraph will help prosecutors make the best case possible. If a victim is lying, then an innocent person will not got to jail. And if a victim is exaggerating the circumstances of a story, then it will be detected."

Source: Shecter, J. (1996). "Fighting for Rape Victims." *The Chronicle of Higher Education,* April 19, p. A8.

## Shield Provisions

Under common law, the burden of proof in a rape case fell squarely upon the victim. It was up to the victim to show that the accused forced her to engage in behavior to which she objected. A common tactic that many aggressive defense attorneys invoked was to attack the victim's credibility by making an issue of her sexual past. A typical strategy was to imply promiscuity from prior consensual sexual activity with men other than the defendant. Presumably, this information suggested a lack of chastity and, therefore, amply proved the victim's willingness to engage in sexual activity without any reliance on force. In essence, the criminal justice system placed the victim on trial and dealt with her in a callous fashion.

Many victims were reluctant to pursue formal charges under these skewed conditions. No other type of crime victim had to endure this kind of intense scrutiny. For example, lawyers did not probe the history of burglary or robbery victims to show they had a particular reputation or a proclivity for becoming victimized. As a result, reformers sought to introduce new standards that would protect or shield sexual assault victims from further trauma. To do so required a very delicate balance. As one group of experts explains (Call et al., 1991: 784-785):

> The controversy over rape shield laws has presented policy makers with a difficult dilemma: should they permit a defense strategy based on destroying the victim's reputation, a strategy that compounds victim trauma, may discourage reporting rapes, and may enable rapists to avoid punishment. Conversely, a strong shield law may generate complaints that it limits defendants' ability to have an adequate defense, thus violating due process.

The states varied in their approach to revising this portion of their sexual battery statutes. Three primary dimensions sprang from these efforts. First, there was the general issue of whether the victim's prior sexual history with others was relevant. Second, there was the more specific concern of whether the victim's prior sexual history with the accused should be admissible. Finally, the court would judge the relevancy of any evidence about the victim's sexual history *in camera*, that is, well out of public earshot. As you can see, the aim of these reforms was to protect the victim's privacy from any unnecessary public invasion.

One can rate a state's shield provisions as either strong (very restrictive and protective of victims) or weak (virtually no change from past practices) depending on how each of these three concerns are handled. While one might guess that more progressive states would respond more favorably to feminist pressures by embracing these changes, such is not the case. There is some indication that having a feminist agenda or strong lobbying efforts has not influenced these evidentiary reforms. Instead, it seems that these modifications reflect the much broader crime control strategy that was presented in Chapter 1 (Berger et al., 1988; Berger et al., 1991; Call et al., 1991).

## Sex Offender Registration

The final legislative reform we will discuss is the proliferation of sex offender registration laws. These laws, often referred to as "Megan's Law" (which will be discussed further in Chapter 7), exist in every state and seek to provide both past victims and the general public with information regarding the presence of a convicted sex offender in the community. The premise underlying these laws is twofold. First, treatment protocols for sex offenders are far from perfect. The recidivism rates of these criminals are quite high. Second, warning the public that a sex offender is living in their community alerts residents to take appropriate precautions and to be watchful of these people's activities. As the purpose section of the Ohio statute explains:

> Sexual Predators and Habitual Sex Offenders pose a high risk of engaging in further offenses, and . . . protecting the public from sexual predators and habitual sex offenders is a paramount government interest. . . . a sexual predator or a habitual sex offenders has a reduced expectation of privacy because of the public's interest in public safety. . . . (Ohio Revised Code, 1997, Title 2950.02(A)).

One example of a *sex offender registration* law appears in Figure 5.6. Taking effect in 1997, the Ohio law shares many of the same features found in other state statutes. The precipitating offense need not be a violent rape. Instead, a host of "sexually oriented offenses" can trigger registration. Such crimes as rape, sexual battery, gross sexual imposition, other offenses that fulfill sexual needs of the offender (e.g. murder, kidnapping) and various sex crimes against children (e.g. kidnapping, pandering obscenity, compelling prostitution) can trigger these legal provisions. In addition, judges can impose registration requirements on convicted sex offenders because of the likelihood of there being future violations. Factors that judges can use when making this determination include multiple past convictions, evidence of deviant (not necessarily criminal) sexual behavior, past offenses involving torture or ritualistic acts, or prior nonsexual violent acts.

These laws instruct two main parties to take action. First, the offender must register with the local law enforcement agency where he (or she) intends to settle. This stipulation includes both the agency that has jurisdiction over the offender's permanent residence and any agency with jurisdiction over a temporary residence. Registration generally must occur within seven days of release from custody, movement into a new jurisdiction or following a change of address. Second, the law enforcement agency with whom the registration occurs must notify a wide range of constituencies about the presence of the offender. Parties to be notified include neighbors of the offender, local educational institutions, agencies that deal with children, and other local law enforcement agencies. The notification typically includes the name and address of the offender, as well as the nature of the conviction offense.

**FIGURE 5.6**
**Excerpts from Ohio's Sexual Predator Law**

Section 2950.01 Definitions.

I.   Habitual Sex Offender

A person who is convicted of or pleads guilty to a Sexually Oriented Offense and who previously has been convicted of or pleaded guilty to one or more Sexually Oriented Offenses.

J.   Sexual Predator

A person who has been convicted of or pleaded guilty to committing a Sexually Oriented Offense and is likely to engage in the future in one or more Sexually Oriented Offenses.

Section 2950.04 Registration.

A.   [A]n offender shall register with the Sheriff of a County in which he is temporarily domiciled for more than seven days and the Sheriff of the County in which he resides:

1.   Within 7 days of release from prison or confinement;

2.   Within 7 days of the date of entry of the Judgment of Conviction.

Section 2950.11 Community Notification.

A.   This provision applies only to Sexual Predators and to Habitual Sex Offenders upon whom the Judge has imposed the Community Notification requirements.

B.   The Sheriff . . . shall provide written notice to the following:

1.   All occupants of residences adjacent to the offender's residence . . . ;

2.   The Executive Director of the Public Children Services Agency that has jurisdiction;

3.   The Superintendent of each Board of Education . . .;

4.   The Director, Principal or Head Teacher of each preschool program . . .;

5.   The Administrator of each Child Day Care Center . . .;

6.   The President or Chief Officer of each college or university and the Chief Law Enforcement Officer of the college or university;

7.   The Chief of Police of the municipality. . . .

Source: Ohio Revised Code (1997).

The move to offender registration has not been limited to state action. The federal government passed the Jacob Wetterling Crimes Against Children and Sexually Violent Offender Registration Act in 1995. What this legislation requires, among other things, is that states must establish registries of convicted sex offenders or face a reduction in federal criminal justice funding.

As with any new legislation, several questions and challenges have arisen. One concern deals with the potential of these laws to further punish an offender once he or she has completed his or her sentence. This concern over double-jeopardy, however, has fallen on deaf ears so far, with the U.S. Supreme Court upholding the right of the state to protect citizens in this way (*Kansas v. Hendricks*, 1997). A related concern involves attempts to impose the new laws on those already convicted and serving their sentences. Another issue relates to the impact of such laws on the offender's ability to find a home and work, and to be free from intimidation and harassment. There have been several well-known cases in which an offender loses his job and must move due to actions taken by community members against the offender. At what point does the community's right to know impinge on the rights of the offender to be secure in his (or her) home and to hold a job free from harassment? Each of these various concerns will be addressed in greater detail in Chapter 7.

When dealing with legislative change, the genesis of the reform may be not as important as the impact of the new law. The real question is whether enacted legislative remedies are achieving the desired effects. The following section visits this question of whether legal reforms have worked as intended.

## THE IMPACT OF LEGAL REFORM

Chapter 4 introduced two concepts that can be of use in addressing the question of whether these legal reforms have had the desired impact. Earlier, we talked about whether victim compensation legislation produced any macro-level or micro-level effects. If you will recall, a *macro-level effect* looks to see if there have been any changes in such global indicators as crime reporting rates, clearance rates, prosecution rates, conviction rates, and the like. The emphasis is on a broad societal impact. In contrast, a *micro-level effect* looks at a much smaller unit to see if there have been changes in such things as worker attitudes, client satisfaction, and so forth.

Both types of effects are helpful to look at when trying to evaluate whether legal reforms have worked. The following material examines whether changes in sexual assault laws have had the anticipated macro-level and micro-level effects.

### Macro-Level Effects

The changes that legislators have made in the sexual assault regulations were designed to make the criminal justice system more "victim-friendly." Modifying the elements of what constitutes sexual assault, removing some of the overly restrictive evidentiary barriers and establishing shield provisions should lessen some of the trauma victims experience when seeking justice. These attempts to counteract biases that had come to typify sexual assault cases should encourage greater system participation. As a result, reformers were expecting to find increased crime reporting, higher arrest rates, more effective prosecution and enhanced conviction rates.

Early studies gave hope that these legal reforms held promise. For example, it appeared that Michigan had experienced some significant gains in arrests and convictions (Caringella-MacDonald, 1984; Marsh et al., 1982). However, subsequent evaluations have been less than enthusiastic about these changes (Bachman and Paternoster, 1993).

One research team studied the effect of definitional and evidentiary reforms in Illinois (Spohn and Horney, 1990). Using court cases from the Cook County Circuit Court allowed the researchers to monitor (1) charges filed by the prosecutor, (2) conviction records, and (3) sentencing outcomes. What Spohn and Horney found was that legislative reforms had very limited, if any, direct impact. They explained that "passage of the rape shield law in 1978 had no significant effects on reports of rape or the processing of rape cases in Chicago. The results of the analysis of the 1984 definitional changes are inconclusive" (Spohn and Horney, 1990: 14).

Conclusions based upon data from a single jurisdiction suffer from an inability to generalize to other locations. One does not know whether the results are idiosyncratic or whether they accurately reflect broad trends. Such a shortcoming points out the need to look at several jurisdictions and various degrees of reform efforts.

After closely examining a number of state statutes, Spohn and Horney (1991) selected six evaluation sites: Atlanta, Detroit, Chicago, Houston, Philadelphia and Washington, DC. Using records from 1970 until 1984, the researchers gathered information regarding filed reports, indictments, convictions and sentencing practices. Even after isolating the different types of changes in the various locations, there was no evidence of any systematic or dramatic impact. Another study that looked at the impact of legal reform in Canada upon arrests and subsequent prosecution also found no effect (Schissel, 1996). In other words, it appears that rape reforms have not introduced any sweeping changes into system operations.

## Micro-Level Effects

The lack of any noticeable macro-level effects perplexed some observers. However, others did not regard these dismal outcomes as being out of the ordinary. They pointed out that the system has a long history of failures in attempting to mend flaws. Whenever outsiders try to amend current practices, system officials have ample opportunities to circumvent the desired goals.

Mindful of the gap between how the law appears on the books and how it is implemented, Spohn and Horney (1991) interviewed judges, prosecutors and defense attorneys in six cities for clues. What they found was instructive.

While shield provisions outline what types of evidence are considered relevant and provide for *in camera* hearings, private side bars rarely occur. Instead, informal courtroom norms govern the players. Prosecutors, well aware of how the judge eventually would rule, simply concede and do not try to block the admission of certain kinds of evidence. As Spohn and Horney (1991: 155-156) explain:

> If a defendant is acquitted because the judge ignored the law and either admitted potentially relevant evidence without a hearing or allowed the defense attorney to use legally inadmissible evidence, the victim cannot appeal the acquittal or the judge's decisions. If, on the other hand, the judge followed the law and refused to admit seemingly irrelevant sexual history evidence, the defendant can appeal his conviction. All of the consequences, in other words, would lead judges and prosecutors to err in favor of the defendant.

What this finding seems to indicate is that the major players in the courtroom drama have the capability to thwart reform efforts. The results show a huge gap between the law as it appears on the books and the law in action.

## Summary of Legal Reform Efforts

Legislative reform does not guarantee improvement in the plight of the victim or the activity of the criminal justice system. Simply changing the law neither guarantees compliance nor impact. In some cases, the system can accommodate the change by altering procedure rather than outcome. In more recent actions, such as offender registration laws, enough time has not yet gone by for an impact to materialize. In still other instances, there has been little, if any, systematic study devoted to the effect of the legislation.

## RESPONDING TO SEXUAL ASSAULT VICTIMS

The criminal justice system normally responds to sexual assault cases in the manner outlined in Figure 5.7. After the dispatcher sends a patrol car to the scene, he or she will stay on the telephone with the victim until the responding officer arrives. After arrival, the officer must assess the victim's physical and emotional condition and then initiate appropriate actions. Once this stage is concluded, the officer usually tries to get some details on what has taken place. Victims normally go to a medical facility for treatment. Evidence collection takes place at the crime scene, as well as at the hospital. At this point, the initial investigation usually concludes with an interview to gather more information about the incident and the assailant.

**FIGURE 5.7**
**Ten Stages in a Typical Sexual Battery Investigation**

1. Dispatch Officer to Scene

2. Officer Arrival at Scene

3. Initial Assessment at the Scene

4. Transportation to a Medical Facility

5. Initial Police Report

6. Evidence Processing

7. Subsequent Interview

8. Ongoing Investigation

9. Maintenance of Case File

10. Preparation for Prosecution

Source: Carrow, D.M. (1980). *Rape: Guidelines for a Community Response.* Washington, DC: U.S. Department of Justice, pp. 84-87.

During the ongoing investigation phase, the police will try to locate witnesses and follow other leads. Building and maintaining case files are important for finding patterns and attempting to link suspects to unsolved crimes. In the event that a suspect is identified and arrested, the final step is to relay all case materials to the prosecutor.

This brief overview of case handling emphasizes three groups that become involved in sexual assault matters: (1) the police, (2) medical personnel, and (3) the prosecutor. The following materials examine the role of each in greater detail.

## The Police

The view of police indifference and insensitivity toward rape victims is widespread and not without some empirical support. A national survey of police officers uncovered a prevailing attitude of suspicion and lack of concern for rape victims (LeDoux and Hazelwood, 1985). A significant number of police officers, like the general population, subscribe to rape myths. Often, police officers classify rape cases as unfounded based on their perceptions of the offender and the victim (Sanders, 1980). While this decisionmaking is not unlike what takes place in other kinds of cases, it does indicate a consistent style of indifference.

One factor that may reflect the criminal justice system's stance toward rape victims is the level of reporting by victims. As noted earlier, the NCVS finds that more than one-half of all rape victims never report their incidents to the police. One possible reason for this nonreporting is the reaction of the police to such allegations. Cumbersome and inappropriate questions can change the emphasis of the case from what the accused did to what the victim did or did not do.

Concern over this callous handling has led many agencies to institute changes in how they process sexual assault cases. Many departments have established specialized investigatory units whose exclusive responsibilities are to handle sexual battery calls. Steps have been taken toward training officers to employ crisis counseling techniques, establishing closer ties with rape crisis centers, deploying victim advocates to the crime scene, dispatching female patrol officers to assist sexual assault victims and developing relationships with doctors and medical services for better treatment of victims. The result of such initiatives is officers who are more sympathetic toward, and hold more positive attitudes about, victims of sexual assault (Campbell, 1995; Campbell and Johnson, 1997; Temkin, 1996).

## The Hospital

A standard procedure when dealing with sexual assault victims is to arrange for the provision of medical care. The recommendations contained in Figure 5.8 underscore the fact that the hospital becomes a very crucial link for many victims. The purpose of seeking emergency medical treatment for sexual assault victims is actually twofold (Gilmore and Evans, 1980; Klapholz, 1980). The first goal is to receive medical assistance; the second is to preserve materials for evidentiary purposes.

### Medical Examination

One of the more pressing needs in a sexual assault case is to attend to the victim's physical well-being. For some victims, this need is rather apparent. There may be bleeding, contusions, bumps, broken bones or other obvious injuries that require immediate medical treatment. Other victims may be hurt even though they do not display any outward signs of injury.

**FIGURE 5.8**
**Recommendations from the U.S. Attorney General's Office to**
**Medical Care Providers Concerning Victims of Crime**

- Hospitals should establish and implement training programs for hospital personnel to sensitize them to the needs of victims of violent crimes, especially the elderly and those who have been sexually assaulted.

- Hospitals should provide emergency medical assistance to victims of violent crime without regard to their ability to pay, and collect payments from state victim compensation plans.

- Hospitals should provide emergency room crisis counseling to victims of crime and their families.

- Hospitals should encourage and develop direct liaison with all victim assistance and social service agencies.

- Hospitals should develop, in consultation with prosecuting agencies, a standardized rape kit for proper collection of physical evidence, and develop a procedure to ensure proper storage and maintenance of such evidence until it is released to the appropriate agency.

Source: U.S. Department of Justice (1986). *Four Years Later: A Report on the President's Task Force on Victims of Crime.* Washington, DC: U.S. Government Printing Office, p. 39.

Many hospitals have established specific procedures aimed at minimizing the emotional trauma that victims experience. A support person—either a victim advocate or a specially trained nurse—will remain with the victim throughout the physical examination. Most hospital procedures allow sexual assault victims to bypass the usual registration procedures in the public intake area. Instead, medical personnel escort the victim to a private room in order to spare the victim further embarrassment and to help the victim reestablish a sense of control.

The medical examination addresses the immediate physical injuries, the prevention or treatment of sexually transmitted diseases and the possibility of pregnancy. The likelihood of becoming pregnant after a sexual assault ranges from 5 to 30 percent (Shulman et al., 1992: 205). In addition to external forms of trauma, it is not unusual for sexual assault victims to sustain internal gynecological injuries. These conditions, if left untreated, could lead to unnecessary long-term complications.

One problem that can have extremely important ramifications is *sexually transmitted disease (STD)*. Because most assailants have not been apprehended or tested at this point, the risk of an STD infection is unknown. Precautionary measures designed to combat gonorrhea, syphilis, chlamydia or other STDs may be warranted. For example, Baker and associates (1990) note that almost one-half of the rape victims in their study identified AIDS as a primary worry. However, there is some concern that detection of exposure to the HIV virus is neither time-ly nor reliable and could impede emotional recovery (Bowleg and Stoll, 1991). Undoubtedly, anxiety over this issue will escalate as the incidence of AIDS continues to grow.

## *Forensic Examination*

Evidence preservation begins long before the victim reaches the hospi-tal doors. Sometimes sexual assault victims may feel defiled or dirty. They may have a strong desire to take a shower, change clothes, brush their teeth or wash their hands before going to the hospital, but doing so could destroy potentially valuable evidence. As a result, police investigators nor-mally advise sexual assault victims to delay these activities. They also ask these victims to carry a fresh set of clothing to the hospital so that items worn during the attack can be impounded and preserved as evidence.

A frequent stumbling block to the forensic portion of the emergency room examination has been that it placed physicians in an awkward position (Best et al., 1992). Once the attending physician finished treat-ing the victim, the *forensic examination* was underway (though the vic-tim might not be cognizant of it). Many doctors lacked appropriate training in evidence collection (Carrow, 1980; Hilberman, 1976: 22; Martin and Powell, 1994; Sproles, 1985) or conveyed a less than sym-pathetic attitude toward the victim (Martin and Powell, 1994; Temkin, 1996). Consequently, they relied upon police investigators for instruc-tions as to what to do in these situations. The outcome, as one might well guess, was often haphazard and far from systematic. These gaps could hinder successful prosecution of the attacker.

Many states responded to a federal initiative and formulated *"rape kits"* to alleviate this evidentiary problem. The Office of the Florida Attor-ney General (1991), for example, has instituted one such standardized protocol. Rape kits include a preprinted set of instructions for the physi-cian to follow, report forms to complete, containers for collecting hair samples and fingernail scrapings, swabs and slides for extracting fluid specimens, blood sample containers and other tools for gathering trace evi-dence. Although one can order prepackaged commercial "rape kits" from manufacturers, local hospitals can assemble these items for slightly more than $2.00 per kit (Carrow, 1980: 109). Once the attending physician completes the forensic examination, the police investigator impounds the kit and submits it to the crime laboratory for evidence analysis.

A related issue that has commanded attention is who should pay for the evidentiary or forensic examination. A follow-up to the 1982 Presi-dent's Task Force on Victims discovered that it was a common practice for hospitals to bill sexual assault victims for the evidence collection. This situation led one federal report to comment that: "Forcing sexual assault victims to bear this cost is tantamount to charging burglary victims for collecting fingerprints" (U.S. Department of Justice, 1986: 17). Today, many state victim compensation programs underwrite the cost of this evidence gathering. If this recourse is not available, then either the investigating agency or the prosecutor's office is responsible for payment (National Victim Center, 1996).

## The Prosecutor

In the past, many prosecutors have been reluctant to take sexual battery cases to trial. Prior to the implementation of the legal reforms presented earlier, prosecutors were leery of pursuing cases in which the victim did not sustain any visible physical injuries. The issue of consent was a huge stumbling block, particularly if there was a jury trial. Often, the determining factor in the case was the victim's demeanor and credibility on the stand.

Critics have not hesitated to question prosecutorial decisions and case attrition. A common complaint is that prosecutors refused to file charges and failed to prosecute an inordinate number of suspects. In very broad terms, it is typical for only about one-half of the victimizations reported to the police to result in an arrest. In turn, only about one-half of the arrests culminate in a prosecution, and far fewer end in a conviction.

Studies by Horney and Spohn (1996), Spohn and Spears (1996) and Spears and Spohn (1996) indicate that the attrition in prosecution and conviction is due to actions of the victim. For example, victims who take "risks," such as hitchhiking, using drugs or alcohol, or going to the offender's home have a greater likelihood of their case being dismissed than other victims. In one sense, these people do not fit the normal profile of a "genuine victim." In terms of the case handling by the system, a detailed comparative analysis has shown that rape cases move through the system just like any other major felony (Galvin and Polk, 1983). Despite this "business as usual" approach, there is still room for improvement in the way prosecutors handle sexual assault cases. Figure 5.9 presents a series of common mistakes for the prosecutor's office to avoid when handling sexual battery cases.

The legal reforms mentioned earlier in this chapter are intended to alter the system's response. Shield provisions have become an important part of most recent legislation dealing with sexual assault. No longer is the sexual history of the victim an issue, except as it directly pertains to past consensual sexual behavior with the accused. In essence, the victim is protected or "shielded" from any irrelevant character assassination attempts.

**FIGURE 5.9**
**Pitfalls to Avoid When Managing the Prosecution of Sexual Assault Cases**

- Failure to consider organizational arrangements which allow rape prosecutions to be handled by only a few designated prosecutors within the office.

- Failure to allow sufficient flexibility within case assignments so that special sexual assault prosecutors are also given assignments to other major crimes.

- Failure to limit the number of prosecutor personnel coming into contact with the victim.

- Assignment of rape cases to personnel who are insensitive to the victim's needs or biased against victims of sexual assault.

- Assignment of junior personnel to rape prosecutions.

- Designation of female prosecutors as "rape prosecutors" without regard to their skills, experience, or sensitivity to the victim.

- Failure to screen personnel trying rape cases to ensure that individuals who are emotionally or intellectually drained by these cases no longer receive rape prosecutions.

Source: Carrow, D.M. (1980). *Rape: Guidelines for a Community Response*. Washington, DC: U.S. Department of Justice, pp. 95, 97.

## SEXUAL HARASSMENT

An additional form of sexual assault that receives a great deal of attention is the problem of *sexual harassment*. Sexual harassment differs from most other forms of sexual assault in two primary ways. First, sexual harassment often does not involve an actual physical assault. Rather, harassment can manifest itself in subtle ways, such as sexually suggestive comments, unwanted touching, risqué jokes, pornography or blatant demands for sexual contact. In most cases, these actions take place within work or educational settings where both the offender and the victim are required to be in close contact. This means that the offender and victim are acquaintances. The second distinguishing feature of sexual harassment is that the criminal justice system rarely deals with these infractions. Instead, sexual harassment falls into the realm of civil or administrative law and remedies.

While no universally accepted definition of sexual harassment exists, most definitions outline unacceptable actions that fall into two broad categories. The first is *quid pro quo* harassment, in which the offender requires sexual contact in exchange for employment, better working conditions, good grades or other favorable treatment. In essence, the offender sets up an exchange arrangement in which sex is the cost to be paid by the victim. Most people would recognize this first category as a violation of the rights of others.

The second category deals with the creation of a hostile environment. In this category, the harassment may be as subtle as displaying calendars of naked people at work, telling crude sexual jokes, touching a person or commenting about how "sexy" a person looks in certain clothing. In each case the victim, intentionally or unintentionally, is made to feel uncomfortable. While some individuals may not perceive these actions as harassment, others will be negatively impacted by the activity. This second form, therefore, is more difficult to identify and requires individuals to express their feelings about such actions to the offending party. The true problem begins when the offender *continues* a practice after he or she has been informed about the problem. The hostile environment situation does not require the loss of a job, benefits or other factors in order to prove harassment (Rubin, 1995).

Both of these forms of sexual harassment can be seen in the definition presented in Figure 5.10. While the definition is specific to employment situations, it has been tailored by many institutions to fit the unique nature of varying environments. Universities, for example, typically add language that applies the same conditions to actions that interfere with the ability of a student to learn. It is not uncommon to see definitional policies developed to meet the specific needs of different agencies and settings.

**FIGURE 5.10**
**The EEOC Definition of Sexual Harassment**

Section 1604.11 Sexual Harassment.

Unwelcome sexual advances, requests for sexual favors, and other verbal or physical conduct of a sexual nature constitute sexual harassment when

(1) submission to such conduct is made either explicitly or implicitly a term or condition of an indivdual's employment,

(2) submission to or rejection of such conduct by an individual is used as the basis for employment decisions affecting such individual, or

(3) such conduct has the purpose or effect of unreasonably interfering with an individual's work performance or creating an intimidating, hostile, or offensive working environment.

Source: 29 *Code of Federal Regulations* Ch. XIV (7-1-96 Edition).

Gauging the extent of sexual harassment depends on the definition used and the target of the investigation. There is no ongoing national data collection program for sexual harassment. Rather, the knowledge we have is based primarily on various surveys. Further complicating the measurement of the problem is the fact that most surveys target specific groups, such as students or faculty at a single university, or heavily female-dominated employee groups like nursing. Thus, the results typically are not generalizable to the overall population. Other measurement problems include the failure of respondents to report harassment due to embarassment or fear of retaliation and the failure of some to define a sexual situation as harassment even though it may fit the legal definition.

Despite these measurement problems, numerous studies provide insight into the frequent occurrence of sexual harassment. In one early study, 17 percent of the female students reported sexual advances and 14 percent claimed to have received unwanted sexual invitations. McKinney (1990), studying 156 faculty at one institution, reported that almost 14 percent of the female respondents and 9 percent of the male respondents felt they had been sexually harassed by a coworker. In a national survey of college faculty, 6.8 percent of the respondents reported harassment, with women reporting almost five times more incidents than men (Dey et al., 1996). Using results from female employees, Gutek (1985) found that 53 percent had been negatively impacted (i.e., fired, denied promotions or raises, etc.) as a result of refusing sexual advances at work. Studies of the general public, while more rare, have uncovered even greater levels of harassment. For example, Wyatt and Riederle (1995) found that 44 percent of women from the Los Angeles area claimed to have been sexually harassed at work and 45 percent reported harassment in social settings. Finally, Swisher (1995) noted that the number of sexual harassment claims made to the Equal Employment Opportunity Commission more than doubled from 1991 to 1993 (3,300 complaints compared to 7,300 complaints). This evidence suggests that harassment is a common problem for many individuals—both females and males—in a host of situations.

As noted earlier, responses to sexual harassment generally fall outside the realm of the criminal justice system. Instead, victims deal with harassment in two major ways. First, many individuals attempt to handle the situation themselves by either avoiding or confronting the offender. This may be effective, particularly when the activity falls into the realm of creating a hostile work environment and the offender was unaware of the impact of his or her actions. Unfortunately, avoidance is problematic in many work settings, and confronting an offender who is in a position of power can create greater problems.

The second avenue of redress is through administrative policies or civil procedures. Most organizations have sexual harassment policies that outline the problem, the expectations for workers and the procedures for resolving these issues. Where these actions fail, victims can invoke various equal employment statutes and protections or take direct action in civil court. No matter what avenue is chosen, however, the victim is put under additional unwarranted stress and inconvenience.

**FIGURE 5.11**
**Selected Internet Sites Dealing with Sexual Assault**

National Clearinghouse on Marital and Date Rape
        http://members.aol.com/ncmdr/index.html

Sexual Assault Information Page
        http://www.cs.utk.edu/~bartley/saInfoPage.html

## SUMMARY

Sexual assault has been an instrumental rallying point in the growth of the victim movement in the United States. Many of these issues led to the revision of the criminal justice system to become more protective of victims. Sexual assault victims suffer much emotional trauma and endure a burdensome recovery process. In order to expedite the healing, new legislation and interventions have emerged. These reforms aim to relocate victims from a position in which they receive blame to one in which they receive help. Due to the relatively short time since rape and sexual assault have emerged as major policy concerns, there is a need for more research, improved training of system workers and further development of informed systems of intervention.

# LEARNING OBJECTIVES

After reading Chapter 6, you should be able to:

- Talk about how historically men have dominated women.

- Address historical trends in spouse abuse.

- Estimate the extent of spouse abuse.

- Explain how researchers measure spousal violence.

- Distinguish spouse abuse from domestic violence.

- Understand what the battered woman syndrome means.

- Link masochism with spouse abuse.

- Outline the learned helplessness perspective.

- Tell how the cycle of violence builds.

- Explore the role of alcohol in spousal violence.

- Summarize how the laws of arrest hamper police intervention.

- Assess the nonarrest options available to the police.

- Summarize the Minneapolis experiment.

- List three criticisms of the Minneapolis experiment.

- Relate pro-arrest policies to the Minneapolis experiment.

- Summarize the replications of the Minneapolis experiment.

- Explain how legislatures have relaxed the misdemeanor rule.

- Talk about why there are refuge houses.

- Explore the prosecutorial response to abuse.

- Discuss what an injunction is.

- Explain the idea of coordinating system responses and their impact.

- Define and discuss the issue of anti-stalking legislation.

- Investigate concerns surrounding court-ordered mandatory counseling for batterers.

# Chapter 6

# Spouse Abuse

## INTRODUCTION

When one thinks of crime and criminals, the image that most often comes to mind is that of stranger-to-stranger violations. In actuality, however, you are more likely to be killed or beaten by a person you know than by a total stranger. Furthermore, the violent offender is probably not just a passing acquaintance or somebody you nod to at the grocery store. More than likely, that person will be an immediate family member or someone with whom you share a very close personal relationship.

Every day hundreds of husbands brutalize their wives. Much of this violence is hidden from the public eye. It frequently takes place in private where no one can see the physical infliction or hear the anguished pleas for help. In addition, if people should hear the muffled sounds of a beating, many would not intervene, based on the belief that "a man's home is his castle."

It is only recently that we have come to realize the amount of human suffering that takes place within families. Gradually, this internal domestic strife is becoming more exposed to public view. Society finally is starting to recognize the problem of family violence as a major public health hazard.

## KEY TERMS

action stage

affidavit

battered woman syndrome

battering episode

celebrity stalkers

contemplation stage

criminogenic effect

cycle of violence

disenchantment through action

disenchantment through avoidance

disinhibition

domestic stalker

domestic violence

domestic violence shelters

ex parte

external validity

full enforcement

hit stalker

incapacitation

injunction

internal validity

learned helplessness

love-scorned stalker

lust stalker

maintenance stage

This chapter deals with violence between husbands and wives, or other conjugal cohabitants. We look at the pervasiveness of this problem and at the types of statutory provisions that govern these behaviors. We also examine how academicians account for spousal violence. As you will see, the spouse abuse problem has dropped into the laps of law enforcement personnel. The primary reason why the police deal with spouse abuse is because no other public agency operates seven days a week, 24 hours a day, 365 days a year. Because they did not anticipate these tasks, law enforcement agencies often lack the resources and skills required to deal with this form of violence. Despite this shortcoming, police departments and the criminal justice community still must find ways to combat this social problem.

## A Brief History of Spousal Violence

The domination of men over women has strong historical roots. Early Roman law treated women as the property of their husbands, a custom reinforced by biblical passages, Christianity, English common law and the mores of American colonists (Dobash and Dobash, 1977-78; Dobash and Dobash, 1979; Edwards, 1989; Pleck, 1989). As property, women were subject to the control of their fathers or husbands, who held the power of life and death over them.

Women have held no legal standing throughout most of history. Any harm committed against a woman was viewed as an offense against the father or husband, not her. Consequently, it was the male "owner" who sought vengeance or compensation for his loss.

At the same time, a female could not be an aggrieved party. The father or the husband was the one held responsible for any injurious action by his woman. Buzawa and Buzawa (1990) point out that husbands or fathers were expected to punish women. In fact, many Western cultures proscribed official punishment of women in their legal codes.

The move in this country to laws restricting wife beating fits into roughly three stages. The first period occurred in the mid-1600s when the Puritans in Massachusetts enacted laws against wife beating and family violence (Pleck, 1989). Pleck points out, however, that these laws were rarely enforced. This laxity was due, in large part, to the strong belief in family privacy and the acceptance of physical force by the husband as a valid form of discipline.

A second upswing in concern over family violence appeared in the late 1800s, when states began passing laws restricting family violence. Worries over immigration, rising crime, the use of alcohol and other factors prompted the passage of laws restricting family conflict and allowing for outside intervention (Pleck, 1989). Some states even mandated public flogging as a punishment for beating women. As with the earlier movement, however, these laws and punishments were seldom enforced (Pleck, 1989).

While these protective actions were evolving, some nineteenth-century state supreme court decisions continued to condone wife beating. However, husbands were advised that physical chastisement should not exceed the boundaries of good taste (Dobash and Dobash, 1977-78: 429-431; Pleck, 1979). It is important to note that it was not until the early part of the twentieth century that women in the United States gained *suffrage*, the right to vote.

The third stage of interest in spousal violence is the one currently in effect. The 1960s saw the beginning of general social unrest and demands for equality. Concerns over rape, spouse abuse and family violence became rallying cries for the emerging women's movement. Calls for greater police intervention into domestic violence replaced family privacy issues (Sherman, 1992). It was during this time that physicians and social workers became vocal about family violence and brought these problems to the attention of society (Pleck, 1989). Remarkably, not a single research article in the *Journal of Marriage and the Family*, a premiere

**KEY TERMS**
*—continued*

mandatory arrest policies
masochism
mediation
Minneapolis experiment
misdemeanor rule
political stalker
precontemplation stage
preparation stage
presumptive arrest policies
pro-arrest policies
probable cause
psychopathic personality
  stalker
psychopathology
psychotic personality
  stalker
reasonable suspicion
reconciliation period
referral
refuge houses
selective enforcement
stalking
suffrage
tension-building phase
warrantless arrest

scholarly outlet in this area, entertained the issue of family violence prior to 1969 (Wardell et al., 1983). Reflecting on the historical paucity of interest in spouse abuse, Dobash and Dobash (1977-78: 427) point out that:

> [W]ife-beating is not, in the strictest sense of the words, a "deviant," "aberrant," or "pathological" act. Rather, it is a form of behavior which has existed for centuries as an acceptable, and, indeed, a desirable part of a patriarchal family system within a patriarchal society, and much of the ideology and many of the institutional arrangements which support the patriarchy through the subordination, domination and control of women are still reflected in our culture and our social institutions.

Perhaps the greatest breakthrough for interest in spouse abuse was the publication in 1984 of the Minneapolis study of arresting abusive husbands. This research, which will be discussed in more detail later in the chapter, generated a great deal of policy change, spawned wide debate in the academic community and prompted a series of replications.

The renewed interest in spousal violence has gone relatively unabated. Spouse abuse continues to be a leading issue within the larger framework and growth of victimology. The criminal justice system has adapted by altering different policies and procedures for dealing with abusive offenders and their victims. Academic interest has also kept pace. A casual inspection of most library holdings will uncover a large selection of materials dealing with spouse abuse.

## THE EXTENT OF SPOUSAL VIOLENCE

Estimates about how often spouse abuse occurs show considerable variation from one study to the next. Figure 6.1 contains one well-known survey instrument, the Conflict Tactics Scale (CTS), used to assess the extent of marital violence.

The CTS represents a range of responses to conflict, extending from nonviolent to violent actions. Respondents are asked to indicate how often each response was used in the past year. Using the CTS, Straus et al. (1980) found that 16 percent of the subjects reported at least one violent episode within the previous year. More than one-fourth of these people acknowledged participating in at least one violent confrontation with their partner during the marriage.

While the CTS enjoys wide usage, it has some limitations (Dobash et al., 1992). First, only one spouse per household is typically surveyed. This shortcoming means that there is no comparison data against which to gauge the responses. Lack of validation is especially problematic because husbands tend to see less violence than do wives (Browning and Dutton, 1986). Second, these data are limited in terms of assessing the degree of conflict. There is no indication as to the kind of object used in various categories, the number of times an act occurred during each instance, the degree of force used or differences in the strength of the combatants (Frieze and Browne, 1989). Third, there is no information on the severity of the actual harm, if any, inflicted. Finally, there is rarely any information gathered on the length of the marriage, age of the parties, family socioeconomic conditions or other demographic characteristics.

Despite these shortcomings, the CTS also carries at least three benefits (Schafer, 1996). First, reliance upon a standardized protocol makes it much easier to compare results from one project to the next and develop a continuous body of knowledge. Second, using a standardized questionnaire may serve as a tool to minimize subject memory decay. If you remember the discussion in Chapter 2, recall problems are a source of constant worry for researchers. Finally, using a standardized set of questions over many different settings makes refinements and improvements possible.

**FIGURE 6.1**
**The Straus Conflict Tactics Scale Used to Measure Self-Reported Family Violence**

---

No matter how well a couple gets along, there are times when they disagree on major decisions, get annoyed about something the other person does, or just have spats or fights because they're in a bad mood or tired or for some other reason. They also use many different ways of trying to settle their differences. I'm going to read a list of some things that you and your (husband/partner) might have done when you had a dispute, and would first like you to tell me for each one how often you did it in the past year (Never, Once, Twice, 3-5 times, 6-10 times, 11-20 times, more than 20 times, Don't Know).

 a.   Discussed the issue calmly
 b.   Got information to back up (your/his) side of things
 c.   Brought in or tried to bring in someone to help settle things
 d.   Insulted or swore at the other
 e.   Sulked and/or refused to talk about it
 f.   Stomped out of the room or house (or yard)
 g.   Cried
 h.   Did or said something to spite the other one
 i.   Threatened to hit or throw something at the other one
 j.   Threw or smashed or hit or kicked something
 k.   Threw something at the other one
 l.   Pushed, grabbed, or shoved the other one
 m.   Slapped the other one
 n.   Kicked, bit, or hit with a fist
 o.   Hit or tried to hit with something
 p.   Beating up the other one
 q.   Threatened with a knife or gun
 r.   Used a knife or gun
 s.   Other (PROBE)

---

Source: Straus, M.A. (1979). "Measuring Intrafamily Conflict and Violence: The Conflict Tactics (CT) Scales." *Journal of Marriage and the Family,* 41: 75-88, pp. 87-88. For a revised version of the CTS, see Straus, M.A., S.L. Hamby, S. Boney-McCoy & D.B. Sugarman (1996). "The revised Conflict Tactics Scales (CTS2): Development and Preliminary Psychometric Data." *Journal of Family Issues,* 17(3):283-316.

Gelles and Straus (1988) claim that approximately 25 percent of all couples will experience abuse during their lifetimes. In terms of numbers, Langen and Innes (1986) estimate that roughly 2.1 million women suffer from abuse each year, while Sherman (1992) reports that police records reflect as many as eight million cases annually. After reviewing the literature, one researcher extrapolated the number of American women beaten at least once by their husbands during their marriage to be somewhere around 20 million (Pagelow, 1984: 45).

Spouse abuse figures, whether official or self-reported, undercount the actual level of abuse and are subject to a great deal of speculation. One reason for inaccuracy may be that many studies fail to register the number of times violence occurs in a relationship, opting instead to simply count whether any abuse has occurred. Looking at the number of times abuse occurred, Straus (1978) reported an average of three beatings a year.

Another problem is that many studies refer only to married couples. Studies of courtship patterns reveal figures of intimate violence ranging from 22 percent to two-thirds of dating partners (Gelles and Cornell, 1985: 65).

Finally, reconciling disparate research results is often difficult due to differences in study design. Besides using different definitions of abuse, the data sources also vary (such as police records, social service agencies, single-city surveys, or estimates by "experts"). As a result, researchers suspect that the actual number of spouse abuse cases involves close to 50 percent of all couples (Feld and Straus, 1989). The inescapable conclusion generated from these and other projects is that intimate violence is a frequent act.

Any discussion of spouse abuse must realize that these incidents sometimes escalate into lethal confrontations. According to the Federal Bureau of Investigation (1996: 17):

> [Almost] half of the murder victims in 1995 were related to or acquainted with their assailants, 11 and 34 percent, respectively. Among all female murder victims in 1995, 26 percent were slain by husbands or boyfriends.

Spousal violence is not restricted to husbands hurting their wives. Sometimes, women batter their mates. When the idea of women battering men was first introduced (Steinmetz, 1977-78; Steinmetz, 1978a), some commentators dismissed this notion as a "red herring" or a misleading distortion of the real problem (Fields and Kirchner, 1978). People who adhere to the family violence perspective would welcome greater attention to this and other related topics. But, those who endorse a feminist viewpoint would reject this call because it does not focus upon the relationship between gender and power (Stalans and Lurigio, 1995). More recently, though, there has been a call for renewed investigation into this phenomenon (Bogard, 1990; Lucal, 1995; McNeely and Mann, 1990) as well as violence within homosexual relationships (Lockhart et al., 1994). Instead of painting the issue of spouse abuse along gender lines, the suggestion these observers make is to recast the issue in terms of *domestic violence* and focus upon violence within intimate relationships.

Women sometimes strike back at their assailants. One analysis of women who killed reveals that 86 percent were carrying on an intimate relationship with the victim whom they murdered (Mann, 1988: 38).

The fact that some of these men had battered these women has led lawyers to raise the *battered woman syndrome* as a self-defense explanation (Eber, 1981; Robinson, 1981). The argument here is that these women were so traumatized by previous beatings that they simply seized the opportunity to kill their batterers to prevent any further victimization episodes. In any event, situations such as those typified here caused one author to remark, "A man's home may be his castle, but a woman's home too often is her dungeon" (Costa, 1984: 8).

## THEORIES OF SPOUSE ABUSE

Although there are several theoretical explanations regarding spouse abuse, no clear consensus has emerged as to the causes of domestic violence. For our purposes, the theoretical arguments can be broken down into three general categories: (1) intraindividual theories, (2) sociocultural explanations (patriarchy), and (3) the learned helplessness perspective. The intraindividual approach tries to reach an understanding of the offender's actions. It entertains the question of what makes some men beat their wives, and addresses the psychological traits of women who endure abuse. A second avenue of thought deals with sociocultural explanations, or what some call a feminist perspective. The emphasis here is on the dominant male orientation of society. The final approach, learned helplessness, is also part of the sociocultural tradition. Learned helplessness questions why women remain in an abusive setting when they can prevent future beatings simply by walking away from the batterer. Despite its intuitive appeal, we shall see that the decision to abandon one's partner is much more complex than just the mere desire to escape a battering relationship.

The status of theorizing on spouse abuse is still haphazard. No single theory has proved the most promising. As a result, the following discussion is meant to be more informative than to advocate the case for any one theoretical perspective.

## Intraindividual Explanations

Intraindividual theories locate the cause of deviant behavior inside a person. These explanations frequently are referred to as theories of *psychopathology*. They focus on what is wrong with the individual and address a variety of specific issues thought to cause abnormal behavior. Some of these items include substance use, mental illness, stress, depression, low self-esteem, intergenerational transmission of abuse, and other problematic areas.

The earliest theories of domestic violence often relied on general opinions that the offender was sick or disturbed. In essence, the offender was an aberration and did not reflect the norm in society. This belief fit well with the idea that domestic violence was a private matter not to be dealt with outside the home. In those instances that domestic violence came into the public spotlight, one could dismiss it easily as an isolated incident and of concern only to the immediate family.

While some writers have attributed spouse abuse to the mental illness of the offender, more precise definition can be given to the topic by looking at individual factors that cause or contribute to the behavior. Drug and alcohol consumption by the offender and/or the victim is a common research finding (Browne, 1987; Collins, 1989; Gelles and Straus, 1979; Hotaling and Sugarman, 1986; Kantor and Straus, 1987). However, the fact that substance use is common in domestic violence cases does not isolate the causal mechanism at work. Two basic possibilities exist. First, the use of drugs or alcohol may cause the offender to become abusive. The second alternative argues that drugs and alcohol act as disinhibitors. They break down the barriers that normally would keep the offender from committing the act. Researchers have not yet learned which of these two possibilities is correct.

Stress, depression, low self-esteem and similar factors are often proposed as causes of domestic violence (Gelles, 1973; Hotaling and Straus, 1989; Pagelow, 1984). The basic argument is that the offender, when striking out against his or her spouse, is venting frustration or anger at other people or things he or she cannot deal with directly. For example, one cannot relieve stress at work by attacking the boss. Instead, one might search for a substitute and turn on an available family member who has little recourse. The abuser simply does not possess the tools with which to channel feelings in a more acceptable fashion. Often, socioeconomic conditions of the family are pointed to as a cause of low self-esteem or stress.

Also considered under the heading of psychopathological causes is the idea that some individuals commit abusive acts because they have learned to do so through past experiences. This intergenerational transmission of violence approach is a learning theory. Proponents maintain that an individual who was the victim of abuse or who witnessed abuse as a child often grows up to be an abuser (Hotaling and Sugarman, 1990; Pagelow, 1984; Straus et al., 1980). The available evidence favoring the intergenerational transmission approach is weak and is the subject of much debate (Pagelow, 1984).

Besides attributing violence to a pathological condition of the offender, some people would counter that wives who tolerate such behavior are also pathological. In other words, if a woman remains in a troubled relationship and still professes to love her husband after he has beaten her, she must be sick or crazy. The problem with this perspective is the identification of which psychological traits are conducive to remaining in a violent relationship. Some observers point to *masochism*, or a desire to suffer, as the key ingredient. For whatever reason, women who stay in a battering relationship harbor guilt feelings or other unresolved psychological problems that seem to welcome punishment. As a result, masochistic women gravitate toward mates who will oblige their needs by hurting them. Another way to rephrase this notion is that these women induce their mates to beat them to satisfy deep-seated inner urges to be beaten and hurt.

As you might imagine, not everyone accepts this orientation unequivocally (Hamberger, 1993; Pagelow, 1992; Pagelow, 1993). One scholar, in assessing this body of literature, notes:

> [T]here is little that would suggest either that women wish to bring the abuse onto themselves or simply that they are trapped in their homes without options. . . . The women were not passively accepting of abuse as most had attempted to get some sort of help but this did not change things. . . . If they are masochistic, they are staying for the abuse. An alternative is that they are staying *in spite* of the abuse or because of the positive aspects of the relationship. A strong possibility is that although women do have options, they do not *feel* that they do (Rounsaville, 1978: 17-18).

## Sociocultural Explanations (Patriarchy)

The sociocultural or feminist perspective views abuse of women as an outcome of their historical treatment and the current patriarchal makeup of society (Brownmiller, 1975; Burgess and Draper, 1989; Dobash and Dobash, 1979). As has already been discussed, throughout much of history women were the property of their fathers or husbands, subject to control and discipline. Today's society remains predominantly patriarchal, prompting many feminist writers to argue that women's concerns and problems receive little attention. Wife abuse, therefore, is largely ignored by the male-dominated criminal justice system and society. The "man's home is his castle" view has kept the public outside and the violence inside.

Coupled with this view of a patriarchal society is the perception that violence is an integral part of modern society. It is socially accepted as a solution to problems (Gelles and Straus, 1979). The increasing level of personal crime, especially among adolescents, is pointed to as evidence of this trend. A world in which violence and aggression is an accepted means of dealing with disputes leads many feminists to conclude that males rely on violence to exert their position of power and to support the status quo. The patriarchal society benefits from violence against women. This sociocultural argument also surfaces in explanations of sexual assault and rape (see Chapter 5). The theme of dominance in the sociocultural viewpoint has gained support from a wide range of groups due to the ability to apply this perspective to social class (upper-class domination) and racial (white domination) issues (Buzawa and Buzawa, 1990).

## The Social Learning Approach: Learned Helplessness

Closely following the historical components of the sociocultural explanations is the idea of learned helplessness. Some professionals contend that battered women remain in destructive relationships for economic reasons. These abused wives may lack the monetary resources that would enable them to depart. They may have no place to go. They may not be able to support themselves financially. They may have young children, which makes support even more difficult. They lack marketable job skills. In short, the circumstances are such that some women are unable to exert control over themselves or their environments. The perceived, or actual, inability to support oneself or gain employment may be an outcome of the historic role of women in society.

According to Lenore Walker (1979), many battered women suffer from the syndrome she identifies as *learned helplessness*. The idea of learned helplessness centers upon three components. The first is the information a person has about what is going to happen. The second aspect is the knowledge or perception about what will happen. This component usually comes from past experiences (or lack thereof). The third portion is the person's behavior toward the event that takes place. Some people believe that they cannot influence or control what is about to happen to them. As these perceptions mount and grow more overwhelming, the woman comes to believe that she is helpless to alter her environment. In other words, she develops a belief that she is not in charge of the events around her and that she cannot change the flow of events. As a result, she becomes helpless in her struggle and may appear apathetic to some viewers.

## The Cycle of Violence

Contributing to this sense of helplessness is the reality that battered women are not beaten every minute of the day. Instead, there is a *cycle of violence*, which gradually builds the feelings of being powerless and unable to alter their plight. Walker sees this cycle as consisting of three distinct stages: (1) the tension-building phase, (2) the battering episode, and (3) the reconciliation period.

The *tension-building phase* may be accompanied by minor assaults. During this period, the woman believes that she can deflect her husband's bullying. She may calm the situation by conceding to his wishes or by staying out of his way. Her goal is not to prevent the battering behavior, but to avoid it. She becomes grateful that small displays of abusive behavior are not as serious as what they could be. Sometimes, she may even make excuses for the man's behavior. Her general perception is that these incidents are isolated events that will end once the irritant is removed. Thus, she is able to rationalize these outbursts.

The second part of the cycle, the *battering episode*, is the culmination of the frustrations experienced in the first stage. At this point, the man is out of control and acts in a rage. As Walker (1979: 55) explains:

> He starts out wanting to teach the woman a lesson, not intending to inflict any particular injury on her, and stops when he feels she has learned her lesson. By this time, however, she has generally been very severely beaten.

A common rationalization to these volatile outbursts is the man's claim that he did not fully realize what he was doing because he had been drinking. This *disinhibition* account acts to transfer responsibility away from the abuser and to characterize alcohol as the real culprit (Collins, 1989). In other words, the alcohol weakened the man's normal behavioral restraints, thus triggering atypical and uncontrollable violence. As noted earlier, however, the evidence for alcohol as a cause of spouse abuse is unclear. This fact has prompted some researchers to conclude that although "there is more than a 'kernel of truth' in the drunken bum theory of wife beating, the findings also provide the basis for demythologizing this stereotype" (Kantor and Straus, 1987: 224).

The final phase is the *reconciliation period*. Here the husband transforms himself into a very apologetic, tender and loving character. Pleas for forgiveness and promises of a better future often cloud the anger and fear the victim has experienced at the hands of her husband. As Walker (1979: 58) puts it:

> The batterer truly believes he will never again hurt the woman he loves; he believes he can control himself from now on. He also believes he has taught her such a lesson that she will never again behave in such a manner, and so he will not be tempted to beat her.

It is not uncommon for a battering husband to shower his wife with tokens of affection during this period. A bouquet of flowers may appear unannounced. Declarations of love abound. There may be many little thoughtful things, reminiscent of romantic days gone by, to prove the insistence of a loving relationship. However, the cycle-of-violence perspective implies that this period too shall pass.

As the couple's relationship proceeds through this cycle again and again, the wife's physical and psychological well-being become compromised. She might assess her marriage as a failure, but not be able to take any remedial steps. There may be strong religious beliefs, family pressures and other social considerations that prevent action. Postponement of any resolution to the beatings permits the cycle to continue without any end in sight (Eisikovits, 1996). The woman is trapped; she simply learns to live with the violent spasms that characterize the relationship.

The learned helplessness perspective centers on the emotional dependency that develops during an intimate relationship. As society expects, the woman becomes more enthralled with her husband. Simultaneously, an economic dependency also surfaces within the household. One writer (Pagelow, 1984: 313) sizes up the situation quite deftly:

> When a woman leaves her abuser, her economic standard of living very likely takes a drastic drop. If she has dependent children, she must take into consideration the lives and welfare of her children, who have roughly one chance out of two of dropping below the poverty level (two out of three for minority children). Is it any wonder that many battered women remain with their abusers for many years, sometimes until the children have grown up and left home?

## POLICE INTERVENTION

The first point at which society typically becomes involved in domestic disputes is when a police officer is summoned to an abusive episode. Officers who respond to a call involving domestic violence have a variety of alternatives at their disposal: making an arrest, counseling the parties, referring the couple to professional counseling, threatening to make an arrest, separating the parties or advising the victim to sign a formal complaint. This portion of the chapter explores some of these options and their limits.

### The Arrest Option

While one of the more awesome powers entrusted to police officers is that of arrest, there are several restrictions that limit its utility. The first consideration is the distinction between reasonable suspicion and probable cause. *Reasonable suspicion* permits an officer to intrude into a situation to investigate whether a crime has been committed, is being committed or is about to occur. *Probable cause*, on the other hand, is more stringent. Probable cause means that the facts and circumstances are sufficiently strong enough to make the officer conclude that the accused is the one who committed the crime under investigation. If probable cause is present, the officer can make a legitimate or lawful arrest. If probable cause is absent, the arrest lacks proper foundation. There is not a lawful custodial situation. Any officer who willfully violates this provision may be the subject of a series of administrative, criminal and civil penalties.

A second major consideration lies in the distinction between a misdemeanor and a felony offense. The general rule of thumb is that an officer may effect a lawful arrest for a felony offense, either with or without an arrest warrant, as long as probable cause exists. In a misdemeanor case, though, an officer can make a *warrantless arrest* only if the transgression has taken place in his or her presence. This restriction, called the *misdemeanor rule*, can hamper effective police intervention, particularly in situations where many offenses are misdemeanors, such as spouse abuse.

One recommendation issued by the U.S. Attorney General's Task Force on Family Violence (1984) called for states to revise their provisions concerning arrests in family violence. Most states have responded by relaxing the misdemeanor rule in spouse abuse situations. In other words, an officer can make a legitimate warrantless arrest even though he or she did not observe the crime being committed. The probable cause element, though, has not changed. It remains the essential ingredient in the decision to take an individual into custody.

Another important determinant in how the police handle a domestic disturbance is whether the suspect is at the scene when the police arrive (Eigenberg et al., 1996; Feder, 1996). If the abuser has left the premises, the officer may not be able to make an immediate arrest. At this point, the officer must assess the extent of injury to the victim. If the injuries are serious and require medical attention, then more than likely the crime is an aggravated battery, which is a felony in most jurisdictions. This classification means that the officer can initiate a warrantless arrest. However, if the injuries are minor or nonvisible, then it might be difficult to establish that a crime took place. If probable cause is lacking or if the misdemeanor rule is in effect, then the officer is powerless to make a legitimate warrantless arrest. The only thing that will enable the police to arrest the abuser is if the victim signs an affidavit.

An *affidavit* is an official complaint in which the victim outlines the details of the offense and swears under oath that the individual named in the accusation is the offender. The completion of this legal document and the issuance of a warrant by a judge give the police proper authority to arrest the suspect on a misdemeanor charge.

Should the suspect be present at the scene when the officer arrives, an evaluation of the arrest option is in order. Bear in mind that if the state legislature has not made spouse abuse an exception to the usual misdemeanor rule, then the officer cannot arrest the abuser for a misdemeanor without observing a violation firsthand. However, if the elements for a felony offense fit, the officer may have probable cause for an immediate arrest.

## Nonarrest Options

If an arrest is not possible or if the officer elects not to pursue the arrest option immediately, a variety of other options are at the officer's disposal. The officer may engage in a *mediation* effort. Ideally, this choice involves talking to each party privately to learn each participant's version of what took place. The officer may suggest one or more ways in which to handle disputes of this nature in the future. Alternatively, he or she may try to extract a promise from the disputants that they will not engage in another confrontation after the officer leaves. The officer then exits, in the belief (or hope) that accord has been reestablished.

In other instances, the officer may suggest that the couple contact a minister, a counselor or some other social service agency. The problem with this *referral* option is

> that it depends upon the efforts of the citizen for initial contact with the agency to which he is referred. Many of those involved in domestic disturbances are prevented from seeking assistance by their own fear, ignorance, or lack of initiative (Parnas, 1967: 934-935).

As one psychologist adroitly recognizes, "Regardless of the potential danger, the parties have the Constitutional right to refuse help" (Bard, 1980: 114). In other words, the police are powerless to compel individuals to seek family counseling—even if this recourse is in the best interests of the couple.

Another common tactic is to either threaten or cajole the parties into peaceful behavior. As one veteran commented, "What can a police officer tell a person who has been married 20-25 years! You just have to be a good con artist" (Parnas, 1967: 948). Usually this option comes with the reminder that a return visit by the police will trigger the arrest of either one or both parties.

Perhaps the most typical response is to separate the combatants. Officers do not have the legal authority to order an inhabitant out of his or her own house. However, one prevalent strategy is to request that the perpetrator leave for a "cooling off" period. Sometimes the request may go unheeded or the occupant might assert the right to remain on the premises. In this situation the officer might try to regain the upper hand by reminding the uncooperative party of the dire consequences of an arrest. Confronted with a hostile subject and a lack of legitimate alternatives, the officer might enlist the help of the woman. The officer might even offer to drive the woman to a relative's house or to place her and the children, if any, in a domestic violence shelter for the evening (Finn and Stalans, 1995).

## THE MINNEAPOLIS EXPERIMENT

Victim advocates and women's groups have long argued that the police need to take a more proactive role in dealing with domestic violence situations. In particular, they have called for the police to make arrests of offenders rather than resorting to nonarrest alternatives. Underlying these arguments is the assumption that arrest will curb future acts of spouse abuse more effectively.

The Minneapolis Police Department, working with the Police Foundation, agreed to serve as a testing site for an investigation into the impact of arrest in domestic violence cases. The purpose of the study was to determine how effective various police responses were in preventing further episodes of domestic violence (Sherman and Berk, 1984). These responses included: (1) an automatic arrest, (2) having one party leave for a "cooling off" period, and (3) counseling or referral to a social service agency.

Each officer participating in the field experiment received a report pad. This pad instructed him or her about which option to invoke on a particular call. While these actions were predetermined in advance via a randomized fashion, officers could deviate from the guidelines whenever the situation demanded a more appropriate response. Situations allowing for deviation included when the offense was a clear felony, when the officer felt threatened and when the victim demanded action. To see how well each intervention strategy worked, staff members telephoned civilian complainants biweekly over the following six-month period. The purpose of these telephone contacts was to elicit information about any more domestic violence by the suspect.

Profiles of victims and suspects revealed that 60 percent were unemployed, a considerably higher figure than the area's general 5 percent unemployment rate. Three out of five suspects had a prior arrest record, and almost one-third of the suspected men had a violent arrest history. Eighty percent of the abusers had assaulted the woman at least once during the previous six months. More than one-half of these earlier violent confrontations had been responded to by the police, and one-half of the couples were not married to each other at the time of the study. In short, these men and women appeared to be tormented couples.

Two outcome measures were analyzed. The first indicator tapped whether the police had to return to the residence for another domestic squabble during the six-month follow-up period. The other measure came from the telephone interviews. It indexed any victim reports of repeated violence with the same suspect.

The police blotters showed that officers returned to 26 percent of the households in cases in which the initial strategy was to issue a warning and separate the parties for a brief "cooling off" period. Recidivism figures reached the 18-percent mark for those settings in which the officer took the counseling approach and reached only 13 percent when the officer exercised the arrest option. The telephone interview results showed a high of 37 percent repeaters stemming from the counseling tactic. The low was 19 percent in the cases in which the initial response was an arrest. In short, arrest appeared to be the most efficient way of preventing more domestic violence between the original combatants.

The researchers combed their data to learn whether an incapacitation effect clouded the results. *Incapacitation* refers to the fact that an offender is unable to recidivate while in confinement. If most of the arrested individuals spent the next six months in jail, the results would not be very impressive. However, further analysis revealed that incapacitation held very little influence. Almost one-half of the detained suspects were released from confinement within 24 hours of the arrest. Only 14 percent remained in jail one week after their arrest. Thus, it does not appear that an incapacitation effect contaminated or impinged upon the results.

These findings contradict the belief that an arrest merely aggravates an already tense domestic situation and that the best course of action is for minimal police involvement. First, there was no indication of a revengeful violent escapade once the arrested male returned home. Second, the separation did not produce economic hardships for these women. (Some observers have commented that many wives shy away from the arrest alternative because they rely upon their husbands for a steady income to maintain the household.) Third, the results are even more impressive when one considers the abundant arrest histories—particularly violent confrontations with their wives—that these men had logged.

While proponents embraced these results and used them to lobby for more sustained police action in spouse abuse cases, the researchers themselves were not quite as enthusiastic. Besides reciting the familiar refrain for replicative studies, Sherman and Berk (1984: 270) issued some conservative remarks:

> [A]rrest and initial incarceration alone may produce a deterrent effect, regardless of how the courts treat such cases. . . . Therefore, in jurisdictions that process domestic assault

offenders in a manner similar to that employed in Minneapolis, we favor a *presumption* of arrest; an arrest should be made unless there are good, clear reasons why an arrest would be counterproductive. We do not, however, favor *requiring* arrests in all misdemeanor domestic assault cases. Even if our findings were replicated in a number of jurisdictions, there is a good chance that arrest works far better for some kinds of offenders than others and in some kinds of situations better than others.

## REACTION TO THE MINNEAPOLIS EXPERIMENT

The recognition of spouse abuse as a social problem, as well as the publicity surrounding the *Minneapolis experiment*, heralded reaction on several fronts. As one might expect, academicians found flaws in the Minneapolis experiment. However, mounting public pressure meant that the legal system could not sit by idly until scholarly debate resolved these questions. As a result, police enforcement policies changed and legislatures revamped their criminal codes. What we shall do in this section of the chapter is explore some of these ramifications.

### Agency Reaction

At one time, many police agencies adhered to a strategy of minimal intervention in domestic disturbances. What this directive amounted to was that officers would not resort to an arrest if they could avoid such action (Jensen, 1977-78). Such a stance did not tend to bother officers, particularly in light of the perception that domestic disturbances were the most dangerous calls for police to handle (Garner and Clemmer, 1986; Hirschel et al., 1994; Stanford and Mowry, 1990). However, advocacy efforts and lawsuits forced agencies to rescind these informal "no arrest" policies.

The findings from the Minneapolis experiment forced law enforcement agencies to reconsider their stance. While some administrators maintain a public image of full enforcement, actual field practices fall short of this mark. *Full enforcement* means that the police arrest every violator for every illegal act whenever possible. Because such a goal is often impractical, officers engage in selective enforcement. *Selective enforcement* means that the police arrest only some violators for some of their actions some of the time. In other words, individual officers are free to exercise their discretion when deciding whom to arrest and whom not to arrest.

Discretion vests officers with considerable latitude in the performance of their duties. It also raises two major concerns. First, the lowest-ranking members of the agency are the ones who determine how official policy translates into action. Second, quite often these decisionmakers are the least accountable members of the agency (that is, their decisions are rarely subject to review). Hence, there are no assurances that actions out in the field correspond to policy guidelines.

One way to circumvent the thorny problem of officer discretion is to remove it. That is exactly what many agencies did when they revamped their domestic violence guidelines. They outlawed selective enforcement. These new directives, sometimes called *pro-arrest policies* or *mandatory arrest policies*, informed police officers that they must make an arrest whenever feasible in spouse abuse situations. Others, known as *presumptive arrest policies*, assume that an arrest will be made in every case. A decision not to arrest requires a written justification by the officer. Probable cause requirements persist in these new policies. Failure to conform to agency rules and regulations can result in disciplinary action and, if appropriate, termination from employment. Thus, officers have an incentive to follow agency expectations.

These changes have not come easily. First, many rank-and-file officers resent what they perceive to be an unwarranted encroachment upon their discretion (Steinman, 1988). There is evidence that officers fail to follow mandatory arrest policies. Mignon and Holmes (1995) note that two-thirds of all domestic violence offenders in 24 Massachusetts communities were *not* arrested, despite the existence of a mandatory arrest statute. While arrests increased after the law took effect, the arrest rate remained well below 100 percent. Second, some suspects taken into custody have sued, claiming that mandatory arrest policies unfairly discriminate against males. In other words, if they were not male, officers would not arrest them for domestic violence.

Some police administrators, in an effort to appease all parties, have shied away from a mandatory arrest policy and have chosen to express a *preference* for an arrest solution. Figure 6.2 contains an example of a written policy directive governing police handling of spouse abuse situations.

## Legislative Reform

Many state legislatures have responded to the problem of domestic violence with reforms on several fronts. As noted earlier, one popular approach has been to relax the misdemeanor rule in spouse abuse cases. To bypass this restriction, some state legislatures have declared spouse abuse to be an exception to the usual misdemeanor rule. This legislative maneuver removes the "in the presence of an officer" requirement. As a result, a police officer may make a bona fide warrantless arrest for a misdemeanor even though he or she did not witness the violation itself.

**FIGURE 6.2**
**An Example of Police Policy Guidelines Regarding Domestic Violence**

---

## PATROL OFFICER RESPONSE/INVESTIGATION

A.  Enforcement of Laws in Domestic Violence Incidents.

   1.  An arrest shall be made in the event that there is reasonable cause to believe that a felony has occurred. All suspects arrested should be booked into the county jail. A pro-arrest policy should be implemented by all agencies.

       If an officer has reasonable cause to believe that a felony has occurred, an arrest shall be made irrespective of whether the officer believes the offense may ultimately be prosecuted as a misdemeanor.

   2.  The suspect should be arrested in the event that a misdemeanor domestic violence incident occurs in the officer's presence. Such situations include, but are not limited to, an officer who witnesses an act of domestic violence, a violation of a restraining order, or illegal possession of a weapon when the officer believes a domestic violence history exists involving the suspect in possession of the weapon.

   3.  When a crime has been committed outside the officer's presence which does not meet the requirements for a felony arrest, the officer shall make a good faith effort to inform the complainant of his/her right to make a private person's arrest. Whenever possible, such discussion should be held out of the presence of the suspect. An officer shall not dissuade complainants from making a private person's arrest.

   4.  The existence of the elements of a crime or the willingness of the victim to make a private person's arrest shall be the sole factors that determine the proper method of handling the incident. The following factors, for example, are not to influence the officer's course of actions in domestic violence incidents except as they relate to the elements of the crime:

       a.  The relationship or marital status of the suspect and the victim, i.e., not married, separated, or pending divorce;
       b.  The fact that the victim and suspect are of the same gender;
       c.  Whether or not the suspect lives on the premises with the complainant;
       d.  The existence or lack of a temporary restraining order;
       e.  The potential financial consequence of arrest;
       f.  The complainant's history or prior complaints;
       g.  Verbal assurances that violence will cease;
       h.  The complainant's emotional state;
       i.  Injuries are not visible;
       j.  The location of the incident, i.e., public or private;
       k.  Speculation that the complainant may not follow through with the criminal justice process or that the arrest may not lead to a conviction.

   5.  Once a suspect is arrested on a misdemeanor offense, he/she should be booked into the county jail unless the officer can identify a strong likelihood that the offense will not continue once the officer leaves the scene and that there has been no prior history of domestic violence.

   6.  An officer shall make no statements which would tend to discourage a victim from reporting an act of domestic violence or requesting a private person's arrest.

   7.  Pursuant to Penal Code section 13700 et seq., an officer responding to an incident of domestic violence shall prepare a Domestic Violence Incident Report irrespective of the wishes of the victim or the presence or absence of the suspect.

---

Source: Police Chiefs' Association of Santa Clara County (1994). *Domestic Violence Protocol for Law Enforcement.* Los Altos, CA: Police Chiefs' Association of Santa Clara County.

Another legislative remedy that provides police officers with an immediate response aims to provide safe temporary housing. One fear that victims harbor is that the arrested husband will return home from jail and embark upon a revengeful rampage. The only alternative available to many women, and one that is often suggested by responding police officers, is to pack their belongings and move their children to a temporary location where they can hide. However, not all women have the resources to pursue this option. Many are poor; others live too far away from family and friends.

Some social service groups have responded by establishing *refuge houses* or *domestic violence shelters*. The purpose of these places is to provide the battered woman a safe haven where she can live until she decides what to do about the abusive marital situation. The location of these refuge houses remains a well-guarded secret to ensure safety from angry husbands who might appear on the premises for retaliation. More recently, some shelters are publicizing their presence in an effort to mobilize greater public support (Belluck, 1997). No matter which approach is taken, these havens require considerable finances for housing, furniture, food, clothing, upkeep and staffing. These escalating costs have prompted some legislatures to mandate surcharges on marriage licenses and divorce settlements to underwrite domestic violence centers.

## Academic Reaction

Partly due to the tremendous popular and legislative interest in the Minneapolis results, many researchers turned a critical eye toward the project and viewed it as more suggestive than definitive. Flaws in the experiment's design, implementation and analysis have proved troublesome. In fact, some people considered these limitations serious enough to "make it more appropriate to consider the Minneapolis study a pilot study rather than an experiment with decisive implications for changing national policy" (Binder and Meeker, 1988: 350).

One issue that generated a skeptical reaction involved external validity. *External validity* is another way of asking how generalizable are the results of a study (Campbell and Stanley, 1963: 5). Are the results obtained in Minneapolis applicable to just Minneapolis or do they apply to other locations? As one critic explains:

> The problem is not that the Minneapolis experiment was a single study; the problem is that it was a *Minneapolis* experiment. Had Sherman and Berk designed a study that collected data from ten cities simultaneously and had the results been consistent across locations, I would not have called for replication. . . . (Lempert, 1989: 155).

A second volley of criticisms focused upon internal validity. *Internal validity* raises the question of whether the treatment caused the outcome or whether outside influences contaminated the experiment (Campbell and Stanley, 1963: 5). For example, the officers who participated in the study volunteered for this duty. Some of these officers became much more extensively involved in producing the data than did others (Binder and Meeker, 1988: 355; Gartin, 1995a). Indeed, three officers supplied the vast majority of all the cases included in the study. Furthermore, officers found it necessary to deviate from the randomly assigned treatment to make an arrest in a number of incidents. While this impact may appear to be negligible (Berk et al., 1988), there is a hint that other complications may be at work (Elliott, 1989: 453-455; Gartin, 1995b; Weiss and Boruch, 1996).

A third area of concern involves a cost-benefit assessment (Binder and Meeker, 1988; Lempert, 1989; Meeker and Binder, 1990). Do the benefits of making a misdemeanor arrest outweigh the costs? What impact do such misdemeanor arrests have on the victim and/or on local jail bed capacities? Is the arrest option an efficient use of scarce police resources? Would other intervention techniques provide more efficient strategies? The following section looks at some of these issues.

## THE MINNEAPOLIS EXPERIMENT REPLICATIONS

The criticisms outlined here, along with a host of other questions, led to the funding of six replication projects. The chosen sites were Milwaukee, Omaha, Charlotte, Colorado Springs, Miami and Atlanta. While the studies were replications, each site employed a slightly different research design. Rather than use the same battery of possible interventions, the replications tested a variety of police responses, including arrest, mediation, varying lengths of jail confinement, protective orders and verbal warnings. The most important departure from the Minneapolis study was the increased control over random assignment of responses. In most sites, the dispatcher (or someone else removed from the scene of the disturbance) assigned the response type to officers. In essence, officer discretion was greatly curtailed in the replications.

The results of the replications failed to confirm the Minneapolis findings. In general, there was little evidence that any treatment was significantly better than another at reducing subsequent domestic violence (Sherman, 1992). In Charlotte, for example, arrest did not reduce domestic assaults (Hirschel et al., 1991; Hirschel et al., 1992) and there is some evidence that recidivism increased after arrests (Sherman, 1992). Similarly, Dunford et al. (1989) reported that there was no difference in recidivism within six months of the initial police contact in Omaha. Further, Sherman (1992) points to evidence of escalating abuse in Omaha at the one-year mark.

Sherman (1992), inspecting the reports and data from five of the six replication sites, suggests that arrest has a possible *criminogenic effect.* That is, arresting an offender may cause greater subsequent offending. The only clear deterrent effect of arrest appears in an analysis of arrests that resulted from the issuance of an arrest warrant (Dunford, 1990). In this instance, arrest warrants were randomly obtained for Omaha cases in which the offender was not present when police initially responded. Those individuals arrested on a warrant were clearly deterred from further abuse compared to those not arrested. With this exception, arrest had either no effect or was found to increase subsequent abuse.

Sherman (1992) attempted to probe the reasons for the discrepancies between the initial Minneapolis study and the replication projects. First, differences may be due to demographic variation from study to study. Offenders who were employed, married (as opposed to cohabiting) and better educated seem to be deterred by arrest. Individuals with lower stakes in conformity may increase their offensive behavior after an arrest. Second, greater recidivism occurs in longer follow-up time frames, indicating that short-term deterrence may precede even greater long-term abuse. Finally, despite differences and flaws in study designs, there were few consistent differences. Therefore, one cannot attribute variations in results to the research methodology.

While the replication projects greatly temper the enthusiasm generated by the initial Minneapolis experiment, Garner et al. (1995) suggest that the conclusions are far from clear. The authors point out a variety of questionable assumptions made in the different analyses. They assert that greater attention to the methodology reveals more favorable results than originally reported. The impact of arrest on domestic violence, therefore, requires further study.

Until such analysis is completed, police responses to domestic violence should attend to the elements of each situation and be informed by both research and practice. Accordingly, Sherman (1992) outlines eight recommendations for "Smart Policing." These recommendations, as shown in Figure 6.3, rely on allowing the police officer the flexibility to choose among different alternatives in different situations.

## PROSECUTORIAL AND JUDICIAL ACTION

While most attention has been paid to the actions of the police in domestic violence cases, the prosecutor and court are another arena to which the victim can turn. Not all cases reach the court through an initial police arrest. Victims can turn directly to the court through the office of the prosecutor. Despite this fact, victims bring few cases (domestic or otherwise) to the prosecutor. The police remain the largest "supplier" of cases for the court.

**FIGURE 6.3**
**Sherman's Recommendations for "Smart Policing"**

1.  Police should be empowered by every state legislature to make warrantless arrests on probable cause for misdemeanor domestic assaults the officer did not witness.

2.  State statutes requiring mandatory arrest upon probable cause in cases of misdemeanor domestic assault should be replaced with mandatory action chosen from a list of options to be specified by each police agency.

3.  The range of approved options for probable cause, offender-present misdemeanor domestic assault should include:

    a.  offering to transport the victim to a shelter
    b.  taking the suspect or victim to a detoxification treatment center
    c.  allowing the victim to decide if an immediate arrest should be made
    d.  mobilizing the victim's social network to provide short-term protection

4.  Police and prosecutors should cooperate on developing the offender-absent warrant procedure demonstrated to be an effective deterrent in Omaha.

5.  Police should not be held civilly liable for failure to prevent domestic homicide or serious injury because of failure to make arrests in one or more prior misdemeanor assaults. . . .

6.  Police should continue the process of trial and error to identify promising approaches to chronically violent couples. . . .

7.  Police should advise victims that orders of protection may have limited practical value. . . .

8.  Police and victims' advocates should lobby the U.S. Congress for further support for research and development on domestic violence control. . . .

Source: Adapted from Sherman, L.W. (1992). *Policing Domestic Violence: Experiments and Dilemmas.* New York: The Free Press, pp. 253-260.

Evidence exists that there is a high level of attrition in domestic violence cases once they reach the prosecutorial stage. Buzawa and Buzawa (1990) identify a number of reasons for this attrition. First, victims see that there are both immediate and potential costs involved in going through with a case. Among these costs are the possibility of retaliation by the accused, lost time from work, lost income from the accused, lack of companionship, and so forth. Second, many victims change their mind about prosecuting after filing charges. They may no longer see the action as important enough to prosecute or may simply lose interest in the case. Third, victims may feel guilty and assume some of the blame for the abusive act. Fourth, some victims may be using the court for purposes other than to prosecute the offender. They may be trying to teach the accused a lesson, gain revenge, confirm their own status as a victim, or they may have other reasons that do not require completion of prosecution (Eisikovits, 1996; Fischer and Rose, 1995; Gondolf et al., 1994). Each of these reasons for case attrition can contribute to yet another factor—pressure by the prosecutor to drop the charges. Based on prior experiences of victims failing to carry through with charges, prosecutors are reluctant to prepare and begin proceedings when they feel it is likely that the victim may withdraw at a later date. Prosecutors, therefore, often influence victims to drop charges by suggesting that the victim was an active participant in the abuse situation. The lack of a clear victim makes a case more difficult to prosecute.

Despite claims that prosecutors often summarily dismiss domestic violence cases, evidence from different jurisdictions reveals that prosecutors make decisions on the basis of case merit more than type of case. For example, Schmidt and Steury (1989) note that in cases in which charges were not brought, 45 percent were a result of the fact that victims did not wish to pursue the case, and another 30 percent of the cases rested on questionable legal grounds. Only 14 percent of the cases were deemed not important enough to pursue. Similarly, Sigler et al. (1990), in a statewide survey of judges and prosecutors, found that the failure to prosecute was due primarily to victims recanting their testimony or a lack of evidence. The most important factor uncovered in the literature is the level of cooperation by the victim. A lack of cooperation often led to dismissals or a failure to bring charges (Elliott, 1989).

This discussion on whether to prosecute presupposes that this intervention will make a difference. There have been few studies of the impact of prosecution in domestic violence cases. Elliott (1989), in a review of such studies, notes that court actions tend to have little impact on subsequent violence. The most notable instance in which prosecution reduces violence is in cases in which past violence was less common and not as serious. These conclusions, however, are drawn from few studies and much more research is needed before suggesting any significant policy changes.

Besides filing criminal charges against an abusive husband or partner, there is the possibility of taking civil action against the offender. Unfortunately, a woman who has made the decision to leave her partner is usually too destitute to pay the attorney fees and filing costs associated with divorce or other civil petitions. Some states now provide a simplified mechanism to secure an *injunction*, or what some people call a restraining order or a protection order, against the abuser. Under these provisions, the clerk of the court supplies a preprinted, fill-in-the-blanks form to request an injunction or court protection order against the violent party. The clerk also explains how to complete the form. He or she can waive the filing fees if the woman is unable to pay court costs. The clerk also assists in the preparation of these materials. The judge can issue a temporary restraining order on an *ex parte* basis. In other words, the offender does not have to be present in order for the judge to take official action. Any violation of a protective order constitutes a contempt of court charge and any law enforcement officer may then arrest the offender, a significant repercussion for men who do not want others to know about their behavior (Eisikovits, 1996; Fischer and Rose, 1995; Wallace and Kelty, 1995). Figure 6.4 displays an example of a petition form for a court injunction.

**FIGURE 6.4**
**Petition for an Injunction for Protection against Domestic Violence**

Before me, the undersigned authority, personally appeared Petitioner ____(name)____ who has been sworn and says that the following statements are true:

(a) Petitioner resides at: _____(address)_____
(Petitioner may furnish address to the court in a separate confidential filing if, for safety reasons, the petitioner requires the location of the current residence to be confidential.)

(b) Respondent resides at: _____(last known address)_____

(c) Respondent's last known place of employment: _____(name of business and address)_____

(d) Physical description of respondent:

Race: _____

Sex: _____

Date of birth: _____

Height: _____

Weight: _____

Eye color: _____

Hair color: _____

Distinguishing marks or scars: _____

(e) Aliases of respondent: _____

(f) Respondent is the spouse or former spouse of the petitioner or is any other person related by blood or marriage to the petitioner or is any other person who is or was residing within a single dwelling unit with the petitioner, as if a family, or is a person with whom the petitioner has had a child in common, regardless of whether the petitioner and respondent are or were married or living together, as if a family.

(g) The following describes any other cause of action currently pending between the petitioner and respondent: _____

The petitioner should also describe any previous or pending attempts by the petitioner to obtain an injunction for protection against domestic violence in this or any other circuit, and the results of that attempt: _____

*Case numbers should be included if available:* _____

(h) Petitioner has suffered or has reasonable cause to fear domestic violence because respondent has: _____

**Figure 6.4**—*continued*

(i) Petitioner alleges the following additional specific facts: (mark appropriate section or sections)

\_\_\_\_ Petitioner is the custodian of a minor child or children whose names and ages are as follows: _____

\_\_\_\_ Petitioner needs the exclusive use and possession of the dwelling that the parties share.

\_\_\_\_ Petitioner is unable to obtain safe alternative housing because: _____

\_\_\_\_ Petitioner genuinely fears that respondent will abuse, remove, or hide the minor child or children from petitioner because: _____

(j) Petitioner genuinely fears domestic violence by respondent.

(k) Petitioner seeks an injunction: (mark appropriate sections or sections)

\_\_\_\_ Immediately restraining the respondent from committing any acts of domestic violence.

\_\_\_\_ Restraining the respondent from committing any acts of domestic violence.

\_\_\_\_ Awarding to the petitioner the temporary exclusive use and possession of the dwelling that the parties share or excluding the respondent from the residence of the petitioner.

\_\_\_\_ Awarding temporary custody of, or temporary visitation rights with regard to, the minor child or children of the parties, or prohibiting or limiting visitation to that which is supervised by a third party.

\_\_\_\_ Establishing temporary support for the minor child or children or the petitioner.

\_\_\_\_ Directing the respondent to participate in a batterers' intervention program or other treatment pursuant to §415.601.

\_\_\_\_ Providing any terms the court deems necessary for the protection of a victim of domestic violence, or any minor children of the victim, including any injunctions or directives to law enforcement agencies.

Source: Florida Statutes, 1997: §741.30(3)(b).

There are a number of other proposals aimed at improving the prosecutorial and judicial responses to domestic violence (Finn and Colson, 1990). One such idea has been the introduction of victim advocates into the prosecutor's office and the courtroom. The availability of such individuals can help demystify the court process, provide support to the victim and assist in the successful prosecution of the case. Closely related to this change is the appointment of specific attorneys to handle domestic violence cases. Another strategy has entailed efforts to curtail the incidence of dropping domestic violence cases at the prosecutorial level. Such "no drop" policies seek to force victims to carry through with the case and have the state assume the burden of the prosecution (Buzawa and Buzawa, 1990; Davis and Smith, 1995). Finally, many jurisdictions have sought to deemphasize punishment in domestic violence cases and to promote treatment for both the offender and victim.

## COORDINATING SYSTEM RESPONSES

Instead of assuming that any single agency can have a major impact on domestic violence, it is more reasonable to assume that coordinated efforts of several agencies will be more effective. Coupling arrest with aggressive prosecution, for example, may reduce subsequent offending more than arrest alone. Indeed, one criticism of the Minneapolis experiment and its replications was the lack of information on what happened to the offender after the arrest. Unfortunately, relatively few analyses look at broader-based system approaches.

Tolman and Weisz (1995) report on one coordinated arrest and prosecution program in Illinois. DuPage County instituted a program that included a pro-arrest policy as well as prosecution based on complaints signed by the police when victims refused to do so. While officers can sign complaints in many jurisdictions, it is not very common because the refusal of victims to sign generally signifies a future lack of cooperation with the prosecution. In the DuPage program, the prosecution actively worked to gain victim participation in the case. Analyzing 690 domestic abuse cases, Tolman and Weisz (1995) found the highest recidivism levels in cases of arrests with no convictions. Conversely, arrests ending in conviction display the lowest recidivism rates. The authors argue that this system approach is more effective than individual agency initiatives.

Another cooperative arrangement holding potential for stemming domestic violence entails coupling victim or social service agencies with the criminal justice system. The use or inclusion of such individuals when dealing with victims is becoming increasingly common in recent years. Many police departments will call on specially trained individuals to assist in responding to domestic violence or sexual assault cases. Similarly, prosecuting attorneys often rely on victim advocates and social service agencies to help guide victims through legal proceedings and encourage victims to carry through with a prosecution.

Relatively little empirical research has been conducted looking at the use of victim advocates and social service agencies. In one report, Davis and Taylor (1997) analyzed the impact of a program that combined the police with social workers in New York City. This program, the Domestic Violence Intervention Education Project (DVIEP), involved crisis response teams in two main functions. One was to follow up on domestic violence calls handled by routine patrol. The second function involved educating the public about family violence and invoking system response. The authors were able to make random assignments of domestic violence cases to either the DVIEP program or normal police intervention. Similarly, the education program was randomly assigned to different households. Unfortunately, the evaluation showed no impact on subsequent self-reports of domestic violence or on the seriousness of subsequent abuse. On the other hand, the project significantly increased the willingness of respondents to call for police assistance (Davis and Taylor, 1997). It would appear that the project had its greatest impact on altering the amenability of victims to recognize their victimization as a problem and one that required some form of intervention. What is missing in the evaluation is any assessment of the quality of the intervention (especially across cases) and the extent to which the program prompted other positive responses on the part of the victims.

More attention needs to be paid to systemic responses to domestic violence. These efforts are not uncommon. Unfortunately, few have undergone rigorous evaluation, leaving the programs with little more than faith in their abilities. It would be advantageous to know what type of cooperative intervention works best and in what settings each is most appropriate.

## NEW LEGISLATIVE RESPONSES

Besides making legislative changes that allow greater police action, such as relaxing the misdemeanor rule, most jurisdictions have responded to domestic violence by enacting laws aimed at threatening behavior and situations. Perhaps the most notable of these efforts is the growth of antistalking laws and court-ordered mandatory counseling for convicted batterers.

### Stalking Laws

While "stalking" may bring an immediate picture to mind, there is no single accepted definition of what the term means. According to Wright and colleagues (1997: 487), *stalking* "is the act of following, viewing, communicating with, or moving threateningly or menacingly toward another person." The inclusion of "viewing" and "communicating with" in the definition may surprise some readers. These kinds of actions, however, can create a great deal of anxiety and fear, especially if they are part of a repeated pattern or coupled with other activities. This combination of action with both fear and repetition can be seen in the "Model Antistalking Code," developed by the Bureau of Justice Assistance and displayed in Figure 6.5.

The three key features of most antistalking codes are the existence of threatening behavior, criminal intent by the offender and repetition in the activity. These three factors are important because there is no other law violation involved in most instances. For example, in the absence of an antistalking code, simply following someone around is not illegal. In fact, some professions, such as private investigation or journalism, typically require one person to follow another. Determining threat or criminal intent is not easy. The typical standard, however, involves recognizing what a "reasonable person" would fear or find acceptable. The requirement for repeated action or a pattern of activity also helps to outline what constitutes stalking. It is important, therefore, for legislation to allow for the distinction between different types of "following" behavior.

**FIGURE 6.5**
**The Model Antistalking Code**

Section 1. For purposes of this code:

a) "Course of conduct" means repeatedly maintaining a visual or physical proximity to a person or repeatedly conveying verbal or written threats implied by conduct or a combination thereof directed toward a person;

b) "Repeatedly" means on two or more occasions; . . . .

Section 2. Any person is guilty of stalking who:

a) purposely engages in a course of conduct directed at a specific person that would cause a reasonable person to fear bodily injury to himself or herself or a member of his or her immediate family or to fear the death of himself or herself or a member of his or her family; and

b) has knowledge or should have knowledge that the specific person will be placed in reasonable fear of bodily injury to himself or herself or a member of his or her immediate family or will be placed in reasonable fear of the death of himself or herself or a member of his or her family; and

c) whose acts induce fear in the specific person of bodily injury to himself or herself or a member of his or her immediate family or induce fear in the specific person of the death of himself or herself or a member of his or her immediate family.

Source: Bureau of Justice Assistance (1996). *Regional Seminar Series on Developing and Implementing Antistalking Codes.* Washington, DC: Bureau of Justice Assistance.

As far as domestic violence goes, stalking often takes place once a battered woman has decided to end the "cycle of violence." The cycle of violence progresses through three distinct stages: (1) the tension-building phase, (2) the battering episode, and (3) the reconciliation period. However, once the woman is determined to abandon the abusive relationship, the male partner may be at a loss as to how best regain control over her. When the mollifying behaviors that worked so well before fizzle, the male may resort to stalking activity or threats in an effort to thwart her escape (Coleman, 1997; Eiskovits, 1996).

The development of antistalking laws is a relatively recent activity. Indeed, the first state antistalking code was passed by California in

1990, largely in response to the highly publicized murder of actress Rebecca Schaeffer. Since that time, every state and the District of Columbia has enacted some form of antistalking legislation.

At the federal level, several pieces of legislation deal with stalking. The 1994 Violence Against Women Act holds offenders civilly liable for violent actions that are based on gender. The Federal Anti-Stalker Act of 1996 addresses stalking that crosses state lines or uses the U.S. mail.

As with any new legislation, many state codes have been challenged on a number of fronts (Bureau of Justice Assistance, 1996). The most strenuous objections have focused on the perceived ambiguity and extensive breadth of the statutes (Bjerregaard, 1996; Sohn, 1994; Thomas, 1997). For example, critics have charged that terminology such as "repeatedly" and "intent to cause emotional distress" is too vague, thus rendering the statutes unconstitutional. Other challenges attack provisions that outlaw such things as "contacting another person . . . without the consent of the other person" or "following" another person. The contention is that this wording is so broad that it criminalizes constitutionally protected behaviors. In almost every case, the courts have rejected these arguments and upheld the constitutionality of stalking laws (Bureau of Justice Assistance, 1996).

Penalties for stalking depend upon past violations, as well as the extent of any injury or threat. Misdemeanor violations typically allow for a jail term of up to one year (Bureau of Justice Assistance, 1996). Felony violations, however, can carry substantial penalties, particularly if there are aggravating circumstances such as the use of a weapon, the violation of a restraining order or a prior conviction. These penalties may include 20 years imprisonment (e.g., Arkansas and Alabama) or fines of $10,000 or more (e.g., Illinois, Kansas and Oregon). It is also possible that stalking may constitute a violent crime for purposes of "three strikes" laws in some states, resulting in life sentences without parole (Bureau of Justice Assistance, 1996).

Despite the sudden growth of stalking legislation, there is relatively little research on the topic. Most discussions point to media accounts of well-known spectacular stalking incidents, typically involving celebrities or politicians, or actions resulting in murder (Hickey, 1997; Wallace and Kelty, 1995). Much more common is stalking of women by ex-husbands or ex-boyfriends. Steinman (1993) claims that 5 percent of all women will be stalked at some point in their lives. Similarly, Beck (1992) reports that 90 percent of all women killed by a former intimate had been stalked by the offender prior to the act.

While there is little documentation about the size of the problem, several authors have developed typologies of stalkers and stalking incidents. Geberth (1992), for example, divides stalkers into two basic groups: psychopathic personality stalkers and psychotic personality stalkers. The *psychopathic personality stalker* group is made up of individuals who tend to dominate women and stalk ex-wives or former girl-friends. These individuals are reacting to their loss of control and often intend to commit violence against the victim. On the other hand, the *psychotic personality stalker* haunts television stars or other well-known personalities out of a misplaced sense of love and desire. These individuals delude themselves into thinking that the victim will reciprocate the affections once the offender makes contact.

Holmes (1993) offers a broader-based stalking typology. *Celebrity stalkers* target famous figures with whom there has been no personal contact in the past. Violence may emerge as a response to perceived rejection by the victim. The *lust stalker* targets a series of victims who fit a specific image. This offender seeks sexual gratification from the victim and turns violent when that expectation is not fulfilled. Stalking that involves victims and offenders who know one another fall into two categories: the love-scorned stalker and the domestic stalker. The *love-scorned stalker* knows his or her quarry, but they do not share a past intimate relationship. The offender, however, believes that the victim eventually will come to admire him or her and return the attention. Failure to do so often results in nonfatal violence. The *domestic stalker* usually crops up after an intimate relationship concludes. The offender haunts the victim as revenge for ending the relationship. A fifth type is the *political stalker*. This offender targets public figures because of their political ideology and often wants to harm the victim. Holmes's (1993) final category is the *hit stalker* who trails his or her prey in the role of a paid, professional killer.

Other authors have embarked on similar typological endeavors (Wright et al., 1997; Zona et al., 1993). In each case, the researchers are attempting to shed some light on a relatively new area of study. Unfortunately, the categories too often are based on small selected samples of cases and have not been validated in other analyses. The extent to which the results are useful, then, remains a matter for further study.

The extent to which stalking laws will impact the level of domestic abuse is unknown at this time. Most statutes are too new to have undergone extensive impact analysis. It is unclear, for example, to what extent these laws are being used by victims and enforced by the police and the courts. The fact that the statutes have withstood constitutional challenges suggests that they should receive attention as a legitimate tool in the fight against domestic violenc

## Court-Ordered Mandatory Counseling

One lingering problem with relying upon mandatory arrest policies as the most appropriate or sole solution to the problem of spouse abuse is that arrest by itself is generally an ineffective response. What an arrest platform amounts to, especially in the absence of any follow-up intervention, is a "scared straight" tactic. In other words, fear becomes the overriding motivational factor. While it is true that the deterrence doctrine is an important underpinning for how the criminal justice system operates, it is not always the most efficient practice. As a result, therapeutic interventions that seek to prevent a relapse become an essential strategy. In fact, Florida, like other states, now requires judges to sentence convicted batterers to participation in a batterer's intervention program (Florida Statutes, 1997: §741.281). What this section explores, then, is whether self-initiated or court-mandated participation works better, whether the counseling should deal with only one or both parties in the relationship and whether therapeutic intervention is a meaningful route to travel.

One scheme for envisioning how treatment produces change within a person is to cast any transformation, whether the topic be abusive action or addictive behavior like cigarettte smoking, into a five-step model (Prochaska and DiClemente, 1984). The initial phase, the *precontemplation stage*, means that although the person may recognize the need to stop engaging in destructive behavior, there is no set timetable nor are there goals in place. The *contemplation stage* gets the person ready for what is to come. Here the subject recognizes the need for modification and starts thinking about the best way to embark upon this process. The *preparation stage* occurs when the individual devises a plan and is ready to implement it. The *action stage* comes when the person achieves the goals and makes headway in terms of eradicating the objectionable behavior. Finally, the *maintenance stage* calls for eternal vigilance. At this point, the person must continue the newly learned behavior and not succumb or give in to pressures to revert to the old destructive behavior.

Abusive partners looking to alter their violent behavior need a supportive therapeutic environment in which to complete this transition. Up until now, abuser participation in therapeutic activities has been largely voluntary or one-sided. Batterers who seek counseling may start with all the best intentions in the world. Given the myriad of defenses that one may conjure to defend previous actions, the therapist faces a herculean task with these clients. Usually, a self-referred patient, no matter how energetic and dedicated, is fragile but amenable to treatment (Dutton and Starzomski, 1994). Should the counselor critically confront the client and abruptly challenge his or her fundamental thinking, the chances are that the self-referred person will not return for a second session (Murphy and Baxter, 1997). In such a case, any hopes for change are dashed.

A second important consideration for the therapist is whether to deal with one or both parties in the abusive relationship. Therapists who engage in couple therapy have several focal points in mind. They are aiming to eliminate any psychological or physical violence, to convince the clients to accept responsibility for escalating to violent behavior when arguing, to have clients learn self-control, to establish better communication between the couple, to promote more enjoyable activity for the couple and to instill the idea that each partner should treat the other with respect (O'Leary, 1996: 451-452).

While this protocol may appear reasonable, critics express serious reservations about it. There is a fundamental disagreement regarding how the problem is conceptualized. As McMahon and Pence (1996: 453) explain, "such terms as *spousal abuse, physically aggressive couples, or abusive relationships* . . . hide the fact that the phenomenon under discussion is primarily men's violence toward their wives or female partners." When the therapist approaches violent behavior as a symptom of a much larger underlying problem, all the counselor does is deflect attention away from treating the violent behavior. What the therapist should be addressing is the abuser's reliance on violence, not probing for tensions within the relationship, and certainly they should not imply that the wife bears responsibility for helping the male partner change his behavior.

There is some evidence that battered women and mental health workers have divergent perceptions of spouse abuse and that this lack of a common definition undermines the utility of seeking help. The therapist's failure to assess the situation appropriately produces two types of victim disenchantment. They are disenchantment through avoidance and disenchantment through action.

According to Eisikovits and Buchbinder (1996), *disenchantment through avoidance* arises when the counselor sidesteps the issue of violence. Rather than initiate a discussion of the battering, many therapists stand back and wait for the victim to broach the topic. This avoidance or lack of guidance leaves many victims wondering about the therapist's interest. Therapists, on the other hand, try hard to maintain some professional distance when dealing with clients. But instead of seeing this stance as a professionalization strategy, victims view it as aloofness or coldness. In other words, what battered women expect from their counselors is quite different from what they receive.

A second avenue, *disenchantment through action*, further cements the woman's frustration with the therapeutic relationship. Many therapists open a couple session by asking the male to give his version of what is taking place within the relationship. Quite often, the male will make some effort to debunk the woman's rendition. Immediately the woman is thrust into the position of having her truthfulness being evaluated. Furthermore, by transforming the battering into an indicator of tensions within the relationship, the therapist paints the woman as a cosource of the disharmony. As Eisikovits and Buchbinder (1996: 436) explain:

For battered women, violence is their life, but for the social worker, it is a symptom. Due to self-disclosure, many battered women tend to develop the illusion of interpersonal closeness, whereas social workers respond with "correct," professional role relationships. Social workers attempt to place violence in context, corroborate the women's story, and bring the men into the process to make them part of the solution rather than the problem. Such behaviors are interpreted by the women as evidence of distance and betrayal.

As you can see, there are many complex issues endemic to the role of therapeutic intervention. While the common assumption is that counseling can cure whatever ails the people in a battering relationship, there are a number of questions that require a critical examination first. At the same time, this discussion has not even delved into the question of which kinds of treatment are more suitable than others and which protocols produce the best success rates. While this area will experience further research and greater development, one thing is certain. While court-mandated therapeutic intervention may appear to be a reasonable and satisfactory solution, it is not a simple universal antidote to the problem of spouse abuse.

**FIGURE 6.6**
**Selected Internet Sites Dealing with Spouse Abuse**

American Bar Association Commission on Domestic Violence
http://www.abanet.org/domviol/home.html

Center on Crime, Communities & Culture
http://www.soros.org/crime/

Family Violence Prevention Fund
http://www.fvpf.org/fund/index.html

Men and Women Against Domestic Violence
http://www.silcom.com/%7Epaladin/madv/

Minnesota Center Against Violence and Abuse
http://www.umn.edu/mincava

National Domestic Violence Hotline
http://www.usdoj.gov/vawo/newhotline.htm

Partners Against Violence Network
http://www.pavnet.org/

Violence Against Women Office (U.S. Department of Justice)
http://www.usdoj.gov/vawo/

## SUMMARY

Spouse abuse is gaining broad recognition as a pressing social problem. People who profess to love one another hurt each other regularly. Abusive behavior appears to be almost an integral part of these marriages. It may be very difficult for an outsider to comprehend why anyone would tolerate being victimized repeatedly in this way. However, as the learned helplessness perspective explains, many women are trapped into staying in an abusive relationship. Fleeing from the abuser is not always a viable option.

Some people look to the criminal justice system—particularly the police—to provide effective relief to battered women. While police folklore holds that nonintervention is a more suitable stance, the Minneapolis study suggested otherwise. That study reported less family violence after the police took the abuser into custody. While there are some doubts over the wisdom of basing public policy upon the outcome of a single study, many law enforcement agencies reacted almost immediately. They instituted policies that instructed officers to make an arrest for domestic violence whenever possible. More recent studies, however, suggest that these policies may have been hastily implemented. The more prudent path for the criminal justice system to pursue in spouse abuse matters is to retain an open mind and be willing to try different approaches as research and practice dictate. As Davis and Smith (1995: 551) explain:

> We have come a long way in changing how the criminal justice sytem responds to domestic violence cases. Significant reforms have included mandatory arrest policies, no-drop prosecution practices, civil restraining orders, and batterer treatment programs. Unfortunately, research findings on these reforms have not been encouraging and it is unclear whether these reforms are making victims safer from harm or changing batterers' violent behavior.

# LEARNING OBJECTIVES

After reading Chapter 7, you should be able to:

- Explain the difference between "abuse" and "neglect."

- Understand what the term "maltreatment" includes.

- Talk about how child maltreatment was discovered.

- Explain why it took so long to recognize child maltreatment.

- Outline the provisions that appear in child maltreatment laws.

- Relate reporting provisions to the "good faith" standard.

- List the items that should be included in a maltreatment report.

- Discuss the intention behind a "central register."

- Identify some problems that still remain in maltreatment laws.

- Gain a feeling for the prevalence of child homicide and child maltreatment.

- Link what we know about maltreatment to its data sources.

- Interpret the relationship between maltreatment and social class.

- Compare and contrast theories of why maltreatment takes place.

- Offer some criticisms of the theories that explain child maltreatment.

- Evaluate the "cycle of violence" thesis.

- Present some coping strategies aimed at fighting maltreatment.

- Understand the issues surrounding the registration of sex offenders.

- Sketch some efforts involving legal reform and maltreatment.

# Chapter 7

# Child Maltreatment

## INTRODUCTION

One of the sadder experiences endured by children are victimizations perpetrated by family members. Some parents routinely beat their offspring. Others deny them food and affection. Still others sexually molest children. Until recently, these victims had no special legal safeguards. Many states placed the welfare of children under "cruelty to animals" provisions. Fortunately, the diligent efforts of children advocacy groups have changed that picture.

Research in the area of child maltreatment has revolved around three questions. First, how widespread or prevalent is child abuse and neglect? Second, what are the correlates of child maltreatment? Third, what causes people to engage in this type of behavior? In addition to these concerns, this chapter probes what is meant by child abuse and neglect, what child abuse laws cover, and some strategies that people have suggested to combat this problem.

## KEY TERMS

abuse
battered child syndrome
central register
child death review teams
countertransference
cycle of violence
double jeopardy
ex post facto
ex post facto law
false negative error
false positive error
good faith
hearsay rule
in camera
legislative immunity
maltreatment
Megan's Law
neglect
patriae potestas
pedophilia
privileged relationship
protective custody
psychopathology
role reversal
sexual offender
sexually violent predator
"sick but slick" parents
substantiated allegation

## THE DISCOVERY OF CHILD MALTREATMENT

Child maltreatment is not of recent vintage. For most of history, children were looked at as family property. The ancient Romans believed that the father was endowed with the power of *patriae potestas* (Thomas, 1972). In other words, fathers had the right to sell, kill or allow their progeny to continue to live. The ancient Greeks, especially the Spartans, practiced infanticide and abandonment of physically deformed newborns (Mause, 1974). The story of Oedipus Rex, who was abandoned at birth, is testimony to the fact that these practices were accepted among both the lower and higher classes in society. Biblical stories also depict instances of child abuse, such as Abraham's aborted sacrifice of his son Isaac and King Herod's slaughter of the innocents. Other accounts of inhumane treatment have persisted down through the ages. Children were treated no differently from other property owned by the father (Whitehead and Lab, 1996).

Why were children treated in such ways? Both emotional and economic factors help explain this high degree of indifference toward children. First, the life expectancy was very short. The majority of infants died during the first year of life. Therefore, emotional attachments to newborns were avoided as a defense mechanism against the highly probable death of the infant. Second, families simply could not bear the burden of feeding and caring for another member. Children, because they could not work in the field and contribute to the household, represented a drain on the already limited family resources. This was especially true for female offspring, who would need a dowry in order to find a suitable husband.

Children who survived the first few years of life quickly found themselves thrust into the position of being "little adults" (Aries, 1962). There was no status of "childhood" as we know it today. As "little adults," children took part in all adult activities. They were expected to go to work and help support themselves. They received no formal education. Rather, schooling often entailed being sold into apprenticeship in order to bring money into the family and to provide a skill for the child.

This situation persisted into the Industrial Revolution. At that time, the severe economic competition for labor was fulfilled by exposing children to long and arduous work hours under unsafe conditions. The identification of "childhood" as a distinct station in life began to emerge slowly. Infant mortality began to diminish. Clergy, educators and other child advocates stepped forward. As the statuses of "child" and "adolescence" emerged, there was a concurrent rise in concern over the treatment of children. Society started to realize that youths needed to be handled differently from adults. Even today, some local school boards are enmeshed in long debates over the merits and utility of corporal punishment (Dorne, 1989: 21-50; Hyman, 1982; Zirkel, 1990).

While the acceptance of maltreatment waned, it did not disappear. The privacy of the home and the assumed sanctity of parental authority allowed much to take place out of sight. What happened within the protected confines of the home was considered to fall beyond the purview of society.

Until recently, child abuse was not easy to detect. John Caffey, a pediatric radiologist, published a study in 1946 outlining bone damage of mysterious origin that he found in some of his young patients. While not accusing parents as the direct source of these injuries, Caffey (1946) noted that some parental explanations of various accidents were preposterous. Caffey's discovery prompted other physicians to conduct similar investigations. These researchers also stopped short of blaming parents for the intentional infliction of the observed injuries. Eventually, Caffey (1957) came to suspect that parents were responsible for this "unspecified trauma." However, this accusation still did not clarify whether the injuries were intentional or nonaccidental.

The first public denunciation of parents as intentional abusers of their offspring appeared in the early 1960s. In a ground-breaking publication, Kempe and his associates abandoned the term "unspecified trauma" and introduced a new phrase, the *battered child syndrome*. The Kempe research team (1962: 107) applied this new terminology to "young children who have received serious physical abuse, generally from a parent or foster parent."

This discovery launched a new movement aimed at eradicating this newly found concern. Before detailing those efforts, though, two questions arise. First, why did it take so long to discover child abuse, especially since it is such a serious problem? Second, why did radiologists, and not some other medical group like pediatricians, discover this phenomenon?

## UNDERSTANDING THE DISCOVERY OF CHILD MALTREATMENT

Four obstacles impeded the recognition of these injured children as victims of abuse (Pfohl, 1977). First, although emergency room physicians dealt with the physical aftermath of brutal beatings, they did not understand what they saw. Second, physicians were unable to bring themselves to realize that parents would beat their children or inflict such severe wounds deliberately. A third hurdle was the confidential doctor-patient relationship. Physicians generally regarded the parent, not the child, as their client. Disclosing confidential information to the authorities would violate ethical standards. Such action could subject the physician to civil liability and professional censure. Finally, testifying in court would place physicians in the awkward position of having to defend their medical expertise and diagnosis to laypersons.

Concerning the question of why radiologists were the discoverers, Pfohl (1977) explains that radiologists differed from physicians in four important ways. First, radiologists examine X-rays, not people. They can be more objective because they have no direct contact with the patient. Second, the goal of radiology is to discover new diagnostic categories, whereas direct care providers simply identify a condition and place it into a logical, already existing category. Third, the doctor-patient relationship was not a stumbling block because the patient is the person being X-rayed. The fourth and most important point deals with the issue of professional control.

Pediatric radiology was a peripheral medical specialty during the 1950s. It lacked professional prestige. Instead of dealing directly with patients, radiologists conducted research alone in isolated laboratories. This separation from patients also meant that radiologists did not make glamorous life-or-death decisions. As a result, child abuse offered a unique opportunity for this marginal branch to become more integrated into the mainstream medical profession. After all, it involved the clinical task of diagnosis, and making the correct assessment could spell the difference between life and death for a young patient.

The term "battered-child syndrome" was born. Adding the word "syndrome" after the term "battered child" created a new medical diagnostic category. These facts, coupled with the advances of other professions whose goal was to "cure" abusers through therapy, elevated the discovery of child abuse to prominence. Child abuse became an integral component of medical parlance.

## A SURVEY OF CHILD MALTREATMENT LAWS

Immediately after the "discovery" of child abuse, state legislatures raced to enact new laws (DeFrancis and Lucht, 1974; Nelson, 1984). A wave of legislative adjustments followed in the late 1960s and early 1970s. The task was to respond to aspects that were overlooked in the hasty lawmaking process. Except for some minor tinkering, maltreatment statutes have remained largely intact since that time. The passage of a federal law dealing with child abuse and neglect brought greater standardization to state statutes.

Although abuse and neglect fall under the broad and more encompassing term of *maltreatment*, they are two distinct phenomena. *Abuse* is the commission of an act upon the child, while *neglect* refers to the omission of a caretaker function (Katz et al., 1975; Katz et al., 1977; Light, 1973; Mayhall and Norgard, 1983).

To gain a more thorough understanding of child maltreatment laws, our analysis focuses upon a limited range of topics. First, we review the statutory definitions of abuse and neglect. Next, we direct our attention to provisions governing who should report such incidents, what the report should contain and the central register. Finally, the discussion concludes by pointing out some problem areas that remain.

## Statutory Definitions

Most state laws define abuse and neglect in very general terms. Some states explain that the purpose behind this approach is to encourage the reporting of as many suspected cases as possible. By casting out a broad net, the hope is to uncover instances of maltreatment that might otherwise go undetected. Critics, though, charge that such an expansive definition invites excessive governmental intervention.

The term "abuse" generally refers to any nonaccidental infliction of injury that seriously impairs a child's physical or mental health. Most statutory definitions outlaw sexual abuse, sexual exploitation, pornography and juvenile prostitution. Some jurisdictions, such as Oklahoma (21 Okl. St. Ann. §844, 1997), go to great lengths to exclude reasonable disciplinary measures such as controlled spanking of a child by a parent, guardian or custodian; in fact, corporal punishment is a common corrective method in this country (Maguire and Pastore, 1996: 243). Most states fail to define emotional abuse explicitly, although virtually every state includes the term in its provisions.

Neglect is the withholding of life's essentials. These necessary ingredients include food, clothing, shelter and medical treatment. Some states [e.g., see Mississippi Code, 1997: §43-21-105(l)(I),(m)] recognize that parents may hold religious beliefs that prohibit them from seeking medical care. They place such persons outside the scope of the neglect definition. Some statutes also mention offenses such as: failure to make child support payments; alcoholic or substance-dependent parents who cannot supervise their offspring properly; permitting a child to be habitually truant from school; and family abandonment.

The federal Child Abuse Prevention and Treatment Act (CAPTA) captures the essence of these statutory details. It defines child maltreatment in terms of three components. First, the act or failure to take appropriate action must produce an unacceptable risk of serious physical or emotional harm, death, sexual abuse or exploitation. Second, the target of this maltreatment is a child, usually a person under the age of 18 years. Finally, the perpetrator is a parent or caretaker who bears responsibility for the child's welfare and well-being.

As one might imagine, there are a variety of behaviors that fall under the rubric of child maltreatment. Figure 7.1 attempts to capture the breadth of these activities by displaying the major types of child maltreatment along with a definition for each category.

**FIGURE 7.1**
**Main Types of Child Maltreatment**

| | |
|---|---|
| Physical Abuse | Infliction of physical injury as a result of punching, beating, kicking, biting, burning, shaking, or otherwise harming a child. The parent or caretaker may not have intended to hurt the child, rather the injury may have resulted from over-discipline or physical punishment. |
| Child Neglect | Failure to provide for the child's basic needs. Neglect can be physical, educational, or emotional. |
| Physical Neglect | Refusal or delay in seeking health care, abandonment, expulsion from the home or refusal to allow a runaway to return home, and inadequate supervision. |
| Educational Neglect | Allowance of chronic truancy, failure to enroll a child of mandatory school age in school, and failure to attend to a special educational need. |
| Emotional Neglect | Marked inattention to the child's needs for affection, refusal of or failure to provide needed psychological care, spouse abuse in the child's presence, and permission of drug or alcohol use by the child. The assessment of child neglect requires consideration of cultural values and standards of care as well as recognition that the failure to provide the necessities of life may be related to poverty. |
| Sexual Abuse | Fondling a child's genitals, intercourse, incest, rape, sodomy, exhibitionism, and commercial exploitation through prostitution or the production of pornographic materials. |
| Emotional Abuse | Acts or omissions by the parents or other caregivers that have caused, or could cause, serious behavioral, cognitive, emotional, or mental disorders. |

Source: National Clearinghouse on Child Abuse and Neglect Information (1997). *What Is Child Maltreatment.* Washington, DC: National Clearinghouse on Child Abuse and Neglect Information.

# The Reporter

A significant element of child abuse laws is the existence of mandatory reporting provisions. Any person who witnesses or learns of a child maltreatment incident has the obligation to report the occurrence to the authorities. Anyone who knowingly fails to make such a report risks a criminal penalty.

As we already mentioned, medical personnel championed the early battle against child maltreatment. However, physicians initially were very reluctant to report suspected cases of abuse or neglect. In fact, when states were drafting their original child abuse laws, the American Medical Association opposed any provision that required doctors to report suspicious cases (No Author, 1964). One reason for this stance was a fear of legal and professional repercussions.

Most states normally regard doctor-patient interaction as a *privileged relationship*. A privileged relationship means there is an inviolable, nonintrudable bond between two parties. The physician cannot reveal any information gathered in that confidential capacity without first obtaining the patient's consent. Should a doctor break that trust, he or she could face a civil lawsuit and professional censure. Some other privileged discussions are those between attorneys and their clients and the confessions that ministers hear from their penitents.

Because the traditional doctor-patient privileged relationship could hinder physician reporting of suspected abuse and neglect, many states created an exemption. Today, the doctor-patient privileged relationship does not exist in child maltreatment cases. In addition, states have extended this protection by granting *legislative immunity* to any person who makes a child maltreatment report in "*good faith*." That is, if a person contacts the authorities out of genuine concern for the child's well-being, he or she cannot be sued if the allegation turns out to be false.

## The Report

State statutes require that reporters contact authorities about alleged maltreatment as quickly as possible. Some states stipulate that the initial disclosure can be an oral statement, followed a short time later by a written report. The purpose of an oral report is to avoid any cumbersome bureaucratic delays when a child is at risk. The written report must include the victim's name, parents' identity, address and nature of the injuries. It should also contain color photographs and X-rays, if possible. It also must indicate whether there are other siblings in jeopardy. Figure 7.2 details some of the evidence that is useful in trying to establish whether an abusive or neglectful situation exists.

One area of intense legislative debate in some jurisdictions has been the issue of to whom to submit the report. Most statutes designate a public social service agency as the primary recipient of child abuse and neglect reports. However, such an arrangement is not satisfactory for at least three reasons. First, most social service agencies conduct their business on a 9-to-5, Monday-through-Friday schedule. Lack of availability and the inability to research family records at night or on weekends or holidays becomes a key concern. Second, although search and seizure guidelines empower the police to make warrantless entries into houses or other structures if an emergency exists, such lawful powers do not extend automatically to nonsworn personnel acting as governmental agents. Third, it is not uncommon for the perpetrator to be present when the social service worker arrives. Because of the potential explosiveness involved here and possible violence directed against the social worker (Littlechild, 1995), many states also include the police as an appropriate agency to handle child maltreatment reports. The offender's presence may fuel antagonisms. For example, if the child is in danger, the investigator may place the minor in *protective custody*. In this situation, the worker terminates parental custody for the time being, removes the child from the home and places him or her in foster care for safekeeping. In addition to arousing parental anger, this step can stir up resentments within the child. As one victim told the U.S. Attorney General's Task Force (1984: 15):

> Why should I have been taken out of my home? I was the victim. I had [done] nothing. I did nothing wrong. My father should have been taken out, not me.

**FIGURE 7.2**
**The Basis for Making a Child Maltreatment Report**

**Direct Evidence**

- Eyewitness observations of a parent's abusive or neglectful behavior

- The child's description of being abused or neglected, unless there is a specific reason for not believing it

- The parent's description of abusive or neglectful behavior, unless it is long past

- Accounts of child maltreatment from a spouse or other family members

- Films, photographs, or other visual material depicting a minor's sexually explicit activity

- Newborns who are denied nutrition, life-sustaining care, or other medically indicated treatment

- Children in physically dangerous situations

- Young children who are left alone

- Apparently abandoned children

- The parent's demonstrated disabilities (for example, mental illness or retardation or alcohol or drug abuse) that are severe enough to make child abuse or child neglect likely

- The parent's demonstrated inability to care for a newborn baby

**Circumstantial Evidence**

- "Suspicious" injuries that suggest physical abuse

- Physical injuries or medical findings that suggest sexual abuse

**Figure 7.2**—*continued*

- For young children, signs of sexual activity

- Signs of severe physical deprivation on the child's body that suggest general neglect

- Severe dirt and disorder in the home that suggest general neglect

- Apparently untreated physical injuries, illnesses, or impairments that suggest medical neglect

- "Accidental" injuries that suggest gross inattention to the child's need for safety

- The parent's apparent indifference to a child's severe psychological or developmental problems

- The parent's apparent condonation of or indifference to the child's misbehavior that suggests improper ethical guidance

- Chronic and unexplained absences from school for which the parent is apparently responsible

- A newborn who shows signs of fetal exposure to drugs or alcohol

Source: Adapted and reprinted with the permission of The Free Press, a Division of Simon & Schuster from *Recognizing Child Abuse: A Guide for the Concerned* by Douglas J. Besharov. Copyright © 1990 by Douglas J. Besharov, p. 175.

## The Central Register

A critical component of child maltreatment laws is the establishment of a central register. A *central register* is a depository that stores records of all allegations of child abuse and neglect. Register users can index cases by the child's name, parent's name and perpetrator's name.

The purpose of this record-keeping system is to help in the diagnosis by tracking relevant case histories. In the past, some enterprising abusers skirted detection by taking the child to a different hospital or doctor every time the child needed medical attention (Fontana, 1973). This strategy usually succeeded because the attending physician lacked access to any previous medical records. Now with the central register, chronic abusers have a more difficult time eluding detection.

## Some Trouble Spots

Although child abuse and neglect laws have undergone much revision, some gaps remain. One troublesome area revolves around definitional aspects. Most states have an expansive construction of what constitutes abuse and neglect. However, not everyone views maltreatment in the same way. Social workers and police officers, for example, may regard instances of maltreatment as being more serious than do doctors and lawyers (Giovannoni and Becerra, 1979; Saunders, 1988). Differences also exist between such groups as police, mental health therapists and child protection services workers (Deisz et al., 1996; Everson et al., 1996). These divergent definitions can strain already scarce resources by compelling a small staff to investigate a large number of allegations. For example, two out of every three reports alleging child maltreatment during 1996 turned out to be unfounded or unsubstantiated (Wang and Daro, 1997). Such a high rate of unfounded allegations has unleashed a round of criticisms and suggestions aimed at improvement (Besharov, 1990a; Besharov, 1990b; Besharov, 1991; Finkelhor, 1990; McCurdy and Daro, 1994; Zellman, 1991).

A second problem is that not all states place the same degree of emphasis on child maltreatment. Designated violations range from misdemeanors in some states to felonies in other states. A third difficulty involves the lack of reporting. Despite statutory protection, many professionals are still reluctant to report suspected instances of maltreatment. Some develop *countertransference*—a sense of guilt, shame or anxiety that leads to nonreporting (Pollak and Levy, 1988). Others either waiver in their initial assessment that the situation is serious or they fear that an interruption in an ongoing treatment program would halt any progress already made (Kalichman et al., 1990; Willis and Wells, 1988; Zellman, 1990a; Zellman, 1990b). Fourth, although some states mandate a central register, the statutes often fail to specify the type of central register. The register might take the form of index cards stashed inside a desk drawer or may be an elaborate online computer retrieval system.

Finally, the issue of training has not received sufficient attention. Teachers, for example, spend much time in direct contact with children. One would think that teacher preparation courses and state licensing requirements would devote detailed attention to the topic of child abuse and neglect. Perhaps one solution would be for legislation to require specific instruction to all workers whose occupational duties involve routine contact with children (Crenshaw et al., 1995; Lamond, 1989; U.S. Attorney General's Task Force, 1984: 74-80).

## THE INCIDENCE OF CHILD MALTREATMENT

Measuring child maltreatment is very difficult. These acts usually take place out of the public eye. As a result, it is a very difficult offense to detect. The neighbors rarely see it. The police have a hard time discovering it. When it is detected, the victim may be too small to explain what happened. As a result, nobody really knows how pervasive child abuse is.

Although the incidence and costs of child maltreatment remain elusive, one estimate is that 5.4 of every 100,000 American children under the age of four die from maltreatment (McClain et al., 1993). Almost three children die from maltreatment every day in this country (McCurdy and Daro, 1994; National Committee to Prevent Child Abuse, 1996; U.S. Department of Health and Human Services, 1997). According to the Uniform Crime Reports, 249 murder victims in 1995 were infants. Another 411 homicide victims came from the one-to-four year-old age bracket, while an additional 103 criminal homicide victims were between the ages of five and eight (Federal Bureau of Investigation, 1996: 16).

Most observers would agree that these numbers underestimate the true extent of child fatalities due to maltreatment. To combat this problem, some jurisdictions employ *child death review teams*. These groups combine the expertise of child protective services workers, law enforcement officers, coroners and medical examiners, health care workers, prosecutors, and the like to investigate child deaths to determine whether maltreatment was involved. Some signs that may suggest abuse or neglect would include severe head trauma, the shaken baby syndrome, injuries to the abdomen or thorax areas, scalding, drowning, suffocation, poisoning or chronic neglect.

The National Committee to Prevent Child Abuse conducts an annual telephone survey of child protective service agencies to compile yearly figures on child maltreatment in the United States. According to the latest available report (Wang and Daro, 1997), there were 3,126,000 children alleged to be maltreatment victims in 1996. This number represents a 45 percent increase in child maltreatment reports since 1987. However, investigators were able to substantiate the allegations in only 31 percent of the cases. A *substantiated allegation* means that sufficient evidence existed to confirm the reporting person's suspicions.

It is important to realize that child maltreatment figures may not reflect actual increases in the level of maltreatment. It is possible that a heightened awareness of child abuse has led to greater reporting of maltreatment by the public, more intensive investigative efforts and better methods for tabulating the data by interested agencies. Given the historical treatment and place of children in society, it is very likely that the growing numbers are the result of better counting rather than escalating instances of abuse. Figure 7.3 contains a visual depiction of the kinds of substantiated maltreatment involved in these cases. As you can see, neglect and physical abuse top the list.

**FIGURE 7.3**
**Substantiated Child Maltreatment Allegations by Type of Case, 1996**

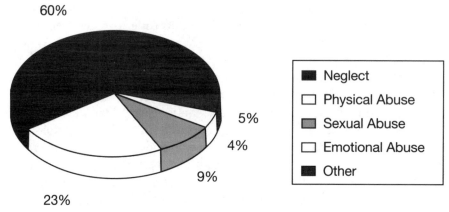

60%

5%

4%

9%

23%

| | Neglect |
| | Physical Abuse |
| | Sexual Abuse |
| | Emotional Abuse |
| | Other |

Source: Wang, C.T. and D. Daro (1997). *Current Trends in Child Abuse Reporting and Fatalities: The Results of the 1996 Annual Fifty State Survey.* Chicago: National Committee to Prevent Child Abuse.

Figure 7.4 lists some child maltreatment statistics. As alarming as these statistics may be, the reader should bear one thing in mind: No one yet has compiled an accurate count of the number of crippling injuries or the physical and mental retardation cases that stem from this kind of violence. All that we can do at this point is to make ballpark estimates of what suffering our children endure (Melton and Flood, 1994).

## CHARACTERISTICS OF MALTREATED CHILDREN

In order to consolidate the myriad of findings in the child maltreatment literature, Maden and Wrench (1977) reviewed a large number of studies. Many people think of child abuse victims as being infants or small children. Quite often, however, the data source itself can influence what one finds. Clinical studies, which are based on counseling records, usually reveal that the very young are victims, yet surveys show that child maltreatment spans all ages. Survey data generally record a high proportion of nonwhite victims, whereas clinical studies do not. This relationship probably reflects differential accessibility. African-Americans, because of their impoverished status, are often unable to afford private therapy.

One common finding in family violence research is the relationship between child maltreatment and social class. Official records show that these cases are concentrated in the lower classes (Fontana, 1973; Garbarino, 1976; Gil, 1971; Maden and Wrench, 1977; Spinetta and Rigler, 1972). Some observers contend that people of the lower classes resort to violence more often to resolve misunderstandings (Gelles, 1973; Wolfgang and Ferracuti, 1967). At the same time, others recognize that official abuse and neglect statistics contain an inherent bias (Gelles, 1975; Gelles, 1980; Handelman, 1979; Socolar et al., 1995). Because members of the lower classes more often come under the watchful eyes of service providers, higher rates of detected maltreatment should come as no surprise. In other words, it is entirely possible that child maltreatment is just as prevalent in the middle and upper classes as it is in the lower classes. The critical difference is that members of the middle and upper classes have the advantage of more resources. They can escape monitoring while those of the lower classes are not as fortunate. As a result, Gelles (1975; 1980) recommends that attention focus more upon the "gatekeepers"—the system personnel who have the power to confer the label of child abuse.

**FIGURE 7.4**
**Some Child Maltreatment Statistics**

- Of the adolescents ages 12-17 in the United States, an estimated 8% have been victims of serious sexual assault; 17% have been victims of serious physical assault; and 40% have witnessed serious violence.

- The probability of child abuse by a violent husband increases from five percent with one act of marital violence to near certainty with fifty or more acts of marital violence.

- Every incident of child sexual abuse costs the victim and society $99,000.

- The risk of being sexually abused does not vary among races, but children from lower income groups or from single parent families are more frequently victims.

- Twenty-nine percent of all forcible rapes occurred when the victim was less than eleven years old.

- A large study of female adults sexually abused as children found that their abuse lasted an average of 7.6 years and began at age six.

- Forty-three percent of responding physicians indicated that multidisciplinary centers responding to child sex abuse were occasionally, rarely, or never adequate.

- In a study of male survivors sexually abused as children, over 80% had a history of substance abuse; 50% had suicidal thoughts; 23% attempted suicide; and 70% received psychological treatment.

- Among children who were sexually abused, the odds are 27.7 times higher that they will be arrested for prostitution as an adult than non-victims.

Source: National Victim Center (1997). *Child Abuse Statistics*.
URL: *http://www.nvc.org/edir/childabu.htm#ca*

At least one researcher has taken this suggestion to heart. Handelman (1979) investigated a variety of alleged maltreatment cases that were referred to a social service agency for official investigation. Taking an organizational approach, Handelman showed how agency emphasis upon certain carefully selected details influenced the degree of intervention required in each case. In other words, the imposition of the label "child abuse" depended upon the presence or absence of certain cues. They included the social worker's interpretation of what constitutes abuse and neglect, the client's amenability to accepting the label of child abuse and the caseload the worker was currently handling.

Handelman's study shows that the definitional ambiguity surrounding child abuse and neglect, coupled with bureaucratic mandates, may influence the official designation of problem families as abusive families. On the other hand, the system may overlook and discard actual cases of child abuse because the workload is sufficiently high to keep all agency workers fruitfully occupied.

## THEORIES OF CHILD MALTREATMENT

Explanations for child maltreatment fall into three popular approaches: (1) intraindividual theories, (2) sociocultural explanations, and (3) the social learning approach. Because each way of looking at child maltreatment has its own implications, this section of the chapter will examine each approach briefly and highlight some problems encountered with each model.

**FIGURE 7.5**
**Who Is Committing These Acts?**

Although no single profile fits every case, researchers have identified several factors that seem to characterize many abusing parents. They have found that frequently an abusive parent:

- Is a young adult in his mid-20's
- Lives near or below poverty level
- Has not finished high school
- Is depressed and unable to cope with stress
- Has experienced violence firsthand

Source: National Clearinghouse on Child Abuse and Neglect Information (1997). *Frequently Asked Questions About Child Fatalities.* Washington, DC: National Clearinghouse on Child Abuse and Neglect Information. *URL: http://www.calib.com/nccanch/pubs/fatality.htm*

## Intraindividual Explanations

The intraindividual approach views child maltreatment as the product of some internal defect or flaw inside the abuser. Supposedly, this personality deficiency leads "to a lack of inhibition in expressing frustration and other impulsive behavior" (Spinetta and Rigler, 1972: 299). If researchers can identify the disturbances present in child abusers, then the next step is to develop appropriate treatment plans (Belsky, 1978). Thus, the psychiatric model is attractive because it tries to locate and treat personality disorders that lead to child abuse.

Steele and Pollock (1974) conducted one of the first attempts to apply the psychiatric model to child abusers. They described their initial patient as a "gold mine of psychopathology." Those insights guided their analyses of 60 families over the next six years. The results revealed that child abusers did not monopolize any one particular diagnostic category. Instead, maltreaters exhibited disorders that spanned the entire spectrum of *psychopathology* or mental disorders. One phenomenon the researchers did focus upon, though, was role reversal.

*Role reversal* occurs when parents switch roles with children, expecting the child to shower them with nurturance and love, rather than vice versa. When the child fails to provide such emotional support (as evidenced by crying for a prolonged period, by soiling diapers or by being unresponsive), the frustrated parent feels unwanted, rejected and not loved by the child. Such feelings trigger an aggressive parental response that culminates in maltreatment. Steele and Pollock (1974) trace this infantilism back to the abuser's relationship with his or her own parents. According to them, parents maltreat children because of the inadequate relationship they had with their own parents.

Later research in this vein led Wright (1976) to coin the phrase *"sick but slick" parents*. Child maltreaters do not exhibit serious deficiencies on a battery of traditional psychological inventories. However, closer inspection shows that these subjects were not answering truthfully. Instead, they gave what they thought were socially desirable responses. Thus, child abusers go to great lengths to project an image of themselves as normal parents—probably in order to deflect detection.

Despite these insights, critics point to four concerns that weaken the intraindividual approach. First, the data source is slanted. Most psychiatric inquiries rely upon clinical information as opposed to a random sample from some larger population. As a result, there is no way of knowing whether abusers who seek help form a typical cross-section of all maltreaters. Second, these studies usually lack an appropriate control group. The absence of a benchmark makes it difficult to determine whether attributes isolated as peculiar to abusers are unique or are shared with members of the larger population. Third, there is very little agreement among psychiatric researchers about which exact characteristics distinguish abusers from nonabusers. Finally, much of the research conducted in this vein is *ex post facto,* that is, it occurs after the abuse has taken place and registers very little predictive power.

## Sociocultural Explanations

The sociological approach looks for events that are external to the individual. This approach emphasizes the amount of stress found within the family. Such irritants as unemployment, family size, child spacing and social isolation become focal points.

One typical characteristic of abusive families is their location in the lower social strata. Although one possibility is that social service agencies maintain more surveillance over these families, the etiological connection still fascinates researchers. Apparently, other variables act together to aggravate this situation. For example, Gil (1971) reports that one-half of the fathers were unemployed when they abused their children. Families that are cut off from neighbors and friends are prime candidates for internal hostilities (Garbarino and Gilliam, 1980). Family size and the amount of spacing between children often create havoc for parents. Unwanted pregnancies, large families, substance abuse and unsupportive spouses may strain family resources and exacerbate an already tense living arrangement (Gelles, 1980; Smithey, 1997).

The social stress model emphasizes parents' lack of coping strategies (Belsky, 1978). In other words, when parents become stressed, their reactions include a sense of frustration and helplessness. This relative lack of power carries a feeling of not being in control, which makes it very easy for parents to lash out and vent their rage on their unprotected offspring.

The sociological approach to explaining child maltreatment has not escaped criticism. One problem is that the model fails to explain why some stressed families do not turn to child abuse as an outlet (Belsky, 1978). The model also overlooks other available coping strategies. Furthermore, it fails to explain why or how abuse is chosen from all the other alternative strategies.

## The Social Learning Approach

Social learning theory focuses upon the absorption of experiences and reinforcement (Akers, 1973; Bandura, 1973). It means that rewarded activities, or those that go unpunished, creep into the observer's repertoire of what is acceptable behavior. Subscribers find this approach very useful when studying family violence.

Social learning theory has led to an interest in examining whether maltreatment leads to subsequent impairment. A review of 29 empirical studies analyzing children who witnessed parental violence does find some connection with certain types of developmental problems (Kolbos et al., 1996). There are other indications that being the victim of child maltreatment leads to subsequent delinquent behavior (Doerner, 1987; Doerner and Tsai, 1990; Kelley et al., 1997; Smith and Thornberry, 1995; Widom, 1989; Zingraff et al., 1993). While researchers have not looked at this linkage thoroughly, it does appear that this relationship might vary according to the kind of maltreatment, the severity of the experience, and the frequency and duration of the victimization episodes. As this body of research becomes more sophisticated over the next several years, investigators should be able to achieve greater closure on this issue.

The principles behind social learning theory also lend credence to the notion of a *cycle of violence*. There is a fear that children who watch their parents engage in violent outbursts toward each other will come to accept these behaviors as permissible. Similarly, children who are maltreated run the risk of thinking that these behaviors are acceptable because their parents performed them. When these children grow up and form their own intimate relationships, these very same acts of violence are likely to surface.

Adherents to the "cycle of violence" thesis commonly apply it to two forms of family violence (Schwartz, 1989). First, there is the popular notion that abused children will grow up to become child abusers. Second, there is the belief that children who witness spousal violence will become spouse abusers in their relationships. The U.S. Attorney General's Task Force on Family Violence (1984: 2-3) summed up this view when it wrote:

> Children in violent homes "learn" violence in much the same way they learn any other behavior. They observe that violence is a normal way for people to treat one another and a normal way to solve problems. The family violence that occurs today is a time bomb that will explode years later as abused children become abusers of their own children or other children, and as children who watch one parent hitting the other repeat the example in their relationships or the community.

Some family violence researchers feel that this assessment is accurate. While there is limited empirical evidence to support this position (Simons et al., 1995), these findings are very tentative. However, this state of affairs did not keep one spokesperson from proclaiming that "The idea that child-abusing parents were themselves victims of abuse, and that wife-beating husbands come from violent families, is now widely accepted" (Straus, 1983).

Not all victimologists share this opinion. There is a great deal of debate over whether past victimization causes future offending. Some scholars maintain that there is still no sound empirical proof for the notion of intergenerational transmission of violence. As far as child mal-treatment goes, Gelles and Cornell (1990: 13-17) refer to the "cycle of violence" as a myth that hinders a full understanding of family violence. They reject this idea because it implies that maltreated children are imprinted or programmed to become abusers later in life. Another author explains that her "search of the literature reveals that many writ-ers repeat the claim but few produce any sound empirical evidence to support it" (Pagelow, 1984: 225). In other words, even if the linkage does exist, the definitive research needed to support this claim has yet to appear (Widom, 1989). Pagelow (1984: 254) further chips away at this very point when she concludes:

> [T]here is no scientifically sound empirical evidence that there is a *causal* relationship between being an abused child and becoming an adult child abuser. There is evidence of a weak association, but when up to 90 percent of child abusers cannot be shown to have been abused in their own childhoods, the association can be considered hardly greater than chance.

The existence of contradictory evidence surrounding this unresolved debate suggests that a great deal of additional research is needed prior to making any final decisions about an intergenerational argument. The fact that past victimization may make the individual either an offender or a further victim indicates that different types of intervention may be useful once the initial victimization episode takes place. There is a clear need to identify the causal forces at work here prior to making any fun-damental policy decisions for addressing future behavior.

## SOME COPING STRATEGIES

What can be done to ensure that all children have a safe home and a loving atmosphere in which to grow and develop? One option that the state does exercise is to rescind parental custody and place children in foster homes or in other alternative housing. Such a procedure comes into play in only the most extreme circumstances and is a last-ditch effort. But what else can be done? Some people have suggested public health screening for detection. Others think parenting classes are the key to prevention. Another group advocates the development of profiles of offenders and victims to enhance detection. Further suggestions include more active law enforcement, self-help groups and legal changes that would increase deterrence. These latter solutions would avoid governmental intrusion into one's domicile. The following materials explore some of these options.

## Health Screening

One social policy option that attracts interest is a health screening program. Proponents suggest that public health workers should conduct routine home visits where there are young children and newborns (National Committee to Prevent Child Abuse, 1996; Wasik and Roberts, 1994). In fact, the U.S. Advisory Board on Child Abuse and Neglect is on record as recommending universal implementation of home visits. These home visits would serve a dual purpose. The first goal would be prevention. Workers could help new parents adjust to their offspring by showing them how to care for infants and allaying parental apprehensions. The second objective would be to uncover hidden cases of maltreatment. Such a strategy would avoid the haphazard detection techniques now in use.

**FIGURE 7.6**
**The Hawai'i Healthy Start Program**

---

Paraprofessional home visitors call on families weekly (or more frequently, if needed) for the first 6 to 12 months. The first 1½ hour visit is spent describing the program and the role of the home visitor.

During the first 3 months of weekly visits, the primary focus is on helping the parents with basic family support, such as learning how to mix formula and wash the baby and understanding the baby's early stages of development and sleep patterns, as well as on answering the most common question, "Why does my baby cry so much?"

A great deal of the home visitor's time is spent listening to parents and providing emotional support, helping them obtain food, formula, and baby supplies; assisting them with housing and job application; getting them to appointments; and providing informal counseling on a wide range of issues, including domestic violence and drug abuse. . . . [E]arly in their relationship, the home visitor and the family develop an Individual Family Support Plan, which lists the services that Healthy Start provides, plus assistance available from other social services. The family checks the services they want to receive during the next 6 months. The plan spells out "What we want," "Ways to get it," "Who can help," "Target date," and "What happened."

---

Source: Earle, R.B. (1995). *Helping To Prevent Child Abuse—and Future Criminal Consequences: Hawai'i Healthy Start*. Washington, DC: U.S. Department of Justice.

Although this proposal is appealing, it has some drawbacks. One criticism is that it invites unwarranted governmental intrusion. Two types of errors would surface (Light, 1973: 569-71; Warner and Hansen, 1994). A *false positive error* would occur when a worker misclassifies a nonabused child as a maltreatment case. A *false negative error* entails not diagnosing a child as abused when that child really is a maltreatment victim. Critics fear that these two errors could be high enough to render this approach questionable at best. Proponents counter that a greater emphasis on personnel training and a multistage checking system would avoid the embarrassment of making false accusations and impugning caretakers.

## Education

The education effort aims to demystify child rearing by providing parents with instruction in child development. Some observers contend that the high school curriculum should contain a family course. Others advocate continuing adult education projects at hospitals, schools, churches and social service agencies (National Committee to Prevent Child Abuse, 1996; U.S. Attorney General's Task Force, 1984: 68-71).

Although this approach appears attractive, it is not the simple cure one might wish it to be. This option could not be implemented within a very short period of time (Light, 1973: 573). There are matters of course content, development and funding. Moreover, once in place, this alternative would require several years before yielding any returns.

## Parents Anonymous

Parents Anonymous is a nonprofit organization with local chapters. Local groups consist of parents who feel they are maltreating (or are in danger of maltreating) their children. The national organization operates a 24-hour hot line that parents can call when they need to vent their frustration or anger. Hopefully, talking to a sympathetic person who has encountered similar feelings will curb any violence directed at a child. In some ways, Parents Anonymous resembles the Alcoholics Anonymous network.

In order to meet the philosophy outlined in Figure 7.7, the members of each local chapter gather for weekly meetings to discuss their successes and failures, both as parents and as crisis interventionists for fellow members. It is not known just how effective this type of program is in the fight against child maltreatment because membership is anonymous. As a result, no definitive evaluations have appeared on this self-help project.

**FIGURE 7.7**
**The Parents Anonymous Principles and Group Standards**

## PARENTS ANONYMOUS PRINCIPLES

Parents Anonymous programs effectively strengthen families based on culturally responsive implementation of the following four guiding principles.

**Parent Leadership:** Parents recognize and take responsibility for their problems, develop their own solutions and serve as role models for other parents.

**Mutual Support:** Help is reciprocal in that parents give and get support from each other, creating a strong sense of community.

**Shared Leadership:** Parents and professionals build successful partnerships to share responsibility, expertise and leadership roles.

**Personal Growth:** Parents make significant long-term positive change through identifying their options, exploring their feelings and acting on their decisions in an atmosphere of belonging, trust and acceptance in which healthy interactions are modeled.

## PARENTS ANONYMOUS GROUP STANDARDS

**Parents Anonymous Groups:**

◆ Have at least one facilitator who is professionally trained in the Parents Anonymous Principles

◆ Have at least one parent group member in an acknowledged leadership role, and all other parent group members are encouraged to take on leadership roles.

◆ Meet weekly at a designated time, in a location that is safe and accessible

**In a Parents Anonymous Group:**

◆ Parents provide nonjudgmental support to each other

◆ Information shared by and among group members remains confidential within the group unless abuse and/or neglect of children is suspected and necessitates a report in accordance with state laws

◆ Parents determine what information they share with the group

◆ No fee is charged for parents or children to attend a group meeting

◆ Parents determine the content of each meeting and shape the agenda to fit their specific needs on any given week

◆ Between weekly meetings, the group leader and facilitator are available for consultation to all group members as are members to each other

◆ Parents participate in Parents Anonymous groups for any length of time they determine to be most useful to them

◆ All parent members receive an *I Am A Parents Anonymous Parent* handbook, available in Spanish and English, which defines the expectations of the group, discusses parenting issues and provides an on-going resource

Source: Parents Anonymous, Inc. (1997). *The Parents Anonymous Principles and Group Standards*. Claremont: CA: Parents Anonymous, Inc.

## Counseling

Another avenue for dealing with child abuse cases emphasizes a treatment or rehabilitation approach. This response seeks to help both the victim and the offender, often involving the entire family. Most treatment interventions revolve around individual and group counseling. Various studies report that treatment programs are successful at engendering more assertiveness in victims and opening up communication about the event and related problems (Maddock et al., 1991; Owen and Steele, 1991; Woodworth, 1991). At the same time, however, some distrust and suspicion of the offender remains after treatment, and therapy can have a negative impact on the family unit (Levitt et al., 1991; Maddock et al., 1991; Woodworth, 1991). Wright (1991) evaluates the impact of removing the offender from the home (a common step in familial sexual abuse) and concludes that this action often leads to divorce, distant relations between the missing parent and children, financial hardship and failed attempts at reconciliation.

Perhaps the most notable result of intervention studies is the almost-universal finding that more services are needed than are typically available. Indeed, it may be the absence of available and appropriate services that is the cause of negative treatment outcomes. Among the needs most often cited are the need for financial assistance, extended treatment and counseling, more clarity and structure in the expectations of all participants and the provision of tangential services for related problems such as drug and alcohol dependence (Levitt et al., 1991; Woodworth, 1991; Wright, 1991).

## Sex Offender Laws

Megan Kanka was a 7-year-old girl who resided in a small New Jersey town. Her neighbor, Jesse K. Timmendequas, lived across the street. Timmendequas had a dark secret that nobody in the neighborhood knew about. He had been convicted twice of sex offenses against children and was just released from prison. He was also living with two other sex offenders whom he had met while in prison.

On July 29, 1994, Timmendequas promised Megan that she could play with his puppy if she went inside his house. She did. It was there that Timmendequas sexually assaulted Megan and strangled her to death with a belt before disposing of her body.

Public outrage over this death spurred state legislatures to pass new laws commonly referred to as "*Megan's Law.*" While the exact details vary from state to state, the core requirement calls for public notification whenever a sex offender is released from prison into the community.

These laws typically classify sex offenders into three risk categories with commensurate notification responsibilities (Brooks, 1996). The lowest tier is reserved for convicted offenders who have made numerous adjustments and are least likely to reoffend. The typical requirement is that the state must notify victims and local law enforcement agencies that the offender has been released from custody and is back in the community. The second level is the *sexual offender*. This person is deemed to be a "moderate risk" and an additional notification is made to local schools and youth organizations (Boy Scouts, Girl Scouts, sports and recreation centers). The highest risk category, *sexually violent predator*, is reserved for the most dangerous offenders with the highest proclivity for recidivism. In these instances, the entire community is alerted about the offender's release. Community meetings, press releases, as well as flyers and posters with photographs, criminal history, the offender's new address, place of employment, and vehicle tag all serve to advertise this person's presence in the area. The hope, of course, is that enhanced community awareness will spur greater parental supervision of their children and reduce any opportunity for the criminal to reoffend.

Balancing the rights of the offender against the community's concern for protection has ignited considerable debate. Critics have raised a number of objections to these new regulations (Cohen, 1995). For one thing, they contend that these practices violate the offender's constitutional right to privacy and the prohibition against cruel and unusual punishment. Completing a term of imprisonment, some people argue, satisfies an individual's debt to society. Another worry concerns vigilantism. Beatings, demonstrations and even arson have greeted some offenders after their much-publicized releases from confinement (Brooks, 1996; Steinbock, 1995). Finally, some commentators maintain that these laws, despite a noble intention, fail to protect children adequately. Steinbock (1995: 5) notes that most child molestation is perpetrated by family members and friends, not by strangers. Furthermore, common plea bargaining practices allow many child molesters to sidestep the label of "sex offender" and avoid registration requirements (Pallone, 1995).

These and other issues have brought the dawning recognition that current ways of dealing with sex offenders are ineffective and represent an emotional knee-jerk reaction (Freeman-Longo, 1996; Lieb, 1996; Myers, 1996; Prentky, 1996). Many sex offenders have lengthy criminal histories, are not amenable to treatment and will recidivate after release. As a result, some states have instituted civil commitment procedures for mentally ill sex offenders in an effort to prevent future victimization. In other words, once a dangerous sex offender completes his or her prison sentence, the state will initiate legal proceedings to confine this person indefinitely in a mental institution.

This strategy came under fire for a number of reasons. First, critics argued that this approach was nothing more than an *ex post facto law*. It imposed additional punishment long after the criminal court had adjudicated the matter. Second, there is the question of *double jeopardy*. Essentially, the offender is being punished twice for the same act. Third, the prospect of a lifetime commitment after completing the terms of incarceration amounts to cruel and unusual punishment. Finally, additional confinement violates plea bargain terms.

The U.S. Supreme Court ruled on this matter in *Kansas v. Hendricks* (1997). Hendricks was a convicted sex offender who had already served a 10-year prison term. As he neared release, the state sought to commit Hendricks to a mental institution as an uncured sexually violent predator. During that trial, Hendricks freely admitted that he quit the therapy program the prison offered, that he had a long history of sexually assaulting children, that he felt that he suffered from *pedophilia* (a sexual attraction toward children) and that he had no control over his urges to molest children. The jury found that Hendricks suffered from a mental abnormality and posed a danger to others; they agreed that he met the criteria for being classified as a sexually violent predator. The judge then issued a civil commitment order, which Hendricks appealed on the grounds that Kansas had violated his due process rights, double jeopardy and *ex post facto* protections.

The Supreme Court ruled against Hendricks in a 5-4 decision. It held that the Kansas statute had built in a sufficient number of procedural checks to provide for due process and protect against overzealous application. Furthermore, the Court found that Kansas had distanced the civil commitment procedures from any criminal proceeding and, therefore, the statute was not punitive in nature. The Justices ruled that Kansas was correct to incapacitate Hendricks as a way of protecting society even though no effective treatment was available for his mental abnormality.

Two days after the Supreme Court rendered this opinion, the New York legislature passed a sexual predator act into law (Myers, 1997b). A safe prediction is that the number of states availing themselves to this protection will grow quite quickly now that the federal Supreme Court has removed some roadblocks.

## Law Enforcement

Law enforcement action against child maltreatment consists of two general types. There are efforts to enhance police detection abilities and projects aimed at preventing maltreatment. These two activities often overlap.

One suggestion is for law enforcement agencies to construct profiles to identify abusive caretakers and their victims. The construction of offender profiles is a recent advance in crime control. Such tactics help spot drug couriers in airports and assist in other kinds of investigations. The Federal Bureau of Investigation, for example, has begun compiling and analyzing data on serial murderers. The hope is that this statistical information would target high-risk families for surveillance and therapy regarding child maltreatment.

Unfortunately, a host of compromising factors plague current efforts. For example, information comes only from known abusers. Without a good data source, this approach has serious limitations. Figures 7.8 and 7.9 display materials developed by one police agency in an effort to increase public awareness.

**FIGURE 7.8**
**Profile of Abusive or Neglectful Parents**

---

Abusive or neglectful parents are likely to share several of the following characteristics:

- They are isolated from family supports, such as friends, relatives, neighbors, and community groups.
- They consistently fail to keep appointments, discourage social contact, rarely or never participate in school activities.
- They seem to trust no one.
- They are reluctant to give information about the child's injuries or condition. They are unable to explain the injuries or they give far-fetched explanations.
- They respond inappropriately to the child's condition, either by overreacting or seeming hostile and antagonistic when questioned; or they underreact showing little concern or awareness and seem more occupied with their own problems than those of the child.
- They refuse to consent to diagnostic studies of the child.
- They delay or fail to take the child for medical care—for routine checkups or for treatment of injury or illness. Or they may choose a different doctor or hospital each time.
- They are overcritical of the child and seldom discuss the child in positive terms.
- They have unrealistic expectations of the child, expecting or demanding behavior that is beyond the child's years or ability.
- They believe in harsh punishment.
- They seldom touch or look at the child.
- They ignore the child's crying or react with impatience.
- They keep the child confined—perhaps in a crib or playpen—for very long periods of time.
- They seem to lack understanding of the child's physical and emotional needs.
- They are hard to locate.
- They may be misusing alcohol or drugs.
- They appear to lack control or fear that they may lose control.
- Their behavior may generally be irrational, they may seem incapable of child-rearing and may seem to be cruel and sadistic.

---

Source: Crime Prevention Unit (no date). *Officer Friendly Training Manual*. Tallahassee, FL: Tallahassee Police Department.

**FIGURE 7.9**
**Profile of Abused or Neglected Children**

Abused or neglected children are likely to share several of the following characteristics:

- They appear to be different from other children in physical and emotional makeup or their parents describe them as being different or bad.

- They seem afraid of their parents.

- They may bear bruises, welts, sores, or other skin injuries, which seem to be untreated.

- They are given inappropriate food, drink, or medication.

- They are left alone or with inadequate supervision.

- They are chronically unclean.

- They exhibit extremes in behavior: cry often or cry very little and show no real expectation of being comforted; they are excessively fearful or seem fearless of adult authority; they are unusually aggressive or extremely passive or withdrawn.

- They are wary of physical contact, especially with an adult. They may be hungry for affection yet have difficulty relating to children and adults. Based on their experiences, they feel they cannot risk getting close to others.

- They exhibit a sudden change in behavior, exhibit regressive behavior, such as wetting their pants or bed, thumb-sucking, whining, or becoming uncommonly shy or passive.

- They have learning problems that cannot be diagnosed. Their attention wanders and they easily become self-absorbed.

- They are habitually truant or late to school. Frequent or prolonged absences from school may result from the parent's keeping an injured child at home until the evidence of abuse disappears. Or they may arrive at school early and remain after classes instead of going home.

- They are tired and often sleep in class.

- They are not dressed appropriately for the weather. Children who wear long sleeves on hot days may be dressed to hide bruises or burns or other marks of abuse or they may be dressed inadequately and suffer frostbite or illness from exposure to the weather.

Source: Crime Prevention Unit (no date). *Officer Friendly Training Manual*. Tallahassee, FL: Tallahassee Police Department.

Another prevention tactic calls for the licensing of all caregivers who have contact with children. Florida, for example, stipulates that all private and public employees who deal with children must undergo a pre-employment background check. They must submit a set of their fingerprints and not be a convicted felon. Applicants must also complete a 30-hour course in child care to become a licensed child care worker. Failure to comply with these standards automatically results in licensing disqualification (Florida Statutes, 1997: §§402.305, 402.3055).

Other nontraditional approaches are surfacing all over the country. One such imaginative venture has been to enlist the help of robots (Norton, 1987). Besides giving the usual safety presentations to school children, some police agencies use robot celebrities to help talk with abuse victims. The robot can be equipped with a video recorder, television monitor, camera and microphone to preserve interview sessions for prosecution.

Other departments rely upon "drawing interviews" in which the child constructs pictures to explain graphically what happened to him or her (Farley, 1987). Puppet shows tend to fascinate children and are useful in explaining "good," "bad" and "secret" touches. Local businesses sometimes sponsor fingerprint programs to help combat the missing children problem. Police agencies have started the School Resource Officer Program in which officers are assigned to school counseling programs. Some departments promote "Officer Friendly" outings where officers meet school-age children and explain how the police like to help children (Klappers, 1985).

The use of anatomically correct dolls as an investigative technique in sexual abuse cases is another frequent approach (Berliner, 1988; Boat and Everson, 1988; Maan, 1991; Walker, 1988). Quite often, the victim is too immature or naive to express himself or herself adequately. The child may also feel confused because he or she is pitted against a parent or other adult for whom he or she may maintain a sense of loyalty, love and concern. The child is faced with denying one set of feelings while emphasizing another. To help quell this trauma, the youngster can indicate what happened by using dolls. Concern that these dolls are sexually suggestive to children has received little empirical support (Conte, 1991; Everson and Boat, 1994; Maan, 1991).

## Legal Reform

Participation in criminal justice system proceedings can be a traumatic experience for children (Lipovksy, 1994). In fact, the American Bar Association (1996) requires attorneys to consider the child's well-being carefully before deciding whether the victim should testify in court. However, victim testimony is a crucial component in an adversarial system of justice. Without a victim's account, most cases are simply not prosecutable. As a result, some jurisdictions employ victim counselors to help combat the emotional upheaval that victims incur and to sustain victim credibility by increasing cognitive recall (Burgess and Laszlo, 1976; Geiselman et al., 1992). Figure 7.10 contains several recommendations issued by the U.S. Attorney General's Task Force when dealing with child abuse cases.

**FIGURE 7.10**
**U.S. Attorney General's Task Force Recommendations for Prosecutors and Judges in Child Abuse Cases**

Prosecutors should adopt special policies and procedures for child victims. These should include:

- Presenting hearsay evidence at preliminary hearings so the child is not required to testify in person;

- Presenting, with consent of counsel, the child's trial testimony on videotape;

- Use of anatomically correct dolls and drawings to describe abuse; and

- Limiting continuances to an absolute minimum.

Judges should adopt special court rules and procedures for child victims. These should include:

- The use of hearsay evidence at preliminary hearings;

- Appointment of a special volunteer advocate for children, when appropriate;

- A presumption that children are competent to testify;

- Allowing the child's trial testimony to be presented on videotape with agreement of counsel;

- Flexible courtroom settings and procedures; and

- Carefully managed press coverage.

Source: U.S. Attorney General's Task Force (1984). *Family Violence*. Washington, DC: U.S. Government Printing Office, pp. 31, 33.

Any reform effort must weigh victim trauma against the defendant's constitutional rights. The defendant has the right to confront and to cross-examine witnesses under the Fourteenth Amendment of the U.S. Constitution. There is the right to a public trial under the Sixth Amendment and the public has the right to access the proceedings under the First Amendment. The difficulty, then, becomes one of balancing victim trauma induced by system participation against the defendant's interests.

Reform efforts in other countries have focused mostly upon the role of the victim in providing testimony. Israel, for example, employs youth examiners who discuss the case with the child. The youth examiner then relays to the court what the child said during their sessions (Reifen, 1975).

Some states in the United States relax the hearsay rule when the following circumstances are present: a child victim is under the age of 11, he or she is involved in a sexual abuse case, and the trustworthiness of a statement made out of court and not under oath can be established (Florida Statutes, 1997: §90.803(23); Levine and Battistoni, 1991). The *hearsay rule* disallows statements made by a third party because the court cannot evaluate a third party's credibility and thus the defense is unable to impeach that testimony. Judges waive the hearsay rule only under very narrow circumstances.

Another mechanism to reduce victim trauma is the use of *in camera* proceedings. One such effort has been to allow child victims to testify outside the courtroom in less formal, less threatening surroundings. This practice allows the judge to interview a child in private and to videotape the testimony for the trial. An example of a state statute allowing for this is reproduced in Figure 7.11.

**FIGURE 7.11**
**An Example of a Statute Allowing Videotaping of Testimony in Child Sexual Abuse Cases**

On motion and hearing *in camera* and a finding that there is a substantial likelihood that a victim or witness who is under the age of 16 would suffer at least moderate emotional or mental harm if he were required to testify in open court or that such victim or witness is otherwise unavailable as defined in §90.804(1), the trial court may order the videotaping of the testimony of the victim or witness in a sexual abuse case or child abuse case, whether civil or criminal in nature, which videotaped testimony is to be utilized at trial in lieu of trial testimony in open court. . . .

The defendant and the defendant's counsel shall be present at the videotaping, unless the defendant has waived this right. The court may require the defendant to view the testimony from outside the presence of the child by means of a two-way mirror or another similar method that will ensure that the defendant can observe and hear the testimony of the child in person, but that the child cannot hear or see the defendant. The defendant and the attorney for the defendant may communicate by any appropriate private method.

Any party, or the court on its own motion, may request the aid of an interpreter, as provided in §90.606, to aid the parties in formulating methods of questioning the child and in interpreting the answers of the child throughout proceedings conducted under this section.

Source: Florida Statutes §92.53, 1997.

Although the use of *in camera* proceedings is innovative, it has encountered some legal objections. First, some defendants have argued that such proceedings violate their constitutional right to confront and cross-examine witnesses. These complaints have been quashed by allowing the defense counsel to attend the out-of-court questioning. However, the courts have ruled that the defendant does not have to be physically present in the same room with the witness. A suitable alternative arrangement is to have the defendant view witness testimony from another location via closed circuit television (Bjerregaard, 1989; Melton, 1980).

A second objection deals with the right of the public to have access to the trial. Sufficient precedent exists that the public has limited access to observe judicial proceedings without jeopardizing the legal process. A similar third objection deals with the defendant's right to a public trial. Precedence is mixed on this point. After reviewing a variety of cases, Melton concluded that "embarrassment and emotional trauma to witnesses simply do not permit a trial judge to close his courtroom to the entire public" (Melton, 1980: 282). While *in camera* proceedings may avoid inducement of unnecessary trauma, not all courts have reached a definitive conclusion about the conditions under which it is permissible.

**FIGURE 7.12**
**Selected Internet Sites Dealing with Child Maltreatment**

American Bar Association Center on Children and the Law
   http://www.abanet.org/child/

American Professional Society on the Abuse of Children
   http://www.apsac.org

Incest Survivors Resource Network International
   http://www.zianet.com/ISRNI/

National Center for Missing and Exploited Children
   http://www.missingkids.org

National Clearinghouse on Child Abuse and Neglect Information
   http://www.calib.com/nccanch/

National Committee to Prevent Child Abuse
   http://www.childabuse.org

National Court Appointed Special Advocate Association
   http://www.nationalcasa.org

National Network of Children's Advocacy Centers
   http://www.nncac.org

The Polly Klaas Foundation
   http://www.pollyklaas.org/

## SUMMARY

It has taken our society much time to recognize that child maltreatment exists. Once discovered, states implemented laws forbidding the victimization of children. Maltreatment, however, tends to take place behind closed doors. It often involves victims who are unable to defend themselves, making detection difficult. While reporting laws aim to remedy this dilemma, they have had a boomerang effect. Almost two-thirds of child maltreatment complaints are graded as unfounded or unsubstantiated.

Other coping strategies have surfaced. Together, they suggest that the eradication of child abuse and neglect is everybody's responsibility. One way to place this mandate in perspective is to realize that somewhere in this country another child died from maltreatment in the time it took to read this chapter.

# LEARNING OBJECTIVES

After reading Chapter 8, you should be able to:

- Explain who the elderly are.

- Talk about age patterns in victimization statistics.

- Discuss the objective odds of elder victimization.

- Separate "fear of crime" into two components.

- Understand what is meant by the fear-crime paradox.

- Demonstrate the "graying" of the American population.

- Link changes in life expectancies with population shifts.

- Tie "vicarious victimization" to fear of crime.

- Comment on the political role of the elderly.

- Distinguish risk from vulnerability.

- List four risk factors for the elderly.

- Outline three vulnerability factors for the elderly.

- Compare and contrast elder abuse with elder neglect.

- Estimate how much elder maltreatment takes place.

- Relay various shortcomings with official estimates of elder maltreatment.

- Provide some characteristics of maltreated adults.

- Sketch out some explanations for elder maltreatment that focus upon individual pathological conditions.

- Explain how situational aspects contribute to maltreatment situations.

- Summarize how role reversal impacts elder maltreatment.

- Discuss the relevancy of social exchange theory for elder abuse and neglect.

- Define ageism and explore how it affects maltreatment.

- Evaluate whether mandatory abuse reporting laws are effective.

- Recognize the limitations of current social service provisions.

# Chapter 8

# Elder Abuse

## INTRODUCTION

Perhaps the most recent concern to emerge in victimology is the topic of elder victimization. The elderly are an expanding segment of the population. Senior citizens comprised only 4 percent of the American citizenry in 1900. Projections hold that this group will make up 20 percent of the population by the year 2030 (Administration on Aging, 1997). These figures show that soon there will be more potential victims in the elderly age bracket than ever before.

Because interest in elder victimization has just begun to sprout, there remain a number of unanswered questions and issues. The entire field of elder victimization is still in the process of defining its parameters. The subject matter can be divided into two major subheadings: criminal victimization and elder maltreatment. For our purposes, criminal victimization refers to the commission of acts against the elderly that would be criminal violations regardless of the victim's age. Certainly, abuse and neglect fall into this category. However, they differ from other crimes in that they specifically target the elderly. The status of being elderly provides the opportunity for this type of victimization.

## KEY TERMS

Adult Protective Services

ageism

elder abuse

elder neglect

exogenous factors

fear of crime

gerontologists

life expectancy

risk

role reversal

Silver Haired Legislature

social exchange theory

symbolic interactionism

vicarious victimization

vulnerability

## DEFINING THE ELDERLY

At one time, it was relatively easy to define elderliness. Most people worked until they reached age 65 and then they retired, subsisting on a pension and social security benefits. Federal legislation eventually lowered the threshold for Medicaid and Medicare to 62 years of age. Suddenly, more and more pension plans opened their retirement windows to younger participants. Companies found themselves in jeopardy of "graying." In order to provide promotional opportunities for younger workers and to restructure their workforce, some businesses began offering special incentives for early retirement packages. They attempted to lure younger persons, who were in the mid- to late-fifties, into retirement. As you can see, gauging elderliness in terms of retirement eligibility soon lost any intrinsic meaning.

*Gerontologists*, people who study the aging process, tend to be critical of efforts to link old age to chronological years of life. Much to their dismay, many researchers quickly adopted calendar age as a convenient reference point (Schaie, 1988). This simple definition overlooked the complexity of the aging process. As Maddox and Wiley (1976: 9) explain: "aging connotes three distinct phenomena: the biological capacity for survival, the psychological capacity for adaptation, and the sociological capacity for the fulfillment of social roles."

Victimologists began to realize that lumping all people over the age of 65 into a single category did not produce a homogeneous group (Fattah and Sacco, 1989). There were significant variations that were being masked by this designation. As a result, efforts were made to expand the senior citizen category. Some researchers separated "early old age" (64-74) from "advanced old age" (75+). Other schemes recognized that there were important differences between the "old," the "very old" and those over 85—the "old old" (Fattah and Sacco, 1989). The reader should be sensitive to this concern and be aware that classifying the elderly into a single group can do more disservice than good.

## CRIMINAL VICTIMIZATION OF THE ELDERLY

As mentioned in Chapter 2, one data source that victimologists rely upon for crime information is the FBI's annual Uniform Crime Reports (UCR). Unfortunately for our purposes, there are very few details about victims given in those reports. Hence, one needs to turn to the National Crime Victimization Survey (NCVS) for materials regarding criminal victimization of the elderly.

While crime pervades much of modern society, it does not reach all social groups equally. In terms of demographic characteristics, the most victimized people are blacks, males, people from the lower economic strata and the young. The elderly, in contrast, experience relatively low levels of victimization.

An inspection of the NCVS data contained in Figure 8.1 bears out this point. Victimization levels are highest among the youngest age categories and consistently decline with each successive age group. While persons age 65 and over make up 14.6 percent of the population age 12 and over, they experience only 2.2 percent of the victimizations reported to the interviewers. Similarly, those age 50-64 comprise 16 percent of the population but report only 5 percent of the total victimizations. Conversely, respondents age 12-19 make up roughly 14 percent of the population but experience almost one-third of the victimizations. These data show a clear negative linear relationship between victimization and age. Thus, one could conclude that the overall objective odds of falling prey to the criminal element are very small for senior citizens.

**FIGURE 8.1**
**National Victimization Rates by Type of Crime and Age of Victims, NCVS, 1994**

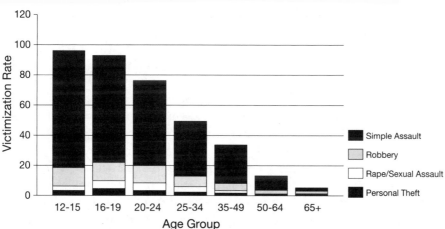

Source: Perkins, C. and P. Klaus (1996). *Bureau of Justice Statistics Bulletin: National Crime Victimization Survey: Criminal Victimization, 1994.* Washington, DC: U.S. Government Printing Office, p. 4.

Further analyses of these victimization data do show some variations. For example, one can divide the age category of the elderly into individuals between 65 and 74 years of age versus those persons who are 75 and older. The 75+ group displays even lower victimization rates than their counterparts in the 65-74 range. In every age group, males have higher victimization rates than do females. Similarly, black elderly are more victimized than are white elderly, while black-white differentials are minimal for those age 16-49. Thus, while one can characterize the elderly in general as having low victimization rates, some elderly citizens are more vulnerable than others.

# FEAR OF CRIME

While the actual victimization experience directly impacts a finite number of people, a much larger portion expresses a genuine fear of becoming crime victims. *Fear of crime* consists of two parts: (1) the actual odds of being victimized, and (2) the subjective or perceived risk of victimization.

Fear of crime has soared over the past 30 years (Erskine, 1974; Hindelang, 1975; Skogan and Maxfield, 1981; Toseland, 1982). Interestingly, the level of fear consistently outdistances both official and victimization measures of actual crime. For example, Skogan and Maxfield (1981) note that while almost one-half of all Americans fear crime, official records show only about 6 percent of the population become actual crime victims.

Not surprisingly, surveys find that fear is not constant across demographic groups. In general, fear is highest among urban dwellers, females, blacks, the poor and the elderly (Baumer, 1985; Clemente and Kleiman, 1977; Erskine, 1974; Gomme, 1986; Greenberg et al., 1985; Hindelang et al., 1978; Lab, 1990; Riger et al., 1978; Skogan and Maxfield, 1981; Smith and Lab, 1991).

Of all the age groups in society, the elderly are the least likely to become crime victims. This relatively small number of actual victims would, in itself, elicit very little interest from researchers. However, senior citizens readily vocalize a tremendous concern about their fear of crime. This paradoxical discrepancy between the objective level of victimization and the subjective perception about the odds of becoming a victim has attracted prolonged debate in the research community.

This gap between elderly victimization and their fear of crime suggests that interest in these issues is disproportionate to the size of the problem. Consequently, a number of questions arise at this point. First, why is there such interest in these problems? Second, how do we explain the discrepancy between the perceived level of fear and the actual risks of becoming a crime victim? Third, are there reasons for this high fear, despite lower victimization levels?

## Explaining the Fear-Crime Paradox

One would expect that because crime against the elderly is relatively low, there should be a corresponding reduced fear of crime for that group. When the level of fear is incongruent with the supposed cause of fear (crime in this case), it becomes necessary to find alternative explanations for that fear. Attempts to explain the fear-crime differential typically fall into three related discussions. Those deal with the way fear is measured, and the issues of differences in both risk and vulnerability (either real or perceived) among the elderly.

## *Measuring Fear*

No universally accepted definition of fear has emerged in the literature. Consequently, measures of fear vary by the definition used by different researchers. Ferraro (1995) provides one of the most recognized definitions. He defines fear as "an emotional response of dread or anxiety to crime or symbols that a person associates with crime" (p. 8). The key to this definition is the required *emotional response* from the victim. As a result, fear can be elicited by different events or situations depending on what evokes emotions in varied individuals. The elderly, therefore, may respond as being fearful in situations that do not evoke the same response in younger respondents.

Ferraro (1995) points out that fear measures often tap more than emotions. For example, many studies ask respondents to rate their assessment of safety in a specific neighborhood or area, or to provide an opinion on whether crime is increasing or decreasing over a period of time. In both of these cases, the research is tapping more of a value judgment or a person's general knowledge than any real emotional reaction to crime. The emotional component is more directly tested in surveys that ask about how much respondents *worry* about being victimized (Ferraro, 1995; Ferraro and LaGrange, 1988). Unfortunately, many studies claiming great fear of crime rely on questions that do not assess the emotional state of the victim. One example of those questions is the key query from the NCVS which asks "How safe do you feel or would you feel being out alone in your neighborhood at night?" While bordering on an emotional response, the question is so broad and hypothetical that it would not fit Ferraro's definition.

Does this mean that the fear data are meaningless? Is there nothing to be gained from surveys purporting to measure fear? Does this mean that the elderly really are not fearful? In each case, the answer is no. While no definitive statement can be made about fear, what the varying measures do offer is some insight into the related issues of risk and vulnerability, at least as they are perceived by the elderly. *Risk* typically refers to the chances of becoming a victim of crime, while *vulnerability* deals more with the susceptibility to crime and the harm that accompanies victimization. In some instances, the same factors enhance both risk and vulnerability. For the elderly, there are particular risk and vulnerability factors that may help explain their inordinate fear of crime. It is to these discussions that we now turn.

## *Risk*

Possible risk factors for the elderly include their economic resources, where they live, whether they live alone and their diminished physical abilities. The economic status of an elderly person can have a great impact on other facets of life. In general, the income of elderly families is roughly two-thirds lower than nonelderly families, with a median income of under $23,000 per year (U.S. Senate, 1991). More than one-fourth of persons over 65 years of age have an income that is at or below 150 percent of the poverty level. For a single individual, this threshold would be roughly $9,000 per year.

Dour economic conditions often dictate that many elderly live in older, deteriorating neighborhoods, in areas that are more ethnically diverse due to turnover of older homes to younger tenants, and in neighborhoods with more transient populations. These types of neighborhoods are often very crime-prone. They frequently attract deviants as residents and draw outsiders who commit crime. The prevalence of crime in these areas, whether directed against the elderly or not, exacerbates feelings of fear and loss of safety among the aged (McCoy et al., 1996).

Additionally, many senior citizens lack financial reserves and live in homes needing repairs. To the extent that confidence games play a role in the level of crime, older people living in run-down housing may respond more favorably to offers of seemingly "bargain" repairs. Economic factors also may force the elderly to walk or to use public transportation, which may increase both real and perceived risks of victimization.

The fact that many elderly live alone also increases risk by making them more suitable crime targets. One-third of all older Americans reside by themselves, with 40 percent of the women over the age of 65 living alone (U.S. Senate, 1991). Dealing with a single individual lessens both resistance and chances of identification of intruders. Hindelang and associates (1978) show a relationship between living alone and victimization. Similarly, Bachman (1992) reports that divorced or separated elderly persons are victimized more often than are married elderly.

The generally diminished physical abilities of the elderly also contribute to actual and perceived risk. If the offender is a young male, an elderly victim is at a clear physical disadvantage. More than one-half of the violent crime victims age 65 and older report that their assailant was under 30 years old; 87 percent of the offenders were strangers (U.S. Department of Justice, 1992). Both the age differential and the anonymity of offenders serve to enhance the fears of the elderly.

Going beyond simply identifying potential risk factors, Stafford and Galle (1984) have considered exposure to risk in assessing fear of crime. They argue that the elderly are overly victimized given their exposure to risk. Stafford and Galle (1984) claim that by adjusting the level of fear in terms of the degree to which different demographic groups are exposed to victimization opportunities, the discrepancy between fear and victimization greatly diminishes. In their study, the elderly still express higher levels of fear than expected, but not to the great extent found in other studies. Ward et al. (1986) present similar evidence that fear is related to the differential risk introduced by varying environmental situations. Warr (1984), however, cautions that fear cannot be totally explained by differences in risk. Age continues to play a role in the level of fear even after accommodations are made for differential risk.

## *Vulnerability*

Because risk alone does not completely explain the level of fear among the elderly, vulnerability helps round out the picture. Vulnerability refers to the ease of being victimized and the impact the crime has upon the victim. The assumption is that people who would suffer the greatest pain or loss from a victimization will be the most fearful. For the elderly, vulnerability is a key concern. Among the many factors that increase elder vulnerability are physical attributes, financial concerns and social connections.

Declining physical strength and increasing health problems contribute much to a sense of vulnerability. While more than two-thirds of the elderly feel they are in good health, they suffer from more chronic ailments than any other age group (U.S. Senate, 1991). Senior citizens are more susceptible to arthritis, hypertension, sight and hearing impairments, heart disease and an overall decreased mobility. Older people also visit physicians more often, are disproportionately represented among the hospitalized and account for more than one-third of the health care expenditures in the United States (U.S. Senate, 1991).

These medical facts suggest that the elderly are not as capable as younger persons of warding off physical attacks, they are likely to be more prone to injury and they are in need of more medical assistance than other segments of the population. Data from victim surveys support this point. For example, the likelihood of injury and medical attention because of a crime increases with victim age (Bachman, 1992; Cook et al., 1978; Hochstedler, 1981; Killias, 1990; Liang and Sengstock, 1983; U.S. Department of Justice, 1992). It is not unusual for crime-related injuries to aggravate preexisting health problems (Burt and Katz, 1985).

Economic liability often accompanies criminal victimization. The elderly have reduced incomes. Much of that money is derived from fixed sources, such as social security, retirement funds and investments (U.S. Senate, 1991). Any loss, no matter how small, can be burdensome to the elderly. Indeed, victimization data reveal that after adjusting for income and insurance, the elderly sustain greater economic losses than any other age group (Cook et al., 1978; Cook et al., 1981). Many elderly cannot afford more medical expenses, insurance premiums and property replacement costs. In addition, elder victimization affects the rest of society. Public funds, primarily in the form of Medicare and Medicaid, cover more than 60 percent of the elderly's health expenditures (U.S. Senate, 1991).

Besides such tangible factors as physical harm and economic losses, social isolation can compound the impact of victimization. As we have discussed elsewhere in this text, social support is an important part of coping with the aftermath of crime. This is no less true for the elderly. Older victims who suffer physical injury may need assistance with normal daily activities during their recuperation. They also may need help repairing damaged property, shopping for replacement goods or straightening up the mess left by intruders. Sometimes victims blame themselves for the crime. Social support is important for placing the event in its proper perspective and alleviating any guilt feelings. The presence of a support network also can help the victim realize that the world is not all bad, and that the victimization should not be the central focus of what to expect in the future.

Many elderly do not have access to a suitable support system. A number of factors contribute to the social isolation of the elderly. First, the transience of today's society means that the families of the elderly are scattered around the country, often due to employment requirements. Second, old age often brings the death of one's spouse and friends, which results in living alone. Third, due to economics, many elderly live in transient and ethnically diverse neighborhoods. Any one, or a combination, of these factors can make a person feel lonely and isolated. A victimization experience can further fuel these feelings. Social isolation, therefore, intensifies the physical and economic impacts by reducing one's sense of well-being.

## ELDER ABUSE AND NEGLECT

Like victimology in general, it is only recently that abuse and neglect of the elderly has surfaced as a topic worthy of study. Some observers credit Steinmetz (1978b) with introducing the idea of *elder abuse* into contemporary focus. This is not to say that maltreatment of the elderly did not exist prior to this time. There have always been tensions between the young and the old that have resulted in various forms of mistreatment.

An examination of pre-modern Western society shows that disagreements over property rights resulted in physical conflict, including death, between parents and their offspring. Pre-industrial American parents often used economic power to control their adult children, leading to strained family relationships (Steinmetz, 1988). Due to this economic bondage, children often despised and isolated their parents, waiting until such a time that they could rid themselves of the parent. The idea that the young have always venerated their elders down through the ages is a myth.

Family patterns changed during the Industrial Revolution (Stearns, 1986). There were fewer households mixing different generations under the same roof. Retirement support systems made their debut, reducing the financial dependency of the older generation on younger family members. Better economic situations also made medical care more accessible. A new industry of caregivers, such as geriatric nurses and social workers, made it possible for people outside the immediate family to provide suitable alternative living arrangements. All these factors spelled a period of relative calm between parents and their grown children. More than likely, it is this ebb that accounted for the lack of attention paid to abuse and neglect of the aged.

## The Re-Emergence of Interest in Elder Abuse

### Demographic Change

Renewed interest in elder abuse and neglect stems from several factors. Perhaps one major reason for the keen interest in elder affairs stems from the graying of the American population. As Table 8.1 shows, there has been a dramatic surge in the number of elderly people in this country since 1900. Experts project that this trend should continue well into the twenty-first century. For instance, in 1900 less than 10 percent of the United States population were 55 years of age or older. By 1990, this group accounted for 21 percent of the population. A further look at Table 8.1 reveals that the size of the population segment exceeding 65 years of age has increased more than threefold since 1900. This cluster is expected to increase by yet another 50 percent over the next 30 years.

**TABLE 8.1**
**Actual and Projected Growth in the Elderly U.S. Population (percent of population)**

| Year | 55-64 | 65-74 | 75-84 | 85+ | Total 65+ |
|---|---|---|---|---|---|
| 1900 | 5.3 | 2.9 | 1.0 | .2 | 4.0 |
| 1950 | 8.8 | 5.6 | 2.2 | .4 | 8.1 |
| 1980 | 9.6 | 6.9 | 3.4 | 1.0 | 11.3 |
| 1990 | 8.5 | 7.3 | 4.0 | 1.3 | 12.6 |
| 2000 | 9.0 | 6.8 | 4.5 | 1.7 | 13.0 |
| 2020 | 14.0 | 10.5 | 4.9 | 2.3 | 17.7 |

Source: U.S. Senate, Special Committee on Aging (1991). *Aging America: Trends and Projections*. Washington, DC: Department of Health and Human Services.

This demographic change is due, in large part, to medical advances that have increased the life expectancy of both men and women. *Life expectancy* refers to the number of years that the average person should live. The life expectancy for a man born in 1900 was 46.3 years; it was 48.3 years for a woman. These numbers soared to 72.1 and 79.0 years, respectively, in 1990. The forecast is that these figures will continue to rise until they peak at 74.9 and 81.8 years, respectively, by the year 2020 (U.S. Senate, 1991). This steady increase in life expectancies suggests that, despite relatively lower odds of victimization, the absolute number of elderly crime victims will continue to grow. This absolute increase in the number of cases will make this problem more noticeable than ever before.

## New Responsibilities

Enhancing the chances of elder abuse and/or neglect in the face of increasing numbers of elderly are stress issues, such as increased stress for caregivers—especially of the very old—as well as increased work-place stress that may contribute to general levels of familial conflict. Adding to stress levels are economic issues that may affect the incidence of elder abuse. The resources of the elderly have decreased, due mainly to the failure of retirement plans and the increasing costs of medical care. In addition, the increasing economic instability of society as a whole has resulted in fewer families being able to provide financial assistance to their elderly relatives. This economic erosion has forced more families to cohabit across generations, which may also serve to raise the potential for intrafamilial conflict.

## Vicarious Victimization

A third possible explanation for the sustained interest in crime against the elderly stems from the influence of the mass media. Victimologists refer to this phenomenon as *vicarious victimization*. People who have had no actual victimization experiences themselves become acutely aware of others who were preyed upon by criminals. The receiver absorbs this information and speculates that "it could have happened to me." This indirect attribution heightens one's fearfulness, even though the actual odds of victimization may be remote.

Patterns of television viewing and newspaper consumption, both of which portray a great deal of sensationalistic reports, contribute to fear of crime. As we have developed into a society attuned to the "crime of the week," victimization of the elderly has emerged as an issue that commands media attention. A news story might cover the situation of an elderly person found dead in a stifling hot home. While proximately due to heat prostration, the ultimate cause of the death is often attributed to the fact that the individual kept the house locked up tight because of a fear of crime.

Similarly, different media routinely present stories or issue warnings about con artists operating scams on area residents, particularly the elderly. While some writers claim that fraud and cons are prevalent against the elderly (Geis, 1977; Levin, 1993; McGhee, 1983; Pepper, 1983), there is little evidence to support these claims. Despite the relative rarity of these crimes, the prominence they receive in the media propels them into the consciousness of the general public.

## Political Action

Another factor for the growth in visibility of elder issues is political astuteness. Given their numbers, the elderly form a considerable voting constituency. Age-based advocacy groups, such as the American Association of Retired Persons (AARP) and other similar organizations, have the resources and savvy to lobby elected officials. One recent innovation, the Silver Haired Legislature, places these efforts well within the political mainstream.

Several states have instituted the idea of a Silver Haired Legislature. The *Silver Haired Legislature* is a mock legislative assembly consisting of elderly persons. These so-called representatives convene periodic meetings to discuss legislative remedies to issues confronting the elderly. The Florida chapter meets annually in the state capital, holds a variety of committee hearings, debates new proposals and eventually passes "bills" aimed at resolving these matters. The outcomes of the Florida mock assembly are conveyed to the governor, cabinet members and state legislators. According to one evaluation, a number of bills supported by the Florida Silver Haired Legislature have picked up sponsors from state politicians and, eventually, have made their way into state statutes (Matura, 1982).

Other political developments, such as statewide task forces, have brought considerable attention to the elderly. The Florida Attorney General, for example, sponsors such endeavors from time to time. An abbreviated version of some recommendations from the Florida Task Force on Crimes and the Elderly appears in Figure 8.2 to give the reader an idea of what these bodies do.

## Social Consciousness

A final reason for increased attention to elder abuse and neglect may be the general trend to take up the causes of oppressed and/or underprivileged segments of society. In this sense, interest in elder abuse is a logical extension of the concern over women's and children's issues.

**FIGURE 8.2**
**Selected Recommendations from the Florida Attorney General's Task Force on Crimes and the Elderly**

- A mandatory/minimum prison sentence of three years be established for a person convicted of aggravated assault or battery upon a person 60 years or older.

- Quite often, private businesses, such as home security systems, prey upon the frailties and weaknesses of recently traumatized victims of crimes by gaining their names and addresses via the public records such as police and accident reports. . . . This bill proposal has been affectionately referred to as the "vulture amendment." [It would] make it unlawful to obtain information of a reported crime or accident in order to solicit for the purposes of financial gain.

- Amend Chapter 92 of the Florida Statutes in order to provide for the videotaping of testimony and the perpetuation of testimony for those suffering the infirmities of aging or mental or physical handicaps which would tend to limit their abilities as witnesses, cause undue hardships, or the inability to proceed with court cases due to the death or permanent incapacitation of the victim.

- That home service providers and the staffs of nursing homes, adult congregate living facilities, and adult day care centers are required to conduct background criminal investigations and abuse registry checks upon all of their employees.

- That procedures governing medical examiners, autopsies and unattended deaths be changed statewide to provide for the notification of appropriate law enforcement and medical examiner agencies when deaths occur in nursing homes or adult congregate living facilities, unless a physician is in actual attendance.

Source: Office of the Florida Attorney General (1989). *Attorney General's Task Force on Crimes and the Elderly*. Tallahassee, FL: State of Florida.

## Defining the Problem

While many commentators point to elder abuse and neglect as a problem, there is little agreement on exactly what constitutes abuse and neglect. A major problem in studying elder abuse is the lack of a clear definition. One of the earliest definitions outlined abuse as:

> the willful infliction of physical pain, injury or debilitating mental anguish, unreasonable confinement or deprivation by a caretaker of services which are necessary to the maintenance of mental and physical health (O'Malley et al., 1979).

A number of objections have risen concerning this type of definition (Hudson, 1989). First, it fails to distinguish abuse from neglect. As we explained in the chapter on child maltreatment, many researchers view abuse as a more active form and neglect as a more passive form of mistreatment. Second, the preceding definition requires the perpetrator to act with "intent." It ignores the possibility of abuse or neglect that is unintentional, yet still problematic, for the victim. Third, there is an assumption that the victim depends upon the perpetrator for physical or mental care. One might construe this feature as a legal requirement to provide care before an act is considered abuse. It also ignores the possibility that a perpetrator may be dependent on the victim and commits abusive acts as a means of exerting power.

Definitions of abuse and/or neglect often include a wide range of diverse items, with varying degrees of agreement among users. Even the term "physical abuse" can mean different things to different people. Few would disagree that physical attacks against the elderly represent abuse, particularly when perpetrated by someone who is responsible for the victim's well-being. However, some consider the deliberate withholding of care as physical abuse, while others might call the same act "neglect" (Wolf and Pillemer, 1989). Even when researchers do separate abuse from neglect, they may disagree on the contents of each (Galbraith, 1989). This definitional ambiguity hampers discussion of the issues and the comparison of findings from one study to the next.

Rather than attempt to identify a single definition of abuse and neglect, most writers have gravitated toward a discussion of different types of abuse and/or neglect. Giordano and Giordano (1984), for example, include bodily harm, sexual assault and restriction of movement under the rubric of physical abuse. Negligence, in their scheme, entails carelessness or the failure of a caretaker to fulfill a duty. Psychological abuse subsumes any threats, fear and/or isolation of the elderly. Giordano and Giordano (1984) also include provisions for financial exploitation, violation of rights guaranteed to all citizens, and self-neglect, which consists of any harm that arises from a failure to care for one's own needs.

Figure 8.3 contains a breakdown of various forms of elder abuse and neglect. Wolf and Pillemer (1989) present these five categories as fairly representative of those found in past research and various state laws. In their categorization, the distinction between abuse and neglect relies mainly on whether the offender is a caretaker of the victim. The failure of a caretaker to fulfill that role generally results in a determination that neglect, either active or passive, is present. Abuse, on the other hand, does not rest on an obligation to provide care. That is, anyone can commit an abusive act. One can divide abuse further into categories of physical, psychological and material misconduct.

**FIGURE 8.3**
**Forms of Elder Abuse and Neglect**

**Physical Abuse**

actual physical harm or coercion of the victim, ranging from slapping to sexual molestation to assault with a weapon

**Psychological Abuse**

anything that causes mental anguish to the victim, including intimidation, threats, isolation, and name calling

**Material Abuse**

exploitation, use or theft of money or property of the victim, through force or deception

**Active Neglect**

a conscious and intentional decision not to fulfill a caretaking obligation, such as denying food, abandonment, failing to provide adequate health care or housing, etc.

**Passive Neglect**

an unconscious or unintentional failure to provide caretaking obligations due to factors such as an inability to provide the care or lack of knowledge

Source: Wolf, R.S. and K.A. Pillemer (1989). *Helping Elderly Victims: The Reality of Elder Abuse.* New York: Columbia University Press.

Instead of compiling a long list of different kinds of abuse or neglect, Hudson (1989) turns to what he considers critical attributes of the concepts. This strategy allows one to distinguish related ideas from one another by highlighting important elements and identifying key commonalities found in many definitions or typologies. Hudson's definition of elder abuse, with critical attributes identified by number, follows:

(1) destructive behavior through the use of physical or psychological force

(2) with improper or indecent use of an elderly's person or property

(3) resulting in harmful physical, psychological, economic and/or social effects

(4) and unnecessary suffering in the elderly.

Using a similar approach, Hudson casts *elder neglect* in terms of:

(1) carelessness in behaviors (commission)

(2) or omission of behaviors

(3) which are reasonably warranted by the elderly's unmet basic needs

(4) and are implicit or explicit in the obligation of the relationship

(5) and which result in unnecessary suffering

(6) as demonstrated by harmful physical, psychological, financial and/or social effects in the elderly.

Today, most researchers rely on categorizations of abuse and neglect rather than viewing them as a single concept. However, these categorizations do not resolve all definitional problems. Using the categories in Figure 8.3 as an example, one can find several apparent problems. First, the components of a caretaking "obligation" are not always clear. Who decides an individual's obligation? What actions are required, as opposed to being simply "nice to do"? Second, some actions may cause more than one type of maltreatment. For example, physically striking an individual can engender fear and intimidation (i.e., psychological abuse) as well as physical abuse. Similarly, material abuse deprives the victim of his or her property and may also result in an inability to provide needed care (i.e., neglect). Third, it is easy to argue that the notion of self-neglect does not fall readily into the neglect categories. Finally, since much research is based on official records of various government and social service agencies, the categories may not correspond to the legal classifications used to define the problem at that location.

Some of these same concerns also apply to the more theoretical definitions outlined by Hudson (1989). It is apparent that definitional problems are an unresolved issue in the study of elder abuse. As a result, we will remind the reader of these issues whenever they affect issues discussed in the chapter.

## THE INCIDENCE OF ELDER MALTREATMENT

Identifying just how much maltreatment of the elderly takes place is not an easy undertaking. The U.S. House Select Committee on Aging (1981) claimed that roughly one million members of the senior population suffer instances of abuse every year. Projections from other studies reveal that this figure is not far-fetched (Pillemer and Finkelhor, 1988; Tatara, 1990), although the actual figure may extend as high as 2.5 million victims (Hudson, 1988). Tatara (1993) reports that Adult Protective Service (APS) agencies from across the United States documented 227,000 cases of abuse and neglect in 1991. While this number is small compared to other figures, it is important to note that these instances reflect only those cases reported to an official government agency. In relation to the earlier figures, official data appear to include a small minority of all cases. Perhaps of greater importance in the APS figures is the finding that official reports of elder abuse have been increasing in recent years (Tatara, 1993).

Besides looking at simple raw numbers, many reports offer estimates of the prevalence of abuse in the elderly population. Most estimates place the number of victims somewhere around 5 percent of the aged population, although some researchers posit levels as high as 10 percent (Giordano and Giordano, 1984). Other studies using small sample sizes from specific locations (Block and Sinnott, 1979; Gioglio and Blakemore, 1983) and from other countries (Schlesinger and Schlesinger, 1988) report victimization rates hovering around 2 to 4 percent of the elderly population.

Attempts to identify the relative level of different kinds of abuse have not been altogether effective. Many of these efforts are plagued by small sample sizes and local databases, precluding generalization. In general, it appears that the most prevalent forms of elder maltreatment are self-neglect (Sprey and Matthews, 1989) and financial abuse (Shell, 1982), with physical abuse being the least common. Data from APS agencies support this finding. According to 1991 data, almost one-half of the cases reported to APS were unsubstantiated and, of those that were, 51 percent involved self-neglect. In cases of abuse by others, only 19 percent involved physical abuse, while almost one-half were neglect situations (Tatara, 1993).

While there may seem to be some consistency across studies in the reported levels of elder abuse, there are many factors that one should keep in mind when considering the extent of maltreatment. Many social service providers and researchers claim that these estimates grossly underreport the actual level of maltreatment. The greatest difficulty with these estimates is that most are based on official statistics.

As you may recall from Chapter 2, official statistics require notification by the victim or someone else. Elder victims may be reluctant to contact the authorities for many reasons. First, the perpetrators of elder abuse often are family members. Under these conditions, the victim may regard the situation as a private matter not meant for outside viewing. The victim, therefore, may be unwilling to notify anyone. Second, the elderly victim, like a child, may depend upon the abuser for daily care and support. In this situation, making an allegation of maltreatment may not only eliminate the abuse, but also the needed care. Third, the elderly individual may feel a sense of shame for allowing himself or herself to be abused. Fourth, the victim may think that he or she somehow contributed to the situation and, therefore, is at fault. Fifth, victims may not recognize the abuse as such or, as often happens in financial theft, may not be aware of what has transpired. Finally, the victim may simply feel compassion for the abusive relative and refrain from contacting the authorities out of a sense of love and concern for the perpetrator. Given these possible influences on reporting behavior, it is safe to conclude that reported estimates mark the lower boundaries of elder abuse and neglect.

## SOME CHARACTERISTICS OF VICTIMS AND OFFENDERS

In addition to looking at the amount of elder maltreatment cases, researchers have tried to learn more about these situations. Some of the more meaningful variables they have examined include the age and sex of the victim, the relationship between the victim and offender, and age and sex of the offender.

Most instigators of abusive or neglectful conditions are related to the victim (O'Malley et al., 1979; Pillemer and Finkelhor, 1988; Quinn and Tomita, 1986; Schlesinger, 1988; Wolf and Pillemer, 1989). Perhaps even more distressing is that the typical violator is not a distant relative or someone who lives outside the household. Instead, the offender usually stays with the victim and is typically a son, daughter or spouse of the victim (O'Malley et al., 1979; Sprey and Matthews, 1989; Wolf and Pillemer, 1989).

Studies portray the typical victim as female and over 75 years old (Pillemer and Finkelhor, 1988; Quinn and Tomita, 1986; Shell, 1982; Steinmetz, 1988; Tatara, 1993; Wolf and Pillemer, 1989). In terms of race, whites are more likely to be victimized than are blacks (Cazenave and Straus, 1979; Wolf and Pillemer, 1989). However, a word of caution is needed here. Most studies of elder maltreatment are based on such small sample sizes that only a handful of minority cases appear in the analysis. This shortcoming makes it difficult to draw any firm or definitive conclusions about the role of race (Griffin and Williams, 1992).

The usual perpetrators of elder abuse and neglect are males (Schlesinger, 1988; Shell, 1982; Wolf and Pillemer, 1989). In many instances, the offender is also an elderly person (Pillemer and Finkelhor, 1988; Steinmetz, 1988; Wolf and Pillemer, 1989). This age factor is self-explanatory in the case of spouses. For offenders who are sons or daughters, however, the elderly status of the offender is not as readily apparent. In these cases, victims are often very old (over 75), with offenders being sons or daughters in their fifties or sixties.

## INSTITUTIONAL ABUSE

The living situation of the victim plays an important role in determining possible correlates of elder abuse and neglect. While many think that strangers commit most elder abuse and that they do so in impersonal institutional surroundings, such is not the case. Indeed, most senior citizens do not even live in institutions. Only about 4 percent of the elderly reside in foster homes or other institutional settings (Administration on Aging, 1997). Consequently, few elders are at risk of being mistreated in these facilities. These small numbers also mean that relatively little research has been directed at the issue of institutional abuse.

This does not mean that elder abuse is not a problem in those settings. While the relative number of elderly residents in institutions is small, 7 percent of the nursing homes in this country were cited for abuse or neglect in 1980 (Doty and Sullivan, 1983). Survey data portray an even greater problem. McDonald (1996) notes that 36 percent of nurses and nursing home aides report having seen at least one act of physical abuse over the course of a year. The most common form of abuse is the use of excessive restraints. Further, more than 80 percent admit to committing psychological abuse, typically yelling at the patient (McDonald, 1996). Other forms of institutional abuse involve theft, fraudulent medical billings, unnecessary physical or chemical restraint, and social isolation.

What factors contribute to abuse in settings that, at least nominally, exist to care for the well-being of the elderly? Pillemer (1988) offers a model containing four interrelated sets of factors. The first of these are *exogenous factors,* which reflect the influence of the larger community on institutional operations. For example, a relatively small number of nursing homes and available beds means that clients have few choices and poor-quality facilities will still be in demand. Similarly, low unemployment in the community may result in fewer qualified workers available for employment in these settings.

The nursing home environment is a second source from which abuse may arise. Institutions that have a custodial orientation and fail to emphasize resident needs will tend to have greater levels of abuse. Similarly, poor supervision, low staff-to-patient ratios, lower pay and high staff turnover can all contribute to less concern for the elderly patient (Pillemer, 1988). A third area of potential concern involves staff characteristics. Pillemer (1988) notes that younger staff members and those with less education tend to show less concern for the elderly. These individuals take a more custodial view toward their duties. Workers who experience higher levels of stress and burnout also contribute to the incidence of abuse.

The final category of factors reflects patient characteristics (Pillemer, 1988). Elderly patients who are in poor health and have poor (or deteriorating) social abilities pose additional challenges and place greater demands on institutional staff. In Ohio, an estimated 600,000 nursing home residents suffer from some form of dementia, making the patient more resistant to care (Ohio State Medical Association, 1994). Consequently, some staff may respond in inappropriate ways. A patient who tends to wander the halls, for example, may be subjected to bed restraints as a means of controlling the behavior. Exacerbating the incidence of abuse may be the social isolation of an elderly person (Pillemer, 1988). The absence of visitors means that abuse and neglect can take place with little chance of discovery.

Most jurisdictions have passed legislation specifically to address the incidence of institutional abuse and neglect. Ohio, for example, passed the Patient Abuse/Neglect Law in 1986. Under this statute, "any person who owns, operates, administers or who is an agent or employee of a care facility in the state shall not abuse or neglect a resident of that facility" (Ohio State Medical Association, 1994). The onus for investigating and enforcing criminal violations of this law falls on the state attorney general, not local law enforcement. Claims for civil liability can be handled at either the state or local level. At the federal level, the 1987 Nursing Home Reform Act outlines various forms of prohibited activity, including abuse, neglect and the unwarranted use of restraints.

## THEORIES OF ELDER ABUSE AND NEGLECT

What causes elder maltreatment? Why does it occur? There are no simple answers to these questions. Researchers have looked at a variety of explanations. Generally speaking, these different approaches fit into five basic groups or categories, based on: (1) intraindividual sources, (2) situational aspects, (3) symbolic interactionism, (4) social exchange, and (5) social attitudes. While some observers might propose alternative groupings, this arrangement is a convenient way to explore the more popular perspectives.

### Intraindividual Explanations

Intraindividual theories reflect the belief that abusers suffer from some underlying pathological condition. In essence, there is something wrong with the perpetrator that forces him or her to act abusively. Some distinctive factors that fall into this category are drug and alcohol dependence, mental illness or retardation, intergenerational causes of behavior and an inability to deal with changing life expectations.

There is considerable support for thinking that abuse stems from intraindividual sources. Perpetrators of physical abuse often have mental and emotional problems, and are more likely to have histories involving psychiatric hospitalization (Wolf and Pillemer, 1989). A heavy reliance upon alcohol or drug use is also a common characteristic among offenders (Anetzberger et al., 1994; Champlin, 1986; O'Malley et al., 1983; Quinn and Tomita, 1986). Fattah and Sacco (1989) point out that substance abuse can impact maltreatment in two ways. In addition to reducing inhibitions against violence or theft, it may limit the caretaker's ability to care properly for the victim. One can make similar claims for the adverse impact of mental illness.

The idea of intergenerational transmission of violence has a fair share of adherents. The notion that parents instill an acceptance of violence in their offspring has appeared in the literature on child abuse and spouse abuse. Applying that same argument to elder abuse and neglect is a logical extension. Indeed, elder abuse researchers rely on child abuse and spouse abuse research to support their arguments (see Quinn and Tomita, 1986). The main difference appears in the outlet for the aggression. Rather than an abused child growing up and abusing his or her child, the abused child grows up and retaliates against the parent who committed the initial abuse (Pillemer, 1986). However, this literature suffers from serious design flaws and weak empirical support. More research needs to be undertaken before reaching a verdict as to whether intergenerational transmission is a reasonable explanation.

## Situational Aspects

Situational explanations of elder abuse and neglect reflect an array of factors that deal with the social, environmental and economic situation of the victim and perpetrator. Some common factors include dependence, stress and social isolation. The potential influence of each is discussed in turn.

Dependency on other people for daily needs and special assistance often emerges as a major cause of maltreatment. Elder persons may become victims because they rely so heavily upon the caregiver for subsistence. In reality, however, abusers tend to be economically dependent upon their victims (Anetzberger, 1989; O'Malley et al., 1983; Wolf and Pillemer, 1989). It appears that maltreatment is most likely to occur when the caregiver harbors a great deal of resentment toward the older person in his or her guardianship.

Some observers link stress as a leading cause of abuse and neglect (Phillips, 1986). Here the perpetrator strikes out at the individual or situation that he or she perceives as causing tension. Some of the more significant stressors include the intensity or burden of caring for another person (O'Malley et al., 1983; Quinn, 1990; Quinn and Tomita, 1986; Schlesinger, 1988; Steinmetz, 1983; Steinmetz, 1988), the economic strain that accompanies extended care (Champlin, 1986; O'Malley et al., 1983; Shell, 1982; Wolf and Pillemer, 1989), insufficient caregiver training (Steinmetz, 1988) and a lack of privacy between cohabiting adults (Anetzberger, 1989; Steinmetz, 1988). Steinmetz (1988) points out that the elderly sometimes feel they must resort to invading privacy, crying, yelling or using guilt and other maneuvers to get what they want from their caregivers. A continued reliance upon these tactics can lead to tension (which the abuser may try to resolve by retaliating against the older person).

Another situational factor that contributes to elder maltreatment is the social isolation experienced by the participating parties. Lack of family support can exacerbate both dependency and stress (Anetzberger, 1989; Steinmetz, 1983; Steinmetz, 1988). For example, an offspring who cares for a parent may resent the fact that other siblings are not providing similar assistance. Indeed, studies have found that abusive situations often involve frustrated caregivers with limited support systems at their disposal (Kosberg, 1988; Pillemer, 1986; Quinn and Tomita, 1986; Wolf and Pillemer, 1989). Taken together, dependence, stress, social isolation and other situational factors can precipitate abuse and neglect as well as contribute to other causes of maltreatment.

## Symbolic Interactionism

The *symbolic interactionism* approach to explaining elder abuse acknowledges that individual roles change over time. Participants alter their expectations and reactions according to the new way in which they see and interpret the changing "reality." In essence, reality is the result of how people interpret what is going on around them and react to their surroundings.

Elder abuse signifies a dramatic *role reversal* for both the parent and the child. At an earlier point in time, the elderly person provided the basic income, made the major decisions and acted as the head of the household. At that time the child was completely dependent on the parent. As years pass, parents relinquish their dominance. Parents whose well-being withers may come to rely heavily on the child—making extensive new demands and requiring more assistance than ever before. In essence, the parent and the child swap positions and take on new roles. Many individuals are either unprepared or unwilling to accept these new responsibilities; this frequently leads to abuse and neglect (Galbraith, 1989; Phillips, 1986).

As the aging person faces changing needs and begins to rely upon others for basic assistance, he or she redefines the situation in a variety of ways. In one sense, the parent may see himself or herself as a burden to the caregiver (Quinn and Tomita, 1986) and, in turn, may tacitly accept any maltreatment. Alternatively, the elderly individual may feel that the caregiver is too demanding, makes unreasonable requests, fails to do things when and how the parent wishes, or simply ignores the parent (Phillips, 1986; Shell, 1982). The older person may fight, yell, throw tantrums, invade the caregiver's privacy or react in other inappropriate ways (Quinn and Tomita, 1986). The caregiver can similarly define the actions and demands of the elderly as inappropriate. These behaviors by both the older person and the caregiver can easily lead to abuse and neglect, or result in the interpretation of actions as abusive (Phillips, 1986).

## Social Exchange

Closely related to both the situational and symbolic interactionist approaches is *social exchange theory*. Parties interact appropriately as long as both sides receive something in the exchange and each side feels that the other is treating him or her fairly (Galbraith, 1989). Typically, there is an assumption of equitable power or resources applied to the situation by both sides of the exchange.

As the elderly grow increasingly dependent on others, they have increasingly less to offer in an exchange relationship (Phillips, 1986). If this inequity continues over a period of time, a strong imbalance may develop between the parties (George, 1986). The parties may allow this imbalance to accumulate because of a past mutual history (Cicirelli, 1986).

The aging person in an imbalanced exchange relationship may respond with feelings of guilt or distress (George, 1986) and recognize that he or she no longer has the power to control the relationship (Phillips, 1986). The caregiver may realize that the relationship is unfair. He or she may resent the fact that a valuable service is being provided with little or no return. That individual may opt to inflict punitive costs on the elderly person through abuse or neglect as a way to rectify the imbalance (Phillips, 1986). The mistreated member of the dyad may quietly accept the abuse or neglect in recognition of his or her dependent position in the exchange.

## Social Attitudes

The final theoretical perspective for explaining maltreatment involves social attitudes toward aging and the elderly. Quinn and Tomita (1986) point out that, while attitudes themselves do not cause abuse or neglect, public opinion does make it easier for maltreatment to take place and thrive. *Ageism*, the stereotyping of older individuals and treating them differently because of their age, basically places the elderly in a devalued position (Hudson, 1988). Various factors contribute to a general malaise about the elderly and their plight. The historical record of interaction between the generations provides some insight, just as the past plays a role in the plight of women and children. As noted earlier, older members of society have often kept rigid control over the family, yielding power only through death or major confrontations (Stearns, 1986; Steinmetz, 1988). The animosity that developed between parents and offspring in the past may be reappearing today when the elderly turn to the independent child for care and support.

A second factor may be that old age, particularly very old age, is an unknown in modern society (Quinn and Tomita, 1986). Families in the past century have moved away from extended households, even to the extent of being scattered across the country. This means that most citizens are isolated from aging family members and cannot readily assist them. Coupled with longer life spans and medical advances that allow humans to live longer, people are faced with unknowns about being old. The elderly lack physical and economic power, and because they tend to be out of the workforce, they face a perception that they are useless. Social attitudes such as ageism make abuse and neglect more tolerable to society.

# RESPONDING TO ELDER ABUSE AND NEGLECT

Societal response to elder abuse and neglect is still very much in the developmental stages. Only within the past decade or so has formal legislation dealt specifically with the rights and needs of older Americans. The Family Violence Prevention and Treatment Act of 1984 was perhaps the earliest legislation to prohibit elder abuse. In the same year, amendments to the Older Americans Act mandated that states assess the need for abuse services, identify existing programs and address the problem of elder abuse (Rinkle, 1989). The reauthorization of the Older Americans Act in 1993 included new initiatives dealing with the protection of the elderly, including an ombudsman program, abuse and neglect prevention programs and legal assistance. Of course, the impact of these initiatives will have to be assessed in the future. Despite growing legislative initiatives for a variety of programs and interventions, the single effort that has received the most attention has been the promotion of mandatory elder abuse reporting laws.

## Mandatory Reporting

At first glance, it appears reasonable to assume that mandatory reporting is a good first step in dealing with elder abuse. Interestingly, however, there has been a great deal of resistance to mandatory reporting and numerous criticisms of these efforts. Most states now have some form of mandatory reporting law for abuse that, either implicitly or explicitly, covers elder abuse (Kapp, 1995; Macolini, 1995; Thobaben, 1989). The greatest criticism of such efforts has been that they do little more than encourage reporting. Often, these reporting laws do not define elder abuse, do not identify to whom abuse is to be reported, do not impose penalties for failure to report abuse and do not outline what to do with the reports once they are made (Blakely and Dolon, 1991; Quinn and Tomita, 1986; Thobaben, 1989).

A number of other problems also have been identified with mandatory reporting laws. First, the laws typically deal only with the reporting of abuse and fail to provide resources to follow up on the reports or to do something about the problem (Anetzberger, 1989). Second, critics claim that these laws intrude into the privacy of the individual. The best example of this contention involves laws requiring physicians to report suspected cases of abuse, which critics contend violates client-physician confidentiality (Crystal, 1986; Macolini, 1995). Third, mandatory reporting is seen as reinforcing ageism by focusing on the victim rather than the offender (Anetzberger, 1989; Quinn, 1990; Quinn and Tomita, 1986). These laws identify the victim of abuse and often prompt reactions that may include removing the victim from the home or blaming the victim for the abuse, rather than focusing on the perpetrator (Crystal, 1986). A fourth criticism is that these efforts place the elderly into a category with children, the mentally ill and others who are incapable of making decisions for themselves. These laws, therefore, fail to treat the elderly as adults and, consequently, degrade the elderly victim.

## Social Service Provision

One expected outcome of mandatory reporting laws is that social service professionals will be alerted to the problem and will take appropriate actions. Surveys of various social service professionals reveal that nurses, social workers and the clergy are among those who most often deal with and who are most knowledgeable about elder abuse (Anderson, 1989; Dolon and Hendricks, 1989). Interestingly, while one might assume that the police would be a primary source of immediate contact and aid, law enforcement is minimally involved—even when mandated to receive reports of abuse (Dolon and Hendricks, 1989; Fiegener et al., 1989). The relative lack of police involvement may be due to the fact that self-neglect is often the most common form of abuse identified by social service workers (Fiegener et al., 1989). The questionable legal status of self-neglect serves to remove the police from the equation.

Beyond identifying which social service workers are most involved in dealing with elder abuse, research has surveyed these professionals about their views of service needs. The need for additional training in elder abuse issues is perhaps the most common response (Blakely and Dolon, 1991; Dolon and Blakely, 1989; Fiegener et al., 1989). A second commonly expressed opinion is that there is room for more and improved resources to deal with abuse. Blakely and Dolon (1991), based on a national survey, identify a number of other needs, including greater cooperation between agencies, more public awareness, increased numbers of staff to deal with elder abuse, and stronger elder abuse legislation. What these responses tell us is that social service efforts to deal with elder abuse are still in their infancy and that much more remains to be done.

In an attempt to address the issues of elder abuse and neglect, many jurisdictions have established agencies, or offices within agencies, with the specific mandate of responding to those needs. One common name for these agencies is *Adult Protective Services* (APS). Often these efforts are backed by state legislation and are attached to agencies such as health and human services departments. Today, every state has some form of protective service devoted to the elderly. While their primary task revolves around investigations of abuse and neglect, these offices also may be responsible for such disparate activities as licensing nursing homes, funding research, and training social service workers. The fact that every jurisdiction has some form of APS is not indicative of a growing consensus on the problems of elder abuse and neglect. There remains a great deal of diversity in definitions, legislation, legal requirements and interventions across the different jurisdictions.

**FIGURE 8.4**
**Selected Internet Sites Dealing with Elder Abuse**

---

Administration on Aging
     http://www.aoa.dhhs.gov

American Association of Retired Persons
     http://www.aarp.org/

Elder Abuse Prevention, Information and Resource Guide
     http://www.aimnet.com/~oaktree/elder/home.html

National Center on Elder Abuse
     http://interinc.com/NCEA/Elder_Abuse

---

# SUMMARY

As the number of elderly persons steadily increases, society faces new problems and issues. For victimology, the elderly emerge as the subject of interest in two broad areas. First, they are victims of the same crimes as everyone else. Second, they occupy a special niche as victims of abuse and neglect.

More is known about general crimes committed against the elderly because of the great similarity to crime against the rest of society. Theft, burglary, assault and other such offenses are traditional realms of interest for the criminal justice system. The greatest difference regarding crime against the elderly falls not in the crime itself, but rather in the impact of that crime upon the victim.

Elder maltreatment, however, poses a relatively new problem for the criminal justice system. While abuse may not be a new occurrence, it is a phenomenon that is just now gaining attention. Victimologists are beginning to identify the intricacies of the problem, probe its causes and offer some solutions. However, a great deal of additional work remains to be done at both the theoretical and practical levels. A short decade of work has not been sufficient to do much more than identify elder abuse and neglect as a major problem and offer the sketchiest of responses.

# Chapter 9

# LEARNING OBJECTIVES

After reading Chapter 9, you should be able to:

- Define criminal homicide.

- Assemble a picture of homicide victimization based upon FBI UCR statistics.

- Give some reasons why African-Americans are overrepresented in homicide statistics.

- Evaluate the need for a national Firearm Fatality Reporting System.

- Distinguish a primary homicide from a nonprimary homicide.

- Separate a felony murder from a nonfelony murder.

- Define a "mushroom shooting."

- Link victim precipitation with the term "situated transaction."

- Describe how routine activities or lifestyle can influence homicide victimization.

- Outline the stages of Luckenbill's situated transaction in a homicide confrontation.

- Convey what is meant by the differential distribution of homicide victimization rates.

- Discuss the "regional culture of violence" thesis.

- Sketch out two sets of challenges to the "regional culture of violence" thesis.

- Introduce the term "trauma" and explain its relevance.

- Establish a connection between trauma and medical resources.

- Offer an explanation as to how medical resources could affect the production of homicide statistics.

- Explore some remaining issues in the medical resources argument.

- Relay the details of the death notification process.

- Discuss the grief process and its different stages.

- Explain some of the adjustments faced by survivors of homicide victims.

- List the five homicide survivor patterns and tell how they differ in response to the homicide event.

# Chapter 9

# Homicide

## INTRODUCTION

One aspect of daily life that sets the United States apart from other industrialized countries is the death toll that continues to mount from criminal violence. Murder is a common fixture in our urban landscapes. Homicide, for example, is a leading cause of death among young African-American males in this country.

This chapter will take a close look at the dynamics that underlie criminal violence. Most killers murder someone they know rather than kill a complete stranger. Victim precipitation and alcohol consumption appear to be almost essential ingredients in any deadly confrontation. While there are different interpretations as to how alcohol actually works in these settings, it is certain that expanding medical resources have done much to keep these mortality figures in check. In fact, one argument developed in this chapter is that medical resources play an important role in the production of homicide statistics.

No treatment of homicide would be complete without looking at the silent or hidden sufferers of homicide: the survivors of the deceased. In this context, we will look briefly at the death notification process and the bereavement process endured by the victim's relatives.

# THE EXTENT OF HOMICIDE VICTIMIZATION

According to the FBI's Uniform Crime Reports (UCR), there were almost 22,000 known homicides in the United States during 1995. Unlike most of the index crimes, the FBI attempts to collect detailed data on reported homicides through the Supplementary Homicide Reports. These reports seek information on both the victim and offender, as well as circumstances about the event. Despite this fact, detailed information is not available for every one of these deaths. As a result, the UCR data offer a sketch based upon information derived from 95 percent of the known victim deaths.

The FBI (1996: 13) defines *criminal homicide* as the "willful (non-negligent) killing of one human being by another. . . . Not included in the count for this offense classification are deaths caused by negligence, suicide, or accident; justifiable homicides; and attempts to murder or assaults to murder. . . ." The FBI also omits from its tabulations traffic fatalities and deaths resulting from gross negligence.

Homicide victims are more likely to be males than females. In 1995, 77 percent of the deceased were males. In terms of race, 48 percent of the homicide victims were African-American and 48 percent white. This racial composition means that African-Americans experience an *over-representation* in homicide victimizations. Considering that African-Americans make up approximately 12 percent of the American population, all things being equal, one would expect that they would account for 12 percent of all murder victims. Because the participation figure of 48 percent clearly exceeds the 12 percent population mark, victimologists regard African-Americans as being excessively represented in homicide victimization statistics.

Table 9.1 displays the age distribution of murder victims for 1995. Those figures show that more than 600 deaths can be attributed to *infanticide* (child homicide). Victims under the age of five made up 3.3 percent of the homicide victimization pool. If we expand the upper limit of childhood to 12 years of age, children account for 4.3 percent of all the homicide victimizations in this country. The most likely perpetrator in the majority of these cases is a parent or parent substitute.

A closer look at Table 9.1 shows that homicide victimization is concentrated among the younger segments of society. Fifty-five percent of all homicide victims were between 17 and 34 years of age. In fact, the leading cause of death among young, African-American males is homicide. As Figure 9.1 suggests, this frightening observation has led some commentators to conclude that violence, particularly with the use of firearms, has reached epidemic proportions among disadvantaged, urban, African-American males (Kellerman, 1994; Pless, 1994; Snyder et al., 1996; Sorenson et al., 1993). Another commentator (Kellerman, 1994: 541) notes, "the number of 15- to 19-year-old African-American males who died from gunshot wounds in 1990 was 4.7 times larger than the number who died from acquired immunodeficiency syndrome, sickle cell disease, and all other natural causes of death *combined*." At the same time, these figures fail to convey the toll sustained from the combined years of potential life lost whenever a person loses his or her life prematurely.

KEY TERMS
—*continued*

routine activities/lifestyle model

situated transaction

Structural Poverty Index

trauma

victim precipitation

**TABLE 9.1**
**Age Distribution of U.S. Murder Victims, 1995**

| Age in Years | Number | Simple Percent | Cumulative Percent |
|---|---|---|---|
| Under 1 | 249 | 1.2% | 1.2% |
| 1-4 | 411 | 2.1 | 3.3 |
| 5-8 | 103 | 0.5 | 3.8 |
| 9-12 | 103 | 0.5 | 4.3 |
| 13-16 | 953 | 4.8 | 9.1 |
| 17-19 | 2,116 | 10.6 | 19.7 |
| 20-24 | 3,559 | 18.8 | 38.5 |
| 25-29 | 2,814 | 14.0 | 52.5 |
| 30-34 | 2,526 | 12.6 | 65.1 |
| 35-39 | 1,966 | 9.8 | 74.9 |
| 40-44 | 1,517 | 7.6 | 82.3 |
| 45-49 | 993 | 5.0 | 87.3 |
| 50-54 | 645 | 3.2 | 90.5 |
| 55-59 | 471 | 2.3 | 92.8 |
| 60-64 | 352 | 1.8 | 94.6 |
| 65-69 | 292 | 1.5 | 96.1 |
| 70-74 | 222 | 1.1 | 97.2 |
| 75+ | 414 | 2.1 | 99.3 |
| Unknown | 337 | 1.7 | 101.0 |
| Total | 20,043 | 101.0% | |

Source: Federal Bureau of Investigation (1996). *Uniform Crime Reports for the United States 1995*. Washington, DC: U.S. Government Printing Office, p. 16.

Weapon involvement, especially of firearms, is a potent predictor of lethal and nonlethal injuries (Saltzman et al., 1992). The data in Table 9.2 show that firearms are used in 68 percent of all homicides. Knives and other sharp objects account for an additional 13 percent of the homicides. In only 6 percent of the cases are hands, feet, fists or other "personal weapons" used (Federal Bureau of Investigation, 1996: 18). Compared to weapon use in aggravated assaults (where, as in homicides, the intent of the offense is bodily harm to the victim), homicides are three times as likely to involve a firearm.

**FIGURE 9.1**
**A Profile of Juvenile Violence in America**

- Juveniles were murdered at a rate of 7 per day in 1994.

- Between 1980 and 1994 most murdered children below age 6 were killed by a family member, while most murdered older juveniles were killed by an acquaintance or a stranger.

- Between 1980 and 1994 most murdered children below age 6 were beaten to death, while most older juveniles were killed with a firearm.

- Black homicide victims were more likely to be killed by a firearm than were white victims.

- While juvenile homicide victimizations not involving firearms remained constant, those involving firearms nearly tripled from 1984 to 1994.

- In 1989 females were less likely than males to carry weapons to school, by 1994 they were nearly as likely to do so.

- The presence of gangs in school greatly increased in four years.

- In 1994 juveniles accounted for 19% of all violent crime arrests and 14% of all violent crimes cleared by law enforcement.

- The number of juvenile homicide offenders tripled between 1984 and 1994—the increase is all firearm-related.

Source: Snyder, H.N., M. Stickmund and E. Poe-Yamagata (1996). *Juvenile Offenders and Victims: 1996 Update on Violence.* Pittsburgh, PA: National Center for Juvenile Justice.

**TABLE 9.2**
**Weapon Use in U.S. Homicides, 1995**

| Weapon | N | % |
|---|---|---|
| Firearm | 13,673 | 68% |
| Knife or cutting instrument | 2,538 | 13% |
| Blunt objects (clubs, hammers, etc.) | 904 | 5% |
| Personal weapons (hands, fists, feet, etc.) | 1,182 | 6% |
| Poison | 12 | 0% |
| Explosives | 190 | 1% |
| Fire | 166 | 1% |
| Narcotics | 22 | 0% |
| Strangulation | 232 | 1% |
| Asphyxiation | 135 | 1% |
| Other | 989 | 5% |

Source: Federal Bureau of Investigation (1996). *Uniform Crime Reports for the United States 1995.* Washington, DC: U.S. Government Printing Office, p. 18.

A growing number of medical experts are becoming increasingly dissatisfied with the lack of a systematic policy addressing the problem of gun violence (Kellerman, 1994; Marwick, 1992; Skolnick, 1992; Teret et al., 1992). One fundamental concern is that the United States does not have a comprehensive national clearinghouse that stockpiles data regarding gun-related deaths. As a result, some physicians are imploring the federal government to establish a *Firearm Fatality Reporting System.* Such an effort would be modeled after the fatal crash data bank operated by the National Highway Traffic Safety Administration. Researchers there have used this information to effect seatbelt laws, child restraint regulations and other safety considerations aimed at reducing vehicle-related deaths. As Figure 9.2 shows, it is hoped that a parallel gun-related database would yield similar dividends. However, one spokesperson (Kellerman, 1994: 542) wryly notes:

> [M]oney seems not to be a problem if an issue is considered important. When Congress passed the Brady bill, $200 million was allocated to help states upgrade their computerized records so that handgun purchasers may eventually be spared the inconvenience of a 5-day waiting period. This total is roughly five times the annual budget of the National Center for Injury Prevention and Control and eight times the annual budget of the National Institute of Justice. A comparable level of concern for the victims of gun-related violence could work wonders.

**FIGURE 9.2**
**Objectives for the Proposed Firearm Fatality Reporting System**

At a minimum, data collected on firearm fatalities should include the following:

- Information on the gun itself, such as type, make, model, caliber, and serial number, which would allow researchers to determine other variables such as year of manufacture.

- Type of death—homicide, suicide, unintended, or undetermined.

- Information on the victim, such as age, race, sex, and drug/alcohol involvement.

- Information on the shooter, such as age, race, sex, relationship to the victim, and drug/alcohol involvement.

- Information on the circumstances of the shooting, such as date, time, type of location, and whether it occurred during commission of another crime.

- Involvement of emergency medical services.

Source: Teret, S.P., G.J. Wintemute and P.L. Beilsenson (1992). "The Firearm Fatality Reporting System: A Proposal." *Journal of the American Medical Association* 267: 3073-3074. Copyright 1992, American Medical Association.

The FBI (1996: 14) also reports that homicide is, for the most part, an intraracial event. In other words, victims and offenders tend to share the same racial backgrounds. African-American offenders killed 94 percent of the African-American homicide victims, and white perpetrators murdered 84 percent of the white homicide victims. Similarly, males were more likely to die at the hands of male killers (but so were female victims).

One important distinction that has emerged in the literature is the notion of nonprimary versus primary homicides (Parker, 1989; Parker and Smith, 1979; Smith and Parker, 1980). A *nonprimary homicide* is a situation in which the victim did not know the offender very well, if at all. A *primary homicide* means that both the victim and the offender shared a primary, or face-to-face, relationship.

Primary homicides span a variety of relationships. Some examples of primary relationships would include spouses, parents and their children, siblings, and people who are very close to one another. One researcher has dubbed cases involving men who murder their wives or lovers as *intimate femicide* (Stout, 1991). Recognition of the "battered woman syndrome," discussed in Chapter 6, has unearthed situations in which women retaliate by killing their husbands or lovers (Mann, 1988; Mann, 1990). The act of *parricide*, children who kill their parents, has not escaped scholarly attention (Berliner, 1993; Fine, 1993; Heide, 1989; Heide, 1993; Mones, 1993). One can subdivide parricide into cases involving *patricide* (where the father is the victim) or *matricide* (where the mother is the victim).

Another useful dichotomy is the difference between a felony murder and a nonfelony murder. A *felony murder* takes place when "a person dies during the course of a felony that is dangerous to life (usually robbery, burglary, sexual battery, arson, kidnapping)" (Doerner, 1998: 189). A *nonfelony murder* occurs when a person dies either during the course of a misdemeanor or when no other crime is being committed.

Table 9.3 applies these homicide classifications to 1995 homicides. Two important points emerge from a reading of this table. First, most murderers know their victims. A person is more likely to be killed by someone he or she knows rather than by a complete stranger. Ignoring type of homicide, family members commit 24 percent of homicides, while acquaintances commit twice as many offenses (51%). Second, strangers are more likely to engage in felony murders than are family members. Family members are more likely to commit nonfelony murders than felony murders (2,559 nonfelony versus 164 felony). This distinction reflects the fact that different events lead up to homicide when family members are involved than when strangers are involved.

One disturbing trend is the recent proliferation of innocent bystander shootings associated with gang feuds and drug trafficking (Sherman et al., 1989). *Mushroom shootings*, stray bullets that are not intended for any one particular person, are a continuing urban phenomenon.

**TABLE 9.3**
**Murder Circumstances by Victim-Offender Relationship, 1995**

| Victim-Offender Relationship | Felony Type n | Felony Type % | Nonfelony Type n | Nonfelony Type % | Unknown Type n | Unknown Type % | Total n | Total % |
|---|---|---|---|---|---|---|---|---|
| Family Member[1] | 164 | 7% | 2,559 | 30% | 249 | 20% | 2,972 | 24% |
| Acquaintance[2] | 1,047 | 46% | 4,494 | 52% | 590 | 47% | 6,131 | 51% |
| Stranger | 1,052 | 46% | 1,576 | 18% | 408 | 33% | 3,036 | 25% |
| Total | 2,263 | 99% | 8,629 | 100% | 1,247 | 100% | 12,139 | 100% |
| Unknown Cases | 1,272 | | 1,963 | | 4,670 | | 7,905 | |

[1] Includes husband, wife, mother, father, son, daughter, brother, sister, other family, boyfriend, and girlfriend.

[2] Includes acquaintance, friend, neighbor, employer, and employee.

Source: Adapted from Federal Bureau of Investigation (1996). *Uniform Crime Reports for the United States 1995.* Washington, DC: U.S. Government Printing Office, p. 19.

# THEORIES OF HOMICIDE VICTIMIZATION

Most criminological theories attempt to understand why some people resort to criminal behavior while others do not. Victimologists, on the other hand, take a slightly different approach by focusing upon the not-so-victorious portion of the criminal-victim dyad. As we saw in Chapter 1, this concentration upon the victim led to an early reliance upon the notion of victim precipitation. What did the victim do to deserve this type of treatment? While this idea does have some very real limits, victim involvement has yielded some fruitful insights when it comes to homicide victimization. As a result, the following materials focus upon theories that are based upon social interactionism and a cultural perspective.

## Social Interactionism

As we mentioned before in Chapter 1, early victimologists gave serious consideration to the idea of *victim precipitation.* They sought to learn what the victim did that triggered such a violent reaction. While Hans von Hentig and others debated how the dynamics of the criminal-victim dyad led to the victim's ultimate demise, it was Wolfgang's (1958) analysis of Philadelphia homicides that provided the necessary empirical support.

Wolfgang (1958) undertook an extensive review of police homicide records for all murders committed in Philadelphia during the five-year period of 1948-1952. The one thing that struck Wolfgang was the realization that there was a significant amount of victim participation in some of these homicide events. Wolfgang (1958: 254) categorized 150 cases (26% of all the homicides) as victim-precipitated. In other words, the victims in these incidents initiated the violent encounter. They were the first party to display a weapon, throw a punch or take other physically aggressive actions. When the other party retaliated, the violence escalated to a lethal response.

As we explained in Chapter 1, Amir, one of Wolfgang's students, applied the same thinking to forcible rape situations. The reaction to Amir's treatment of victim precipitation in sexual battery cases drew an intense and bitter reaction. Consequently, this concept remained dormant for many years. It took two decades before other homicide researchers revived this idea.

## Homicide as a Situated Transaction

Luckenbill (1977) rekindled interest in victim actions when he addressed homicide as a "situated transaction." What he meant by a *situated transaction* was that the homicide culminated from a chain (or series) of discrete actions and reactions by the participants. The combination of the two actors, and possibly an audience, contributed to the development of a violent interaction. Luckenbill became intrigued by how the parties reacted to each other and whether the dynamics progressed in any regular patterns.

Tracing the hostilities, as well as the moves and countermoves displayed by the participants, led Luckenbill to conclude that these deadly struggles evolved in a series of predictable stages. What initiated these encounters was some type of an insult. The eventual victim may have said something rude, made an unwelcomed remark or issued an obnoxious gesture toward the other party. The second stage consists of the recipient's assessment of these actions as offensive. The next stage, the response, appears to be absolutely critical to the final resolution of this conflict. The recipient's response could be to ignore the apparent insult, to dismiss the issuer as inconsequential or to deal with the matter immediately. For instance, direct confrontation could involve a dare for the victim to restate the insult, an issuance of a retaliatory remark or gesture by the aggrieved party, or a physical challenge. The goal at this point is to do something to save face, degrade the initiator or demonstrate superiority.

If the attempt to salvage one's social appearance fails, then the situation escalates to the fourth stage. At this point both parties have elected not to turn away, nor to defuse the mounting disagreement. There could be more verbal challenges, accompanied by minor scuffling or further insults. Should neither party break off or end the grievance, a battle is imminent. A common strategy at this point is to assume an intimidating stance as a demonstration of pugilistic superiority or to display a weapon as proof of a tactical advantage. A failure to heed such a warning results in the ultimate demise of one of the parties. Thus, Luckenbill (1977) sees murder as the final outcome in a series of moves and counterstrategies negotiated continuously by the combatants.

Following the lead of Luckenbill (1977), Felson and Steadman (1983) reconstructed the criminal episode that resulted in imprisonment on charges of homicide and aggravated assault. A refinement of Luckenbill's stages lent clarification to the analysis. Victim precipitation was a very prominent characteristic of homicide situations. Combatants who were armed, intoxicated and aggressive were more likely to be killed than those who were sober. As Luckenbill (1977) explained, these violent episodes usually began with a verbal confrontation. They then moved to the next stages with more threats and evasive actions. If a serious outcome is to be avoided, this is the time to deescalate matters. However, for those incidents that do continue, the physical attack ensues next.

Victim precipitation is a major contributing factor in serious violence. The key feature of these violent encounters is that they are provoked by an attack on one's "honor" and systematically evolve into a deadly "character contest." In essence, the nature of the instigating act is trivial compared to the final outcome. To verify whether this conceptualization was correct, Savitz and associates (1991) reviewed 381 homicides that took place in Philadelphia during 1978. Each homicide was dissected, paying close attention to how the quarrel began and who initiated the challenge or "character contest." Almost two-thirds of the killings fit Luckenbill's description of a "situated transaction"; one-half of these cases involved victim-initiated circumstances.

## The Routine Activities/Lifestyle Model

An alternative approach for explaining homicide events is through the inspection of routine activities. Routine activities refers to the fact that individuals may be placed at risk of victimization by their everyday behavior. Cohen and Felson (1979) demonstrate this possibility by examining social changes that have led to increasing property crime. They point out that the move to two-income households has left homes unprotected during the day and allows for the purchase of more valuable and portable items. At the same time, increased mobility has led to increased numbers of targets for offenders. Taken together, this convergence of suitable targets, lack of guardianship and the increased motivation of offenders has allowed for greater levels of theft. Hindelang et al. (1978) refer to this as a function of the lifestyle of the parties involved. That is, an individual's choice of behavior (i.e., lifestyle) influences the chances of becoming a victim. This is referred to as the *routine activities/lifestyle model.*

A similar explanation can be used for personal offenses such as homicide. For a homicide to occur, it is necessary that the offender and victim be in the same place and that some event or occurrence precipitate the act. One example of this would be the following scenario:

> Two acquaintances frequent a bar where fights are a common occurrence. On one visit both individuals are cheering for opposing sports teams and make a wager on the outcome. Towards the end of a close contest, a questionable call by an official determines the outcome of the game. Coupled with a good amount of alcohol consumption, the two parties come to blows; one person pulls a knife and stabs the other.

From a routine activities perspective, this offense is partly attributable to the routine of the parties involved.

One example of the applicability of a routine activities/lifestyle model is the apparent tie to the seasonality of homicide. It has long been argued that homicide varies by season of the year (Dexter, 1904; Ferri, 1882; Lombroso, 1968; Quetelet, 1835) and that this variation is attributable to changes in heat and humidity (Baron and Bell, 1975; Durkheim, 1951; Lombroso, 1968). Rather than credit changes in homicide to fluctuating temperature, recent research has relied more on routine activities as an explanation. For example, the warm summer months draw people out of doors and prompt increased use of alcohol. This change in routine activities escalates the chances for personal victimization. Conversely, it can be argued that inclement weather reduces outdoor activity, which may lead to greater intrafamilial conflict. Indeed, research has demonstrated that personal crime, including homicide, varies with heat and humidity (Baron and Bell, 1976; Cotton, 1983; Lab and Hirschel, 1988; LeBeau and Langworthy, 1986). Thus, it is feasible to assume that it is changing routines that explain alterations in the level of homicide.

The value of routine activities/lifestyle explanations is in understanding the social situations in which homicide occurs. These perspectives argue that our choices of where to go, what to do and how to proceed (even when made innocently) influence the chances of becoming a victim. Recognition of this process may provide insight into homicide events.

## Mass Media Influences

One way that culture influences both individual outlooks and behavior is through the images produced in the mass media. The pervasiveness of violence on television and in other popular outlets has led many spokespersons to condemn what they see as an unhealthy trend in our society. A number of professional and "self-appointed" watchdog groups routinely monitor the level of violence displayed in television broadcasts, movies and books. Every year these organizations issue counts regarding the number of violent acts shown on television. Their verdict is that the level of violence available for public consumption has climbed beyond any acceptable limit. What these groups fear is that the widespread depiction of violence will desensitize viewers (especially younger and more impressionable children), render turbulent outbursts of behavior more acceptable, and prompt violent actions. In many respects, this argument is a simple extension of social learning theories. Among the various learning theories that would apply here are the ideas behind: (1) modeling (Bandura and Walters, 1963), (2) differential association (Sutherland, 1939), and (3) differential identification (Glaser, 1956).

*Modeling* is perhaps the simplest form of learning theory. It suggests that people learn by copying or imitating the behavior of others. While it is assumed that most people will duplicate the actions of significant others, it is possible that some nondiscriminating media viewers will mimic the activity of characters in the media.

Sutherland's (1939) *differential association* theory argues that most learning comes from interpersonal contacts that vary in frequency, duration, priority and intensity. Individuals will act in accordance with the dominant input from the people with whom they have direct contact. Sutherland, however, paid very little attention to the media—primarily because television did not yet exist in those days.

Glaser (1956), however, recognized the growing potential of the mass media to influence or mold behavior. *Differential identification* proposes that personal contact is not necessary for the transmission of behavioral guidelines. Both real and fictional presentations in the media (particularly television) can serve to define behaviors as either acceptable or unacceptable. In essence, differential identification is an explicit recognition that viewers can "model" or "imitate" what they see on the screen. This transference becomes problematic when the media grows preoccupied with depicting violence.

There is no dispute that the mass media is enamored with crime and violence. Violent crime is a major theme in both news and fictional media presentations, with 20 percent or more of television broadcast time often devoted to crime-related topics (see, e.g., Dominick, 1978; Graber, 1977; Hofstetter, 1976). Even a casual observer cannot escape the centrality of crime to television. Recent years have seen a steady diet, as evidenced by shows such as "Top Cops," "America's Most Wanted," "Unsolved Mysteries," "Law and Order," "NYPD Blue," and the influx of telecasts such as "Court TV."

Perhaps the most disturbing aspect of this proliferation of crime-related programming is that the presentations rarely resemble reality. Only the most sensational and horrific offenses make their way into the media. Violent crime, particularly murder, is overrepresented in comparison to its actual occurrence in the real world (Dominick, 1978; Gerbner et al., 1980; Graber, 1980; Hofstetter, 1976; Skogan and Maxfield, 1981). In addition, it is rare for a story to focus on the consequences of the crime (e.g., being caught, prosecuted and punished). Crime is glorified to some extent through its simple dominance in the stories. Such exposure may desensitize the public toward violence.

Various researchers have examined the potential of media presentations to influence behavior. At the simplest level, Gerbner et al. (1978; 1980) and Barrile (1980) have demonstrated that the general public gives answers about crime that are more consistent with what is presented in the media than what actually occurs. A more important concern, though, is whether media presentations can promote similar behavior among viewers. Belson (1978) reports that individuals with higher levels of exposure to realistic depictions of violence tend to commit more serious acts of violence. Similarly, studies of prize fights and fictionalized suicides find significant increases in homicide and suicide after these media presentations have aired (Phillips, 1982; Phillips, 1983).

There are some claims that exposure to aggressive/violent pornography is coupled with violent criminal behavior (Donnerstein, 1980; Donnerstein and Hallam, 1978; Meyer, 1972; U.S. Attorney General's Commission on Pornography, 1986; Zillman et al., 1981). For example, just before his execution, serial killer Ted Bundy blamed pornography for his violent escapades. Finally, Andison's (1977) review of television violence research concluded there was a positive correlation between media presentations and violence. This relationship has grown stronger in more recent years, possibly due to accumulated exposure to media violence over time (Andison, 1977).

Apart from these macro-level attempts to unravel a media-behavior link, there are numerous individual accounts of instances in which an individual imitates an act of violence seen on television or is prompted to violence by media presentations. While evidence on the media-violence link is not conclusive, there is at least qualified support for a causal connection. Huesmann and Malamuth (1986) suggest that, at the very least, excessive exposure to media violence can force some viewers to become more aggressive. It is uncertain, however, just how this causal mechanism actually works. While it is logical to assume that mass media depictions of violence prod some individuals to be violent, it is equally plausible that people who commit aggressive acts simply enjoy watching violence in the media. Despite the fact that the direction of this relationship has not been firmly established, there is little doubt that the mass media plays a major role in the high levels of violence in society.

## The "Regional Culture of Violence" Thesis

For years, the southern portion of the United States has had the dubious distinction of leading the country in terms of homicide victimization rates. As one might imagine, this *differential distribution of homicide rates* has attracted considerable scholarly interest. What the phrase "differential distribution of homicide rates" refers to is the fact that murder rates are not uniformly dispersed throughout time and space. In other words, if all things were equal, then all regional homicide victimization rates should be equivalent to each other. The observed imbalance leads one to the question of how to account for these differences in murder rates.

A variety of theoretical accounts have cropped up in the literature. Some criminologists have tried to explain regional victimization differences by looking at such things as the size of the minority population (Dollard, 1949), the frustration-aggression hypothesis (Henry and Short, 1954) and childhood socialization practices (Gold, 1958). However, a penetrating critique of these and other theories uncovered a number of inadequacies and led to their dismissal. That assessment forced Hackney (1969) to speculate that one promising approach would be to look at the role of culture in the production of homicide victimization rates. That pronouncement opened the door for Gastil (1971) to build upon the Wolfgang and Ferracuti (1967) subculture of violence framework by posing such a theoretical perspective.

Gastil (1971) began his inquiry by mapping state homicide victimization rates over a number of years. What he found was a stable and intriguing pattern. Murder rates were quite pronounced in the South. Moreover, these rates declined with distance away from this area. States bordering the South had elevated homicide rates, but these figures were not quite as high as what was found in the Southern states. Areas located just beyond these border states exhibited even lower homicide victimization rates. Finally, the states located furthest away from the South consistently showed the lowest homicide victimization rates. These observations led Gastil (1971: 414) to suspect that "persistent differences in homicide rates seem best explained by differences in regional culture."

According to Gastil (1971), there exists a distinctive Southern culture predating the Civil War that tolerates violence. Gastil points to a number of cultural vestiges as supporting evidence of this area's propensity toward violence, including slavery, gun ownership, dueling, a strong military tradition, frontier living and an exaggerated sense of honor among males. This violent heritage renders Southerners very distinctive from other Americans. The net impact of these cultural remnants is a desensitization toward the use of violence as an acceptable behavioral response.

People who are born and bred in the South become carriers of this "Southernness" culture. Not only do Southerners inculcate their offspring into this normative value system, they transport these violent tendencies wherever they go. What this contagion model stipulates is that areas settled by Southerners become infected and, in turn, are characterized by corresponding homicide victimization rates.

Gastil (1971) traced migration patterns out of the South to see how state murder rates mirrored settlement origins. To help track population shifts, Gastil constructed an *Index of Southernness*. States colonized by Southern-born persons receive top scores on this measure. Areas with sparse settlements of Southerners rank at the bottom of the scale. Thus, Gastil's Index of Southernness is an attempt to track cultural diffusion through migratory patterns.

An empirical analysis of 1960 homicide victimization rates and census materials revealed a dramatic empirical relationship between the Index of Southernness and murder. As a result, Gastil (1971: 425) concluded that Southernness was responsible for the differential distribution of homicide victimization rates throughout the United States. This pronouncement, referred to as the *"regional culture of violence" thesis*, eventually spawned a large body of empirical studies.

## Challenges to the "Regional Culture of Violence" Thesis

Gastil's broad assertion linking Southern culture with higher homicide victimization rates sparked several lines of research. The first approach questioned the cultural aspect of this explanation. The second strategy focused on the tenability of the regional component. The following materials examine each of these developments.

### Cultural Challenges

The "regional culture of violence" thesis drew an immediate challenge from Loftin and Hill (1974). They noted that instead of measuring culture directly, Gastil (1971) opted to substitute geographical location as a surrogate. These researchers reanalyzed state homicide rates, adding their own *Structural Poverty Index*, which reflected variables such as high infant mortality, low education and low income. They also added a measure of income inequality to the analysis. Loftin and Hill (1974) found that the statistical power of Gastil's Index of Southernness diminished to virtually nothing. Instead, the Structural Poverty Index and the income inequality measure were the strongest predictors of homicide levels. Essentially, then, these researchers raised serious doubts as to whether Southernness was the key to understanding the differential distribution of homicide victimization rates.

Another tack that researchers took moved away from the macro-level and concentrated on the micro-level. The thinking here is that

Gastil's notion of a "culture of violence" hinges on the existence of a divergent normative value system. In other words, members of a subculture adhere to a distinctive attitudinal system that allows violence as a legitimate behavioral response. This belief system differs from the dominant culture and is directly responsible for higher rates of interpersonal violence among Southerners.

Despite repeated attempts, researchers have not been able to identify a separate Southern tradition conducive to violence (Doerner, 1978c; Doerner 1979; Erlanger, 1974; Erlanger, 1975). In fact, there appears to be no attitudinal differences toward violence between Southerners and non-Southerners, or between non-Southerners and migrants who have left the region. Under these conditions, there does not appear to be any support for the existence of a divergent regional attitudinal structure. Thus, Gastil's contagion idea (that Southerners are carriers of a violent tradition who infect receiving areas) lacks foundation.

## Regional Challenges

A second line of inquiry has remained at the macro-level. The focus here has been on examining the ecological distribution of homicide victimization rates. A close look at Gastil's Index of Southernness reveals that all the Southern states receive the same score. What this means, then, is that Southernness must be distributed uniformly throughout the entire Southern region. Consequently, if Southernness is responsible for variations in murder rates, the South should display homogeneous or similar homicide victimization rates across the states.

A look at homicide rates from 1940 through 1970 in 10-year intervals uncovers significant intraregional variation (Doerner, 1980). In other words, grave dissimilarities abound. A longitudinal analysis using the same data source that Gastil studied, the same point in time that Gastil examined and the same spatial unit of analysis did not substantiate the assumption of regional homogeneity. When coupled with an earlier study of regional homicide rates (Doerner, 1975), the following conclusion emerges:

> [I]f a *regional* culture of violence" ever existed in the South, it existed prior to 1940. Thus, while the term *"regional* culture of violence" is a misnomer when applied to the contemporary South, it does not preclude the possibility that "Southernness" did exist at one time and that remnants exist in scattered pockets throughout the South (Doerner, 1978b: 93).

## Medical Resources as an Emerging Theoretical Dimension

While the empirical evidence mustered in response to Gastil's (1971) formulation was strong enough to cast heavy doubts regarding the adequacy of a cultural explanation, the original concern still remained. Some commentators chided researchers for failing to address the primary question in a meaningful way (Gastil, 1978; Loftin and Hill, 1978). That is, how can victimologists account for the differential distribution of homicide rates? If cultural values are not the answer, then what is? All the scholarly quibbling had yet to generate a meaningful alternative explanation (Hawley and Messner, 1989).

### *Conceptual Obstacles*

Up to this point, past research efforts were hampered because they had glossed over some very important points. For example, the typical conceptualization of homicide was of homicide as a finite and distinctive legal category. This approach overlooked its underlying relationship to other proscribed behaviors. Illegal violent acts range from mere threats or verbal taunts (assault) to minor injuries (simple battery) to very serious bodily harm (aggravated battery) to death (homicide). When viewed in this context, one can locate violent behavior on a continuum. To illustrate this, the FBI definition of an aggravated assault is "an unlawful attack . . . for the purpose of inflicting severe or aggravated bodily injury" usually with "use of a weapon or by means likely to produce death or great bodily harm." In one sense, homicide is nothing more than a successful aggravated battery, while an aggravated battery could very well be a failed murder attempt.

A second pertinent point is the obsession with lethality as the only theoretically meaningful outcome of violent social interaction. Riveting attention entirely upon the outcome of an event ignores the fact that violence is a process and that death is only one possible consequence. Just because two combatants engage in a physical confrontation, with or without weapons, does not mean that this clash will automatically culminate in a death. Wounded fighters often sustain nonfatal injuries. Furthermore, when they do incur critical, life-threatening damage, death is not necessarily imminent. Timely and appropriate medical intervention can play a key role in keeping an aggravated battery from slipping into a homicide statistic. Firearms are evident in three times as many homicides as aggravated assaults (Federal Bureau of Investigation, 1996). This may be due to the fact that firearm incidents require more medical attention than other injuries. Thus, it would seem that further examination should be given to the potential impact of medical resources upon the production of lethality rates stemming from criminal violence.

## *The Impact of Medical Resources*

One specialty area in the medical literature is trauma management. *Trauma*, in the medical sense, refers to any physical injury without any concern for the origin of the damage. Some examples of trauma include traffic accident injuries, industrial mishaps, suicide, poisoning, drowning, heart attacks, burns, stabbings, gunshots, and so forth. One prominent goal of trauma management is to reduce trauma-induced mortality.

In a review of the trauma management literature, Doerner (1983) looked at emergency transportation, field treatment, hospital emergency treatment and postoperative recovery. One generalization that emerged was that rapid ambulance response time, coupled with the deployment of specially trained paramedics, increased the odds of patient survival. Medical experts refer to a period called the *"golden hour,"* the time period in which seriously injured people need medical attention if they are to survive. A second finding is that quick delivery of a salvageable patient to a hospital emergency room does not ensure survival. Most hospitals are not equipped sufficiently to handle serious trauma cases. They lack the appropriate technological facilities and do not have uniquely trained persons on staff. Instead, an ambulance with a critical injury case would be better advised to reroute cases to a specially designated trauma center. There the patient would receive more intensive care from specialized medical teams acquainted with the most current technology. However, all these measures still do not guarantee an automatic "save" from death. There is the ever-present danger of postoperative infection and other long-term complications.

It is important to realize that medical resources, just like homicide rates, are differentially distributed throughout time and space. In fact, many states aim to correct physical imbalances by offering financial incentives to doctors who agree to practice in certain locations (Rivo et al., 1995). There is recognition, of course, that the concentration and distribution of physicians is influenced by such considerations as degree of urbanization, community size, quality of life and availability of hospital facilities (Anderson, 1977; Begun, 1977; Eyles and Woods, 1983; Frenzen, 1991; Marden, 1966; Reskin and Campbell, 1974; Rushing, 1975; Rushing and Wade, 1973). One known outcome of greater medical specialization is a reduction in infant mortality rates and alterations in morbidity (sickness) patterns (Anderson, 1977; Begun, 1977; Friedman, 1973). Given this evidence, it would not be unreasonable to expect that areas characterized by relatively fewer medical resources would exhibit higher lethality rates stemming from criminal violence, not because of the impact of Southernness, but due to the limited availability of adequate emergency medical care.

## *Empirical Evidence*

Given this orientation, Doerner (1983) pitted the Index of Southern-ness against several indicators of medical care in an examination of state homicide rates. While the results were not entirely conclusive, they did offer some encouraging support for this line of reasoning. Spurred on by these results, a second study was undertaken using Florida counties (Doerner and Speir, 1986). Once again, modest support for the medical resources argument emerged. Buoyed by these findings, a third study employing more detailed measures of medical resources was initiated (Doerner, 1988). Yet again, there was some indication that medical resources, particularly emergency transportation, partially affected criminally induced mortality.

Concern that the accumulating evidence might be peculiar to the state of Florida prompted Long-Onnen and Cheatwood (1992) to look at the medical resources argument in five states: Delaware, Maryland, Pennsylvania, Virginia and West Virginia. Their data showed limited support for the notion that medical resources contribute to the production of homicide rates. In a similar vein, an examination of female homicide offender records in Alabama links racial inequities in emergency medical care with victim demise (Hanke and Gundlach, 1995). In addition, Giacopassi and Sparger (1992) combed through Memphis police homicide files for the years 1935, 1960 and 1985. Looking at the circumstances surrounding these nonsalvageable cases, Giacopassi and Sparger (1992: 256-257) concluded:

> Although the present data are subject to varying interpretations and do not prove that medical care has saved the lives of many who earlier would have become homicide statistics, the evidence seems heavily weighted in favor of this argument. Logic says that increasingly efficient ambulance services, better roads and highways, better trained paramedics, improved communications systems, more hospitals and trauma centers, more skillful physicians, and advances in medicine and medical care all have served to suppress America's homicide rate.

## *Some Remaining Issues*

This initial wave of research activity suggests that the medical resources argument is plausible and deserves further consideration. However, it is also evident that much more work remains before any worthwhile theoretical advances can materialize. Some possible directions include a closer look at the role of alcohol, application of the "autopsy method" and use of an *injury-severity index*.

Both the victimological and emergency medical literatures acknowledge that alcohol is a common ingredient in trauma incidents (Jurkovich et al., 1993; Lowenstein et al., 1990; Riedel et al., 1985; Rivara et al., 1997; Soderstrom and Smith, 1993; Sutocky et al., 1993; Wilbanks, 1984; Wolfgang, 1958; Woolf et al., 1991). Criminologists typically characterize alcohol as a social lubricant. They maintain that alcohol consumption relaxes people, lowers their social inhibitions, weakens restrictions governing the use of force and triggers the release of any pent-up hostilities (Hepburn, 1973; Kantor and Straus, 1987; Wolfgang, 1958). A somewhat related corollary is that alcohol ingestion dulls the reflex system and compromises one's physical readiness. It distorts perceptions and increases reaction time, leaving the person incapable of mounting a sufficient self-defense in the event of a violent attack.

One frequently overlooked aspect of alcohol consumption is that it can also hinder timely medical intervention. Drinking can impede the cardiocirculatory system and depress the central nervous system. Sometimes when time is of the essence, these physical reactions make it difficult to reach an accurate or conclusive diagnosis. For example, a common physical reaction after drinking alcohol is for the pupils to dilate. An attending physician concerned with the possibility of a closed-head injury has to decide whether alcohol is masking the patient's true physical status or if the physical conditions are valid symptoms of brain-related damage (Horton, 1986; Jurkovich et al., 1993; Stone et al., 1986; Woolf et al., 1991). In the absence of any further information, the doctor may delay treatment pending more conclusive blood tests or risk error by choosing one course of intervention over another. Indeed, the general consensus in the emergency medical literature is that 20 to 30 percent of all in-hospital trauma-associated deaths are avoidable (Chan et al., 1980; Davis et al., 1991; Dove et al., 1980; Kreis et al., 1986). While not cognizant of this effect, some criminological studies do show higher alcohol or drug levels in deceased victims compared to survivors of aggravated battery situations (Felson and Steadman, 1983; Pittman and Handy, 1964).

A common hospital administrative practice is to conduct periodic post-mortem reviews to determine whether patients are receiving adequate medical care. This tool is what medical researchers call the *autopsy method* (Pollock et al., 1993; Stothert et al., 1990; West et al., 1983). If a systematic problem surfaces, there might be a suggestion that the institution adopt a different treatment protocol as the standard operating procedure in these instances (Enderson et al., 1990; Ivatury et al., 1991). This constant case monitoring enables trauma centers to take advantage of breaking medical developments and new equipment.

Emergency room admissions generally do not receive medical attention on a "first come, first served" basis. Usually, medical personnel triage patients or conduct a screening during the admissions phase. That is, incoming patients receive a grade regarding the extent and seriousness of their injuries. This strategy creates a queue in which the more seriously wounded are assigned a higher treatment priority over less injured persons (Thayer, 1997).

There have been very few victimological efforts that measure the degree of physical injury incurred by violent crime victims. One researcher suggests that application of the "Abbreviated Injury Scale" and an "Injury Severity Score" could provide immense benefits to this line of inquiry. Allen (1986) explains that these trauma scales were developed to help vehicular crash investigators determine automotive safety standards. His suggestion is that one could use these indices to grade the type of and amount of injuries sustained by crime victims and then to monitor survival patterns. While some researchers have expressed qualms about applying these scales retroactively to archived medical records (Giacopassi and Sparger, 1992: 252-253), these criticisms are not insurmountable. With proper training and adequate documentation, these tools could be incorporated into ongoing patient registration procedures. As you can see, it is quite possible that a sustained interdisciplinary effort, such as what is described here, would enhance our understanding of the production of homicide victimization statistics.

## SURVIVORS OF HOMICIDE VICTIMIZATION

Death is a topic that many people prefer to avoid discussing. In fact, mortality is a taboo subject. Thinking about it can generate a sense of anxiety, so many people shun the subject.

Whenever a person dies, someone must inform the next-of-kin or other survivors of the deceased. The notifier who delivers this message must be prepared to deal with a wide range of responses. The recipients of this communication start the coping process immediately upon hearing of the news. The manner in which the initial notification is made can impact the grieving process. This portion of the chapter will discuss death notification procedures and then move to a treatment of the bereavement process.

### Death Notification

*Death notification* is not a pleasant responsibility. Often, this task falls to law enforcement officers, victim advocates or representatives from the medical examiner's or coroner's office. Many agencies have adopted formal policies similar to what appears in Figure 9.3 to help their personnel with the delivery of death-related news. Even if an explicit policy does not exist, death notification procedures usually follow a four-step process (Byers, 1991; Hendricks, 1984). They include (1) information gathering, (2) control and direction, (3) assessment, and (4) referral.

**FIGURE 9.3**
**An Example of a Law Enforcement Agency Policy Regarding**
**Death Notification Procedures**

A. Notification Within the City

1. When the next-of-kin of a deceased, seriously injured or seriously ill person lives in the City, the officer should make all notifications in person whenever practical. However, if this is not practical, the officer should contact the Communications Center and request another officer be dispatched to the residence for notification.

2. The officer delivering the notification should have as much information as possible to enable him or her to carry out the notification in a professional and considerate manner. When possible, contact between officers or with the Communications Center should be via telephone.

3. The officer should make every reasonable effort to notify the next-of-kin during his or her tour of duty.

    a. The officer shall not leave notification up to the hospital or other authorities.

    b. The officer shall note in the offense report the name of the person notified, relationship and time accomplished.

4. The officer, when possible, should stand by after the notification has been made and render additional assistance to the next-of-kin and, when necessary,:

    a. contact clergy;

    b. contact medical assistance;

    c. contact other family members.

Source: Tallahassee Police Department (no date). *Policy Manual*. Tallahassee, FL: City of Tallahassee.

The first step in any death notification is the information-gathering phase. The person who is to deliver the news should anticipate the types of questions that the recipients may ask and determine the appropriate response to those inquiries. The most important element here is to obtain and verify the identification of the deceased. The name of the person, gender, age, address and any other personal identifiers are of paramount importance. Similar information about the survivor(s) is also essential. Also valuable is information on the circumstances surrounding the death, including time and place. Prior to making the actual notification, the deliverer should confirm that he or she is at the correct location and has reached the appropriate party.

Step two in the death notification process is control and direction. It is the responsibility of the notifier to define the situation for the survivor by informing him or her of the unfortunate news. The deliverer should be factual, honest and deliberate in his or her choice of words. Experts advise that it is best to avoid such euphemisms as "He's gone to a better place" or "She is looking down upon us now" (Byers, 1991; Hendricks, 1984). As the impact begins to take effect upon the survivor, the third phase—the assessment stage—begins to unfold.

The primary task of the notifier during the assessment stage is to gauge how well the bereaved reacts to the disturbing message. Should the recipient show signs of self-blame, or self-destructive behavior such as suicide, the deliverer will need to rechannel, guide or prod the person out of this frame of mind. If the situation worsens, other resources (such as a clergy member, a physician, another survivor or a neighbor) might be in a better position to assist. The objective of this phase is to ensure the well-being of the survivor(s).

The last stage is called referral. Survivors will become flooded with a number of concerns. They will need immediate information about how to make funeral arrangements, how to get the body released from the medical examiner's office, what police procedures must transpire, and the like. Once the situation is under control, the notifier has completed his or her assignment and may leave the scene.

It is important to realize that leaving the scene does not mean that the situation has ended for the notifier. Emergency responders sometimes become deeply immersed in these events and have their own feelings to sort through once the formal assignment is completed (Hendricks, 1984; McCarroll et al., 1993; Walker, 1990). Many agencies will hold a debriefing session for members after a huge disaster or a major catastrophe has subsided. The intent is to relieve any stress reactions that workers may have developed during the crisis. These sessions allow workers to ventilate their feelings, receive information that they may have lacked during the incident and begin adjusting back to the daily routine.

## The Bereavement Process

As we learned in Chapter 5, people who experience a calamity inevitably find themselves in the midst of a crisis. The death of a significant other, particularly through a homicide, qualifies as a sudden, emotionally shattering event that can quickly propel survivors deep into a crisis state. Based upon what experts know about the crisis reaction repair cycle, recovery usually proceeds in a very predictable fashion.

The complete lack of any warning associated with most homicides denies survivors a chance to prepare beforehand for such excruciating news. Survivors do not have the luxury of *anticipatory grief*—the preparations that people can make to cushion the impact of death when a loss is imminent or expected to take place. For example, the diagnosis of a terminal illness in an elderly relative permits family members to brace themselves for the inevitable. This advance warning alerts people to what is coming, gives them time to search for appropriate coping mechanisms and enables survivors to adapt expeditiously to the loss. Homicide survivors lack this preparation. They are thrust into a crisis state unexpectedly without any prior warning or any chance to adjust their readiness.

Most homicide victims are men under the age of 40. This demographic profile means that the survivors of homicide victims will face a host of challenges. Generally speaking, it is easier to cope with timely (as opposed to "off-time") deaths (Detmer and Lamberti, 1991; Parry and Thornwall, 1992). At this point in the life cycle, most men have established a family unit. Their children will grow up without their father. The widow must assume all family responsibilities, including financial burdens. While social security and insurance may help defray some expenses, the role structure of the nuclear family unit often changes. Older children may take on more caretaking functions for younger siblings. Some women may find that they must reenter the job market on a more sustained basis. In short, the survivors must make many adaptations to compensate for the loss of a loved one.

Relatively little research has been devoted to the response of homicide survivors to the loss of a loved one. Kubler-Ross (1969) outlines four stages to the *grief process*: (1) shock and denial, (2) anger, (3) isolation, and (4) acceptance/recovery. The first stage is shock and denial. Immediately after being informed of the death, the survivor reacts by denying that the information is true and tends to shut out all input concerning the event. This is a short-term self-protection mechanism that serves to cushion the blow. The second stage is anger. In this stage the survivor vents his or her rage, frustration and anger toward anyone or anything available. This anger may be toward the bearer of the news, the doctors who could not save the victim, the offender, society or even himself or herself. Third, the survivor tends to isolate himself or herself from others. Isolation reflects different emotions ranging from the uncertainty of how to deal with others to the feeling that there is no one to whom the survivor can turn. Finally, the survivor begins to resume some form of normal activities in the acceptance/recovery stage. While the death remains with the individual, the event is incorporated into the daily routine of the individual as he or she realizes that life must continue.

As mentioned in Chapter 5, there is no predetermined timetable for grief resolution. It may take years before survivors can put the incident behind them. The bereavement process may be continuous and fluid, with members sometimes regressing to early stages. Recovery may be prolonged because of case processing by the criminal justice system. What little research that does exist on homicide survivors, though, suggests that these intense feelings diminish over time and the healing eventually tracks a typical recovery pattern (Kitson et al., 1991; Range and Niss, 1990 ).

There is also evidence that different survivors adapt and cope with the homicide in different ways. Key (1992) identified five *homicide survivor patterns* based on his clinical experience with such individuals. These patterns are highly related to the lifestyle and social setting of the victim and the survivor. The five survival patterns correspond to (1) the drug/alcohol-related murder, (2) the domestic violence homicide, (3) the gang-related murder, (4) the isolated sudden murder, and (5) the serial murder. The survivor in each of these reacts differently.

For example, in the drug/alcohol-related murder survivor pattern, the survivor typically knew of the victim's use and/or trafficking behavior. The survivor had some warning ahead of time that the victim was involved in potentially dangerous behavior and, consequently, was able to prepare somewhat for the loss of the victim. The survivor may even actually feel a sense of relief once the event occurs.

In the domestic violence homicide survival pattern, the survivor may feel some personal guilt for failing to intervene when early signs of abuse and problems emerged. The survivor may believe that if he or she had become involved, the victim may still be alive.

The gang-related homicide survival pattern is typically expected by the survivor who feels he or she had no control over the event. In many cases the survivor may believe that the victim was also a homicide offender and it was only a matter of time until the offender became a victim.

The final two, isolated sudden murder survival pattern and the serial murder survival pattern, both reflect situations in which the death was totally unexpected. These are the scenarios that correspond to the classic image of an unsuspecting homicide victimization. Here, the survivor experiences the typical grief pattern outlined earlier. There are feelings of denial, anger, self-blame, guilt, isolation and eventual reemergence to everyday reality. Key (1992) notes that these survival patterns are not exhaustive; not all possible patterns are included. Rather, he offers these patterns as illustrations of how various people respond to a homicide event in different ways based on the circumstances and background of both the victim and the survivor.

Critical to the bereavement process is the provision of support to the survivor. This support may very well begin with the police officer or physician who notifies the survivor, and may last for a long period of time. An ideal support network can help with a myriad of different things facing the survivor. It certainly would include some offer of counseling, whether in an individual or group setting. While one might assume that these services are common in our society, such assistance is often unknown to the survivor. One method that has emerged in many communities in recent years has been homicide support groups. These groups serve many immediate and long-term needs. In addition, they may involve themselves in community outreach programs, such as those teaching youths about the impact of homicide (Johnson and Young, 1992). Inevitably, the homicide survivor goes on with his or her life. The degree to which survivors receive assistance in that process, however, differs greatly from place to place.

**FIGURE 9.4**
**Selected Internet Sites Dealing with Homicide**

---

Center for Disease Control and Prevention
        http://www.cdc.gov/

Homicide Research Working Group
        http://www.icpsr.umich.edu/NACJD/HRWG/

Parents of Murdered Children
        http://metroguide.com/~world/pomc/

---

## SUMMARY

Homicide, the deliberate killing of one human being by another, claims the lives of thousands of people every year. For some segments of society, murder has reached epidemic levels. For instance, homicide is a leading cause of death for young African-American males in United States cities. Further compounding the alarming spread of violence is the fact that it does not appear that this bloodshed will decrease any time soon. As a result, our theories are in need of greater refinement. So far, the victimization data have experienced some serious limitations, and policy developments have been negligible. It is the homicide survivors, though, (particularly young children) who carry the worst emotional scars. They are forced to make efforts to reclaim their shattered lives and make sense out of the aftermath of the homicide.

# LEARNING OBJECTIVES

After reading Chapter 10, you should be able to:

- Explain the constitutional changes proposed by the President's Task Force.

- Understand the pros and cons behind this proposal.

- Outline the strategy behind the proposed 26th Amendment to the U.S. Constitution.

- Provide details as to what the proposed 26th Amendment encompassed.

- Convey why some people were opposed to the proposed amendment to the Constitution.

- Understand why the strategy switched to targeting state constitutional reform.

- Discuss the revived interest in a federal victim rights constitutional amendment.

- Trace legislative reforms at the federal level.

- Tell what some of the guidelines are regarding the treatment of federal victims and witnesses.

- Relay the provisions of the federal victims' "Bill of Rights."

- Explore some of the guarantees that the states have extended to crime victims.

- List some of the concerns that critics have voiced about victim rights.

- Describe what a victim impact statement contains.

- Communicate the effect that victim impact statements have had.

- Outline case developments regarding federal Supreme Court rulings about victim impact statements.

- Specify the goals of dispute resolution.

- Describe what takes place during dispute resolution.

- Summarize the goals of victim-offender reconciliation programs.

- Explain the ideas behind restorative justice.

# Chapter 10

# Victim Rights

## INTRODUCTION

The historic trend in formal systems of justice has been to look at crimes as transgressions against society and victims as witnesses for society. Recent years, though, have seen a gradual movement toward more victim participation in the justice process. Victims are gaining rights that restore them to greater prominence in the criminal justice system. Some of these rights are as simple as recognizing the victim's human dignity. Others outline procedures for victims to address the court and parole boards. Even more subtle changes include moving cases out of the formal justice system and into informal settings in which victims seek to settle problems with the offenders.

Reasons for these new victim rights are easily identified. First, special interest groups have championed victim causes. They have pushed to balance the rights of the offender with the needs of the victim. Second, the justice system has experienced a great deal of dissatisfaction with how it handles victims. As we demonstrated in Chapter 3, victims derive little, if any, value from contact with the system. Except for fulfilling some vague notion of a "civic duty," victims have very little to gain—and much to lose—from system participation. Many victims never even have the satisfaction of knowing the outcome of their cases. The move toward procedures that give victims a louder voice is a way to make the system more responsive and to lure victims back into the system. Third, the justice system is overwhelmed by the volume of cases. Plea bargaining strategies, failure to file charges, time delays, inadequate sentences and early prisoner releases due to overcrowding indicate that the system is not working well. Alternatives need to be developed. A final, and somewhat unexpected, rationale for giving victims a more active and integral role is its rehabilitative impact. Many advocates point to the potential positive influence that a victim-offender meeting can have on both parties. The growth of victim rights, in this instance, also holds promise for those interested in the offender's well-being.

This final chapter looks at the attempt to reverse the historic trend of alienating victims from the resolution of criminal matters. Specifically, the chapter looks at two general trends that seek to make the victim an active participant at various stages of the justice system. We turn first to the passage of constitutional and statutory provisions for victim rights. Then, we discuss more informal alternatives aimed at resolving victim-offender problems, including dispute mediation, victim-offender reconciliation and restorative justice.

## Victim Rights Amendment

Victim rights reform has taken several different paths in the United States. One strategy has involved efforts to gain passage of a constitutional amendment, commonly referred to as a *Victim Rights Amendment* (VRA), at the federal level to guarantee victims certain rights when involved in the criminal justice system. A parallel movement involved bids to change state constitutions by incorporating VRAs there as well. What we shall do in this section is look at how this movement has fared.

### Federal Constitutional Reform

At the conclusion of its work, The President's Task Force on Victims of Crime (1982) issued a strong, stirring call for action. The Task Force (1982: 114) explained that "government must be restrained from trampling the rights of the individual citizen. The victims of crime have been transformed into a group oppressively burdened by a system designed to protect them." As a result, the Task Force proposed that the Sixth Amendment to the U.S. Constitution be modified to incorporate a new clause guaranteeing explicit rights to crime victims. As Figure 10.1 shows, advocates envisioned that the addition of a single sentence would balance the constitutional standing of crime victims.

Supporters feel that a strong parallel exists between the historical conditions that spawned the original Bill of Rights and the current predicament of crime victims. Constitutional safeguards originally emerged from the colonists' determination to combat what they considered to be an unjust and oppressive system. The drafters of this document wove the notion of fair treatment for persons accused of crimes into a series of protections. This new formulation promised Americans such things as the right to a speedy trial, the right to confront one's accusers, the right to counsel and the freedom from cruel and unusual punishment. As one writer (Eikenberry, 1987: 33) put it, "The founding fathers wanted to ensure that the evils experienced by many innocent citizens at the hands of the English did not find their way into the newly found government."

**FIGURE 10.1**
**Proposed Change to the Sixth Amendment of the U.S. Constitution***

---

In all criminal prosecutions the accused shall enjoy the right to a speedy and public trial, by an impartial jury of the State and district wherein the crime shall have been committed, which district shall have been previously ascertained by law, and to be informed of the nature and cause of the accusation; to be confronted with the witnesses against him; to have compulsory process for obtaining witnesses in his favor and to have the Assistance of Counsel for his defense. **Likewise, the victim, in every criminal prosecution shall have the right to be present and to be heard at all critical stages of judicial proceedings.**

---

* Proposed changes are highlighted for the reader.

---

Source: The President's Task Force on Victims of Crime (1982). *Final Report*. Washington, DC: U.S. Government Printing Office, p. 114.

Crime victims today find themselves in a posture reminiscent of the situation that this country's early settlers faced. The elevation of rights for the accused, coupled with the declining status of the victim, have left victims in a predicament. Even though victims have endured suffering through no fault of their own, the state is more concerned with protecting the rights of their transgressors.

The proposed change to the federal Constitution aims to restore the victim's legal standing and guarantee a certain degree of justice. The inclusion of a VRA in the Constitution, just like the extension of suffrage and the abolition of slavery, would provide a corrective mechanism for undoing past harms (Eikenberry, 1987: 48). However, modifying the Constitution involves a slow, deliberate and tedious process. This was part of the problem with the Equal Rights Amendment, which attempted to resolve gender inequities. As these initial efforts floundered, advocates embraced a new tactic.

A change of direction was heralded during a conference sponsored by the National Organization of Victim Assistance (NOVA) during January of 1986. After reviewing the recommendations proposed by the President's Task Force on Victims of Crime, participants offered an alternate strategy. Rather than trying to add language to embellish the Sixth

Amendment, the suggestion was to create an entirely new 26th Amendment. This new amendment stated:

> Victims of crime are entitled to certain basic rights including, but not limited to, the right to be informed, to be present, and to be heard at all critical stages of the federal and state criminal justice process to the extent that these rights do not interfere with existing Constitutional rights (Young, 1987: 66-67).

Sponsors were in favor of a new amendment for at least three reasons (Young, 1987: 67). First, forming a separate entry that dealt only with victims made the entire issue less confusing and objectionable. Victim gains would not hinge upon offender rights. Second, the new language was broader and much more inclusive. For example, it earmarked participation throughout the entire criminal justice process as its goal rather than restricting such participation to judicial proceedings. Third, it did not tamper with any rights of the accused. As a result, critics could not argue that victim rights were detrimental to existing protections afforded the accused.

These attempts to tamper with the federal Constitution drew resistance. Some observers countered that the entire effort to establish a VRA was misdirected. Dolliver (1987) argued that the purpose behind the federal Bill of Rights is to protect against governmental infringement upon personal liberties. Because victim issues do not involve questions of freedom, they simply do not fit here. While one might commiserate with the unfortunate plight of crime victims, the "lack of uniformity in state statutes should hardly be an automatic recipe for a constitutional amendment" (Dolliver, 1987: 91).

Others found the proposed language to be too vague and overly encompassing. Lamborn (1987), for example, raised a number of perplexing questions as to the meaning of each phrase in the proposed federal amendments. His analysis ended with the following pronouncement (1987: 220):

> The failure of the proponents of the various proposals for a constitutional amendment on behalf of the victim to address the many complex issues raised by their proposals does not diminish the need for an enhanced role for the victim in the criminal justice process. That failure does, however, suggest that the campaign for a constitutional amendment is premature.

## State Constitutional Reform

Given the lukewarm reception, support for any kind of national constitutional reform quickly dwindled. In fact, an assessment of the inroads gained after the 1982 President's Task Force (U.S. Department of Justice, 1986) ignored the entire issue of a federal VRA. Clearly, a new direction was needed.

The method of reform was revisited and revised. Representatives from several victim advocacy groups had established an informal network for sharing ideas and information. Early in 1987, members of these groups decided to create a coalition called the Victims' Constitutional Amendment Network (Victim CAN). This group dedicated itself to promoting VRAs at the state level rather than the federal level.

Targeting states became the preferred option for many reasons (Lamborn, 1987: 201; Spencer, 1987). First, state VRAs would generate greater interest and more local support. Second, even though many states already had victim rights statutes on the books, there was no way to enforce these provisions. A state VRA would reinforce these arrangements. Finally, because state constitutions already protected criminals, it was reasonable to extend the same courtesy to crime victims.

At the present time there are no provisions in the federal constitution that deal with victim rights. However, 29 states, starting with California in 1982, have approved such constitutional measures. The map contained in Figure 10.2 shows the states that have endorsed VRAs in their state constitutions as of June, 1997.

**FIGURE 10.2**
**States with Victim Rights Constitutional Provisions as of June, 1997**

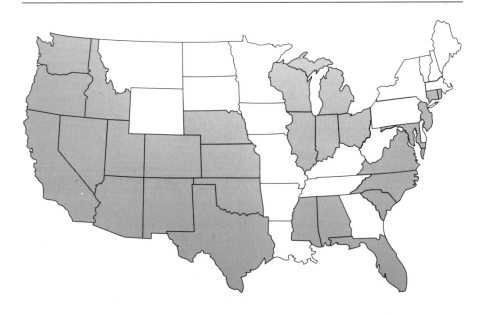

States that are shaded have victim rights constitutional provisions. Alaska (not shown) has such a constitutional provision, while Hawaii (not shown) does not.

State constitutional provisions typically address a set of common rights. As Gaboury and Myers (1997: 40) explain, these guidelines usually mention the right to be treated fairly and with dignity, notification of and attendance at criminal proceedings, opportunity to address the court, notification of the defendant's release from prison, and the availability of restitution or compensation. Figure 10.3 contains the Victims' Rights Amendment from the Wisconsin state constitution.

**FIGURE 10.3**
**The Wisconsin Victims' Rights Constitutional Amendment**

The rights of crime victims, as defined by law, to be treated with fairness, dignity and respect for their privacy, shall be recognized by wholesome laws. Statutes created pursuant to this section shall include, but not be limited to, provisions for

- timely disposition of the case,
- reasonable protection from the accused throughout the criminal justice process,
- notification of court proceedings,
- the right to attend court proceedings unless the trial court finds sequestration is necessary to a fair trial,
- the right to confer with the prosecution,
- the right to make a statement to the court at the disposition,
- rights to restitution and compensation, and
- rights to information about the outcome of the case and the release of the accused.

Victims of crime shall be entitled to rights and remedies as provided by the legislature. Nothing in this section or in any statute enacted pursuant to this section may be construed as creating a basis for vacating a conviction or a ground for appellate relief in a criminal case.

Source: Wisconsin Constitution, Article I, Section 9(m).

The opposition to state constitutional amendments reflects concern over making changes to a document that serves as the basic foundation of our laws. Lamborn (1987) points out that many amendments are proposed without thorough investigation and discussion. Critics fear that victim rights bills tend to be more gut-level reactions than well thought out proposals. Consequently, there appears to be a conservative ideology underlying these amendments that favors a "lock-em up" philosophy.

Opponents of constitutional provisions also warn against eroding the rights of the accused in the haste to assist crime victims. Viano (1987) suggests that passage of constitutional amendments favoring crime victims will result in increased litigation over the treatment of victims, similar to what accompanied civil rights legislation. In essence, such constitutional amendments foster conflict between groups in society.

# Rekindling Federal Constitutional Reform

The momentum achieved through state level efforts was bolstered by a series of rulings issued by the trial court judge in the Oklahoma City bombing case. There the defendant, Timothy McVeigh, was accused of detonating an explosion that toppled the federal building, killing 168 persons and injuring hundreds of other people. During pretrial motions, Judge Matsch announced that he would set aside 45 courtroom seats for media representatives, 37 for public observers, and 16 chairs for the defense. There were no plans to accommodate any victims or survivors (Howlett, 1997). After the government provided a dozen places for victims, Matsch issued an order on June 26, 1996, barring factual witnesses from the trial proceedings. What this ruling meant was that any victim who did not testify but exerted his or her right to attend the deliberations was not eligible to make a victim impact statement before the court during the sentencing phase.

This controversial decision ignited a number of reactions. The Department of Justice intervened, asking the judge to reconsider his decision. Victims and survivors filed their own motion, arguing that the judge's ruling abrogated or set aside the protections guaranteed under the federal "Victims' Bill of Rights" (see Figure 10.6 in this chapter). One victim explained "as it stands, I have to make the excruciating choice between testifying only in the sentencing phase and attending even one minute's worth of the trial" (Cassell, 1997).

The judge upheld his original position in a subsequent hearing, and an appeal to the federal district court on October 4, 1996, produced no change. Bringing the case before the U.S. Court of Appeals for the 10th Circuit provided no immediate relief either. Other efforts, though, proved more successful. Eventually, Congress passed a new measure, signed into law by President Clinton, that removed some of these legal obstacles. However, Matsch warned all parties that a potential avenue of appeal would be opened for the defendant if any victim attended the trial proceedings and gave victim impact testimony later during the sentencing phase. Essentially, then, the legal protections contained in the federal "Victims' Bill of Rights" held a deep, hollow clang for the Oklahoma City bombing victims and their survivors.

These actions propelled a number of victim groups and other interested parties to merge into a unified force. Buoyed by successful campaigns to introduce state VRAs, lobbying efforts resurrected the earlier strategy of seeking support to amend the United States Constitution. This work culminated in Senate Joint Resolution 6 (shown in Figure 10.4).

**FIGURE 10.4**
**Proposed Victim Rights Amendment to the U.S. Constitution**

SECTION I. Each victim of a crime of violence, and other crimes that Congress may define by law, shall have the rights to notice of, and not to be excluded from all public proceedings relating to the crime;

> To be heard, if present, and to submit a statement at a public pre-trial or trial proceeding to determine a release from custody, an acceptance of a negotiated plea, or a sentence;

> To the rights described in the preceding portions of this section at a public parole proceeding, or at a non-public parole proceeding to the extent they are afforded to the convicted offender;

> To notice of a release pursuant to a public or parole proceeding or an escape;

> To a final disposition of the proceedings relating to the crime free from unreasonable delay;

> To an order of restitution from the convicted offender;

> To have the safety of the victim considered in determining any release from custody; and

> To notice of the rights established by this article; however, the rights to notice under this section are not violated if the proper authorities make a reasonable effort, but are unable to provide the notice, or if the failure of the victim to make a reasonable effort to make those authorities aware of the victim's whereabouts prevents that notice.

SECTION 2. The victim shall have standing to assert the rights established by this article. However, nothing in this article shall provide grounds for the victim to challenge a charging decision or a conviction; to obtain a stay of trial; or to compel a new trial. Nothing in this article shall give rise to a claim for damages against the United States, a State, a political subdivision, or a public official, nor provide grounds for the accused or convicted offender to obtain any form of relief.

SECTION 3. The Congress and the States shall have the power to enforce this article within their respective Federal and State jurisdictions by appropriate legislation, including the power to enact exceptions when required for compelling reasons of public safety or for judicial efficiency in mass victim cases.

SECTION 4. The rights established by this article shall apply to all proceedings that begin on or after the 180th day after the ratification of this article.

SECTION 5. The rights established by this article shall apply in all Federal and State proceedings, including military proceedings to the extent that Congress may provide by law, juvenile justice proceedings, and collateral proceedings such as habeas corpus, and including proceedings in any district or territory of the United States not within a State.

Source: Congressional Record, Senate Joint Resolution 6, 105th Congress, 1st Session, January 21, 1997.

A mounting wave of criticism quickly surfaced and opponents echoed many of the concerns mentioned earlier. An editorial in the *New York Times* wondered whether support for constitutional reform amounted to anything more than mere political posturing by elected officials (Lewis, 1996). However, Kansas Attorney General Stovall (1997) counters that the framers of the Constitution never intended for this document to be so sacrosanct as to not undergo modification. In fact, Congress has altered the Constitution 27 times already, extending protections to persons accused of crimes in 15 of these changes. In Stovall's (1997) view, "I do not believe it just that within our system no rights are guaranteed by the very same document to the victims of the very acts for which the accused have been arrested and guaranteed rights."

Obviously, the final page in these recent developments has yet to be written. The forthcoming debate over constitutional reform will continue to highlight the plight of crime victims and may elevate these concerns to the national forefront. It will be interesting to see whether the transition from the *criminal's* justice system to a *justice* system will be realized in the very near future.

## VICTIM RIGHTS LEGISLATION

Another avenue to secure victim rights called for the passage of new laws and regulations that spelled out exact protections. Just like VRA reform, legislation was enacted mandating certain rights and privileges for crime victims and witnesses at the federal level. This activity also prompted a parallel response at the state level. Both the federal and state arenas are visited in this section.

### Federal Legislative Reform

One alternative to making constitutional changes is to promote legislation that addresses victim concerns. This approach is clearly more palatable to many people. In addition to federal efforts, virtually every state has taken parallel steps.

Over the past 25 years, the federal government has undertaken a variety of initiatives dealing with crime victims. Perhaps the earliest indication of a concern for victims appeared in 1974 with the establishment of the Citizen's Initiative Program by the Law Enforcement Assistance Administration (LEAA). This program, like most LEAA actions, entailed funding state and local projects. In this instance, monies were earmarked to establish victim-witness programs. As Chapter 3 explained, the expectation was that such efforts would lure victims and witnesses back into the criminal justice system.

Two major events in 1982 brought victim issues to the forefront of federal actions. The first milestone was the passage of the Omnibus Victim/Witness Protection Act. The second was the release of the Final Report from the President's Task on Victims of Crime.

The Omnibus Victim/Witness Protection Act (VWPA) was the first federal legislation to address victim and witness rights involved in the criminal justice process. The Act's provisions included the right of victims to supply impact statements to the court, the right to freedom from intimidation by the offender, the right to consultation about plea bargaining agreements, and a number of other items. While this legislation applied only to the federal courts, it prompted several states to enact similar legislation.

The President's Task Force on Victims of Crime offered 68 recommendations that touched virtually all parts of society. Forty-five recommendations addressed various components of the criminal justice system—the police, prosecutors, the judiciary and parole boards. The remainder focused upon hospitals, the ministry, the bar, schools, the mental health community and the private sector. Some of these suggestions dealt with:

- keeping victim and witness addresses confidential
- establishing a privileged relationship between victims and counselors
- requiring victim impact statements
- enacting federal victim compensation regulations
- sensitizing criminal justice personnel to victim issues
- notifying victims of parole hearings and decisions
- instituting victim counseling at hospitals
- undertaking background checks for all school employees
- developing mental health responses to victimization

However, the Task Force was an advisory board only and did not have the authority to mandate these changes. While some recommendations have found their way into action, many others still lie dormant. However, one should not forget that the Task Force was the first major federal effort to focus exclusively on the plight of crime victims. As such, it gave instant legitimacy to a struggling victim movement.

These developments encouraged further action. For example, in 1983 the U.S. Attorney General promulgated a set of guidelines for dealing with and assisting federal victims and witnesses. Figure 10.5 lists those actions mandated by the VWPA and those voluntarily undertaken by the Department of Justice as an extension of the Act. These rules attempt to make federal criminal procedures more accommodating and inviting to victims and witnesses.

**FIGURE 10.5**
**U.S. Attorney General's Guidelines for Victim/Witness Assistance**

---

Guidelines Mandated by the Victim/Witness Protection Act:

Victim referral to medical services, social services, and compensation programs.

Victim/witness notification (upon request) of:
- right to be protected from intimidation/harassment
- arrest or release of accused
- judicial proceedings/scheduling changes or continuances
- pleas, plea agreements
- trial results
- sentencing hearing dates
- right to be heard at sentencing
- date sentence imposed

Victim consultation services:
- pretrial release or diversion
- reduction or dismissal of any or all charges
- plea agreements/sentencing recommendations
- restitution

Other victim services:
- waiting areas for victims separate from other witnesses
- prompt return of property held as evidence
- employer intervention services
- assistance with transportation, parking and translating

Victim assistance training for Federal law enforcement personnel and attorneys.

Provisions by the Department of Justice:

Prevention of the disclosure of victims' and witnesses' addresses, if possible.

Notification to creditors of victims and witnesses if cooperation affects the ability to make timely payments.

Establishment of programs to assist Department of Justice employees who are victims of crime.

Assure that U.S. Probation Officers are fully advised of the victim impact statement requirements.

Provision of training for Department of Justice employees concerning these responsibilities.

---

Source: Adapted from Office for Victims of Crime (1990). *Report to Congress, April 1990.* Washington, DC: U.S. Department of Justice.

Perhaps the most significant federal legislation during this period was the Victims of Crime Act (VOCA) of 1984. A major contribution of VOCA was the establishment of the Crime Victim's Fund. This fund, originally capped at $100 million, financed grants to state victim compensation and victim assistance programs. Penalties, fines and forfeitures levied on federal offenders serve as the ongoing endowment for this fund. These sources have played an important role in the adoption and expansion of victim compensation programs throughout the United States.

The "strings" that the federal government attached to the receipt of these monies are responsible for standardized compensation statutes across the country. These regulations have also released funds to victims previously excluded under various state guidelines. Amendments to VOCA in the late 1980s and early 1990s refined the process of safeguarding victim rights, altered the amounts and distribution of monies from the Crime Victims Fund and enhanced the status of victims involved in the criminal justice system.

Strong gains in victims rights came with the passage of the Crime Control Act (CCA) of 1990. Two important components of the CCA were the "Victims' Rights and Restitution Act" and the "Victims of Child Abuse Act." This legislation went beyond VOCA by mandating specific actions and responsibilities of federal personnel in dealing with crime victims. Rather than leaving things to chance, the CCA requires specific services and treatment for federal crime victims. Probably the most noteworthy feature was the creation of the federal Crime Victims' Bill of Rights (reprinted in Figure 10.6). It is important to note that although it is called a Bill of Rights, it is *not* a national constitutional provision. As a result of the CCA and its various components, the federal government has expanded its policies and procedures for informing crime victims of their rights and for protecting their interests (Office of the U.S. Attorney General, 1992b).

One of the more heralded pieces of victim legislation came in the form of the "Victim Rights Clarification Act of 1997" (VRCA). A series of judicial rulings in the Oklahoma City bombing case brought a number of issues to the forefront. If you recall from our earlier discussion, the judge in that case sequestered victims from the criminal trial. In other words, if a victim planned to make an impact statement during the penalty portion of the trial, then he or she could not view the criminal trial. The court maintained that Rule 615 of the Federal Rules of Evidence superseded the provisions of the Victims' Bill of Rights. The fear was that exposure to other victims' testimony during the trial might slant or taint the independent recollection of victims at the later sentencing phase (Cassell, 1997; Myers, 1997a).

**FIGURE 10.6**
**Federal Crime Victims' Bill of Rights**

A crime victim has the following rights:

1.  The right to be treated with fairness and with respect for the victim's dignity and privacy.

2.  The right to be reasonably protected from the accused offender.

3.  The right to be notified of court proceedings.

4.  The right to be present at all public court proceedings related to the offense, unless the court determines that testimony by the victim would be materially affected if the victim heard other testimony at trial.

5.  The right to confer with attorney for the Government in the case.

6.  The right to restitution.

7.  The right to information about the conviction, sentencing, imprisonment, and release of the offender.

Source: Victims' Rights and Restitution Act of 1990.

The VRCA removes this obstacle and permits victims to observe both portions of the criminal trial. The thinking behind this legislation is that while sequestering witnesses is intended to protect the defendant's basic right to a fair trial, impact statements deal with sentencing and bear no relationship to adjudication. As a result, the VRCA clarifies the victim's right to attend the full criminal trial and preserves the victim's right to address the court during sentencing proceedings.

## State Legislative Reform

While these federal actions were taking place, many states were devising steps to protect and assist their own crime victims. One prime example of these inroads is that most states have active victim compensation programs. Virtually every state in the union has passed its own legislation dealing with victim rights. In many respects, these provisions mirror federal efforts. As Figure 10.7 outlines, Wisconsin victims are to be kept informed about the status of cases, they are to be notified about pleas, they are to be protected from intimidation or harassment, their participation in case proceedings is encouraged and they have the right to compensation or restitution. Victims also often have the right to make or provide impact statements at sentencing and parole determinations.

**FIGURE 10.7**
**Selected Victim Rights in Wisconsin**

Victims and their survivors have the right to:

- information from law enforcement as to the final case disposition
- information from the prosecutor as to the final case disposition
- information of the defendant's release from custody if the crime is a felony
- notification of a pardon application by the defendant
- notification of a cancellation in court proceedings to which they are subpoenaed
- provide the court with a victim impact statement
- protection against witness intimidation
- information about and help getting financial assistance and other social services
- witness fees
- secure waiting conditions during court proceedings
- prompt property return when it is no longer needed as evidence
- appropriate employer intercession to minimize loss of pay and other benefits
- have input into parole decision-making
- notification whenever an offender is placed into community residential confinement
- notification regarding an offender's escape from custody
- notification regarding an offender's sentence expiration or release from confinement
- notification in sex crimes about whether the defendant has a communicable disease
- have their names and addresses withheld

Source: Wisconsin Statutes (1997).

One unfortunate feature of victim rights legislation in many jurisdictions is that these provisions are scattered throughout the statutes, rather than being compiled under a single statutory heading. The Ohio Revised Code, for example, lists various victim rights under more than one dozen sections and a myriad of subsections. While this disarray does not reduce the legality of the measures, it does hinder public awareness. Certainly, most victims learn about their rights only if they are informed by the prosecutor, a victim advocate or someone else.

The introduction of victim rights legislation has not gone without criticism. For one thing, these additional measures and responsibilities translate into increased loads for beleaguered criminal justice workers. These actions may bring about some delays and greater costs in the court process.

Some people fear that greater participation may exacerbate harm to the victim. The victim must relive the traumatic events surrounding the crime during both the fact-finding and sentencing phases of a court case. Pointed questions by the defense can be a further detriment. This experience might be a cleansing event for some victims, but for others it may only intensify and prolong the hurt.

Another question involves the situation in which a victim is not notified or accorded his or her statutorily guaranteed rights. What avenues can victims pursue should the system not honor these rights? Although many statutes spell out the steps expected of system personnel, there is little recourse if the prosecution does not comply with these procedures. In fact, some states include an explicit disclaimer that victims cannot take any legal action against system personnel who fail to follow the statute. Other jurisdictions rely on a more general immunity clause that prohibits the public from suing governmental agents for actions undertaken in good faith or without malice. One possible solution lies in the area of ethics standards. Victims may be able to file complaints with a state ethics board that can levy disciplinary action for failure to comply with the law. However, it is likely that this recourse would bring little satisfaction to the victim.

A more perplexing issue involves a debate over the goals of the criminal justice system. Increased attention to victim harm shifts sentencing from a preoccupation with rehabilitation to an emphasis on retribution and restitution. What this change does is to refocus attention upon the needs of the victim. Critics protest that this creates an imbalance and invites a diminution of offender rights. Others note that the call for harsher sanctions stretches an already overextended correctional system beyond its capacity (Acker, 1992; Erez, 1989; Ranish and Shichor, 1985). As one writer adroitly put it:

> [I]n some respects, a new battle has replaced the old. Now, it is not victims fighting for a place in the system; the current consensus is that they belong. But a new battle now rages between the state and its own limited resources. Vying for these resources are overcrowded jails, rising crime rates, and competing welfare and infrastructure programs. Clearly, the rights of crime victims will not be secure until these issues are resolved (Calcutt, 1988: 834).

## THE EFFECT OF VICTIM RIGHTS LEGISLATION

One would expect that the proliferation of victim rights legislation over the past two decades would have had a great impact on crime victims and the criminal justice system. Unfortunately, there has been relatively little research on the effect of these legal and administrative changes.

One way to assess the impact of these measures is to examine reports from system personnel. The Office for Victims of Crime (OVC) undertook one such study. The OVC surveyed U.S. Attorneys about their compliance with the Attorney General's guidelines. As Table 10.1 shows, the respondents reported a high degree of compliance with victim rights provisions and directives. Likewise, Table 10.2 shows there was a general feeling that their offices provided the utmost service to victims.

**TABLE 10.1**
**U.S. Attorney Responses on Service Provision**

| General Office Policy or Practice | % Yes Responses |
|---|---|
| When requested, notify creditors of victims and witnesses if their cooperation affects their ability to pay? | 100 |
| Provide general information to victims and witnesses about transportation, parking, translator services, and other information related to court-room appearance? | 99 |
| Maintain accurate, up-to-date resource material which identifies available victim counseling and treatment programs in the jurisdiction? | 98 |
| Advise victims and witnesses of their right to be protected from intimidation/harassment? | 98 |
| Resist defense attempts to obtain addresses of victims and witnesses? | 96 |
| Provide training to your employees concerning compliance with the Attorney General's Guidelines for the Victim and Witness Protection Act? | 96 |
| Assist your own employees who are victims of crime? | 95 |
| Provide victims and witnesses for the prosecution a waiting area separate from the defendant and defense witnesses? | 92 |
| When requested, notify employers of victims and witnesses if their cooperation causes absence from work? | 91 |
| Ensure that sexual assault victims do not pay for the cost of forensic examinations? | 91 |

Source: Office for Victims of Crime (1990). *Report to Congress, April 1990.* Washington, DC: U.S. Department of Justice.

**TABLE 10.2**
**Perceived Quality of Services Provided by U.S. Attorney's Offices**

| Service Provided | Ratings of "Very Well" or "Well" |
|---|---|
| Notification on: | |
| Protection from intimidation or harassment | 91 |
| Arrest or release of the accused | 90 |
| Scheduling changes of judicial proceedings | 91 |
| Pleas or plea agreements | 87 |
| Trial results | 90 |
| Sentencing hearing dates | 85 |
| Right to be heard at sentencing | 84 |
| Date sentence imposed | 83 |
| Notification to Bureau of Prisons of names of victims/witnesses desiring notification of prisoner transfer, escape and/or release | 83 |
| Consultation on: | |
| Declination or dismissal of any or all charges | 73 |
| Plea agreements/sentencing recommendations | 72 |
| Restitution | 89 |
| Victim referral to: | |
| Emergency medical assistance | 80 |
| Social services | 87 |
| Counseling or support groups | 88 |
| State crime victim compensation program | 87 |

Source: Office for Victims of Crime (1990). *Report to Congress, April 1990.* Washington, DC: U.S. Department of Justice.

While these results suggest that system personnel comply with the various guidelines, there is a lack of clear evidence from victims corroborating these high levels of service provision. Forst and Hernon (1985) reported that victims did not think they were kept informed about the case. Furthermore, many victims felt that what information they did receive was due to their own initiative, rather than that of criminal justice personnel. While this experience contradicts the OVC study, it does predate much of the recent federal and state legislation. There is an obvious need for more up-to-date information on this topic.

# VICTIM IMPACT STATEMENTS

Perhaps one of the more significant steps in the crusade for victim rights has been the idea of a victim impact statement. A *victim impact statement* (VIS) allows the victim the opportunity to let the court know how the incident has influenced his or her life. Victims can describe the emotional and financial costs associated with the victimization and can outline what they consider to be an appropriate punishment.

A VIS takes one of two forms. The first is a written account that usually accompanies the presentence investigation report. The second format, called *allocution*, is an oral presentation. Here the victim addresses the court in person during the sentencing phase.

Two major streams of interest have trailed the VIS: (1) the research dealing with the effect of a VIS upon case processing, and (2) the legal challenges that have risen regarding the use of a VIS in death penalty cases. Both topics are addressed in the following sections.

## The Effect of Victim Impact Statements

The most surprising finding in virtually all victim impact statement studies is that large numbers of victims do not avail themselves of this opportunity. For example, while one-half of the felony victims over a four-year span in Ohio provided a VIS, only 6 percent exercised the right of allocution at sentencing (Erez and Tontodonato, 1990; Erez and Tontodonato, 1992). Other studies concur that fewer than 10 percent of all victims make statements at sentencing hearings or parole board deliberations (Erez and Guhlke, 1988; McLeod, 1987; Ranish and Shichor, 1985; Villmoare and Neto, 1987).

One reason for this stunning lack of participation is that many victims are not aware of the right to be present. Also, in some instances, they cannot be located when the case reaches that stage of the criminal justice process (McLeod, 1987; Villmoare and Neto, 1987). But even when victims *do* know about this opportunity, they refrain from using it. Many victims are dissatisfied with the system, they do not think their input is critical, they fear retaliation or they are concerned for their own emotional well-being (Erez and Tontodonato, 1992; Villmoare and Neto, 1987).

For victims who do use the system, contrary to what skeptics had forecasted, not all of them use the VIS vindictively to seek the harshest punishment possible (Acker, 1992). Critics were concerned that VISs would supersede legal factors and that judicial punishment would comply with these subjective "victim pleas." One study found that the victim's presence in court, a VIS and a request for incarceration all influenced the use of imprisonment (Erez and Tontodonato, 1990). However, the VIS carried far less weight than legal variables and prior offense history in sentence determination. Other studies report that VISs have no impact on sentences, restitution orders, the speed of court procedures, or victim satisfaction (Davis et al., 1990; Davis and Smith, 1994; Davis and Smith, 1995; Erez, 1990; Erez and Roeger, 1995; Erez and Tontodonato, 1992). In fact, one victimologist caustically commented that "requiring a victim impact statement and recommendation as part of the presentence report is a mere genuflection to ritualistic legalism" (Walsh, 1986: 1139).

There is an emerging body of literature that appears to contradict some of these earlier findings. Parsonage and his colleagues (1994) found that parole boards are less likely to recommend inmates for release prior to sentence expiration when victims oppose such action. Luginbuhl and Burkhead (1995), in an experimental design that utilized college students as subjects, uncovered a tendency for these simulated jurors to vote for the death penalty when they had access to victim impact statements like the one the prosecution proffered in the *Booth v. Maryland* case (see the following section).

Despite a number of empirical studies that find that sentencing practices remain largely unaffected by victim input, VISs have generated tremendous legal concern. As the following section explains, even the federal Supreme Court became embroiled in the use of VISs during capital cases.

## Federal Supreme Court Rulings

The practice of allowing a VIS has resulted in three significant U.S. Supreme Court cases. Initially, the Court barred the use of a VIS in death penalty cases. However, the Court recently reversed itself and now permits such information to be heard during the sentencing phase. A brief look at these three cases will illustrate how case law has evolved in this area.

The Supreme Court first addressed the issue of the VIS in *Booth v. Maryland* (1987). Booth was convicted of two counts of first-degree murder in a case involving an elderly couple. During the sentencing portion of the trial, the judge allowed the admission of a written VIS that was read to the jury.

According to Booth's lawyer, the VIS contained a number of inflammatory statements. For example, the VIS described the victims as "loving parents and grandparents" as well as "extremely good people who wouldn't hurt a fly." Family members also stated their parents were "butchered like animals" and that nobody "should be able to do something like that and get away with it." Furthermore, the victim's daughter said that she "could never forgive anyone for killing them that way." Given the tone of these statements, Booth's lawyer argued that such characterizations were unduly prejudicial to his client.

The Supreme Court delivered a 5-4 judgment and ruled that a capital sentencing jury should not be exposed to a VIS during its deliberations. Drawing upon previous death penalty decisions, the Court noted that a VIS was not a statutorily defined aggravating circumstance. Introducing testimony about the sterling character of the victim runs the risk that the jury could make an arbitrary decision. In other words, instead of focusing completely upon the defendant, the jury might be tempted to impose the death penalty solely because the victim was an outstanding member of the community.

In *South Carolina v. Gaithers* the U.S. Supreme Court extended this embargo to cover prosecutor comments made to a jury during the sentencing portion of a death penalty case. During closing arguments, the prosecutor emphasized repeatedly that the deceased was an extremely religious person and a self-styled minister. The South Carolina Supreme Court, relying upon the *Booth* decision, overturned the sentence of death. It reasoned that the prosecutor's remarks implied that the death sentence was appropriate because the victim was such a religious person.

An appeal to the U.S. Supreme Court brought a similar rebuff. The federal justices, in another 5-4 split decision, ruled that the prosecutor's description of the victim violated the standards erected in *Booth*. However, the dissenting opinions made it quite clear there was considerable disenchantment with *Booth* itself. Justice O'Connor, for example, wrote "I remain persuaded that *Booth* was wrong when decided and stand ready to overrule it if the Court would do so. . . ." Justice Scalia also echoed a similar sentiment in his remarks.

The VIS controversy continued until the Court reversed itself in the 1991 *Payne v. Tennessee* decision. Payne had been sentenced to death for murdering a mother and her child. A three-year-old survived the attack and the jury received a VIS that documented the duress the child was facing. The jury imposed the death penalty upon Payne. However, Payne's lawyer appealed the sentence, arguing that any reliance upon a VIS in a capital case clearly violated both *Booth* and *Gathers*.

The federal Supreme Court granted *certiorari*, heard the case and overturned its earlier rulings. As the majority opinion explained:

> We thus hold that if the State chooses to permit the admission of victim impact evidence and prosecutorial argument on that subject, the Eighth Amendment erects no *per se* bar. A State may legitimately conclude that evidence about the victim and about the impact of the murder on the victim's family is relevant to the jury's decision as to whether or not the death penalty should be imposed. There is no reason to treat such evidence differently than other relevant evidence is treated.

As a result of *Payne*, the courts are no longer required to suppress a VIS in a capital penalty case. If state law permits the prosecution to explain what repercussions the survivors have shouldered because of the incident, that information is appropriate for the jury to hear. Nothing in the Eighth Amendment forbids such testimony from consideration.

The controversy surrounding the issue of a VIS in a death penalty case prompted one commentator to recommend a slightly different tack. Finn-DeLuca (1994: 427-428) suggests that a more beneficial route would be for state legislatures to construct guidelines governing the types of victim impact evidence considered admissible and what kind of information would be inappropriate for juries to hear during the penalty phase. Such a strategy wold avoid sentencing practices that rely heavily upon emotional or inflammatory appeal (Newman, 1995).

## INFORMAL VICTIM PARTICIPATION

The unprecedented rise in the number of offenders passing through the doors of the justice system has helped to cultivate the concern about victim rights. This tandem should come as no surprise because victim issues and offender issues are often different sides of the same coin. As crime increases, so does the number of victims. The criminal justice system, mandated to provide offenders with due process, must also contend with new rules and regulations that focus on another constituency: victims. Despite these expanding demands, additional funds are not forthcoming. Under these circumstances, the scarce resources allocated to the justice system are being stretched further. In essence, the system is being exhorted to do more with less.

There have been many suggestions designed to ease the load being placed upon the justice system. One promising avenue is the shifting of some matters out of the system and into a less rigid forum. These various efforts include dispute resolution, victim-offender mediation, victim-offender reconciliation programs and restorative justice. The remainder of this chapter will examine the emergence of these alternatives for addressing victim needs.

### Background

One can trace modern dispute resolution back to the 1970s. During this time, a number of jurisdictions started programs to divert minor disputes out of the formal court system. While many programs were adjuncts to prosecutor offices and the judiciary, others were sponsored by outside groups or organizations. These initial programs provided an arena in which victims and offenders could meet and work out mutually agreeable solutions. The goal, of course, was to avoid going to court.

Dispute resolution is a mechanism for achieving a number of goals simultaneously. First, the parties involved in the situation work together to resolve the problem rather than having some outside authority impose a solution. Second, any dispute that reaches a settlement is one less case with which the formal justice system must contend. This alternative alleviates some congestion in the court system. Third, this informal approach empowers victims by giving them a direct voice in their own matters. Victims retain complete veto power over the final outcome. Finally, dispute resolution provides the victim with a face-to-face encounter with the offender. This meeting enables the victim to vent anger and to seek understanding—something that many victims deeply desire.

The approach of these programs appeals to a diverse audience. Consequently, dispute resolution garners support from many corners and has spread rapidly. Prosecutors and judges welcome the chance to reduce overcrowded dockets, while victim advocates see a tremendous potential to help their clients. More than 80 United States cities had dispute resolution programs in place in 1980 (Garofalo and Connelly, 1980a). Six years later, that number swelled to 350 (Ray et al., 1986). Its popularity is evident in the proliferation of similar arrangements now operating in Canada, Great Britain, Australia, Denmark, Finland, Germany, and many other countries (Umbreit, 1997).

## Dispute Resolution Programs

The basic idea behind dispute resolution is to bring opposing parties together in an attempt to work out a mutually agreeable solution. The early programs of this type were typically referred to as *dispute resolution* or dispute mediation. While there are several different types of dispute resolution programs, they all share five traits in common (Garofalo and Connelly, 1980a):

1) A third-party mediator is involved.

2) Disputants usually know each other.

3) Participation must be voluntary.

4) Processes are informal.

5) Disputants are usually referred to the process by someone in the criminal justice system.

First, these programs involve a third-party mediator who monitors participant interaction. This arbitrator keeps the discussion focused and makes suggestions whenever the need arises. Most mediators are volunteers who are not affiliated with the formal justice system. Because of this independence, some people call these programs "neighborhood dispute resolution."

A second characteristic is that many disputants have known each other for a period of time. Often, they are neighbors, friends or family members (although store owners and customers can utilize such a program). This familiarity can be helpful when trying to forge a compromise.

Third, most programs insist that participation be completely voluntary. Both disputants must agree to handle the problem through the program. If either party declines to take part, the dispute moves back to the realm of more formal legal action.

Fourth, the actual resolution of a dispute follows a very informal process. Rules of evidence are not enforced and attorneys are not allowed to attend these sessions. Instead, the process calls for discussion rather than rigid fact-finding. As one might expect, the mediator has a free hand to conduct each meeting as he or she sees fit.

The fifth and final common aspect is that most disputants enroll in the program after being referred to it by a member of the criminal justice system. Most often, the prosecutor has reviewed the case and decided that the interests of justice can be better served in a nontraditional manner.

The idea of dispute resolution has been extended in recent years to include meetings between convicted offenders and their victims. These programs, typically referred to as *Victim-Offender Reconciliation Programs (VORPs)*, are meant to achieve many of the same ends as the less formal initiatives. A common outcome of a VORP meeting is an agreement to some form of offender restitution to the victim. At the same time, it is hoped that the offender will benefit from meeting the victim. In some jurisdictions, VORP participation has worked so well that it has become a condition of probation or parole.

The ability to arrive at a suitable settlement is a key element for victims. Evaluation efforts typically reveal that more than two-thirds of all participants report a satisfactory resolution and that both parties live up to the agreement (Anderson, 1982; Coates and Gehm, 1989; Cook et al., 1980; Felstiner and Williams, 1982; McGillis and Mullen, 1977; Roehl and Cook, 1982). Similar results have been found for programs geared to juvenile offenders (Bridenback et al., 1980; Reichel and Seyfrit, 1984; Umbreit and Coates, 1993).

Outcome studies that use official data do not paint as consistently optimistic a portrait. These investigations compare recidivism levels for offenders who participate in dispute resolution against those who undergo normal system processing. Various studies report that both adults and juveniles handled through dispute resolution programs have lower recidivism rates (McGillis and Mullin, 1977; Sarri and Bradley, 1980; Smith and Smith, 1979; Vorenberg, 1981). However, other research finds no difference in subsequent court involvement between those who underwent mediation and those who did not (Davis, 1982; Davis et al., 1980; Felstiner and Williams, 1979) .

Two factors temper these findings. As we mentioned earlier, participation in dispute resolution is voluntary. What this suggests is that those persons who agree to use this process are hopeful and extremely motivated to find a workable solution. One might expect, then, that voluntary participants would be more likely to abide by the decision and to refrain from similar behavior in the future.

Another stumbling block is that dispute resolution evaluations typically include only successful cases in which both parties agree to a solution. Subsequent program appraisals are based solely on information supplied by "these parties." There is no input from the failures, that is, the people who dropped out because they could not reach a mutually agreeable solution. The inclusion of only successful mediation efforts virtually guarantees a positive outcome.

Additional considerations challenge the use of dispute resolution from a victim's point of view. First, because both parties must agree to participate, many victims never have the opportunity to avail themselves of this service. A hefty number of case referrals never result in a meeting between the parties (Anderson, 1982; Coates and Gehm, 1989; Cook et al., 1980; McGillis and Mullen, 1977). In other words, some victims find themselves shut out of this means of redress. Only those projects that mandate offender participation, such as some VORP programs, can guarantee the willing victim a chance to meet with his or her offender.

Another concern is that dispute resolution efforts appear to arrive at lasting solutions only for property matters (Garofalo and Connelly, 1980b). When a property dispute is settled and the victim is made whole again, there is no ongoing problem with which to deal. Personal offenses, on the other hand, are often deeply traumatic events. In many instances, victims and offenders are related to one another or know each other. Dispute resolution settlements are engineered to provide immediate, short-term solutions. They tend not to address long-term root causes of the problem. Thus, dispute resolution may not be an appropriate remedy for all kinds of crime victims.

## Restorative Justice

Most arguments favoring dispute resolution alternatives have focused upon victim needs and concerns. A more recent debate suggests that such arrangements serve a broader audience. The concept of *restorative (reparative) justice* seeks to use interventions that return the victim and offender to their pre-offense states. For offenders, this means an assurance that the action will not be repeated.

Any restorative justice intervention should seek to repair the harm done to the victim and to remove the causes of the offender's actions (Wright, 1991). The community, the victim and the offender all need to be intimately involved in dealing with the problems and solutions. By so doing, society becomes a better place for everyone, not just the immediate victim and offender. Programs such as VORP, restitution and dispute resolution procedures aim to repair the harm done to all parties involved.

Restorative justice involves various constituencies (Van Ness, 1990; Umbreit, 1997; also see Van Ness and Strong, 1997). Under this approach victims are compensated through restitution, are given a voice in the case handling and become an integral part of the treatment or intervention provided to the offender. The offender is held accountable for his or her transgressions and may be subjected to a wide array of possible interventions. These responses may include incarceration, restitution orders, meetings with victims, involvement in rehabilitation programs (e.g., educational or vocational training, drug treatment, etc.) and/or community service. The offender makes amends and is assisted in order to mitigate the chances of future deviance. Communities also may be compensated through offender payments or services. At the same time, the community is expected to assist the victim, work with the offender and seek to eliminate causes of crime. Finally, the government (particularly in the form of the criminal justice system) is to provide fair and equitable procedures for all parties, while receiving the support and assistance of the public in these efforts (Van Ness, 1990). In essence, restorative justice seeks to bring all parties to the table in a mutual assistance pact. Everyone who comes in with a need is to depart with some degree of satisfaction.

It is difficult for anyone to argue against the notion that the offender, victim, criminal justice system or the community all need and deserve attention. One appeal of restorative justice is the recognition of these varied needs and a concerned effort to address them.

Restorative justice certainly speaks to the concerns and interests of victim advocates. It is not surprising that the move toward restorative justice is being led by prominent proponents of victim rights. At the same time, many individuals traditionally concerned with offender rights and treatment can see restorative justice as a means of maintaining concern for offenders amidst the growth of victim rights. The criminal justice system, which is caught in the middle of a tug-of-war between victims and offenders, benefits from a proposal that does not seek to elevate one group's concerns over those of another.

Despite its appeal, restorative justice raises some concerns. First, the admission of victims into the criminal justice process is threatening to a system that traditionally has been oriented toward offender rights and that identifies society as the victim. Those favoring harsh punishment and those promoting rehabilitation or treatment tend to view the victim as getting in the way of dealing with offenders. The victim may want restitution and community service in lieu of punishment or may be looking for harsh punishment instead of treatment.

Beyond the inherent competition for attention lies concern about the proper role of the criminal justice system. This second worry relates to the fact that restorative justice proposes a new philosophy for the criminal justice system—particularly the corrections component. The offender-centered correctional system would be replaced by a system that attempts to accommodate diverse needs.

Finally, restorative justice is promoted as an integral part of the formal system of justice. As such, it will increase the number of clients being served (victims and offenders) and the tasks to be carried out by the criminal justice system. This imposes an increased burden to an already overburdened system. Opponents also object to the formalization of the role of victims in criminal justice processing.

Restorative justice is the most recent entry in a long debate about the proper role of victims in the criminal justice system. Despite the intuitive appeal behind these ideas, many of the same concerns voiced about more specific victim rights legislation are resurrected in this debate. The challenging nature of restorative justice, particularly in terms of how it would affect the workings of the existing system, suggests that its adoption as a guiding principle lies in the distant future.

## SOME CLOSING THOUGHTS

Chapter 1 framed this book in the context of Mendelsohn's rendition of the field as "general victimology." At that point, readers were advised that this book was going to concentrate on a single component of that typology: criminal victimology. After considering so many different topics and broad issues, we think our readers would agree that this restriction certainly did not hinder the amount of material we have visited and digested.

Several themes have formed the organizational backbone of this text. Perhaps the most important guiding point is the notion of "double-victimization" introduced in Chapter 3. The whole idea that the system intensifies—rather than rectifies—victim suffering is a pivotal concern. Each subsequent chapter continued this dialogue by addressing various reform efforts intended to help transform the *criminal* justice system into a more meaningful *victim* justice system. While many of these efforts have blossomed and are making the "halls of justice" more user-friendly, we have tried to retain a critical (but not overly skeptical) eye. Simply put, some legal reforms have not worked. As a consequence, many troublesome areas are still in need of solutions.

Another recurring concept that we have been careful to include wherever possible is the idea of victim precipitation. As the opening chapter explained, the original thrust within victimology was to unveil how victims contribute to their own demise. Despite an intense ideological backlash, remnants of victim blaming continue to haunt victimological developments. We saw this when we turned to sexual assault, spouse abuse, child maltreatment, elder abuse and homicide victimization. Rather than shy away from these accounts, we have included them for the reader's own evaluation. In many instances, this intense scrutiny of victim actions has acted as a springboard. It has stimulated a number of theoretical viewpoints. Sexual assault is now interpreted in terms of power and domination instead of sexual gratification. The question of "why doesn't she leave him?" paves the way for understanding how learned helplessness and the cycle of violence immobilize spouse abuse victims. A reinterpretation of how alcohol influences social interaction patterns and impedes the delivery of medical services sheds a different light on homicide victimization. As you can see, the criticisms and flaws associated with the victim precipitation argument have launched many new perspectives.

Another common unifying thread that weaves its way throughout the text has been the inclusion of a distinct practitioner orientation. For example, the sexual assault chapter places the victim's experience within the context of a crisis reaction. It also explores the activities that take place at different junctures throughout the criminal investigation process. Similarly, the spouse abuse chapter addresses how research has prompted policy changes in the ways that the police and the courts now provide services to battered women. Coping strategies for lessening the incidence of child maltreatment and elder abuse also make an appearance. Information on the steps involved in a death notification, as well as the bereavement stages that loved ones will encounter, helps to provide a more intense view of what service providers and their clients face during the aftermath of a horrible victimization episode. Finally, progress already made is evident in the efforts to secure victim rights, the debate over the propriety of victim impact statements and the efforts to search for informal remedies that address individual victim concerns.

Those contemplating a possible career in the field of criminal justice should keep in mind that, while the victim movement has been responsible for many changes, the ultimate success of these efforts hinges upon the people who work within the justice community. Remaining sensitive and compassionate to each victim's tragedies is the most essential ingredient to any meaningful social service delivery.

**FIGURE 10.8**
**Selected Internet Sites Dealing with Victim Legal Issues**

FedLaw, Legal Resources on the Internet
http://www.legal.gsa.gov/

National Victims' Constitutional Amendment Network
http://www.nvc.org/nvcan/

U.S. Code
http://www.law.cornell.edu/uscode

U.S. Federal Courts' Home Page
http://www.uscourts.gov/

U.S. House of Representatives
http://www.house.gov/

U.S. Senate
http://www.senate.gov/

U.S. Supreme Court Decisions
http://supct.law.cornell.edu/supct/index.html

Victim Offender Mediation Association
http://www.igc.apc.org/voma/

## Summary

The victim movement is maturing. Throughout the past two decades, there have been a number of serious initiatives to provide victims with rights. These efforts have continued to gather momentum. Laws now cover a wide range of areas, such as restitution, victim compensation, victim impact statements, notification of system procedures, protection of victims and witnesses, and consultation with victims. This suggests that victim rights will continue to gain even more prominence.

Two issues must be kept in mind as this trend continues. First, there is still much to be learned about the plight of victims. Good intentions, no matter how noble, do not automatically guarantee that recipients are better off than they were in the past. Only through constant monitoring and evaluation is it possible to gauge the effects of change.

Second, in our zeal to help victims, it is important to seek an equitable balance. In the past, many commentators have argued that the system has erred by becoming overly concerned with offender rights. The same argument can be used against victim rights if appropriate precautionary steps are not taken. A middle ground that balances everyone's interests must be sought. Only when victims attain equitable footing with offenders will we be able to talk about a true justice system, rather than a *"criminal's* justice system." That is the challenge facing victimology.

# References

Abbey, A., L.T. Ross, D. McDuffie and P. McAuslan (1996). "Alcohol, Misperception, and Sexual Assault: How and Why Are They Linked?" In D.M. Buss and N.M. Malamuth (eds.), *Sex, Power, Conflict: Evolutionary and Feminist Perspectives.* New York: Oxford University Press.

Acker, J.R. (1992). "Social Sciences and the Criminal Law: Victims of Crime—Plight vs. Rights." *Criminal Law Bulletin* 28:64-77.

Administration on Aging (1997). *A Profile of Older Americans: 1997.*

Akers, R.L. (1973). *Deviant Behavior.* Belmont, CA: Wadsworth.

Alexander, R., Jr. (1992). "Victims' Rights and the Son of Sam Law: Implications for Free Speech and Research on Offenders." *Criminal Justice Policy Review* 6:275-290.

Allen, R.B. (1986). "Measuring the Severity of Physical Injury Among Assault and Homicide Victims." *Journal of Quantitative Criminology* 2:139-156.

American Bar Association (1996). *Standards of Practice for Lawyers Who Represent Children in Abuse and Neglect Cases.* Chicago: American Bar Association.

Amir, M. (1971). *Patterns in Forcible Rape.* Chicago: University of Chicago Press.

Anderson, J.G. (1977). "A Social Indicator Model of a Health Services System." *Social Forces* 56:661-687.

Anderson, K. (1982). "Community Justice Centers: Alternatives to Prosecution." Paper presented at the National Symposium on Victimology.

Anderson, T.B. (1989). "Community Professionals and Their Perspectives on Elder Abuse." In R. Filinson and S.R. Ingman (eds.), *Elder Abuse: Practice and Policy.* New York: Human Sciences Press.

Andison, F.S. (1977). "TV Violence and Viewer Aggression: A Culmination of Study Results, 1956-76." *Public Opinion Quarterly* 41:314-331.

Anetzberger, G.J. (1989). "Implications of Research on Elder Abuse Perpetrators: Rethinking Current Social Policy and Programming." In R. Filinson and S.R. Ingman (eds.), *Elder Abuse: Practice and Policy.* New York: Human Sciences Press.

————, J.E. Kobrin and C. Austin (1994). "Alcoholism and Elder Abuse." *Journal of Interpersonal Violence* 9:184-193.

Aries, P. (1962). *Centuries of Childhood.* New York: Knopf.

Ash, M. (1972). "On Witnesses: A Radical Critique of Criminal Court Procedures." *Notre Dame Lawyer* 48:386-425.

Atkeson, B.M., K.S. Calhoun, P.A. Resick and E.M. Ellis (1982). "Victims of Rape: Repeated Assessment of Depressive Symptoms." *Journal of Consulting and Clinical Psychology* 50:96-102.

Bachman, R. (1992). "Elderly Victims." *Bureau of Justice Statistics Special Report.* Washington, DC: U.S. Government Printing Office.

_____ (1993). "Predicting the Reporting of Rape Victimizations: Have Rape Reforms Made a Difference?" *Criminal Justice and Behavior* 20:254-270.

_____ (1995). "Is the Glass Half Empty or Half Full?: A Response to Pollard (1995)." *Criminal Justice and Behavior* 22:81-85.

_____ and R. Paternoster (1993). "A Contemporary Look at the Effects of Rape Law Reform: How Far Have We Really Come?" *Journal of Criminal Law and Criminology* 84:554-574.

_____ and L.E. Saltzman (1995). *Bureau of Justice Statistics: Special Report: Violence against Women: Estimates from the Redesigned Survey.* Washington, DC: Bureau of Justice Statistics.

_____ and B.M. Taylor (1994). "The Measurement of Family Violence and Rape by the Redesigned National Crime Victimization Survey." *Justice Quarterly* 11:499-512.

Baker, T.C., A.W. Burgess, E. Brickman and R.C. Davis (1990). "Rape Victims' Concerns about Possible Exposure to HIV Infection." *Journal of Interpersonal Violence* 5:49-60.

Bandura, A. (1973). *Aggression: A Social Learning Analysis.* Englewood Cliffs, NJ: Prentice-Hall.

_____ and R.H. Walters (1963). *Social Learning and Personality Development.* New York: Holt, Rinehart and Winston.

Barbieri, M.K. (1989). "Civil Suits for Sexual Assault Victims: The Down Side." *Journal of Interpersonal Violence* 4:110-113.

Bard, M. (1980). "Functions of the Police and the Justice System in Family Violence." In M.R. Green (ed.), *Violence and the Family.* Boulder, CO: Westview Press, Inc.

_____ and D. Sangrey (1986). *The Crime Victim's Book,* 2nd ed. New York: Brunner/Mazel Publishers.

Barnett, R.E. (1981). "Restitution: A New Paradigm of Criminal Justice." In B. Galaway and J. Hudson (eds.), *Perspectives on Crime Victims.* St. Louis, MO: Mosby.

Baron, R.A. and P.A. Bell (1975). "Aggression and Heat: Mediating Effects of Prior Provocation and Exposure to Any Aggressive Model." *Journal of Personality and Social Psychology* 31:825-832.

_____ (1976). "The Influence of Ambient Temperature, Negative Affect, and a Cooling Drink on Physical Aggression." *Journal of Personality and Social Psychology* 33:245-255.

Barrile, L.G. (1980). "Television and Attitudes about Crime." Ph.D. Dissertation. Boston, MA: Boston College.

Bassuk, E.L. (1980). "A Crisis Theory Perspective on Rape." In S.L. McCombie (ed.), *The Rape Crisis Intervention Handbook: A Guide for Victim Care.* New York: Plenum Press.

Baumer, T.L. (1985). "Testing a General Model of Fear of Crime: Data from a National Survey." *Journal of Research in Crime and Delinquency* 22:239-255.

Beck, J. (1992). "Murderous Obsession." *Newsweek* July 13:60.

Begun, J.W. (1977). "A Causal Model of the Health Care System: A Replication." *Journal of Health and Social Behavior* 18:2-9.

Belluck, P. (1997). "Women's Shelters Disclosing Their Locations, Despite Risk." *The New York Times* August 10:A1, A17.

Belsky, J. (1978). "Three Theoretical Models of Child Abuse: A Critical Review." *Child Abuse & Neglect* 2:37-49.

Belson, W. (1978). *Television Violence and the Adolescent Boy*. Westmead, England: Saxon House.

Berger, R.J., W.L. Neuman and P. Searles (1991). "The Social and Political Context of Rape Law Reform: An Aggregate Analysis." *Social Science Quarterly* 72:221-218.

———, P. Searles and W.L. Neuman (1988). "The Dimensions of Rape Reform Legislation." *Law & Society Review* 22:329-349.

Berk, R.A., G.K. Smyth and L.W. Sherman (1988). "When Random Assignment Fails: Some Lessons from the Minneapolis Spouse Abuse Experiment." *Journal of Quantitative Criminology* 4:209-223.

Berliner, L. (1988). "Anatomical Dolls." *Journal of Interpersonal Violence* 3:468-470.

——— (1989). "Another Option for Victims: Civil Damage Suits." *Journal of Interpersonal Violence* 4:107-109.

——— (1993). "When Should Children Be Allowed to Kill Abusers?" *Journal of Interpersonal Violence* 8:296-297.

Bernard, M.L. and J.L. Bernard (1983). "Violent Intimacy: The Family as a Model for Love Relationships." *Family Relations* 32:283-286.

Besharov, D.J. (1990a). "Gaining Control Over Child Abuse Reports." *Public Welfare* 48:34-40.

——— (1990b). *Recognizing Child Abuse: A Guide for the Concerned*. New York: The Free Press.

——— (1991). "Reducing Unfounded Reports." *Journal of Interpersonal Violence* 16:112-115.

Best, C.L., B.S. Dansky and D.G. Kilpatrick (1992). "Medical Students' Attitudes About Female Rape Victims." *Journal of Interpersonal Violence* 7:175-188.

Biderman, A. and A. Reiss (1967). "On Exploring the 'Dark Figure' of Crime." *Annals of the American Academy of Political and Social Sciences* 374:1-15.

Binder, A. and J.W. Meeker (1988). "Experiments as Reforms." *Journal of Criminal Justice* 16:347-358.

Bjerregaard, B. (1989). "Televised Testimony as an Alternative in Child Sexual Abuse Cases." *Criminal Law Bulletin* 25:164-175.

——— (1996). "Stalking and the First Amendment: A Constitutional Analysis of State Stalking Laws." *Criminal Law Bulletin* 32:307-341.

Blakely, B.E. and R. Dolon (1991). "Elder Nistreatment." In J.E. Hendricks (ed.), *Crisis Intervention in Criminal Justice/Social Service*. Springfield, IL: Charles C Thomas.

Block, M.R. and J.D. Sinnott (1979). *The Battered Elder Syndrome: An Exploratory Study*. College Park, MD: University of Maryland.

Block, R.L. and C.R. Block (1995). "Space, Place and Crime: Hot Spot Areas and Hot Places of Liquor-Related Crime." In J.E. Eck and D. Weisburd (eds.), *Crime and Place*. Monsey, NY: Criminal Justice Press.

Blomberg, T.G., G.F. Waldo and C.A. Bullock (1989). "An Assessment of Victim Service Needs." *Evaluation Review* 13:598-627.

Blumberg, M. (1989). "Transmission of the AIDS Virus Through Criminal Activity." *Criminal Law Bulletin* 25:454-465.

———— and D. Langston (1991). "Mandatory HIV Testing in Criminal Justice Settings." *Crime & Delinquency* 37:5-18.

Boat, B.W. and M.D. Everson (1988). "Use of Anatomical Dolls Among Professionals in Sexual Abuse Evaluations." *Child Abuse and Neglect* 12:171-179.

Bogard, M. (1990). "Why We Need Gender to Understand Human Violence." *Journal of Interpersonal Violence* 5:132-135.

*Booth v. Maryland*, 107 S. Ct. 2529 (1987), 482 U.S. 496 (1987).

Bourke, L.B. (1989). *Defining Rape*. Durham, NC: Duke University Press.

Bowleg, L. and K.D. Stoll (1991). *More Harm Than Help: The Ramifications for Rape Survivors of Mandatory HIV Testing of Rapists*. Washington, DC: Center for Women Policy Studies.

Bridenback, M.L., P.L. Imhoff and J.P. Blanchard (1980). *The Use of Mediation/Arbitration in the Juvenile Justice Process: A Study of Three Programs*. Tallahassee, FL: Office of the State Court Administrator.

Brien, V.O. (1992). *OVC Bulletin: Civil Legal Remedies for Crime Victims*. Washington, DC: U.S. Department of Justice.

Brooks, A.D. (1996). "Megan's Law: Constitutionality and Policy." *Criminal Justice Ethics* 15:56-66.

Brooks, J.A. (1975). "How Well Are Criminal Injury Boards Performing?" *Crime & Delinquency* 21:50-56.

Browne, A. (1987). *When Battered Women Kill*. New York: The Free Press.

Browning, J. and D. Dutton (1986). "Assessment of Wife Assault with the Conflict Tactics Scale: Using Couple Data to Quantify the Differential Reporting Effect." *Journal of Marriage and the Family* 48:375-379.

Brownmiller, S. (1975). *Against Our Will: Men, Women and Rape*. New York: Simon and Schuster.

Bruinsma, G.J.N. and J.P.S. Fiselier (1982). "The Poverty of Victimology." In H.J. Schneider (ed.), *The Victim in International Perspective*. New York: de Gruyter.

Bureau of Justice Assistance (1996). *Regional Seminar Series on Developing and Implementing Antistalking Codes*. Washington, DC: Bureau of Justice Assistance.

Bureau of Justice Statistics (1997). *Criminal Victimization in the United States, 1994*. Washington, DC: U.S. Government Printing Office.

Burgess, A.W. (1995). "Rape Trauma Syndrome." In P. Searles and R.J. Berger (eds.), *Rape and Society: Readings on the Problem of Sexual Assault*. Boulder, CO: Westview Press.

_____ and P. Draper (1989). "The Explanation of Family Violence: The Role of Biological, Behavioral, and Cultural Selection." In L. Ohlin and N. Tonry (eds.), *Family Violence*. Chicago: University of Chicago Press.

_____ and L.L. Holmstrom (1974). "Rape Trauma Syndrome." *American Journal of Psychiatry* 131:981-986.

_____ and A.T. Laszlo (1976). "When the Prosecutrix Is a Child: The Victim Consultant in Cases of Sexual Assault." In E.C. Viano (ed.), *Victims & Society*. Washington, DC: Visage Press.

Burt, M.R. and R.E. Estep (1981). "Who Is a Victim?: Definitional Problems in Sexual Victimization." *Victimology* 6:15-28.

_____ and B.L. Katz (1985). "Rape, Robbery, and Burglary: Responses to Actual and Feared Criminal Victimization, with Special Focus on Women and Elderly." *Victimology* 10:325-358.

Buzawa, E.S. and C.G. Buzawa (1990). *Domestic Violence: The Criminal Justice Response*. Newbury Park, CA: Sage.

Byers, B. (1991). "Death Notification." In J.E. Hendricks (ed.), *Crisis Intervention in Criminal Justice/Social Service*. Springfield, IL: Charles C Thomas.

Caffey, J. (1946). "Multiple Fractures in the Long Bones of Infants Suffering from Chronic Subdural Hemotoma." *American Journal of Roentgenology* 56:163-173.

_____ (1957). "Traumatic Lesions in Growing Bones Other Than Fractures and Lesions: Clinical and Radiological Features." *British Journal of Radiology* 30:225-238.

Calcutt, P.B. (1988). "The Victims' Rights Act of 1988, the Florida Constitution, and the New Struggle for Victims' Rights." *Florida State University Law Review* 16:811-834.

Call, J.E., D. Nice and S.M. Talarico (1991). "An Analysis of State Rape Shield Laws." *Social Science Quarterly* 72:774-788.

Campbell, D.T. and J.C. Stanley (1963). *Experimental and Quasi-Experimental Designs for Research*. Chicago: Rand McNally.

Campbell, R. (1995). "The Role of Work Experience and Individual Beliefs in Police Officers' Perceptions of Date Rape: An Integration of Quantitative and Qualitative Methods." *American Journal of Community Psychology* 23:249-277.

_____ and C.R. Johnson (1997). "Police Officers' Peception of Rape: Is There Consistency Between State Law and Individual Beliefs?" *Journal of Interpersonal Violence* 12:255-274.

Cannavale, F.J., Jr. and W.D. Falcon (1976). *Improving Witness Cooperation: Summary Report of the District of Columbia Witness Survey and a Handbook for Witness Management*. Washington, DC: U.S. Department of Justice.

Caringella-MacDonald, S. (1984). "Sexual Assault Prosecution: An Examination of Model Rape Legislation in Michigan." *Women and Politics* 4:65-82.

Carrington, F. (1981). "Victims' Rights Litigation: A Wave of the Future?" In B. Galaway and J. Hudson (eds.), *Perspectives on Crime Victims*. St. Louis, MO: Mosby.

Carrow, D.M. (1980). *Rape: Guidelines for a Community Response*. Washington, DC: U.S. Department of Justice.

Cassell, P.G. (1997). *Statement before the Committee on the Judiciary, United States Senate, Concerning a Constitutional Amendment Protecting the Rights of Crime Victims on April 16, 1997*. Washington, DC: U.S. Government Printing Office.

Castillo, R., T.W. Dressler, R. Foglia and M.J. Faber (1979). "The Use of Civil Liability to Aid Crime Victims." *Journal of Criminal Law & Criminology* 70:57-62.

Cate, R.M., J.M. Henton, J. Kaval, F.S. Christopher and S. Lloyd (1982). "Premarital Abuse: A Social Psychological Perspective." *Journal of Family Issues* 3:79-90.

Cazenave, N.A. and M.A. Straus (1979). "Race, Class, Network Embeddedness and Family Violence: A Search for Potent Support Systems." *Journal of Comparative Family Studies* 10:281-300.

Challeen, D.A. and J.H. Heinlen (1978). "The Win-Onus Restitution Program." In B. Galaway and J. Hudson (eds.), *Offender Restitution in Theory and Action*. Lexington, MA: D.C. Heath.

Champlin, L. (1986). "The Battered Elderly." *Geriatrics* 37:115-116, 121.

Chan, R.N., D. Ainscow and J.M. Sikorski (1980). "Diagnostic Failures in the Multiple Injured." *Journal of Trauma* 20:684-687.

Chappel, D. and L.P. Sutton (1974). "Evaluating the Effectiveness of Programs to Compensate the Victims of Crime." In I. Drapkin and E.C. Viano (eds.), *Victimology: A New Focus, Volume 2*. Lexington, MA: D.C. Heath.

Chelimsky, E. (1981). "Serving Victims: Agency Incentives and Individual Needs." In S.E. Salasin (ed.), *Evaluating Victim Services*. Beverly Hills, CA: Sage.

Cicirelli, V.G. (1986). "The Helping Relationship and Family Neglect in Later Life." In K.A. Pillemer and R.S. Wolf (eds.), *Elder Abuse: Conflict in the Family*. Dover, MA: Auburn House.

Clemente, F. and M.B. Kleiman (1977). "Fear of Crime in the United States: A Multivariate Analysis." *Social Forces* 56:519-531.

Coates, R.B. and J. Gehm (1989). "An Empirical Assessment." In M. Wright and B. Galaway (eds.), *Mediation and Criminal Justice: Victims, Offenders and Community*. Newbury Park, CA: Sage.

*Code of Federal Regulations, 7-1-96 Edition*. Washington, DC: U.S. Government Printing Office.

Cohen, F. (1995). "Sex Offender Registration Laws: Constitutional and Policy Issues." *Criminal Law Bulletin* 31:151-160.

Cohen, L.E. and M. Felson (1979). "Social Changes and Crime Rate Trends: A Routine Activities Approach." *American Sociological Review* 44:588-608.

Coleman, F.L. (1997). "Stalking Behavior and the Cycle of Domestic Violence." *Journal of Interpersonal Violence* 12:420-432.

Collins, J.J. (1989). "Alcohol and Interpersonal Violence: Less than Meets the Eye." In N.A. Weiner and M.E. Wolfgang (eds.), *Pathways to Criminal Violence*. Newbury Park, CA: Sage.

Conte, J.R. (1991). "Child Sexual Abuse: Looking Backward and Forward." In M.Q. Patton (ed.), *Family Sexual Abuse: Frontline Research and Evaluation*. Newbury Park, CA: Sage.

Cook, R.F., J.A. Roehl and D.I. Sheppard (1980). *Neighborhood Justice Centers Field Test, Executive Summary*. Washington, DC: National Institute of Justice.

_____, W.G. Skogan, T.D. Cook and G.E. Antunes (1978). "Criminal Victimization of the Elderly: The Physical and Economic Consequences." *The Gerontologist* 18:338-349.

Cook, T.D., J. Flemming and T.R. Tyler (1981). "Criminal Victimization of the Elderly: Validating the Policy Assumptions." In G.M. Stephenson and J.M. Davis (eds.), *Progress in Applied Social Psychology.* New York: Wiley.

Costa, J.J. (1984). *Abuse of Women: Legislation, Reporting, and Prevention.* Lexington, MA: Lexington Books.

Costin, F. and N. Schwarz (1987). "Beliefs about Rape and Women's Social Roles: A Four- Nation Study." *Journal of Interpersonal Violence* 2:46-56.

Cotton, J.L. (1983). "Violence and High Temperature." *USA Today* August 12:13.

Crenshaw, W.B., L.M. Crenshaw and J.W. Lichtenberg (1995). "When Educators Confront Child Abuse: An Analysis of the Decision to Report." *Child Abuse & Neglect* 19:1095-1113.

Crew, R.E., Jr. and M. Vancore (1994). "Managing Victim Restitution in Florida: An Analysis of the Implementation of FS 775.089." *Justice System Journal* 17:241-248.

Crime Prevention Unit (no date). *Officer Friendly Training Manual.* Tallahassee, FL: Tallahassee Police Department.

Crystal, S. (1986). "Social Policy and Elder Abuse." In K.A. Pillemer and R.S. Wolf (eds.), *Elder Abuse: Conflict in the Family.* Dover, MA: Auburn House.

Curtis, L.A. (1974). *Criminal Violence: National Patterns and Behavior.* Lexington, MA: D.C. Heath.

Dane, D.M. (1991). "Rape Intervention." In J.E. Hendricks (ed.), *Crisis Intervention in Criminal Justice/Social Service.* Springfield, IL: Charles C Thomas.

Davis, J.W., D.B. Hoyt, M.S. McArdle, R.C. Mackersie, S.R. Shackford and A.B. Eastman (1991). "The Significance of Critical Care Errors in Causing Preventable Death in Trauma Patients in a Trauma System." *Journal of Trauma* 31:813-819.

Davis, R.C. (1982). "Mediation: The Brooklyn Experiment." In R. Tomasic and M.M. Feeley (eds.), *Neighborhood Justice: Assessment of an Emerging Idea.* New York: Longman.

——— (1983). "Victim/Witness Noncooperation: A Second Look at a Persistent Phenomenon." *Journal of Criminal Justice* 11:287-299.

———, M. Henley and B. Smith (1990). *Victim Impact Statements: Their Effects on Court Outcomes and Victim Satisfaction.* Washington, DC: National Institute of Justice.

——— and B.E. Smith (1994). "Victim Impact Statements and Victim Satisfaction: An Unfulfilled Promise?" *Journal of Criminal Justice* 22:1-12.

——— and B. Smith (1995). "Domestic Violence Reforms: Empty Promises or Fulfilled Expectations?" *Crime & Delinquency* 41:541-552.

——— and B.G. Taylor (1997). "A Proactive Response to Family Violence: The Results of a Randomized Experiment." *Criminology* 35:307-334.

———, M. Tishane and D. Grayson (1980). *Mediation and Arbitration as Alternatives to Criminal Prosecution in Felony Arrest Cases: An Evaluation of the Brooklyn Dispute Resolution Center (First Year).* New York: Vera Institute.

Dawson, R.K. (1989). "Civil Suits for Sexual Assault Victims: The Up Side." *Journal of Interpersonal Violence* 4:114-115.

DeFrances, C.J., S.K. Smith and L.V.D. Does (1996). *Prosecutors in State Courts, 1994.* Washington, DC: U.S. Department of Justice.

DeFrancis, V. and C.L. Lucht (1974). *Child Abuse in the 1970's*. Denver: The American Humane Association.

Deisz, R., J.H. Doueck and N. George (1996). "Reasonable Cause: A Qualitative Study of Mandated Reporting." *Child Abuse & Neglect* 20:275-287.

DeKeseredy, W.S. and K. Kelly (1995). "Sexual Abuse in Canadian University and College Dating Relationships: The Contribution of Male Peer Support." *Journal of Family Violence* 10:41-53.

Detmer, C.M. and J.W. Lamberti (1991). "Family Grief." *Death Studies* 15:363-374.

Dexter, E.G. (1904). *Weather Influences*. New York: Macmillan.

Dey, E.L., J.S. Korn and L.J. Sax (1996). "Betrayed by the Academy: The Sexual Harassment of Women College Faculty." *Journal of Higher Education* 67:149-173.

Dible, D.A. and R.H.C. Teske, Jr. (1993). "An Analysis of the Prosecutory Effects of a Child Sexual Abuse Victim-Witness Program." *Journal of Criminal Justice* 21:79-85.

Dobash, R.E. and R.P. Dobash (1977-78). "Wives: The 'Appropriate' Victims of Marital Violence." *Victimology* 2:426-442.

————— (1979). *Violence Against Wives: A Case Against the Patriarchy*. New York: The Free Press.

—————, R.E. Dobash, M. Wilson and M. Daly (1992). "The Myth of Sexual Symmetry in Marital Violence." *Social Problems* 39:71-91.

Dodge, R.W. (1985). *Bureau of Justice Statistics Technical Report: Response to Screening Questions in the National Crime Survey*. Washington, DC: U.S. Government Printing Office.

Doerner, W.G. (1975). "A Regional Analysis of Homicide Rates in the United States." *Criminology* 13:90-101.

————— (1977). "State Victim Compensation Programs in Action." *Victimology* 2:106-109.

————— (1978a). "A Quasi-Experimental Analysis of Selected Canadian Victim Compensation Programs." *Canadian Journal of Criminology* 20:239-251.

————— (1978b). "An Examination of the Alleged Latent Effects of Victim Compensation Programs upon Crime Reporting." *LAE Journal* 41:71-76.

————— (1978c). "The Index of Southernness Revisited: The Influence of Wherefrom upon Whodunnit." *Criminology* 16:47-56.

————— (1978d). "The Deadly World of Johnny Reb: Fact, Foible, or Fantasy?" In J.A. Inciardi and A.E. Pottieger (eds.), *Violent Crime: Historical and Contemporary Issues*. Beverly Hills, CA: Sage.

————— (1979). "The Violent World of Johnny Reb: An Attitudinal Analysis of the 'Regional Culture of Violence' Thesis." *Sociological Forum* 2:61-71.

————— (1980). "Trends in Southern Homicide: Is the South a 'Regional Culture of Violence?'" *Journal of Crime and Justice* 3:83-94.

————— (1983). "Why Does Johnny Reb Die When Shot? The Impact of Medical Resources upon Lethality." *Sociological Inquiry* 53:1-15.

————— (1987). "Child Maltreatment Seriousness and Juvenile Delinquency." *Youth & Society* 19:197-244.

———— (1988). "The Impact of Medical Resources on Criminally Induced Lethality: A Further Examination." *Criminology* 26:171-179.

———— (1998). *Introduction to Law Enforcement: An Insider's View*. Boston, MA: Butterworth-Heinemann.

————, M.S. Knudten, R.D. Knudten and A.C. Meade (1976a). "Correspondence Between Crime Victim Needs and Available Public Services." *Social Service Review* 50:482-490.

————, M.S. Knudten, R.D. Knudten and A.C. Meade (1976b). "An Analysis of Victim Compensation Programs as a Time-Series Experiment." *Victimology* 1:295-313.

———— and S.P. Lab (1980). "The Impact of Crimes Compensation upon Victim Attitudes Toward the Criminal Justice System." *Victimology* 5:61-67.

———— and J.C. Speir (1986). "Stitch and Sew: The Impact of Medical Resources upon Criminally Induced Lethality." *Criminology* 24:319-330.

———— and T. Tsai (1990). "Child Maltreatment and Juvenile Delinquency in Taiwan." *International Journal of Comparative and Applied Criminal Justice* 14:225-238.

Dollard, J. (1949). *Caste and Class in a Southern Town*. New Haven, CT: Yale University Press.

Dolliver, J.M. (1987). "Victims' Rights Constitutional Amendment: A Bad Idea Whose Time Should Not Come." *The Wayne Law Review* 34:87-93.

Dolon, R. and B. Blakely (1989). "Elder Abuse and Neglect: A Study of Adult Protective Service Workers in the United States." *Journal of Elder Abuse and Neglect* 1:31-49.

———— and J.E. Hendricks (1989). "An Exploratory Study Comparing Attitudes and Practices of Police Officers and Social Service Providers in Elder Abuse and Neglect Cases." *Journal of Elder Abuse and Neglect* 1:75-90.

Dominick, J.R. (1978). "Crime and Law Enforcement in the Mass Media." In C. Winick (ed.), *Deviance and Mass Media*. Beverly Hills, CA: Sage.

Donnerstein E. (1980). "Aggressive Erotica and Violence Against Women." *Journal of Personality and Social Psychology* 39:269-277.

———— and J. Hallam (1978). "Effects of Erotic Stimuli on Male Aggression Toward Females." *Journal of Personality and Social Psychology* 32:237-244.

Dorne, C.K. (1989). *Crimes Against Children*. New York: Harrow and Heston.

Doty, P. and E.W. Sullivan (1983). "Community Involvement in Combating Abuse, Neglect and Mistreatment in Nursing Homes." *Milbank Memorial Fund Quarterly/Health and Society* 37:115-121.

Dove, D.B., W.M. Stahl and L.R.M. Delbuercio (1980). "A Five-Year Review of Deaths Following Urban Trauma." *Journal of Trauma* 20:760-765.

Dunford, F.D. (1990). "System Initiated Warrants for Suspects of Misdemeanor Domestic Assault: A Pilot Study." *Justice Quarterly* 7:631-653.

Dunford, F.D., D. Huizinga and D.S. Elliott (1989). *The Omaha Domestic Violence Police Experiments: Final Report*. Washington, DC: National Institute of Justice.

Durkheim, E. (1951). *Suicide*. Glencoe, IL: The Free Press.

Dutton, D.G. and A.J. Starzomski (1994). "Psychological Differences Between Court-Referred and Self-Referred Wife Assaulters." *Criminal Justice and Behavior* 21:203-221.

Earle, R.B. (1995). *Helping To Prevent Child Abuse—and Future Criminal Conse-quences: Hawai'i Healthy Start.* Washington, DC: U.S. Department of Justice.

Eber, L.P. (1981). "The Battered Wife's Dilemma: To Kill or To Be Killed." *Hastings Law Journal* 32:895-931.

Edelhertz, H. and G. Geis (1974). *Public Compensation to Victims of Crime.* New York: Praeger.

Edwards, S.S.M. (1989). *Policing "Domestic" Violence: Women, the Law and the State.* Newbury Park, CA: Sage.

Ehrhart, J.K and B.R. Sandler (1985). *Myths and Realities About Rape.* Washington, DC: Project on the Status and Education of Women.

Eigenberg, H.M. (1990). "The National Crime Survey and Rape: The Case of the Miss-ing Question." *Justice Quarterly* 7:655-671.

———, K.E. Scarborough and V.E. Kappeler (1996). "Contributory Factors Affect-ing Arrest in Domestic and Non-Domestic Assaults." *American Journal of Police* 15:27-54.

Eikenberry, K. (1987). "Victims of Crime/Victims of Justice." *The Wayne Law Review* 34:29-49.

Eisikovits, Z. (1996). "The Aftermath of Wife Beating: Strategies of Bounding Violent Events." *Journal of Interpersonal Violence* 11:459-474.

——— and E. Buchbinder (1996). "Pathways to Disenchantment: Battered Women's Views of Their Social Workers." *Journal of Interpersonal Violence* 11:425-440.

Elias, R. (1990). "Which Victim Movement?: The Politics of Victim Policy." In A.J. Luri-gio, W.G. Skogan and R.C. Davis (eds.), *Victims of Crime: Problems, Policies and Programs.* Newbury Park, CA: Sage.

Elliott, D.S. (1989). "Criminal Justice Procedures in Family Violence Crimes." In L. Ohlin and M. Tonry (eds.), *Family Violence.* Chicago: University of Chicago.

Ellis, D. (1992). "Toward a Consistent Recognition of the Forbidden Inference: The Illi-nois Rape Shield Statute." *Journal of Criminal Law & Criminology* 83:395-436.

Ellis, L. (1989). *Theories of Rape.* New York: Hemisphere.

Enderson, B.L., D.B. Reath, J. Meadors, W. Dallas, J.M. DeBoo and K.I. Maull (1990). "The Tertiary Trauma Survey: A Prospective Study of Missed Injury." *Journal of Trauma* 30:666-670.

Ennis, P. (1967). *Criminal Victimization in the United States: A Report of a National Survey.* Chicago: National Opinion Research Center.

Erez, E. (1989). "The Impact of Victimology on Criminal Justice Policy." *Criminal Jus-tice Policy Review* 3:236-256.

——— (1990). "Victim Participation in Sentencing: Rhetoric and Reality." *Journal of Criminal Justice* 18:19-31.

——— and V. Guhlke (1988). "Victims in Court." Paper presented at the World Soci-ety of Victimology Sixth Annual Symposium.

——— and L. Roeger (1995). "The Effect of Victim Impact Statements on Sentencing Patterns and Outcomes: The Australian Experience." *Journal of Criminal Justice* 23:363-375.

_____ and P. Tontodonato (1990). "The Effect of Victim Participation in Sentencing on Sentence Outcome." *Criminology* 28:451-474.

_____ and P. Tontodonato (1992). "Victim Participation in Sentencing and Satisfaction with Justice." *Justice Quarterly* 9:393-417.

Erlanger, H.S. (1974). "The Empirical Status of the Subculture of Violence Thesis." *Social Problems* 20:280-292.

_____ (1975). "Is There a 'Subculture of Violence' in the South?" *Journal of Criminal Law and Criminology* 66:483-490.

Erskine, H. (1974). "The Polls: Fear of Violence and Crime." *Public Opinion Quarterly* 38:131-145.

Ervin, L. and A. Schneider (1990). "Explaining the Effects of Restitution on Offenders: Results from a National Experiment in Juvenile Courts." In B. Galaway and J. Hudson (eds.), *Criminal Justice, Restitution, and Reconciliation*. Monsey, NY: Criminal Justice Press.

Everson, M.D. and B.W. Boat (1994). "Putting the Anatomical Doll Controversy in Perspective: An Examination of the Major Uses and Criticisms of the Dolls in Child Sexual Abuse Evaluations." *Child Abuse & Neglect* 18:113-129.

_____, B.W. Boat, S. Bourg and K.R. Robertson (1996). "Beliefs Among Professionals About Rates of False Allegations of Child Sexual Abuse." *Journal of Interpersonal Violence* 11:541-553.

Eyles, J. and K.J. Woods (1983). *The Social Geography of Medicine and Health*. New York: St. Martin's Press.

Farley, R.H. (1987). "'Drawing Interviews: An Alternative Technique." *Police Chief* 54:37-38.

Farrell, G. (1995). "Preventing Repeat Victimization." In M. Tonry and D.P. Farrington (eds.), *Building a Safer Society: Strategic Approaches to Crime Prevention*. Chicago: University of Chicago Press.

Fattah, E.A. and V.F. Sacco (1989). *Crime and Victimization of the Elderly*. New York: Springer-Verlag.

Feder, L. (1996). "Police Handling of Domestic Calls: The Importance of Offender's Presence in the Arrest Decision." *Journal of Criminal Justice* 24:481-490.

Federal Bureau of Investigation (1995). *Uniform Crime Reports for the United States 1994*. Washington, DC: U.S. Government Printing Office.

_____ (1996). *Uniform Crime Reports for the United States 1995*. Washington, DC: U.S. Government Printing Office.

Feld, L.S. and M.A. Straus (1989). "Escalation and Desistance of Wife Assault in Marriage." *Criminology* 27:141-161.

Felson, R.B. and H.J. Steadman (1983). "Situational Factors in Disputes Leading to Criminal Violence." *Criminology* 21:59-74.

Felstiner, W.L.F. and L.A. Williams (1979). *Community Mediation in Dorchester, Massachusetts: Final Report*. Los Angeles, CA: University of Southern California.

_____ and L.A. Williams (1982). "Community Mediation in Dorchester, Massachusetts." In R. Tomasic and M.M. Feeley (eds.), *Neighborhood Justice: Assessment of an Emerging Idea*. New York: Longman.

Ferraro, K.F. (1995). *Fear of Crime: Interpreting Victimization Risk.* Albany, NY: SUNY Press.

_____ and R.L. LaGrange (1988). "Are Older People Afraid of Crime?" *Journal of Aging Studies* 2:277-287.

Ferri, E. (1882). "Das Verbrechen in Seiner Abhangigkeit van Jahrlichen Temperaturewechse." *Zeitschrfit für die Gesammte Strafrechtswissenschaft* 2:38.

Fiegener, J.J., M. Fiegener and J. Meszaros (1989). "Policy Implications of a Statewide Survey on Elder Abuse." *Journal of Elder Abuse and Neglect* 1:39-58.

Fields, M.D. and R.M. Kirchner (1978). "Battered Women Are Still in Need: A Reply to Steinmetz." *Victimology* 3:216-226.

Fine, S.A. (1993). "Do Not Blur Self-Defense and Revenge." *Journal of Interpersonal Violence* 8:299-301.

Finkelhor, D. (1990). "Is Child Abuse Being Over-Reported? A Reply to Besharov." *Public Welfare* 48:22-29.

_____ and K. Yllo (1983). "Common Features of Family Abuse." In D. Finkelhor, R.J. Gelles, G.T. Hotaling and M.A. Straus (eds.), *The Dark Side of Families: Family Violence Research.* Beverly Hills, CA: Sage.

Finn, M.A. and L.J. Stalans (1995). "Police Referrals to Shelter and Mental Health Treatment: Examining Their Decisions in Domestic Assault Cases." *Crime & Delinquency* 41:467-480.

Finn, P. and B.N.W. Lee (1987). *Serving Crime Victims and Witnesses.* Washington, DC: U.S. Department of Justice.

_____ and S. Colson (1990). *Civil Protection Orders: Legislation, Current Court Practice, and Enforcement.* Washington, DC: U.S. Department of Justice.

Finn-DeLuca, V. (1994). "Victim Participation at Sentencing." *Criminal Law Bulletin* 30:403-428.

Fischer, K. and M. Rose (1995). "When 'Enough Is Enough': Battered Women's Decision Making Around Court Orders of Protection." *Crime & Delinquency* 41:414-429.

Florida Statutes (1997).

Fontana, V.J. (1973). *Somewhere a Child is Crying.* New York: Macmillan.

Forst, B.E. and J.C. Hernon (1985). *The Criminal Justice Response to Victim Harm.* Research in Brief. Washington, DC: National Institute of Justice.

Franklin, C.W, II and A.P. Franklin (1976). "Victimology Revisited: A Critique and Suggestions for Future Direction." *Criminology* 14:177-214.

Frazier, P.A. and E. Borgida (1992). "Rape Trauma Syndrome: A Review of Case Law and Psychological Research." *Law and Human Behavior* 16:293-311.

Freeman-Longo, R.E. (1996). "Feel Good Legislation: Prevention or Calamity." *Child Abuse & Neglect* 20:95-101.

Frenzen, P.D. (1991). "The Increasing Supply of Physicians in U.S. Urban and Rural Areas, 1975 to 1988." *American Journal of Public Health* 81:1141-1147.

Friedman, J.J. (1973). "Structural Constraints on Community Action: The Case of Infant Mortality Rates." *Social Problems* 21:230-245.

Frieze, I.H. and A. Browne (1989). "Violence in Marriage." In L. Ohlin and M. Tonry (eds.), *Family Violence.* Chicago: University of Chicago Press.

Gaboury, M.T. and R. Myers (1997). "Legal Developments in the Legislatures and the Courts." *The Crime Victims Report* 1:40-43.

Galaway, B. (1981). "The Use of Restitution." In B. Galaway and J. Hudson (eds.), *Perspectives on Crime Victims*. St. Louis, MO: Mosby.

Galbraith, M.W. (1989). "A Critical Examination of the Definitional, Methodological and Theoretical Problems of Elder Abuse." In R. Filinson and S.R. Ingman (eds.), *Elder Abuse: Practice and Policy*. New York: Human Sciences Press.

Gallup, G., Jr. (1992). *The Gallup Poll Monthly, No. 318*. Princeton, NJ: The Gallup Poll.

Galvin J. and K. Polk (1983). "Attrition in Case Processing: Is Rape Unique?" *Journal of Research in Crime and Delinquency* 20:126-154.

Gandy, J.T. (1978). "Attitudes Toward the Use of Restitution." In B. Galaway and J. Hudson (eds.), *Offender Restitution in Theory and Action*. Lexington, MA: D.C. Heath.

———— and B. Galaway (1980). "Restitution as a Sanction for Offenders: A Public's View." In J. Hudson and B. Galaway (eds.), *Victims, Offenders, and Alternative Sanctions*. Lexington, MA: D.C. Heath.

Garbarino, J. (1976). "A Preliminary Study of Some Ecological Correlates of Child Abuse: The Impact of Socioeconomic Stress on Mothers." *Child Development* 47:178-185.

———— and G. Gilliam (1980). *Understanding Abusive Families*. Lexington, MA: Lexington Books.

Garner, J. and E. Clemmer (1986). *Danger to Police in Domestic Disturbances—New Look*. Washington, DC: U.S. Department of Justice.

————, J. Fagan and C. Maxwell (1995). "Published Findings from the Spouse Assault Replication Program: A Criminal Review." *Journal of Quantitative Criminology* 11:3-28.

Garofalo, J. (1981). "Victimization Surveys." In B. Galaway and J. Hudson (eds.), *Perspectives on Crime Victims*. St. Louis, MO: Mosby.

———— and K.J. Connelly (1980a). "Dispute Resolution Centers, Part I: Major Features and Processes." *Criminal Justice Abstracts* 12:416-436.

———— and K.J. Connelly (1980b). "Dispute Resolution Centers, Part II: Outcomes, Issues, and Future Directions." *Criminal Justice Abstracts* 12:576-611.

Gartin, P.R. (1995a). "Examining Differential Officer Effects in the Minneapolis Domestic Violence Experiment." *American Journal of Police* 14:93-110.

———— (1995b). "Dealing with Design Failures in Randomized Field Experiments: Analytic Issues Regarding the Evaluation of Treatment Effects." *Journal of Research in Crime and Delinquency* 32:425-445.

Gastil, R.D. (1971). "Homicide and a Regional Culture of Violence." *American Sociological Review* 36:412-427.

———— (1978). "Comments." *Criminology* 16:60-64.

Geberth, V.J. (1992). "Stalkers." *Law and Order* 40:138-143.

Geis, G. (1977). "The Terrible Indignity: Crimes against the Elderly." In M.A.Y. Rifai (ed.), *Justice and Older Americans*. Lexington, MA: D.C. Heath.

Geiselman, R.E., G. Bornstein and K.J. Saywitz (1992). "New Approach to Interviewing Children: A Test of Its Effectiveness." *NIJ Research in Brief*. Washington, DC: U.S. Department of Justice.

Gelles, R.J. (1973). "Child Abuse as Psychopathology: A Sociological Critique and Reformulation." *American Journal of Orthopsychiatry* 43:611-621.

———— (1975). "The Social Construction of Child Abuse." *American Journal of Orthopsychiatry* 45:363-371.

———— (1980). "Violence in the Family: A Review of Research in the 70's." *Journal of Marriage and the Family* 42:873-885.

———— and C.P. Cornell (1985). *Intimate Violence in Families*. Beverly Hills, CA: Sage.

———— and C. P. Cornell (1990). *Intimate Violence in Families*. Beverly Hills, CA: Sage.

———— and M.A. Straus (1979). "Determinants of Violence in the Family: A Theoretical Integration." In W. Burr (ed.), *Contemporary Theories about the Family*. New York: The Free Press.

———— and M.A. Straus (1988). *Intimate Violence*. New York: Simon and Schuster.

George, L.K. (1986). "Caregiver Burden: Conflict Between Norms of Reciprocity and Solidarity." In K.A. Pillemer and R.S. Wolf (eds.), *Elder Abuse: Conflict in the Family*. Dover, MA: Auburn House.

Gerbner, G., L. Gross, M. Jackson-Beeck, S. Jeffries-Fox and N. Signorielle (1978). "Cultural Indicators: Violence Profile No. 9." *Journal of Communication* 29:177-196.

————, L. Gross, N. Signorielle and M. Morgan (1980). "Television Violence, Victimization, and Power." *American Behavioral Scientist* 23:705-716.

Gerner, J., J. Fagan and C. Maxwell (1995). "Published Findings from the Spouse Assault Replication Program: A Critical Review." *Journal of Quantitative Criminology* 11:3-28.

Gerstenfeld, P.B. (1997). "'Net Justice': Using the Internet for Teaching and Research in Criminal Justice." *ACJS Today* 16:1, 3, 24-25.

Giacopassi, D.J. and J.R. Sparger (1992). "The Effects of Emergency Medical Care on the Homicide Rate: Some Additional Evidence." *Journal of Criminal Justice* 20:249-259.

Giannelli, P. (1997). "Rape Trauma Syndrome." *Criminal Law Bulletin* 33:270-279.

Gil, D. (1971). *Violence Against Children: Physical Child Abuse in the United States*. Cambridge, MA: Harvard University Press.

Gilbert, N. (1993). "Examining the Facts: Advocacy Research Overstates the Incidence of Date and Acquaintance Rape." In R.J. Gelles and D.R. Loseke (eds.), *Current Controversies on Family Violence*. Newbury Park, CA: Sage.

Gilmore, S.G. and J.W. Evans (1980). "The Nursing Care of Rape Victims." In S.L. McCombie (ed.), *The Rape Crisis Intervention Handbook: A Guide for Victim Care*. New York: Plenum Press.

Gioglio, G.R. and P. Blakemore (1983). *Elder Abuse in New Jersey: The Knowledge and Experience of Abuse Among Older New Jerseyans*. Trenton, NJ: New Jersey Department of Human Services.

Giordano, N. and J. Giordano (1984). "Elder Abuse: A Review of the Literature." *Social Work* 29:232-236.

Giovannoni, J.M. and R.M. Becerra (1979). *Defining Child Abuse*. New York: The Free Press.

Glaser, D. (1956). "Criminality Theories and Behavioral Images." *American Journal of Sociology* 61:433-444.

Gold, M. (1958). "Suicide, Homicide, and the Socialization of Aggression." *American Journal of Sociology* 63:651-661.

Gomme, I.M. (1986). "Fear of Crime Among Canadians: A Multi-Variate Analysis." *Journal of Criminal Justice* 14:249-258.

Gondolf, E.W., J. McWilliams, B. Hart and J. Stuehling (1994). "Court Response to Petitions for Civil Protection Orders." *Journal of Interpersonal Violence* 9:503-517.

Gottfredson, M.R. (1984). *Victims of Crime: The Dimensions of Risk*. London: H.M. Stationery Office.

Graber, D. (1977). "Ideological Components in the Perceptions of Crime and Crime News." Paper presented to the meeting of the Society for the Study of Social Problems.

———— (1980). *Crime News and the Public*. New York: Praeger.

Greenberg, S.W., W.M. Rohe and J.R. Williams (1985). *Informal Citizen Action and Crime Prevention at the Neighborhood Level: Synthesis and Assessment of the Research*. Washington, DC: National Institute of Justice.

Greer, D.S. (1994). "A Transatlantic Perspective on the Compensation of Crime Victims in the United States." *Journal of Criminal Law & Criminology* 85:333-401.

Griffin, L.W. and O.J. Williams (1992). "Abuse Among African-American Elderly." *Journal of Family Violence* 7:19-35.

Griffin, S. (1971). "Rape: The All-American Crime." *Ramparts* 10:26-36.

Gross, J.J. (1991). "Marital Rape—A Crime? A Comparative Law Study of the Laws of the United States and the State of Israel." *International Journal of Comparative and Applied Criminal Justice* 15:207-216.

Groth, A.N. and H.J. Birnbaum (1980). "The Rapist: Motivations for Sexual Violence." In S.L. McCombie (ed.), *The Rape Crisis Intervention Handbook: A Guide for Victim Care*. New York: Plenum Press.

Gutek, B. (1985). *Sex and the Workplace*. San Francisco: Jossey-Bass.

Hackney, S. (1969). "Southern Violence." In H.D. Graham and T.R. Gurr (eds.), *Violence in America*. New York: Signet.

Hamberger, L.K. (1993). "Comments on Pagelow's Myth of Psychopathology in Woman Battering." *Journal of Interpersonal Violence* 8:132-136.

Handelman, D. (1979). "The Interpretation of Child Abuse: Bureaucratic Relevance in Urban Newfoundland." *Journal of Sociology and Social Welfare* 6:70-88.

Hanke, P.J. and J.H. Gundlach (1995). "Damned on Arrival: A Preliminary Study of the Relationship Between Homicide, Emergency Medical Care, and Race." *Journal of Criminal Justice* 23:313-323.

Harland, A.T. and C.J. Rosen (1990). "Impediments to the Recovery of Restitution by Crime Victims." *Violence and Victims* 5:127-140.

Harrington, N.T. and H. Leitenberg (1994). "Relationship Between Alcohol Consumption and Victim Behaviors Immediately Preceding Sexual Aggression by an Acquaintance." *Violence and Victims* 9:315-324.

Hawley, F.F. and S. Messner (1989). "The Southern Violence Construct: A Review of Arguments, Evidence, and the Normative Context." *Justice Quarterly* 6:481-511.

Healey, K.M. (1995). "Victim and Witness Intimidation: New Developments and Emerging Responses." *National Institute of Justice: Research in Action*. Washington, DC: U.S. Department of Justice.

Hearst, N. and S.B. Hulley (1988). "Preventing the Heterosexual Spread of AIDS: Are We Giving Our Patients the Best Advice?" *Journal of the American Medical Association* 259:2428-2432.

Heide, K.M. (1989). "Parricide: Incidence and Issues." *The Justice Professional* 4:19-41.

––––––– (1993). "Parents Who Get Killed and the Children Who Kill Them." *Journal of Interpersonal Violence* 8:531-544.

Hendricks, J.E. (1984). "Death Notification: The Theory and Practice of Informing Survivors." *Journal of Police Science and Administration* 12:109-116.

Henry, A.F. and J.F. Short, Jr. (1954). *Homicide and Suicide*. Glencoe, IL: The Free Press.

Hepburn, J.R. (1973). "Violent Behavior in Interpersonal Relationships." *Sociological Quarterly* 14:419-429.

Hickey, E.W. (1997). *Serial Murderers and Their Victims*, 2nd ed. Belmont, CA: Wadsworth.

Hilberman, E. (1976). *The Rape Victim*. New York: Basic Books.

Hillenbrand, S. (1990). "Restitution and Victims Rights in the 1980s." In A.J. Lurigio, W.G. Skogan and R.C. Davis (eds.), *Victims of Crime: Problems, Policies, and Programs*. Newbury Park, CA: Sage.

Hindelang, M.J. (1975). *Public Opinion Regarding Crime, Criminal Justice, and Related Topics*. Washington, DC: U.S. Department of Justice.

––––––– (1976). *Criminal Victimization in Eight American Cities: A Descriptive Analysis of Common Theft and Assault*. Cambridge, MA: Ballinger.

–––––––, M.R. Gottfredson and J. Garofalo (1978). *Victims of Personal Crime: An Empirical Foundation for a Theory of Personal Victimization*. Cambridge, MA: Ballinger.

Hirschel, J.D., C.W. Dean and R.C. Lumb (1994). "The Relative Contribution of Domestic Violence to Assault and Injury of Police Officers." *Justice Quarterly* 11:99-117.

–––––––, I.W. Hutchinson III and C.W. Dean (1992). "The Failure of Arrest to Deter Spouse Abuse." *Journal of Research in Crime and Delinquency* 29:7-33.

–––––––, I.W. Hutchinson, C.W. Dean, J.J. Kelley and C.E. Pesackis (1991). *Charlotte Spouse Assault Replication Project: Final Report*. Washington, DC: National Institute of Justice.

Hochstedler, E. (1981). *Crimes Against the Elderly in 26 Cities*. Washington, DC: U.S. Department of Justice.

Hofrichter, R. (1980). "Techniques of Victim Involvement in Restitution." In J. Hudson and B. Galaway (eds.), *Victims, Offenders, and Alternative Sanctions*. Lexington, MA: D.C. Heath.

Hofstetter, C.R. (1976). *Bias in the News*. Columbus, OH: Ohio State University Press.

Hogben, M., D. Byrne and M.E. Hamburger (1996). "Coercive Heterosexual Sexuality in Dating Relationships of College Students: Implications of Differential Male-Female Experiences." In E.S. Byers and L.F. O'Sullivan (eds.), *Sexual Coercion in Dating Relationships*. New York: Hayworth Press.

Holmes, R.M. (1993). "Stalking in America: Types and Methods of Criminal Stalkers." *Journal of Contemporary Criminal Justice* 9:317-327.

Holmstrom, L.L. and A.W. Burgess (1978). *The Victim of Rape: Institutional Reactions*. New York: Wiley Interscience.

Horney, J. and C. Spohn (1991). "Rape Law Reform and Instrumental Change in Six Urban Jurisdictions." *Law & Society Review* 25:117-153.

———— and C. Spohn (1996). "The Influence of Blame and Believability Factors on the Processing of Simple Versus Aggravated Rape Cases." *Criminology* 34:135-162.

Horton, J.W. (1986). "Ethanol Impairs Cardiocirculatory Function in Treated Canine Hemorrhagic Shock." *Surgery* 100:520-530.

Hotaling, G.T. and D.B. Sugarman (1986). "An Analysis of Risk Markers in Husband to Wife Violence: The Current State of the Evidence." *Violence and Victims* 1:101-124.

———— and M.A. Straus (1989). "Intrafamily Violence, and Crime and Violence Outside the Family." In L. Ohlin and N. Tonry (eds.), *Family Violence*. Chicago: University of Chicago Press.

Howlett, D. (1997). "Oklahoma Families Expand Victmis' Rights." *USA Today* March 21:11A.

Hudson, J. and S. Chesney (1978). "Research on Restitution: A Review and Assessment." In B. Galaway and J. Hudson (eds.), *Offender Restitution in Theory and Action*. Lexington, MA: D.C. Heath.

———— and B. Galaway (1980). "A Review of the Restitution and Community-Service Sanctioning Research." In J. Hudson and B. Galaway (eds.), *Victims, Offenders, and Alternative Sanctions*. Lexington, MA: D.C. Heath.

Hudson, J.E. (1988). "Elder Abuse: An Overview." In B. Schlesinger and R. Schlesinger (eds.), *Abuse of the Elderly: Issues and Annotated Bibliography*. Toronto: University of Toronto Press.

Hudson, M.F. (1989). "Analyses of the Concepts of Elder Mistreatment: Abuse and Neglect." *Journal of Elder Abuse and Neglect* 1:5-25.

Huesmann, L.R. and N.M. Malamuth (1986). "Media Violence and Antisocial Behavior: An Overview." *Journal of Social Issues* 42:1-6.

Hyman, I.A. (1982). "Corporal Punishment in the Schools: America's Officially Sanctioned Brand of Child Abuse." In G.J. Williams and J. Money (eds.), *Traumatic Abuse and Neglect of Children at Home*. Baltimore: John Hopkins University Press.

Ivatury, R.R., J. Kazigo, M. Rohman, J. Gaudino, R. Simon and W.M. Stahl (1991). "'Directed' Emergency Room Thoracotomy: A Prognostic Prerequisite for Survival." *Journal of Trauma* 31:1076-1082.

Jacob, B. (1976). "The Concept of Restitution: An Historical Overview." In J. Hudson (ed.), *Restitution in Criminal Justice*. St. Paul: Minnesota Department of Corrections.

Jensen, G.F. and M.A. Karpos (1993). "Managing Rape: Exploratory Research on the Behavior of Rape Statistics." *Criminology* 31:363-385.

Jensen, R.H. (1977-78). "Battered Women and the Law." *Victimology* 2:585-590.

Jerin, R.A., L.J. Moriarty and M.A. Gibson (1995). "Victim Service or Self Service? An Analysis of Prosecution Based Victim-Witness Assistance Programs and Providers." *Criminal Justice Policy Review* 7:142-154.

Johnson, K.W. (1996). "Professional Help and Crime Victims." *Social Service Review* 71:89-109.

Johnson, N.C. and S.D. Young (1992). "Survivors' Response to Gang Violence." In R.C. Cervantes (ed.), *Substance Abuse and Gang Violence.* Newbury Park, CA: Sage.

Jurkovich, G.J., F.P. Rivara, H.G. Gurney, C. Fligner, R. Ries, B.A. Mueller and M. Copass (1993). "The Effect of Acute Alcohol Intoxication and Chronic Alcohol Abuse on Outcome from Trauma." *Journal of the American Medical Association* 270:51-56.

Kalichman, S.C., M.E. Craig and D.R. Follingstad (1990). "Professionals' Adherence to Mandatory Child Abuse Reporting Laws: Effects of Responsibility Attribution, Confidence Ratings, and Situational Factors." *Child Abuse & Neglect* 14:69-77.

Kanin, E.J. (1957). "Male Aggression in Dating-Courtship Relations." *American Journal of Sociology* 63:197-204.

*Kansas v. Hendricks*, 117 S. Ct. 2072 (1997).

Kantor, G.K. and M.A. Straus (1987). "The 'Drunken Bum' Theory of Wife Beating." *Social Problems* 34:213-230.

Kapp, M.B. (1995). "Elder Mistreatment: Legal Interventions and Policy Uncertainties." *Behavioral Sciences and the Law* 13:365-380.

Katz, S.N., L. Ambrosino, M. McGrath and K. Sawitsky (1977). "Legal Research on Child Abuse and Neglect: Past and Future." *Family Law Quarterly* 11:151-184.

————, R.W. Howe and M. McGrath (1975). "Child Neglect Laws in America." *Family Law Quarterly* 9:1-372.

Keldgord, R. (1978). "Community Restitution Comes to Arizona." In B. Galaway and J. Hudson (eds.), *Offender Restitution in Theory and Action.* Lexington, MA: D.C. Heath.

Kellerman, A.L. (1994). "Editorial: Firearm-Related Violence—What We Don't Know Is Killing Us." *American Journal of Public Health* 84:541-542.

Kelley, B.T., T.P. Thornberry and C.A. Smith (1997). *In the Wake of Childhood Maltreatment.* Washington, DC: Office of Juvenile Justice and Delinquency Prevention.

Kelly, D.P. (1984). "Delivering Legal Services to Victims: An Evaluation and Prescription." *The Justice System Journal* 9:62-86.

———— (1987). "How Can We Help the Victim without Hurting the Defendant?" *Criminal Justice* 2:14-18, 38-39.

———— (1991). "Have Victim Reforms Gone Too Far—or Not Far Enough?" *Criminal Justice* 6:22-28, 38.

Kempe, C.H., F.N. Silverman, B.F. Steele, W. Droegemuller and H.K. Silver (1962). "The Battered-Child Syndrome." *Journal of the American Medical Association* 181:105-112.

Key, L.J. (1992). "A Working Typology of Grief Among Homicide Survivors." In R.C. Cervantes (ed.), *Substance Abuse and Gang Violence.* Newbury Park, CA: Sage.

Kigin, R. and S. Novack (1980). "A Rural Restitution Program for Juvenile Offenders and Victims." In J. Hudson and B. Galaway (eds.), *Victims, Offenders, and Alternative Sanctions*. Lexington, MA: D.C. Heath.

Killias, M. (1990). "Vulnerability: Towards a Better Understanding of a Key Variable in the Genesis of Fear of Crime." *Violence and Victims* 5:97-108.

Kilpatrick, D.G., C.L. Best, C.J. Veronen, A.E. Amick, L.A. Villenponteaux and G.A. Ruff (1985). "Mental Health Correlates of Criminal Victimization: A Random Community Survey." *Journal of Consulting and Clinical Psychology* 53:873-886.

Kindermann, C., J. Lynch and D. Cantor (1997). *Bureau of Justice Statistics: National Crime Victimization Survey: Effects of the Redesign on Victimization Estimates*. Washington, DC: U.S. Government Printing Office.

Kitson, G.C., R.D. Clark, D.S. DeGarmo, H. Dyches and N. Rao (1991). "Bereavement in Natural and Violent Death." Paper presented at the Theory Construction and Research Methodology Workshop, National Council on Family Relations Annual Meeting.

Klapholz, H. (1980). "The Medical Examination: Treatment and Evidence Collection." In S.L. McCombie (ed.), *The Rape Crisis Intervention Handbook; A Guide for Victim Care*. New York: Plenum Press.

Klappers, D. (1985). "Ident-A-Kid." *Police Chief* 52:30-31.

Knudten, R.D., A.C. Meade, M.S. Knudten and W. Doerner (1976). "The Victim in the Administration of Criminal Justice: Problems and Perceptions." In W.F. McDonald (ed.), *Criminal Justice and the Victim*. Beverly Hills, CA: Sage.

_____, A.C. Meade, M.S. Knudten and W.G. Doerner (1977). *Victims and Witnesses: Their Experiences with Crime and the Criminal Justice System: Executive Summary*. Washington, DC: National Institute of Law Enforcement and Criminal Justice.

_____ and M.S. Knudten (1981). "What Happens to Crime Victims and Witnesses in the Justice System?" In B. Galaway and J. Hudson (eds.), *Perspectives on Crime Victims*. St. Louis, MO: Mosby.

Kolbos, J.R., E.H. Blakely and D. Engleman (1996). "Children Who Witness Domestic Violence: A Review of Empirical Literature." *Journal of Interpersonal Violence* 11:281-293.

Koop, C.E. and G.D. Lundberg (1992). "Violence in America: A Public Health Emergency: Time to Bite the Bullet Back." *Journal of the American Medical Association* 267:3075-3076.

Kosberg, J.I. (1988). "Preventing Elder Abuse: Identification of High Risk Factors Prior to Placement Decisions." *The Gerontologist* 28:43-50.

Koss, M.P. (1995). "Hidden Rape: Sexual Aggression and Victimization in a National Sample of Students in Higher Education." In P. Pearles and R.J. Berger (eds.), *Rape and Society: Readings on the Problem of Sexual Assault*. Boulder, CO: Westview Press.

_____ and H.H. Cleveland (1997). "Stepping on Toes: Social Roots of Date Rape Lead to Intractability and Politicization." In M.D. Schwartz (ed.), *Researching Sexual Violence Against Women: Methodological and Personal Perspectives*. Thousand Oaks, CA: Sage.

_____ and J.A. Gaines (1993). "The Prediction of Sexual Aggression by Alcohol Use, Athletic Participation, and Fraternity Affiliation." *Journal of Interpersonal Violence* 8:94-108.

————, C.A. Gidycz and N. Wisniewski (1987). "The Scope of Rape: Incidence and Prevalence of Sexual Aggression and Victimization in a National Sample of Students in Higher Education." *Clinical Psychology* 55:162-170.

———— and K.E. Leonard (1984). "Sexually Aggressive Men: Empirical Findings and Theoretical Implications." In N. Malamuth and E. Donnerstein (eds.), *Pornography and Sexual Aggression*. New York: Academic Press.

Kreis, D.J. Jr., G. Plascencia, D. Augenstein, J.H. Davis, M.Echenique, J. Vopal, P. Byers and G. Gomez (1986). "Preventable Trauma Deaths: Dade County, Florida." *Journal of Trauma* 26:649-654.

Kubler-Ross, E. (1969). *On Death and Dying*. New York: Macmillan.

Lab, S.P. (1990). "Citizen Crime Prevention: Domains and Participation." *Justice Quarterly* 7:467-492.

———— and J.D. Hirschel (1988). "Climatological Conditions and Crime: The Forecast is . . .?" *Justice Quarterly* 5:281-300.

Lamborn, L.L. (1987). "Victim Participation in the Criminal Justice Process: The Proposals for a Constitutional Amendment." *The Wayne Law Review* 34:125-220.

Lamond, D.A.P. (1989). "The Impact of Mandatory Reporting Legislation on Reporting Behavior." *Child Abuse & Neglect* 13:471-480.

Langen, P. and C. Innes (1986). *Preventing Domestic Violence Against Women*. Washington, DC: U.S. Department of Justice.

Largen, M.A. (1988). "Rape-Law Reform: An Analysis." In A.W. Burgess (ed.), *Rape and Sexual Assault, II*. New York: Garland.

Lauritsen, J.L. and K.F.D. Quinet (1995). "Repeat Victimization Among Adolescents and Young Adults." *Journal of Quantitaive Criminology* 11:143-166.

Lawrence, R. (1990). "Restitution as a Cost-Effective Alternative to Incarceration." In B. Galaway and J. Hudson (eds.), *Criminal Justice, Restitution, and Reconciliation*. Monsey, NY: Criminal Justice Press.

LeBeau, J.L. and R.H. Langworthy (1986). "The Linkages Between Routine Activities, Weather, and Calls for Police Service." *Journal of Police Science and Administration* 14:137-145.

LeDoux, J.C. and R.R. Hazelwood (1985). "Police Attitudes and Beliefs Toward Rape." *Journal of Police Science and Administration* 13:211-220.

Lee, L. (1997). "Courts Begin to Award Damages to Victims of Parking-Area Crime." *The Wall Street Journal* April 23:A1, A8.

Lempert, R.O. (1989). "Humility Is a Virtue: On the Publicization of Policy-Relevant Research." *Law & Society Review* 23:145-161.

Lerner, M.J. (1980). "The Desire for Justice and Reactions to Victims." In M. Walker and S. Brodsky (eds.), *Altruism and Helping Behavior*. New York: Academic Press.

Levin, J. (1993). "Swindled Seniors Testify on the Hill." *USA Today* May 26:4B.

Levine, K. (1978). "Empiricism in Victimological Research: A Critique." *Victimology* 3:77-90.

Levine, M. and L. Battistoni (1991). "The Corroboration Requirement in Child Sex Abuse Cases." *Behavioral Sciences and the Law* 9:3-20.

Levitt, C.J., G. Owen and J. Truchsess (1991). "Families after Sexual Abuse: What Helps?" In M.Q. Patton (ed.), *Family Sexual Abuse: Frontline Research and Evaluation*. Newbury Park, CA: Sage.

Lewis, A. (1996). "Mr. Clinton's Vicitms." *New York Times* June 28:A15.

Liang, J. and M.C. Sengstock (1983). "Personal Crimes against the Elderly." In J.I. Kosberg (ed.), *Abuse and Mistreatment of the Elderly: Causes and Interventions*. Littleton, MA: John Wright.

Lieb, R. (1996). "Community Notification Laws: 'A Step Toward More Effective Solutions.'" *Journal of Interpersonal Violence* 11:298-300.

Light, R.J. (1973). "Abused and Neglected in America: A Study of Alternative Policies." *Harvard Educational Review* 43:556-598.

Lindemann, E. (1944). "Symptomatology and Management of Acute Grief." *American Journal of Psychiatry* 101:141-148.

Lipovsky, J.A. (1994). "The Impact of Court on Children: Research Findings and Practical Recommendations." *Journal of Interpersonal Violence* 9:238-257.

Littlechild, B. (1995). "Violence Against Social Workers." *Journal of Interpersonal Violence* 10:123-130.

Lively, G.M. (1996). "Thinking Globally to Act Locally: NIJ Improves Worldwide Access to Criminal Justice Information." *National Institute of Justice Journal* 230:2-8.

_____ and J.A. Reardon (1996). "Justice on the Net: The National Institute of Justice Promotes Internet Services." *National Institute of Justice: Research in Action*. Washington, DC: U.S. Department of Justice.

Lockhart, L.L., B.W. White, V. Causby and A. Isaac (1994). "Letting Out the Secret: Violence in Lesbian Relationships." *Journal of Interpersonal Violence* 9:469-492.

Loftin, C. and R.H. Hill (1974). "Regional Subculture and Homicide: An Examination of the Gastil-Hackney Thesis." *American Sociological Review* 39:714-724.

_____ (1978). "Comments." *Criminology* 16:56-59.

Lombroso, C. (1968). *Crime, Its Causes and Remedies*. Montclair, NJ: Patterson.

Long-Onnen, J. and D. Cheatwood (1992). "Hospitals and Homicide: An Expansion of Current Theoretical Paradigms." *American Journal of Criminal Justice* 16:57-74.

Lottes, I.L. (1988). "Sexual Socialization and Attitudes Toward Rape." In A.W. Burgess (ed.), *Rape and Sexual Assault, II*. New York: Garland.

Lowenstein, S.R., M.P. Weissberg and D. Terry (1990). "Alcohol Intoxication, Injuries, and Dangerous Behaviors—and the Revolving Emergency Department Door." *Journal of Trauma* 30:1252-1258.

Lucal, B. (1995). "The Problem with 'Battered Husbands.'" *Deviant Behavior* 16:95-112.

Luckenbill, D.F. (1977). "Criminal Homicide as a Situated Transaction." *Social Problems* 25:176-186.

Luginbuhl, J. and M. Burkhead (1995). "Victim Impact Evidence in a Capital Trial: Encouraging Votes for Death." *American Journal of Criminal Justice* 20:1-16.

Lundberg-Love, P. and R. Geffner (1989). "Date Rape: Prevalence, Risk Factors, and a Proposed Model." In M.A. Pirog-Good and J.E. Stets (eds.), *Violence in Dating Relationships: Emerging Social Issues*. New York: Praeger.

Maan, C. (1991). "Assessment of Sexually Abused Children with Anatomically Detailed Dolls: A Critical Review." *Behavioral Sciences and the Law* 9:43-51.

Macolini, R.M. (1995). "Edler Abuse Policy: Considerations in Research and Legislation." *Behavioral Sciences and the Law* 13:349-363.

Maddock, J.W., P.R. Larson and C.F. Lally (1991). "An Evaluation Protocol for Incest Family Functioning." In M.Q. Patton (ed.), *Family Sexual Abuse: Frontline Research and Evaluation.* Newbury Park, CA: Sage.

Maddox, G.L. and J. Wiley (1976). "Scope, Concepts and Methods in the Study of Aging." In R.H. Binstock and E. Shanas (eds.), *Handbook of Aging and the Social Sciences.* New York: Van Nostrand Reinhold Company.

Maden, M.F. and D.F. Wrench (1977). "Significant Findings in Child Abuse Research." *Victimology* 2:196-224.

Maguire, K. and A.L. Pastore (1996). *Sourcebook of Criminal Justice Statistics—1995.* Washington, DC: U.S. Department of Justice.

Makepeace, J.M. (1981). "Courtship Violence Among College Students." *Family Relations* 30:97-102.

——— (1983). "Life Events Stress and Courtship Violence." *Family Relations* 32:101-109.

Mann, C.R. (1988). "Getting Even? Women Who Kill in Domestic Encounters." *Justice Quarterly* 5:33-51.

——— (1990). "Black Female Homicide in the United States." *Journal of Interpersonal Violence* 5:176-201.

Marden, P.G. (1966). "A Demographic and Ecological Analysis of the Distribution of Physicians in Metropolitan America." *American Journal of Sociology* 72:290-300.

Marhofer-Dvorak, A., P.A. Resick, C.K. Hutter and S.A. Girelli (1988). "Single- Versus Multiple-Incident Rape Victims: A Comparison of Psychological Reactions to Rape." *Journal of Interpersonal Violence* 3:145-160.

Marsh, J.C., A. Geist and N. Caplan (1982). *Rape and the Limits of Law Reform.* Boston, MA: Auburn House.

Martin, P.Y. and R. Hummer (1989). "Fraternities and Rape on Campus." *Gender & Society* 3:357-373.

——— and R.M. Powell (1994). "Accounting for the 'Second Assault': Legal Organizations' Framing of Rape Victims." *Law & Social Inquiry* 19:853-890.

Marwick, C. (1992). "Guns, Drugs Threaten to Raise Public Health Problem of Violence to Epidemic." *Journal of the American Medical Association* 267:2993.

Matura, R.C. (1982). *The Politics of Aging in Florida: A Case Study of the Silver Haired Legislature.* Gainesville, FL: University of Florida.

Mause, L. (1974). *The History of Childhood.* New York: Psycho-History Press.

Mawby, R.I. and S. Walklate (1994). *Critical Victimology.* Thousand Oaks, CA: Sage.

Mayhall, P.D. and K.E. Norgard (1983). *Child Abuse and Neglect: Sharing Responsibility.* New York: Wiley.

Mayhew, P., N.A. Maung and C. Mirrlees-Black (1993). *The 1992 British Crime Survey.* London: H.M. Stationery Office.

McAnany, P.D. (1978). "Restitution as Idea and Practice: The Retributive Prospect." In B. Galaway and J. Hudson (eds.), *Offender Restitution in Theory and Action*. Lexington, MA: D.C. Heath.

McCarroll, J.E., R.J. Ursano, K.M. Wright and C.S. Fullerton (1993). "Handling Bodies after Violent Death: Strategies for Coping." *American Journal of Orthopsychiatry* 63:209-214.

McClain, P., J. Sacks and R. Frohlke (1993). "Estimates of Fatal Child Abuse and Neglect, United States, 1979 through 1988." *Pediatrics* 91:338-343.

McCleary, R., B.C. Nienstedt and J.M. Erven (1982). "Uniform Crime Reports as Organizational Outcomes: Three Time-Series Experiments." *Social Problems* 29:361-372.

McCormack, R.J. (1991). "Compensating Victims of Violent Crime." *Justice Quarterly* 8:329-346.

McCoy, H.V., J.D. Wooldredge, F.T. Cullen, P.J. Dubeck and S.L. Browning (1996). "Lifestyles of the Old and Not So Fearful: Life Situation and Older Persons' Fear of Crime." *Journal of Criminal Justice* 24:191-205.

McCurdy, K. and D. Daro (1994). "Child Maltreatment: A National Study of Reports and Fatalities." *Journal of Interpersonal Violence* 9:75-94.

McDonald, L. (1996). "Abuse and Neglect of Elders." In J.E. Birren (ed.), *Encyclopedia of Gerontology*, Vol. 1. San Diego: Academic Press.

McGhee, J.R. (1983). "The Vulnerability of Elderly Consumers." *International Journal of Aging and Human Development* 17:223-246.

McGillis, D. and J. Mullen (1977). *Neighborhood Justice Centers: An Analysis of Potential Models*. Washington, DC: Law Enforcement Assistance Administration.

_____ and P. Smith (1983). *Compensating Victims of Crime: An Analysis of American Programs*. Washington, DC: U.S. Department of Justice.

McGuire, K.A. (1991). "AIDS and the Sexual Offender: The Epidemic Now Poses New Threats to the Victim and the Criminal Justice System." *Dickinson Law Review* 96:95-123.

McKinney, J.C. (1950). "The Role of Constructive Typology in Scientific Sociological Analysis." *Social Forces* 28:235-240.

_____ (1969). "Typification, Typologies, and Sociological Theory." *Social Forces* 48:1-12.

McKinney, K. (1990). "Sexual Harassment of University Faculty by Colleagues and Students." *Sex Roles* 23:421-438.

*McKinney's Consolidated Laws of New York Annotated* (1997).

McLeod, M. (1987). "An Examination of the Victim's Role at Sentencing: Results of a Survey of Probation Administrators." *Judicature* 71:162-168.

McMahon, M. and E. Pence (1996). "Replaying to Dan O'Leary." *Journal of Interpersonal Violence* 11:452-455.

McNeely, R.L. and C.R. Mann (1990). "Domestic Violence is a Human Issue." *Journal of Interpersonal Violence* 5:129-132.

McShane, M.D. and F.P. Williams III (1992). "Radical Victimology: A Critique of the Concept of Victim in Traditional Victimology." *Crime & Delinquency* 38:258-271.

Meeker, J.W. and A. Binder (1990). "Experiments as Reforms: The Impact of the 'Minneapolis Experiment' on Police Policy." *Journal of Police Science and Administration* 17:147-153.

Meiners, R.E. (1978). *Victim Compensation: Economic, Legal, and Political Aspects.* Lexington, MA: Lexington Books.

Melton, G.B. (1980). "Psycholegal Issues in Child Victims' Interaction with the Legal System." *Victimology* 5:274-284.

———— and M.F. Flood (1994). "Research Policy and Child Maltreatment: Developing the Scientific Foundation for Effective Protection of Children." *Child Abuse & Neglect* 18:1-28.

Mendelsohn, B. (1956). "The Victimology." *Etudes Internationale de Psycho-sociologie Criminelle* July:23-26.

———— (1976). "Victimology and Contemporary Society's Trends." *Victimology* 1:8-28.

———— (1982). "Socio-Analytic Introduction to Research in a General Victimological and Criminological Perspective." In H.J. Schneider (ed.), *The Victim in International Perspective.* New York: de Gruyter.

Meyer, T.P. (1972). "The Effects of Sexually Arousing and Violent Films on Aggressive Behavior." *Journal of Sex Research* 8:324-331.

Mignon, S.I. and W.M. Holmes (1995). "Police Response to Mandatory Arrest Laws." *Crime & Delinquency* 41:430-442.

Miller, T.R., M.A. Cohen and B. Wiersema (1996). *Victim Costs and Consequences: A New Look.* Washington, DC: National Institute of Justice.

Mississippi Code Annotated (1997).

Mones, P. (1993). "When the Innocent Strike Back: Abused Children Who Kill Their Parents." *Journal of Interpersonal Violence* 8:297-299.

Monson, C.M., G.R. Byrd and J. Langhinrichsen-Rohling (1996). "To Have and to Hold: Perceptions of Marital Rape." *Journal of Interpersonal Violence* 11:410-424.

Murphy, C.M. and V.A. Baxter (1997). "Motivating Batterers to Change in the Treatment Context." *Journal of Interpersonal Violence* 12:607-619.

Murphy, S.M., A.E. Amick-McMullan, D.G. Kilpatrick, M.E. Haskett, L.J. Veronen, C.L. Best and B.E. Saunders (1988). "Rape Victims' Self-Esteem: A Longitudinal Analysis." *Journal of Interpersonal Violence* 3:355-370.

Myers, J.E.B. (1996). "Societal Self-Defense: New Laws to Protect Children from Sexual Abuse." *Child Abuse & Neglect* 20:255-258.

Myers, R.K. (1997a). "Victim Rights Clarification Act of 1997 Affects Victim Bill of Rights Act, Violent Crime Control Act, and Rule of Evidence." *The Crime Victims Report* 1:17, 29.

———— (1997b). "Supreme Court Finds Sexually Violent Predator Law Constitutional." *The Crime Victims Report* 1:56, 58-59.

National Clearinghouse on Child Abuse and Neglect Information (1997). *Frequently Asked Questions About Child Fatalities.* Washington, DC: National Clearinghouse on Child Abuse and Neglect Information. *URL: http://www.calib.com/nccanch/pubs/fatality.htm*

———— (1997). *What is Child Maltreatment?* Washington, DC: National Clearinghouse on Child Abuse and Neglect Information.

National Committee to Prevent Child Abuse (1996). *An Approach to Preventing Child Abuse.* Chicago: National Committee to Prevent Child Abuse. *URL: http://www.childabuse.org/fs15.html*

National Victim Center (1991). *America Speaks Out: Citizens' Attitudes About Victims' Rights and Violence.* Fort Worth, TX: National Victim Center.

──────── (1996). *The 1996 Victims' Rights Sourcebook: A Compilation and Comparison of Victims' Rights Laws.* Arlington, VA: National Victim Center. *URL: http://www.nvc.org/IDIR/SBOOK*

──────── (1997). *Child Abuse Statistics. URL: http://www.nvc.org/edir/childabu.htm#ca*

Nelson, B.J. (1984). *Making an Issue of Child Abuse: Political Agenda Setting for Social Problems.* Chicago: University of Chicago Press.

Newman, D.W. (1995). "Jury Decision Making and the Effect of Victim Impact Statements in the Penalty Phase." *Criminal Justice Policy Review* 7:291-300.

No Author (1964). "Editorial." *Journal of the American Medical Association.* 188 April 27:386.

No Author (1993). "Been a Crime Victim? The Pace of Compensation Can Be Glacial." *Tallahassee Democrat* December 6:6B.

Norris, J. and S. Feldman-Summers (1981). "Factors Related to the Psychological Impacts of Rape on the Victim." *Journal of Abnormal Psychology* 90:562-567.

Norton, J. (1987). "Robots Unlock Secrets of Child Sexual Abuse." *Police Chief* 54:31-36.

Norton, L. (1983). "Witness Involvement in the Criminal Justice System and Intention to Cooperate in Future Prosecutions." *Journal of Criminal Justice* 11:143-152.

Novack, S., B. Galaway and J. Hudson (1980). "Victim and Offender Perceptions of the Fairness of Restitution and Community-Service Sanctions." In J. Hudson and B. Galaway (eds.), *Victims, Offenders, and Alternative Sanctions.* Lexington, MA: D.C. Heath.

O'Brien, R.M. (1985). *Crime and Victimization.* Beverly Hills, CA: Sage.

Office of the Florida Attorney General (1989). *Attorney General's Task Force on Crimes and the Elderly.* Tallahassee, FL: State of Florida.

──────── (1991). *Sexual Assault: Evidence Collection Protocol.* Tallahassee, FL: State of Florida.

Office of the U.S. Attorney General (1992a). *Combating Violent Crime: 24 Recommendations to Strengthen Criminal Justice.* Washington, DC: U.S. Government Printing Office.

──────── (1992b). *Attorney General Guidelines for Victim and Witness Assistance.* Washington, DC: U.S. Department of Justice.

Office for Victims of Crime (1990). *Report to Congress, April 1990.* Washington, DC: U.S. Department of Justice.

──────── (1996). *OVC Fact Sheet: Victims of Crime Act: Crime Victims Fund Fact Sheet.* Washington, DC: U.S. Department of Justice. *URL: http://www.ojp.usdoj.gov/ovc/here/cvfund2.htm*

──────── (1997). *Civil Legal Remedies for Crime Victims,* 2nd ed. Washington, DC: U.S. Department of Justice. *URL: http://www.ncjrs.org.txtfiles/clr.txt*

O'Grady, K., J. Waldon, W. Carlson, S. Street and C. Cannizzaro (1992). "The Importance of Victim Satisfaction: A Commentary." *The Justice System Journal* 15:759-764.

O'Leary, K.D. (1996). "Physical Aggression in Intimate Relationships Can Be Treated Within a Marital Context Under Certain Circumstances." *Journal of Interpersonal Violence* 11:450-452.

Ohio Revised Code (1997).

Ohio State Medical Association (1994). *Ohio Physicians' Elder Abuse Prevention Project: Trust Talk*. Columbus, OH: Ohio State Medical Association.

Oklahoma Statutes Annotated (1997).

O'Malley, H., H. Segers, R. Perez, V. Mitchell and C. Knuepfel (1979). *Elder Abuse in Massachusetts: A Survey of Professional and Paraprofessionals*. Boston, MA: Legal Research and Services for the Elderly.

O'Malley, T.A., D.F. Everitt, H. O'Malley and E. Campion (1983). "Identifying and Preventing Family-Mediated Abuse and Neglect of Elderly Persons." *Annals of Internal Medicine* 98:998-1004.

Orcutt, J.D. and R. Faison (1988). "Sex-Role Attitude Change and Reporting of Rape Victimization, 1973-1985." *Sociological Quarterly* 29:589-604.

Osborn, D.R., D. Ellingworth, T. Hope and A. Trickett (1996). "Are Repeatedly Victimized Households Different?" *Journal of Quantitative Criminology* 12:223-245.

Owen, G. and N.M. Steele (1991). "Incest Offenders After Treatment." In M.Q. Patton (ed.), *Family Sexual Abuse: Frontline Research and Evaluation*. Newbury Park, CA: Sage.

Pagelow, M.D. (1984). *Family Violence*. New York: Greenwood Press.

———— (1992). "Adult Victims of Domestic Violence: Battered Women." *Journal of Interpersonal Violence* 7:87-120.

———— (1993). "Response to Hamberger's Comments." *Journal of Interpersonal Violence* 8:137-139.

Pallone, N.J. (1995). "A View from the Front Line." *Crime Justice Ethics* 14:9-16.

Parent, D.G., B. Auerbach and K.E. Carlson (1992). *Compensating Crime Victims: A Summary of Policies and Practices*. Washington, DC: U.S. Department of Justice.

Parents Anonymous, Inc. (1997). *The Parents Anonymous Principles and Group Standards*. Claremont, CA: Parents Anonymous, Inc.

Parker, R.N. (1989). "Poverty, Subculture of Violence, and Type of Homicide." *Social Forces* 67:983-1007.

———— and M.D. Smith (1979). "Deterrence, Poverty, and Type of Homicide." *American Journal of Sociology* 85:614-624.

Parnas, R.I. (1967). "The Police Response to the Domestic Disturbance." *Wisconsin Law Review* 31:914-960.

Parry, J.K. and J. Thornwall (1992). "Death of a Father." *Death Studies* 16:173-181.

Parsonage, W.H., F.P. Bernat and J. Helfgott (1994). "Victim Impact Testimony and Pennsylvania's Parole Decision Making Process: A Pilot Study." *Criminal Justice Policy Review* 6:187-206.

Patterson, M. (1978). "The Oklahoma Restitution Program." In B. Galaway and J. Hudson (eds.), *Offender Restitution in Theory and Action*. Lexington, MA: D.C. Heath.

*Payne v. Tennessee*, 111 S. Ct. 2597 (1991).

Pease, K. and G. Laycock (1996). "Revictimization: Reducing the Heat on Hot Victims." *National Institute of Justice: Research in Action*. Washington, DC: National Institute of Justice.

Penick, B.K. and M.B. Owens III (1976). *Surveying Crime: Panel for the Evaluation of Crime Surveys*. Washington, DC: National Academy of Sciences.

Pepper, C.D. (1983). "Frauds Against the Elderly." In J.I. Kosberg (ed.), *Abuse and Maltreatment of the Elderly: Causes and Interventions*. Littleton, MA: John Wright.

Perkins, C. and P. Klaus (1996). *Bureau of Justice Statistics Bulletin: National Crime Victimization Survey: Criminal Victimization, 1994*. Washington, DC: U.S. Government Printing Office.

Pfohl, S.J. (1977). "The 'Discovery' of Child Abuse." *Social Problems* 24:310-323.

Phillips, D.P. (1982). "The Impact of Fictional Television Stories on U.S. Adult Fatalities: New Evidence on the Effect of Mass Media on Violence." *American Journal of Sociology* 87:1340-1359.

————— (1983). "The Impact of Mass Media Violence on U.S. Homicides." *American Sociological Review* 48:560-568.

Phillips, L.R. (1986). "Theoretical Explanations of Elder Abuse: Competing Hypotheses and Unresolved Issues." In K.A. Pillemer and R.S. Wolf (eds.), *Elder Abuse: Conflict in the Family*. Dover, MA: Auburn House.

Pillemer, K.A. (1986). "Risk Factors in Elder Abuse: Results from a Case-Control Study." In K.A. Pillemer and R.S. Wolf (eds.), *Elder Abuse: Conflict in the Family*. Dover, MA: Auburn House.

————— (1988). "Maltreatment of Patients in Nursing Homes: Overview and Research Agenda." *Journal of Health and Social Behavior* 29:227-238.

————— and D. Finkelhor (1988). "The Prevalence of Elder Abuse: A Random Sample Survey." *The Gerontologist* 28:51-57.

Pirog-Good, M.A. and J.E. Stets (eds.) (1989). *Violence in Dating Relationships: Emerging Social Issues*. New York: Praeger.

Pittman, D.J. and W. Handy (1964). "Patterns in Criminal Aggravated Assault." *Journal of Criminal Law, Criminology, and Police Science* 55:462-470.

Pleck, E. (1979). "Wife Beating in Nineteenth-Century America," *Victimology* 4:60-74.

————— (1989). "Criminal Approaches to Family Violence, 1640-1980." In L. Ohlin and M. Tonry (eds.), *Family Violence*. Chicago: University of Chicago Press.

Pless, I.B. (1994). "Editorial: Reducing Violence—How Do We Proceed?" *American Journal of Public Health* 84:539-541.

Police Chiefs' Association of Santa Clara County (1994). *Domestic Violence Protocol for Law Enforcement*. Los Altos, CA: Police Chiefs' Association of Santa Clara County.

Pollak, J. and S. Levy, (1988). "Countertransference and Failure to Report Child Abuse and Neglect." *Child Abuse & Neglect* 13:515-522.

Pollock, D.A., J.M. O'Neill, R.G. Parrish, D.L. Combs and J.L. Annest (1993). "Temporal and Geographic Trends in the Autopsy Frequency of Blunt and Penetrating Trauma Deaths in the United States." *Journal of the American Medical Association* 269:1525-1531.

Poppen, J. and N.J. Segal (1988). "The Influence of Sex and Sex-Role Orientation on Sexual Coercion." *Sex Roles* 19:689-701.

Prentky, R.A. (1996). "Community Notification and Constructive Risk Reduction." *Journal of Interpersonal Violence* 11:295-298.

The President's Commission on Law Enforcement and Administration of Justice (1967). *Task Force Report: Crime and Its Impact—An Assessment.* Washington, DC: U.S. Government Printing Office.

The President's Task Force on Victims of Crime (1982). *Final Report.* Washington, DC: U.S. Government Printing Office.

Prochaska, J.O. and C.C. DiClemente (1984). *The Transtheoretical Approach: Crossing the Traditional Boundaries of Therapy.* Homewood IL: Dow Jones Irwin.

Quetelet, A. (1978). *A Treatise on Man.* New York: Burt Franklin.

Quinn, M.J. (1990). "Elder Abuse and Neglect: Treatment Issues." In S.M. Stith, M.B. Williams and K. Rosen (eds.), *Violence Hits Home.* New York: Springer.

_____ and S.K. Tomita (1986). *Elder Abuse and Neglect: Causes, Diagnosis and Intervention Strategies.* New York: Springer.

Rand, M.R., J.P. Lynch and D. Cantor (1997). *Bureau of Justice Statistics: National Crime Victimization Survey: Criminal Victimization, 1973-95.* Washington, DC: Bureau of Justice Statistics.

Range, L.M. and N.M. Niss (1990). "Long-Term Bereavement from Suicide, Homicide, Accidents, and Natural Deaths." *Death Studies* 14:423-433.

Ranish, D.R. and D. Shichor (1985). "The Victim's Role in the Penal Process: Recent Developments in California." *Federal Probation* 49:50-57.

Rapoport, L. (1962). "The State of Crisis: Some Theoretical Considerations." *Social Service Review* 36:211-217.

Ray, L., P. Kestner and L. Freedman (1986). "Dispute Resolution: From Examination to Experimentation." *Michigan Bar Journal* 65:898-903.

Reichel, P. and C. Seyfrit (1984). "A Peer Jury in Juvenile Court." *Crime & Delinquency* 30:423-438.

Reifen, D. (1975). "Court Procedures in Israel to Protect Child-Victims of Sexual Assaults." In I. Drapkin and E. Viano (eds.), *Victimology: A New Focus. Volume 3: Crimes, Victims, and Justice.* Lexington, MA: Lexington Books.

Reiss, A.J. (1980). "Victim Proneness in Repeat Victimization by Type of Crime." In S.E. Fienberg and A.J. Reiss (eds.), *Indicators of Crime and Criminal Justice: Quantitative Studies.* Washington, DC: Bureau of Justice Statistics.

Resick, P.A. (1987). *Reactions of Female and Male Victims of Rape or Robbery.* Washington, DC: National Institute of Mental Health.

_____ (1990). "Victims of Sexual Assault." In A.J. Lurigio, W.G. Skogan and R.C. Davis (eds.), *Victims of Crime: Problems, Policies, and Programs.* Newbury Park, CA: Sage.

_____ (1993). "The Psychological Impact of Rape." *Journal of Interpersonal Violence* 8:223-255.

_____, K.S. Calhoun, B.M. Atkeson and E.M. Ellis (1981). "Social Adjustment in Victims of Sexual Assault." *Journal of Consulting and Clinical Psychology* 49:705-712.

Reskin, B. and F. Campbell (1974). "Physician Distribution Across Metropolitan Areas." *American Journal of Sociology* 79:981-988.

Riedel, M., M.A. Zahn and L.F. Mock (1985). *The Nature and Patterns of American Homicide.* Washington, DC: U.S. Department of Justice.

Riger, S., M.T. Gordon and R. LeBailly (1978). "Women's Fear of Crime: From Blaming to Restricting the Victim." *Victimology* 3:274-284.

Rinkle, V. (1989). "Federal Initiatives." In R. Filinson and S.R. Ingman (eds.), *Elder Abuse: Practice and Policy.* New York: Human Sciences Press.

Rivara, F.P., B.A. Mueller, G. Somes, C.T. Mendoza, H.B. Rushforth and A.L. Kellerman (1997). "Alcohol and Illicit Drug Abuse and the Risk of Violent Death in the Home." *Journal of the American Medical Association* 278:569-575.

Rivo, M.L., T.M. Henderson and D.M. Jackson (1995). "State Legislative Strategies to Improve the Supply and Distribution of Generalist Physicians, 1985 to 1992." *American Journal of Public Health* 85:405-407.

Roberts, A.R. (1991). "Delivery of Services to Crime Victims: A National Survey." *American Journal of Orthopsychiatry* 6:128-137.

——— (1992). "Victim/Witness Programs: Questions and Answers." *FBI Law Enforcement Bulletin* 61:12-16.

Robinson, J. (1981). "Defense Strategies for Battered Women Who Assault Their Mates: *State v. Curry.*" *Harvard Women's Law Journal* 4:161-175.

Roehl, J.A. and R.F. Cook (1982). "The Neighborhood Justice Centers Field Test." In R. Tomasic and M.M. Feeley (eds.), *Neighborhood Justice: Assessment of an Emerging Idea.* New York: Longman.

Rounsaville, B.J. (1978). "Theories in Marital Violence: Evidence from a Study of Battered Women." *Victimology* 3:17-18.

Rowley, M.S. (1990). "Recidivism of Juvenile Offenders in a Diversion Restitution Program." In B. Galaway and J. Hudson (eds.), *Criminal Justice, Restitution, and Reconciliation.* Monsey, NY: Criminal Justice Press.

Rubin, P.N. (1995). "Civil Rights and Criminal Justice: Primer on Sexual Harassment." *National Institute of Justice: Research in Action.* Washington, DC: National Institute of Justice.

Rushing, W.A. (1975). *Community, Physicians and Inequality.* Lexington, MA: Lexington Books.

——— and G.I. Wade (1973). "Community-Structure Constraints on the Distribution of Physicians." *Health Services Research* 8:283-297.

Russell, D.E.H. (1982). *Rape in Marriage.* New York: Macmillan.

Saltzman, L.E., J.A. Mercy, P.W. O'Caroll, M.L. Rosenberg and P.H. Rhodes (1992). "Weapon Involvement and Injury Outcomes in Family and Intimate Assaults." *Journal of the American Medical Association* 267:3043-3047.

Sanders, W.B. (1980). *Rape and Woman's Identity.* Beverly Hills, CA: Sage.

Sarri, R. and P.W. Bradley (1980). "Juvenile Aid Panels: An Alternative to Juvenile Court Processing in South Australia." *Crime & Delinquency* 26:42-62.

Saunders, E.J. (1988). "A Comparative Study of Attitudes Toward Child Sexual Abuse Among Social Work and Judicial System Professionals." *Child Abuse & Neglect* 17:83-90.

Savitz, L.D., K.S. Kumar and M.A. Zahn (1991). "Quantifying Luckenbill." *Deviant Behavior* 12:19-29.

Schafer, J. (1996). "Measuring Spousal Violence with the Conflict Tactics Scale: Notes on Reliability and Validity Issues." *Journal of Interpersonal Violence* 11:572-585.

Schafer, S. (1968). *The Victim and His Criminal: A Study in Functional Responsibility.* New York: Random House.

_____ (1970). *Compensation and Restitution to Victims of Crime.* Montclair, NJ: Patterson Smith.

Schaie, K.W. (1988). "Methodological Issues in Aging Research: An Introduction." In K.W. Schaie, R.T. Campbell, W. Meredith and S.C. Rawlings (eds.), *Methodological Issues in Aging Research.* New York: Springer.

Schissel, B. (1996). "Law Reform and Social Change: A Time-Series Analysis of Sexual Assault in Canada." *Journal of Criminal Justice* 24:123-138.

Schlesinger, B. and R. Schlesinger (1988). "Abuse of the Elderly: Knowns and Unknowns." In B. Schlesinger and R. Schlesinger (eds.), *Abuse of the Elderly: Issues and Annotated Bibliography.* Toronto: University of Toronto Press.

Schlesinger, R.A. (1988). "Grannybashing." In B. Schlesinger and R. Schlesinger (eds.), *Abuse of the Elderly: Issues and Annotated Bibliography.* Toronto: University of Toronto Press.

Schmidt, J. and E.H. Steury (1989). "Prosecutorial Discretion in Filing Charges in Domestic Violence Cases." *Criminology* 27:487-510.

Schneider, A.L. (1986). "Restitution and Recidivism Rates of Juvenile Offenders: Results from Four Experimental Studies." *Criminology* 24:533-552.

_____, J.M. Burcart and L.A. Wilson II (1976). "The Role of Attitudes in the Decision to Report Crimes to the Police." In W.F. McDonald (ed.), *Criminal Justice and the Victim.* Beverly Hills, CA: Sage.

_____, W.R. Griffith, D.H. Sumi and J.M. Burcart (1978). *Portland Forward Records Check of Crime Victims.* Washington, DC: National Institute of Law Enforcement and Criminal Justice.

_____ and P.R. Schneider (1984). "A Comparison of Programmatic and 'Ad Hoc' Restitution in Juvenile Courts." *Justice Quarterly* 1:529-548.

Schneider, H.J. (1987). "Rape in Criminological and Victimological Perspective." *Eurocriminology* 1:15-29.

Schwartz, M.D. (1989). "Family Violence as a Cause of Crime: Rethinking Our Priorities." *Criminal Justice Policy Review* 3:115-132.

_____ and V.L. Pitts (1995). "Exploring a Feminist Routine Activities Approach to Explaining Sexual Assault." *Justice Quarterly* 12:9-32.

Schwendinger, J.R. and H. Schwendinger (1983). *Rape and Inequality.* Beverly Hills, CA: Sage.

Scully, D. (1990). *Understanding Sexual Violence.* Boston, MA: Unwin Hyman.

Searles, P. and R.J. Berger (eds.) (1995). *Rape and Society: Readings on the Problem of Sexual Assault.* Boulder, CO: Westview Press.

Shah, R. (1991). "Multiple Victimization: A Secondary Analysis of the 1988 British Crime Survey." Master's thesis. Manchester: University of Manchester.

Shapiro, B.L. and J.C. Schwarz (1997). "Date Rape: Its Relationship to Trauma Symptoms and Sexual Self-Esteem." *Journal of Interpersonal Violence* 12:407-419.

Shapiro, C. (1990). "Is Restitution Legislation the Chameleon of the Victims' Movement?" In B. Galaway and J. Hudson (eds.), *Criminal Justice, Restitution, and Reconciliation.* Monsey, NY: Criminal Justice Press.

Shapland, J. (1983). "Victim-Witness Services and the Needs of the Victim." *Victimology* 8:233- 237.

Shecter, J. (1996). "Fighting for Rape Victims." *The Chronicle of Higher Education,* April 19:A8.

Shell, D.J. (1982). *Protection of the Elderly: A Study of Elderly Abuse.* Winnipeg, Manitoba: Manitoba Council on Aging.

Sherman, L.W. (1992). *Policing Domestic Violence: Experiments and Dilemmas.* New York: The Free Press.

————— (1995). "Hot Spots of Crime and Criminal Careers of Places." In J.E. Eck and D. Weisburd (eds.), *Crime and Place.* Monsey, NY: Criminal Justice Press.

————— and R.A. Berk (1984). "The Specific Deterrent Effects of Arrest for Domestic Assault." *American Sociological Review* 49:261-272.

—————, P.R. Gartin and M.E. Buerger (1989). "Hot Spots of Predatory Crime: Routine Activities and the Criminology of Place." *Criminology* 27:27-56.

—————, L. Steele, D. Laufersweiler, N. Hoffer and S.A. Julian (1989). "Stray Bullets and 'Mushrooms': Random Shootings of Bystanders in Four Cities, 1977-1988." *Journal of Quantitative Criminology* 5:297-316.

Shulman, L.P., D. Muran and P.M. Speck (1992). "Counseling Sexual Assault Victims Who Become Pregnant after the Assault: Benefits and Limitations for First-Trimester Paternity Determination." *Journal of Interpersonal Violence* 7:205-210.

Siegel, J.M., J.M. Golding, J.A. Stein, M.A. Burnam and S.B. Sorenson (1990). "Reactions to Sexual Assault: A Community Study." *Journal of Interpersonal Violence* 5:229-246.

Sigler, R.T., J.M. Crowley and I. Johnson (1990). "Judicial and Prosecutorial Endorsement of Innovative Techniques in the Trial of Domestic Abuse Cases." *Journal of Crime and Justice* 18:443-454.

Silverman, S.S. and W.G. Doerner (1979). "The Effect of Victim Compensation Programs upon Conviction Rates." *Sociological Symposium* 25:40-60.

*Simon & Schuster v. Members of the New York State Crime Victims Board et al.,* 112 S. Ct. 501 (1991).

Simons, R.L., C. Wu, C. Johnson and R.D. Conger (1995). "A Test of Various Perspectives on the Intergenerational Transmission of Domestic Violence." *Criminology* 33:141-171.

Skogan, W.G. (1981). *Issues in the Measurement of Victimization.* Washington, DC: U.S. Department of Justice.

————— (1990). "The National Crime Survey Redesign." *Public Opinion Quarterly* 54:256-272.

————— and M.G. Maxfield (1981). *Coping with Crime: Individual and Neighborhood Reactions.* Beverly Hills, CA: Sage.

Skolnick, A.A. (1992). "Congress Acts to Resuscitate Nation's Financially Ailing Trauma Care Systems." *Journal of the American Medical Association* 267:2994.

Smith, C. and T.P. Thornberry (1995). "The Relationship Between Childhood Maltreatment and Adolescent Involvement in Delinquency." *Criminology* 33:451-477.

Smith, D.L. and K. Weis (1976). "Toward an Open-System Approach to Studies in the Field of Victimology." In E.C. Viano (ed.), *Victims & Society*. Washington, DC: Visage Press.

Smith, G.B. and S.P. Lab (1991). "Urban and Rural Attitudes Toward Participating in an Auxiliary Policing Crime Prevention Program." *Criminal Justice and Behavior* 18:202-216.

Smith, M.D. and R.N. Parker (1980). "Types of Homicide and Variation in Regional Rates." *Social Forces* 59:136-147.

Smith, R. and T. Smith (1979). "An Evaluation of the Akron 4-A Project." Paper presented to the Subcommittee on Courts, Civil Liberties, and the Administration of Justice, U.S. House of Representatives.

Smithey, M. (1997). "Infant Homicide at the Hands of Mothers: Toward a Sociological Perspective." *Deviant Behavior* 18:255-272.

Smotas, L. (1991). "In Search of a Balance: AIDS, Rape, and the Special Needs Doctrine." *New York University Law Review* 66:1881-1928.

Snelling, H.A. (1975). "What is Rape?" In L.G. Schultz (ed.), *Rape Victimology*. Springfield, IL: Charles C Thomas.

Snyder, H.N, M. Stickmund and E. Poe-Yamagata (1996). *Juvenile Offenders and Victims: 1996 Update on Violence*. Pittsburgh, PA: National Center for Juvenile Justice.

Socolar, R.R.S., D.K. Runyan and L. Amaya-Hackson (1995). "Methodological and Ethical Issues Related to Studying Child Maltreatment." *Journal of Family Issues* 16:565-586.

Soderstrom, C.A. and G.S. Smith (1993). "Alcohol's Effect on Trauma Outcomes: A Reappraisal of Conventional Wisdom." *Journal of the American Medical Association* 270:93-94.

Sohn, E.F. (1994). "Antistalking Laws: Do They Actually Protect Victims?" *Criminal Law Bulletin* 30:203-241.

Sorenson, S.B., B.A. Richardson and J.G. Peterson (1993). "Race/Ethnicity Patterns in the Homicide of Children in Los Angeles, 1980 through 1989." *American Journal of Public Health* 83:725-727.

*South Carolina v. Gathers*, 490 U.S. 805 (1989).

Spears, J.W. and C.C. Spohn (1996). "The Genuine Victim and Prosecutor's Charging Decisions in Sexual Assault Cases." *American Journal of Criminal Justice* 20:183-205.

Spelman, W. (1995). "Criminal Careers of Public Places." In J.E. Eck and D. Weisburd (eds.), *Crime and Place*. Monsey, NY: Criminal Justice Press.

Spencer, B.J. (1987). "A Crime Victim's Views on a Constitutional Amendment for Victims." *The Wayne Law Review* 34:1-6.

Spinetta, J.J. and D. Rigler (1972). "The Child-Abusing Parent: A Psychological Review." *Psychological Bulletin* 77:296-304.

Spohn, C. (1991). "'The Law's the Law, but Fair is Fair': Rape Shield Laws and Officials' Assessment of Sexual History Evidence." *Criminology* 29:137-161.

———— and J. Horney (1990). "A Case of Unrealistic Expectations: The Impact of Rape Reform Legislation in Illinois." *Criminal Justice Policy Review* 4:1-18.

———— and J. Spears (1996). "The Effect of Offender and Victim Characteristics on Sexual Assault Case Processing Decisions." *Justice Quarterly* 13:649-680.

Sprey, J. and S.H. Matthews (1989). "The Perils of Drawing Policy Implications from Research: The Case of Elder Mistreatment." In R. Filinson and S.R. Ingman (eds.), *Elder Abuse: Practice and Policy*. New York: Human Sciences Press.

Sproles, E.T., III (1985). *The Evaluation and Management of Rape and Sexual Abuse: A Physician's Guide*. Rockville, MD: U.S. National Center for Prevention and Control of Rape.

Stafford, M. and O.R. Galle (1984). "Victimization Rates, Exposure to Risk, and Fear of Crime." *Criminology* 22:173-185.

Stalans, L.J. and A.J. Lurigio (1995). "Responding to Domestic Violence Against Women." *Crime & Delinquency* 41:387-398.

Stanford, R.M. and B.L. Mowry (1990). "Domestic Disturbance Danger Rate." *Journal of Police Science and Administration* 17:244-249.

Stearns, P.J. (1986). "Old Age Family Conflict: The Perspective of the Past." In K.A. Pillemer and R.S. Wolf (eds.), *Elder Abuse: Conflict in the Family*. Dover, MA: Auburn House.

Steele, B.F. and C.B. Pollock (1974). "A Psychiatric Study of Parents Who Abuse Infants and Small Children." In R.E. Helfer and C.H. Kempe (eds.), *The Battered Child*, 2nd ed. Chicago: University of Chicago Press.

Steinbock, B. (1995). "A Policy Perspective." *Criminal Justice Ethics* 14:4-9.

Steinman, L.I. (1993). "Despite Anti-stalking Laws, Stalkers Continue to Stalk: Are These Laws Constitutional and Effective?" *St. Thomas Law Review* 6:213-245.

Steinman, M. (1988). "Anticipating Rank and File Police Reactions to Arrest Policies Regarding Spouse Abuse." *Criminal Justice Research Bulletin* 4:1-5.

Steinmetz, S.K. (1977-78). "The Battered Husband Syndrome." *Victimology* 2:499-509.

———— (1978a). "Services to Battered Women: Our Greatest Need. A Reply to Field and Kirchner." *Victimology* 3:222-226.

———— (1978b). "Battered Parents." *Society* July/August:54-55.

———— (1983). "Dependency, Stress and Violence Between Middle-Aged Caregivers and their Elderly Parents." In J.I. Kosberg (ed.), *Abuse and Maltreatment of the Elderly*. Boston, MA: John Wright.

———— (1988). *Duty Bound: Elder Abuse and Family Care*. Newbury Park, CA: Sage.

Stine, G.J. (1996). *AIDS Update*. Englewood Cliffs, NJ: Prentice-Hall.

Stitt, B.G. and S.A. Lentz (1996). "Consent and Its Meaning to the Sexual Victimization of Women." *American Journal of Criminal Justice* 20:237-257.

Stombler, M. (1994). "'Buddies' or 'Slutties:' The Collective Sexual Reputation of Fraternity Little Sisters." *Gender & Society* 8:297-323.

Stone, J.L., R.J. Lowe, O. Jonasson, R.J. Baker, J. Barrett, J.B. Oldershaw, R.M. Crowell and R.J. Stein (1986). "Acute Subdural Hematoma: Direct Admission to a Trauma Center Yields Improved Results." *Journal of Trauma* 26:445-450.

Stothert, J.C., G.B.M. Gbaanador and D.N. Herndon (1990). "The Role of Autopsy in Death Resulting from Trauma." *Journal of Trauma* 30:1021-1026.

Stout, K.D. (1991). "Intimate Femicide: A National Demographic Overview." *Journal of Interpersonal Violence* 6:476-485.

Stovall, C.J. (1997). Statement before the Committee on the Judiciary, United States Senate, concerning a Constitutional Amendment Protecting the Rights of Crime Victims, April 16, 1997.

Straus, M.A. (1978). "Wife-Beating: How Common and Why." *Victimology* 2:443-458.

_____ (1979). "Measuring Intrafamily Conflict and Violence: The Conflict Tactics (CT) Scales." *Journal of Marriage and the Family* 41:75-88.

_____ (1983). "Ordinary Violence Child Abuse, and Wife-Beating: What Do They have in Common?" In D. Finkelhor, R.J. Gelles, G.T. Hotaling and M.A. Straus (eds.), *The Dark Side of Families: Current Family Violence Research*. Beverly Hills, CA: Sage.

_____, R. Gelles and S. Steinmetz (1980). *Behind Closed Doors: Violence in the American Family*. Garden City, NY: Anchor Press.

Struckman-Johnson, C. (1988). "Forced Sex on Dates: It Happens to Men, Too." *Journal of Sex Research* 24:234-240.

Sutherland, E.M. (1939). *Principles of Criminology*, 3rd ed. Philadelphia: Lippincott.

Sutocky, J.W., J.M. Shultz and K.W. Kizer (1993). "Alcohol-Related Mortality in California, 1980 to 1989." *American Journal of Public Health* 83:817-823.

Swisher, K. (1995). "Businesses Should Clearly Define Sexual Harassment." In K.L. Swisher (ed.), *What is Sexual Harassment?* San Diego: Greenhaven Press.

Tallahassee Police Department (no date). *Policy Manual*. Tallahassee, FL: City of Tallahassee.

Tatara, T. (1990). *Summaries of National Elder Abuse Data: An Exploratory Study of Statistics Based on a Survey of State Adult Protective Service and Aging Agencies*. Washington, DC: National Aging Resource Center on Elder Abuse.

_____ (1993). "Understanding the Nature and Scope of Domestic Elder Abuse with the Use of State Aggregate Data: Summaries of the Key Findings of a National Survey of State APS and Aging Services." *Journal of Elder Abuse and Neglect* 5(4):35-57.

Taylor, B.M. (1989). *Bureau of Justice Statistics Technical Report: New Directions for the National Crime Survey*. Washington, DC: U.S. Government Printing Office.

_____ (1997). *Bureau of Justice Statistics: National Crime Victimization Survey: Changes in Criminal Victimization, 1994-95*. Washington, DC: U.S. Government Printing Office.

Temkin, J. (1996). "Doctors, Rape and Criminal Justice." *The Howard Journal* 35:1-20.

Teret, S.P., G.J. Wintemute and P.L. Beilenson (1992). "The Firearm Fatality Reporting System: A Proposal." *Journal of the American Medical Association* 267:3073-3074.

Thayer, T.A. (1997). "Triage: History and Horizons." *Topics in Emergency Medicine* 19:1-11.

Thobaben, M. (1989). "State Elder/Adult Abuse and Protection Laws." In R. Filinson and S.R. Ingman (eds.), *Elder Abuse: Practice and Policy*. New York: Human Sciences Press.

Thomas, K.R. (1997). "How to Stop the Stalker: State Antistalking Laws." *Criminal Law Bulletin* 29:124-136.

Thomas, M.P., Jr. (1972). "Child Abuse and Neglect, Part I: Historical Overview, Legal Matrix, and Social Perspectives." *North Carolina Law Review* 50:293-349.

Thorvaldson, A. (1989). "Compensation by Offenders in Canada: A Victim's Right?" In E.A. Fattah (ed.), *The Plight of Crime Victims in Modern Society*. New York: Macmillan.

———— (1990). "Restitution and Victim Participation in Sentencing: A Comparison of Two Models." In B. Galaway and J. Hudson (eds.), *Criminal Justice, Restitution, and Reconciliation*. Monsey, NY: Criminal Justice Press.

Tittle, C. (1978). "Restitution and Deterrence: An Evaluation of Compatibility." In B. Galaway and J. Hudson (eds.), *Offender Restitution in Theory and Practice*. Lexington, MA: Lexington Books.

Toennies, F. (1957). *Community and Society*. Trans. C.P. Loomis. East Lansing: Michigan State University.

Tolman, R.M. and A. Weisz (1995). "Coordinated Community Intervention for Domestic Violence: The Effects of Arrest and Prosecution on Recidivism of Woman Abuse Perpetrators." *Crime & Delinquency* 41:481-495.

Tomz, J.E. and D. McGillis (1997). *Serving Crime Victims and Witnesses*, 2nd ed. Washington, DC: U.S. Department of Justice.

Toseland, R.W. (1982). "Fear of Crime: Who is Most Vulnerable?" *Journal of Criminal Justice* 10:199-210.

Ullman, S.E. and J.M. Siegel (1993). "Victim-Offender Relationship and Sexual Assault." *Violence and Victims* 8:121-133.

Umbreit, M.S. (1997). "Victim-Offender Dialogue: From the Margins to the Mainstream Throughout the World." *The Crime Victims Report* 1:35-36, 48.

———— and R.B. Coates (1993). "Cross-Site Analysis of Victim-Offender Mediation in Four States." *Crime & Delinquency* 39:565-585.

United Nations (1985). *Declaration of Basic Principles of Justice for Victims of Crime and Abuse of Power*. Adopted November 29, 1985.

U.S. Attorney General's Commission on Pornography (1986). *Final Report*. Washington, DC: U.S. Government Printing Office.

U.S. Attorney General's Task Force on Family Violence (1984). *Family Violence*. Washington, DC: U.S. Government Printing Office.

U.S. Department of Health and Human Services (1997). *Child Maltreatment 1995: Reports from the States to the National Child Abuse and Neglect Data System*. Washington, DC: National Center on Child Abuse and Neglect.

U.S. Department of Justice (1986). *Four Years Later: A Report on the President's Task Force on Victims of Crime*. Washington, DC: U.S. Government Printing Office.

———— (1989). *Redesign of the National Crime Survey*. Washington, DC: U.S. Government Printing Office.

———— (1992). *Criminal Victimization in the United States, 1991*. Washington, DC: U.S. Government Printing Office.

———— (1996). *National Crime Victimization Survey, 1995: Preliminary Findings*. Washington, DC: U.S. Government Printing Office.

_____ (1997). *Criminal Victimization in the United States, 1994.* Washington, DC: U.S. Government Printing Office.

U.S. House of Representatives Select Committee on Aging (1981). *Elder Abuse: An Examination of a Hidden Problem.* Washington, DC: U.S. Government Printing Office.

U.S. Senate, Special Committee on Aging (1991). *Aging America: Trends and Projections.* Washington, DC: Department of Health and Human Services.

Van Ness, D.W. (1990). "Restorative Justice." In B. Galaway and J. Hudson (eds.), *Criminal Justice, Restitution, and Reconciliation.* Monsey, NY: Criminal Justice Press.

Van Ness, D.W. and K.H. Strong (1997). *Restoring Justice.* Cincinnati: Anderson.

Viano, E.C. (1976a). "Conclusions and Recommendations: International Study Institute on Victimology, Bellagio, Italy, July 1-12, 1975." In E.C. Viano (ed.), *Victims & Society.* Washington, DC: Visage Press.

_____ (1976b). "From the Editor: Victimology: The Study of the Victim." *Victimology* 1:1-7.

_____ (1979). *Victim/Witness Services: A Review of the Model.* Washington, DC: U.S. Department of Justice.

_____ (1987). "Victims' Rights and the Constitution: Reflections on a Bicentennial." *Crime & Delinquency* 33:438-451.

Villmoare, E. and V.V. Neto (1987). *Victim Appearances at Sentencing Under California's Victims' Bill of Rights.* Research in Brief. Washington, DC: National Institute of Justice.

von Hentig, H. (1941). "Remarks on the Interaction of Perpetrator and Victim." *Journal of Criminal Law, Criminology and Police Science* 31:303-309.

_____ (1948). *The Criminal and His Victim: Studies in the Sociobiology of Crime.* New Haven: Yale University Press.

Vorenberg, E.W. (1981). *A State of the Art Survey of Dispute Resolution Programs Involving Juveniles.* Chicago, IL: National Center for the Assessment of Alternatives to Juvenile Justice Processing, University of Chicago.

Waldner-Haugrud, L.K. and B. Magruder (1995). "Male and Female Sexual Victimization in Dating Relationships: Gender Differences in Coercion Techniques and Outcomes." *Violence and Victims* 10:203-215.

Walker, G. (1990). "Crisis-Care in Critical Incident Debriefing." *Death Studies* 14:121-133.

Walker, L.E. (1979). *The Battered Woman.* New York: Harper & Row.

Walker, L.E.A. (1988). "New Techniques for Assessment and Evaluation of Child Abuse Victims: Using Anatomically Correct Dolls and Videotape Procedures." In L.E.A. Walker (ed.), *Handbook on Sexual Abuse of Children.* New York: Springer-Verlag.

Wallace, H. and K. Kelty (1995). "Stalking and Restraining Orders: A Legal and Psychological Perspective." *Journal of Crime and Justice* 18:99-111.

Walsh, A. (1986). "Placebo Justice: Victim Recommendations and Offender Sentences in Sexual Assault Cases." *Journal of Criminal Law & Criminology* 77:1126-1141.

Wang, C.T. and D. Daro (1997). *Current Trends in Child Abuse Reporting and Fatalities: The Results of the 1996 Annual Fifty State Survey.* Chicago: National Committee to Prevent Child Abuse.

Ward, R.A., M. LaGory and S.R. Sherman (1986). "Fear of Crime Among the Elderly as Person/Environment Interaction." *Sociological Quarterly* 27:327-341.

Wardell, L., D.L. Gillespie and A. Leffler (1983). "Science and Violence Against Wives." In D. Finkelhor, R.J. Gelles, G.T. Hotaling and M.A. Straus (eds.), *The Dark Side of Families: Current Family Violence Research*. Beverly Hills, CA: Sage.

Warner, J.E. and D.J. Hansen (1994). "The Identification and Reporting of Physical Abuse by Physicians: A Review and Implications for Research." *Child Abuse & Neglect* 18:11-25.

Warr, M. (1984). "Fear of Victimization: Why Are Some Women and the Elderly More Afraid?" *Social Science Quarterly* 65:681-702.

Wasik, B.H. and R.N. Roberts (1994). "Survey of Home Visiting Programs for Abused and Neglected Children and Their Families." *Child Abuse & Neglect* 18:271-283.

Webster, B. (1988). "Victim Assistance Programs Report Increased Workloads." *National Institute of Justice: Research in Action*. Washington, DC: U.S. Department of Justice.

Weigend, T., (1983). "Problems of Victim/Witness Assistance Programs." *Victimology* 8:91-101.

Weis, K. (1976). "Rape as a Crime Without Victims and Offenders? A Methodological Critique." In E.C. Viano (ed.), *Victims & Society*. Washington, DC: Visage Press.

_____ and S.S. Borges (1973). "Victimology and Rape: The Case of the Legitimate Victim." *Issues in Criminology* 8:71-115.

Weiss, A. and R.F. Boruch (1996). "On the Use of Police Officers in Randomized Field Experiments: Some Lessons from the Milwakee Domestic Violence Experiment." *Police Studies* 19:45-52.

West, J.G., R.H. Cales and A.B. Gazzaniga (1983). "Impact of Regionalization: The Orange County Experience." *Archives of Surgery* 118:740-744.

Whitaker, C.J. (1989). *Bureau of Justice Statistics Special Report: The Redesigned National Crime Survey: Selected New Data*. Washington, DC: U.S. Government Printing Office.

Whitehead, J.T. and S.P. Lab (1996). *Juvenile Justice: An Introduction*, 2nd ed. Cincinnati: Anderson.

Widom, C.S. (1989). "Child Abuse, Neglect, and Violent Criminal Behavior." *Criminology* 27:251-271.

Wilbanks, W. (1984). *Murder in Miami: An Analysis of Homicide Patterns and Trends in Dade County (Miami). Florida, 1917-1983*. Lanham, MD: University Press of America.

Willis, C.L. and R. H. Wells (1988). "The Police and Child Abuse: An Analysis of Police Decisions to Report Illegal Behavior." *Criminology* 26:695-715.

Wisconsin Statutes (1997).

Wolf, R.S. and K.A. Pillemer (1989). *Helping Elderly Victims: The Reality of Elder Abuse*. New York: Columbia University Press.

Wolfgang, M.E. (1958). *Patterns in Criminal Homicide*. Montclair, NJ: Patterson Smith, Reprinted 1975.

_____ and F. Ferracuti (1967). *The Subculture of Violence: Towards an Integrated Theory of Criminology*. London: Tavistock.

Woodworth, D.L. (1991). "Evaluation of a Multiple-Family Incest Treatment Program." In M.Q. Patton (ed.), *Family Sexual Abuse: Frontline Research and Evaluation*. Newbury Park, CA: Sage.

Woolf, P.D., C. Cox, J.V. McDonald, M. Kelly, D. Nichols, T. Hamill and D.V. Feliciano (1991) "Effects of Intoxication on the Catecholamine Response to Multisystem Injury." *Journal of Trauma* 31:1271-1276.

Worth, D.M., P.A. Matthews and W.R. Coleman (1990). "Sex, Role, Group Affiliation, Family Background, and Courtship Violence in College Students." *Journal of College Student Development* 31:250-254.

Wright, J.A., A.G. Burgess, A.W. Burgess, A.T. Laszlo, G.O. McCrary and J.E. Douglas (1997). "A Typology of Interpersonal Stalking." *Journal of Interpersonal Violence* 11:487-502.

Wright, L. (1976). "The 'Sick but Slick' Syndrome as a Personality Component of Parents of Battered Children." *Journal of Clinical Psychology* 32:41-45.

Wright, M. (1991). *Justice for Victims and Offenders: A Restorative Response to Crime*. Philadelphia: Open University Press.

Wyatt, G.E. and M. Riederle (1995). "The Prevalence and Contact of Sexual Harassment Among African American and White American Women." *Journal of Interpersonal Violence* 10:309-321.

Young, M.A. (1987). "A Constitutional Amendment for Victims of Crime: The Victim's Perspective." *The Wayne Law Review* 34:51-68.

Zalichin, D.W., S.Y. Schraga and J. Chytilo (1980). "Restitution in Brooklyn and Bronx Courts: A Victim-Oriented Approach." In J. Hudson and B. Galaway (eds.), *Victims, Offenders, and Alternative Sanctions*. Lexington, MA: D.C. Heath.

Zellman, G.L. (1990a). "Child Abuse Reporting and Failure to Report Among Mandated Reporters: Prevalence, Incidence, and Reasons." *Journal of Interpersonal Violence* 5:3-22.

———— (1990b). "Report Decision-Making Patterns Among Mandated Child Abuse Reporters." *Child Abuse & Neglect* 14:325-336.

———— (1991). "Reducing Underresponding: Improving System Response to Mandated Reporters." *Journal of Interpersonal Violence* 16:115-118.

Zillman, G.L., J. Bryant and R.A. Carveth (1981). "The Effects of Erotica Featuring Sadomasochism and Bestiality on Motivated Intermale Aggression." *Personality and Social Psychology Bulletin* 7:153-159.

Zingraff, M.T., J. Leiter, K.A. Myers and M.C. Johnson (1993). "Child Maltreatment and Youthful Problem Behavior." *Criminology* 31:173-202.

Zirkel, P.A. (1990). "You Bruise, You Lose." *Phi Delta Kappan* 71:410-411.

Zona, M.A., K.K. Sharma and J.L. Lane (1993). "A Comparative Study of Erotomania and Obsessional Subjects in a Forensic Sample." *Journal of Forensic Sciences* 65:894-903.

# Subject Index

# Author Index

# About the Authors

**William (Bill) Doerner** has been a faculty member in the School of Criminology and Criminal Justice at Florida State University since 1977. He earned his M.S. in Sociology at Emory University (1973) and a Ph.D. in Sociology from the University of Tennessee (1977). Doerner is also in his eighteenth year as part-time sworn law enforcement officer with the Tallahassee Police and works there as a one-person uniformed patrol unit. He has served on the Board of Directors for the National Organization of Victim Assistance and was the Founding President of the Florida Network of Victim/Witness Services. He has written a number of journal articles that deal with crime victims, police selection and training, and law enforcement personnel issues.

**Steven P. Lab** is Professor and Director of Criminal Justice at Bowling Green State University. Lab holds a Ph.D. in Criminology from Florida State University. He is the author of *Crime Prevention: Approaches, Practices and Evaluations*, co-author of *Juvenile Justice: An Introduction* and editor of *Crime Prevention at a Crossroads*. A past editor of the *Journal of Crime and Justice*, his research focuses on crime, victimization and crime preventive activity in secondary school settings.